FEDERALISM IN ACTION

The Devolution of Canada's Public Employment Service, 1995–2015

The Institute of Public Administration of Canada Series in Public Management and Governance

Editors:

Peter Aucoin, 2001–2
Donald Savoie, 2003–7
Luc Bernier, 2007–9
Patrice Dutil, 2010–

This series is sponsored by the Institute of Public Administration of Canada as part of its commitment to encourage research on issues in Canadian public administration, public sector management, and public policy. It also seeks to foster wider knowledge and understanding among practitioners, academics, and the general public.

For a list of books published in the series, see page 409.

Federalism in Action

The Devolution of Canada's Public Employment Service, 1995–2015

DONNA E. WOOD

UNIVERSITY OF TORONTO PRESS
Toronto Buffalo London

Toronto Buffalo London
utorontopress.com

ISBN 978-1-4875-0310-9

Library and Archives Canada Cataloguing in Publication

Wood, Donna E., 1948–, author
Federalism in action : the devolution of Canada's public employment service, 1995–2015 / Donna E. Wood.

(Institute of Public Administration of Canada series in public management and governance)
Includes bibliographical references and index.
ISBN 978-1-4875-0310-9 (cloth)

1. Employment agencies - Government policy - Canada - Case studies. 2. Employment agencies - Government policy - Case studies. I. Title. II. Series: Institute of Public Administration of Canada series in public management and governance

HD5879.W66 2018 331.12'80971 C2017-907015-0

This book has been published with the help of a grant from the Federation for the Humanities and Social Sciences, through the Awards to Scholarly Publications Program, using funds provided by the Social Sciences and Humanities Research Council of Canada.

University of Toronto Press acknowledges the financial assistance to its publishing program of the Canada Council for the Arts and the Ontario Arts Council, an agency of the Government of Ontario.

Canada Council for the Arts · Conseil des Arts du Canada

Funded by the Government of Canada · Financé par le gouvernement du Canada

Contents

Figures and Tables

Figures

Tables

Foreword

The Government of Canada will be spending over $330 billion this year and about $3.3 billion of that money (1 per cent) will be spent on provincial, territorial, and Aboriginal programs created to help people who are out of work to find jobs. The funding commitment is captured under various federal-provincial-territorial and federal-Aboriginal labour market agreements. These are crucial government programs, even though they are remarkably small. This money is designed to support job-finding efforts and training. Most of it comes from mandatory contributions made by employers and workers to the Employment Insurance (EI) fund.

Anyone reading this book knows that the labour force is undergoing dramatic changes. The idea that a person can expect to work the same job for an entire career is now strictly reserved for the professions. The same can be said for the idea of working for the same employer (the exception there is the public service). The combined pressures of globalization, mechanization, the rise of artificial intelligence, and technological breakthroughs have steadily eroded the jobs traditionally available to Canadians. Young people are finding it difficult to find full-time employment, and many of my students today will work a variety of temporary jobs simultaneously for many years before they can find a good match to their skills. Older workers are not protected in this new economy. They are finding themselves thrown out of work as industries in search of lower wages move to the Global South or are transformed by the sharing economy. Adaptation and retraining are now the order of the day, and governments are pressed to shoulder at least a part of the burden of ensuring that people have the tools to retrain themselves for the modern economy.

This is not a new policy challenge. The Borden government first felt the responsibility in the last year of the First World War when soldiers started to return to the country in larger numbers, but were less interested in returning to the family farm. As Donna Wood expertly demonstrates, governments have been experimenting with different models ever since. She richly documents how Ottawa's approach has swung between extremes of centralization and decentralization. We are now in a phase where Ottawa plays mostly a funding role and little else. Working with provinces, territories, and Aboriginal labour market organizations, the national government is faced with an urgent policy matter in light of the economic forces that wreak havoc in the labour market. Wood rightly raises important issues of governance for these programs and prompts us to question whether they can respond to future challenges.

The new economy has brought on stresses we thought had been resolved. At the individual level, there is more fear about losing employment, of working for employers who offer no pensions or benefits, and of general uncertainty. Many people argue that there is more at stake than individual angst, that in fact Canada's competitiveness and prosperity is at stake. Industries – including those that are competitive internationally – are not performing to their full potential. Their productivity is lower because they are not adapting to new technologies and are investing comparatively little in employee training. Many industries also report that they are not finding the kinds of employees they want and need. This presents a great challenge as, more and more, one of the best arguments governments can show to potential investors is that an educated and skilled workforce is available to perform the work required.

With Ottawa's role limited primarily to funding, the question becomes whether provinces have the capacity to predict labour market needs and appropriately tailor their programs in order to make their jurisdictions competitive. Readers of this book will also want to ask themselves if Canada indeed has a "traditional" approach to public employment services. If it exists, it certainly is difficult to define. What made and unmade this crucial sector of activity? Donna Wood takes a long view of policy, a welcome perspective in this series on public administration and governance, to explain the successes and failures of these programs.

Serious complaints can be made about these labour market agreements. A regional one is familiar: Ontario grumbles that it suffers a massively disproportional shortage of federal funding – given the size of its economy – of its unemployed workforce, and its needs. Between 2000 and 2010, the workers and businesses of the largest province contributed $20 billion more in EI premiums than they received in EI benefits. Others have focused their criticisms on the workings of the patchwork of programs across the country, noting that fewer than half of Canada's unemployed participate in the programs funded by the labour market agreements. Finally, there's the money argument. Remarkably, critics on both left and right complain that the money is insufficient for retraining and retooling the workforce, that apprenticeships are inadequate, and that industry itself is not an effective partner.

Canada underspends in this sector, compared to other highly competitive countries. According to the OECD, Canada spent 0.12 of its GDP on public employment services (combining both placement and related services and benefits administration) in 2015, 0.02 less than it did in 2010 and 0.04 less than it did in 2005. In 2005, it spent 0.08 of the GDP on training; in 2015 it was a substantial drop to 0.07 per cent. There is no comfort in the recognition that the United States spends even less of its GDP on such programs than Canada. It relies on other instruments to ensure its competitiveness.

By comparison, our key competitors on the global market are spending more. France spent 0.25 of its GDP on public employment services (combining both placement and related services and benefits administration) in 2015, the U.K. spent 0.20 per cent when it last reported in 2011, and Germany spent 0.36 in 2015. Both France and Germany have been increasing their budgets in this area over the past decade, and Germany has done so spectacularly. If Canada is to compete in the European market as a result of the trade agreement signed earlier this year, it is going to have to invest in employment services, training, and crafting effective employment incentives.

As I write this, a round of evaluations of the federal-provincial-territorial and federal-Aboriginal labour market agreements has been completed and there are successes. More good news: the federal government has pledged additional money to improve the agreements in order to make labour market programming more responsive.

Evaluations of programs in this critical area must not stop, so the timing of this book could not be better. Canada's economy – not least the happiness of its children – depends on it.

Patrice Dutil
Ryerson University
Editor, IPAC Series in Public Management and Governance
Labour Day, 2017

Preface

I have wanted to write this book since 2009 when I worked for the Organisation for Economic Cooperation and Development (OECD) on a project examining accountability and flexibility in local employment services. Canada was one of four multilevel countries being compared. The others were Denmark, Belgium, and the Netherlands. Our governance architecture had just gone through dramatic changes: between 1996 and 2010 responsibility for most employment services had been devolved – one jurisdiction at a time – from the Government of Canada to the thirteen provinces and territories. When I joined the OECD project, it had already been decided that Alberta and New Brunswick – two provinces with early devolved agreements – would represent Canada. After the OECD project was done and the reports had been submitted, I wondered what governance regimes the eight other provinces had chosen, especially in my newly adopted home of British Columbia.

This book is my attempt to answer this question and more. My main purpose at the start was to compare the governance choices made by Canadian provinces after they took on the transferred federal employment programs, and to try to understand why they made these choices. Along the way I also ended up looking at provincial outcomes, the federal role post-devolution, Aboriginal employment programming, pan-Canadian coordination, and how Canada's arrangements compare with those of the United States, Australia, and the European Union.

An interest in how public programs are managed and delivered in our complex federation comes from my experience as a civil servant operating on the devolution front lines. I sat in on the Ottawa-Alberta negotiations in 1996 and subsequently became involved in intergovernmental efforts to improve the arrangements. I left government in

2003 to enter academia. As a result, I come to the analysis from a public administration – not a political science or economics – perspective. I also think that history matters – a lot. As such, it is threaded throughout all chapters of this book.

Lying at the heart of any country's workforce development system is the public employment service or PES. Devolution of the PES was implemented starting in 1996 through intergovernmental arrangements called Labour Market Development Agreements or LMDAs. Provincial design and delivery control was reaffirmed in 2008 through supplementary Labour Market Agreements or LMAs. The services provided under these two federal-provincial agreements between 1996 and 2014 frame most of the analysis in the book. This is primarily because comparable data – at the provincial level – were publicly available. Not only did these two agreements frame the PES services that the Government of Canada used to deliver directly, but also most of the federal money made available to provinces flowed through them.

While two other agreements provide provinces with federal funding for employment services – the Labour Market Agreement for Persons with Disabilities and the Targeted Initiative for Older Workers – provincial programs are not examined in detail, as provincial-level data are either non-existent or not comparable. In addition, provincial delivery using federal money under these agreements was in place pre-devolution. The Canada Job Fund Agreements – introduced in the fall of 2014 to replace the LMAs – are too new to assess. Even though provincial employment services under these three other federal-provincial agreements will not be analysed in detail, the programming provided will be addressed as part of the book's overall narrative.

A considerable amount of material used in this book is taken from articles, books, and government reports written by others that describe and analyse past events. However, to understand provincial choices post-1996 and compare them, new primary research was required. This involved interviews with informants in Ottawa and in all ten provinces, as well as a detailed review of government reports outlining program results. In the summer of 2012 I started doing interviews in British Columbia and over the next three years travelled to all provinces, such that by the winter of 2015 I had done 132 interviews and talked to 170 people.

The process of identifying, communicating with, and then meeting with people from across Canada working in this policy field was invigorating and inspiring. Wherever possible, I travelled by train in order to ground myself in the Canadian landscape. I met mostly with "street-level" public service workers directly involved with the management and delivery of Canada's PES programming. This included federal and provincial civil servants, managers of Aboriginal labour market agencies and non-government organizations (who represent the agencies who deliver most of the services), and business and union representatives. Academics and people who work with policy think tanks were also very helpful. Appendix A provides a summary of where the people I talked to worked and lived.

I did not meet with politicians or unemployed people using the services, nor did I conduct interviews in the three territories. Not only do the territories have different constitutional arrangements, but their population is also very small. Since most of their programs are provided to Aboriginal people, territorial activity has been substantially incorporated into the Aboriginal chapter of this book. In order to understand the arrangements in Quebec I spent three months based in Montreal in the fall of 2013. As a Canadian who does not speak or read French, doing this provided valuable insight into the workings of the Quebec labour market system, which is rightly held up as a model to the rest of Canada.

Although unstructured, the interviews followed a consistent framework that I developed from the international literature. As my approach was primarily inductive, a common framework provided a map of theoretical concepts useful for *comparing* provincial approaches. Throughout the course of this research, I became increasingly aware of how averse provinces were to being compared. The main objection of provincial officials is that their labour markets are different and so not comparable. Their second objection is that provinces came to the LMDAs from different starting points in provincial programs on offer, and so they cannot be compared. Their third objection is that the Government of Canada does not possess the legitimacy to compare them, despite the fact that the federal government provides almost all PES program funding. This includes the Canada Employment Insurance Commission, comprising two federal officials as the chair and co-chair, in addition to a commissioner for workers and a commissioner for employers.

I disagree with this perspective. While there are distinct labour markets in Canada, we form a single country operating under basically the same rules. Certainly there are the same – or roughly similar – federal funding rules from one province to another. No public service should expect to operate without effective oversight, including objective, comparative, statistically reliable performance measurement. Without comparison, policy learning and public management improvements do not happen, as those working in the system do not even know if they are doing a good job. Without knowledge of experiences elsewhere, information from a single province cannot be contextualized. We do not seem to have this aversion to comparison in other policy fields – such as education, justice, and health care – where there are highly institutionalized processes and administrative structures that collect data and compare provincial outcomes. In 2016 these kinds of institutions and processes did not exist in most areas relating to the PES.

The interviews and the analysis covered the twenty-year period from 1995 to 2015. It was in December 1995 that new Employment Insurance (EI) legislation was tabled outlining the initial federal devolution offer. I cut off the provincial analysis in March 2014, as that was when the LMAs expired and were replaced, except in Quebec, by new Canada Job Fund Agreements. Focusing explicitly on the LMDAs and LMAs allowed me to examine provincial decision making and results within a defined time period under stable federal-provincial arrangements while the Liberals were in charge from 1995 to 2006 and the Conservatives from 2006 to 2015. My extension of the pan-Canadian analysis into 2016 allowed me to incorporate preliminary information from the 2015 election platform of the Trudeau Liberals and the initial choices of their new government as they moved into 2016.

My second information source was government reports. The most important were the eighteen Canada Employment Insurance *Monitoring and Assessment Report*s (*MAR*s), which have been put out by the Canada Employment Insurance Commission every year since 1997. I decided to focus the provincial analysis on selected years: 1999/2000, 2005/6, 2008/9, 2009/10, 2010/11, 2011/12, 2012/13, and 2013/14. The 1999/2000 report provided the earliest credible information on provincial outcomes under the LMDAs. Information from the mid-years demonstrated results when there was a mixture of federal and provincially delivered programming. The period from 2008/9 onwards (six straight years) was when provinces were exclusively responsible.

While *MAR*s are public documents, they were hard to find. My university library had only hard copies of earlier reports and no electronic access to later reports. The website of the federal department responsible in 2016 – Employment and Social Development Canada, or ESDC – carried only the last three years. It was fortunate that over time I had kept copies of all *MARs*. These reports were invaluable, as they provided results by province and used the same indicators over time.

The fifty-four provincial Labour Market Agreement (LMA) reports released between 2008/9 and 2013/14 were another key data source. All provinces, except for Quebec, agreed to report using the same LMA indicators and release these results to their citizens annually. Provincial LMA reports were also challenging to find. While links to the reports were eventually consolidated on a federal website, they were often broken. While they tracked them, some provinces did not publicly report on all the agreed-to indicators.

I eventually located all provincial LMA reports and – by contacting individual provinces if necessary – got most of the information that I needed for a comparative analysis. Quebec did not explicitly report on LMA funding and did not use the same indicators as in the rest of Canada. The Emploi-Québec annual report and evaluations were reviewed with Quebec officials to try to identify comparable information. Despite a commitment in every LMA agreement, consolidated national reports were released by the Government of Canada only for 2008/9 and 2009/10. Appendix B provides more details on these government reports.

Some readers of this book will question the legitimacy and accuracy of these government reports on LMDA and LMA results, particularly in a comparative context. People whom I talked to, including federal officials, raised questions about the validity of the indicators chosen, the quality of the data collected by the provinces, and their usefulness in comparing provinces or drawing pan-Canadian conclusions. These are all valid concerns. However, these are the only data that exist. Where there are particular limitations, I note it in the text.

My third source of information was ESDC performance and evaluation reports, federal budget documents, and parliamentary committee reports. Especially valuable was evidence provided at hearings held between 2011 and 2015 by the House of Commons Committee on Human Resources, Skills, and Social Development and the Status of Persons with Disabilities (HUMA), the reports released, as well as government responses. I used OECD reports a lot, as they comprise a credible source with the capacity to put the Canadian arrangements in a comparative context. The available OECD studies related to this policy area are referenced extensively in this book.

The international literature was also invaluable, especially the recent work undertaken by researchers on a European Union–wide unemployment insurance (UI) benefits scheme. I contributed Canadian expertise to background research examining how UI was managed across governments in eight federations. My previous work on the European Employment Strategy and the Open Method of Coordination – the means by which the twenty-eight European Union member states coordinate their PES and employment programming – has been highly influential in shaping my thinking on how to make federal political systems work better.

Many, many people have helped me in the writing of this book. My first thanks go to Tom Klassen at York University, who encouraged me to do a PhD, got me hooked into the OECD work, and encouraged me every step along the way to write this book by reviewing chapters as they were written. He said it was like reading a serialized novel. Amy Verdun from the University of Victoria has been another mentor and key supporter. She helped me think about how Canada can be compared to the European Union and connected me to the extensive international scholarship on multilevel governance. Patrik Marier from Concordia University was a gracious host during my Montreal stay. Ed Whitcomb's little books on the provinces provided valuable insight into their political history. Brigid Hayes, Norma Strachan, and Wayne Helgason are valued colleagues who have supported me throughout the writing.

I would especially like to thank the 170 people who agreed to be interviewed for the book, including the 10 people who read first drafts of various chapters, and the eight public servants who helped me assemble and explain their data. Validation of my international descriptions from Chris O'Leary (United States), Tom Bevers (European Union), David Thompson (Australia), and Chris Luigjes (commenting on all the countries) was critical, as I needed to get the analysis and comparisons to Canada right. The detailed comments received from two peer reviewers significantly tightened up the book's focus, facts, and storyline. Finally, I would like to thank my long-suffering friends and family from Victoria and other places who have supported me every step along the way. Special thanks go to Patrick, Samantha, and Daniel, who not only endured my many absences but also helped develop some of the book's tables, charts, and figures.

Donna E. Wood
August 2017

Abbreviations

AANDC	Aboriginal Affairs and Northern Development Canada
AB	Alberta
AETWG	Aboriginal Employment and Training Working Group
AFN	Assembly of First Nations
AHRC	Aboriginal Human Resource Council
AHRDS	Aboriginal Human Resource Development Strategy
AHS	Alberta Human Services
AJC	American Jobs Centers
AJSTL	Alberta Jobs, Skills, Training and Labour
ALMP	Active Labour Market Policy
ASEP	Aboriginal Skills and Employment Partnership
ASETS	Aboriginal Skills and Employment Training Strategy
ASPECT	Association of Service Providers for Employability and Career Training
BC	British Columbia
BCCfEE	British Columbia Centre for Employment Excellence
BCJTST	British Columbia Jobs, Tourism and Skills Training
BCSDSI	British Columbia Social Development and Social Innovation
BNA	British North America
CAF	Canadian Apprenticeship Forum
CAP	Congress of Aboriginal People
CAP	Canada Assistance Plan
CASE	Canadian Association for Supported Employment
CCCBET	Canadian Coalition of Community-Based Employability Training
CCCD	Canadian Council for Career Development

CCDA	Canadian Council of Directors of Apprenticeship
CCDF	Canadian Career Development Foundation
CDP	Career Development Practitioner
CEC	Canada Employment Centre
CEIAC	Canada Employment and Immigration Advisory Council
CEIC	Canada Employment Insurance Commission
CERIC	Canadian Education and Research Institute for Counselling
CHST	Canada Health and Social Transfer
CJFA	Canada Job Fund Agreement
CJS	Canadian Jobs Strategy
CLE	Centres locaux d'emploi
CLFDB	Canadian Labour Force Development Board
CLMPC	Canadian Labour Market and Productivity Centre
CMC	Canada Manpower Centres
CMEC	Council of Ministers of Education Canada
CNSC	Careers Nova Scotia Centre
COAG	Council of Australian Governments
CPMT	Commission des partenaires du marché du travail
CRPMT	Des conseils régionaux des partenaires du marché du travail
CSCES	Canada-Saskatchewan Career and Employment Service Centre
CSMO	Les comités sectoriels de main-d'œuvre
EAPD	Employability Assistance for Persons with Disabilities
EAS	Employment Assistance Services
EBSMs	Employment Benefits and Support Measures
EES	European Employment Strategy
EI	Employment Insurance
EIC	Employment and Immigration Canada
EMCO	Employment Committee
ENS	Employment Nova Scotia
EO	Employment Ontario
EPBC	Employment Program of British Columbia
EPSCO	Employment, Social Policy, Health, and Consumer Affairs Council
EQ	Emploi-Québec
ESC	Employment Service of Canada
ESD	Enhanced Service Delivery
EU	European Union

FLMM	Forum of Labour Market Ministers
FNJF	First Nations Job Fund
HRSDC	Human Resources and Skills Development Canada
HRDC	Human Resources Development Canada
HUMA	House of Commons Committee on Human Resources, Skills, and Social Development and the Status of Persons with Disabilities
ITA	Industry Training Authority
ILO	International Labour Office
ITK	Inuit Tapiriit Kanatami
LAE	Labour and Advanced Education
LMA	Labour Market Agreement
LMAPD	Labour Market Agreement for Persons with Disabilities
LMDA	Labour Market Development Agreement
MAR	Monitoring and Assessment Report
MB	Manitoba
ME	Ministry of the Economy
MCSS	Ministry of Community and Social Services
MJE	Manitoba Jobs and the Economy
MLG	Multilevel Governance
MJSD	Manitoba Jobs and Skills Development Centre
MNC	Metis National Council
MTESS	Ministère du Travail, de l'Emploi et de la Solidarité sociale
MTCU	Ministry of Training, Colleges, and Universities
NAEDB	National Aboriginal Economic Development Board
NAO	National Aboriginal Organization
NASWA	National Association of State Workforce Agencies
NB	New Brunswick
NES	National Employment Service
NESA	National Employment Services Association
NDP	New Democratic Party
NF	Newfoundland and Labrador
NGO	non-government organization
NS	Nova Scotia
NWAC	Native Women's Association of Canada
ODSP	Ontario Disability Support Program
OECD	Organisation for Economic Cooperation and Development
OF	Opportunities Fund
OMC	open method of coordination

ON	Ontario
ONESTEP	Ontario Network of Employment Skills Training Projects
OTAB	Ontario Training and Adjustment Board
OW	Ontario Works
PBO	Parliamentary Budget Office
PEI	Prince Edward Island
PES	Public Employment Service
PETL	Post-Secondary Education, Training, and Labour
PLMPs	Passive Labour Market Policy
PQ	Parti Québécois
QC	Quebec
RBA	Regional Bilateral Agreement
RCAP	Royal Commission on Aboriginal Peoples
RECWOWE	Reconciling Work and Welfare in Europe
RFP	Request for Proposal
RQuODE)	Le Regroupement québécois des organismes pour le développement de l'employabilité
SA	Social Assistance
SK	Saskatchewan
SNAP	Supplemental Nutrition Assistance Program
SPF	Skills and Partnership Fund
SQDM	Société Québécoise de développement de la main-d'oeuvre
SST	Social Security Tribunal
SUFA	Social Union Framework Agreement
TANF	Temporary Assistance for Needy Families
TILMA	Trade, Investment and Labour Mobility Agreement
TIOW	Targeted Initiative for Older Workers
UI	Unemployment Insurance
UIC	Unemployment Insurance Commission
UIDU	Unemployment Insurance Developmental Uses
U.K.	United Kingdom
U.S.	United States
VRDP	Vocational Rehabilitation for Disabled Persons
WAPES	World Association of Public Employment Services
WIA	Workforce Investment Act
WIOA	Workforce Investment and Opportunity Act
YES	Youth Employment Strategy

FEDERALISM IN ACTION

The Devolution of Canada's Public Employment Service, 1995–2015

Chapter One

Introduction

Since the beginning of the twentieth century, every developed country has created a public employment service (PES) as a way to combat unemployment and help people find work. Although structured differently in each country, all public employment services help match supply and demand in the labour market through information, placement, and active support measures at a local, regional, and national level. As a cornerstone of the modern welfare state, an effective and well-run PES is essential to keeping a country's unemployment rates low and labour market participation rates high.

Canada's PES formally started in 1918 as a provincial service, supported by federal funding. It then got caught up in the constitutional wrangling during the depression in the 1930s on which order of government should provide income support to the unemployed. When the federal government and all provinces[1] finally agreed in 1940 to assign constitutional responsibility for a contributory unemployment insurance (UI) program (but not last-resort relief) to the Government of Canada, the provincial employment offices closed and federal ones were opened in conjunction with the new unemployment insurance scheme. Over time the federal government expanded its role. By the late 1980s Ottawa was operating over five hundred Canada Employment Centres across the country, delivering both UI and employment services.

Since 1996 the picture has changed and now provinces are again mostly responsible for the PES as well as related labour market programming through entities called (among other names) Alberta Works,

1 When the term *province* is used in this book, it generally also includes territorial governments. When the term *Ottawa* is used, it means the Government of Canada.

WorkBC, Employment Ontario, and Emploi-Québec. Triggered primarily by a need for the Chrétien Liberal government to show "flexible federalism" following the 1995 Quebec referendum, the transfer of federal responsibilities to the provinces was negotiated one jurisdiction at a time over a period of fourteen years. It was authorized through legislation transforming Unemployment Insurance (UI) into Employment Insurance (EI).

Alberta was the first jurisdiction to take back PES responsibilities in 1996, and the Yukon Territory was the last to take it on in 2010. Ottawa has kept defined national responsibilities as well as a steering role and continues to be the primary funder of the provincial programming. It has also retained direct responsibility for immigrant, youth, and disability employment programming as well as oversight of Aboriginal employment services. In 2015 programs for Aboriginal people were delivered through a network of eighty-five Aboriginal labour market organizations operating across the country under the Aboriginal Skills and Employment Training Strategy (ASETS) banner.

In 2015 provinces, territories, and Aboriginal organizations were responsible for the delivery of 87 per cent of Canada's PES programming. As a result of these changes we now have a much more decentralized and complex PES system, with considerable interdependence among all of the actors who fund, manage, and deliver programs for Canadians who either failed in their early years to make a smooth transition from school to work or later became unemployed or underemployed. These "second-chance" or "remedial" employment services are like a third system that runs alongside our more established and recognizable K–12, postsecondary education, and skills development systems that have always been under provincial control.

Canada's welfare state was built after the Second World War through cooperative federalism and the federal spending power. These gave the Government of Canada a larger role in defining the parameters of key programs than was constitutionally assigned in the 1867 confederation bargain. Over time the provinces started to resist. Starting with the "Quiet Revolution" in the 1960s, Quebec in particular was determined to assert its autonomy to the point of separation from Canada. The devolution of federal PES programming was nested within this broader decentralization trajectory that accelerated during the 1990s in response to federal fiscal retrenchment. By 2005 Canada was already considered the most decentralized welfare state in the Organisation for Economic Cooperation and Development (OECD) world (Obinger,

Leibfried, and Castles 2005). By 2015 this had increased even further as a result of the Harper Conservatives' "open federalism" commitment to strong provinces, limiting the federal spending power, and addressing the fiscal balance.

Devolution of the public employment service provides a clear example of what Canadian political scientists characterize as "province-building." It was also a natural experiment in governance, as each province was free to choose the arrangements that suited it best, including program design and delivery approaches, and the means to achieve the desired outcomes. However, all were guided by largely similar provisions agreed to in bilateral federal-provincial Labour Market Development Agreements or LMDAs (that detailed services for EI clients), as well as supplementary Labour Market Agreements (LMAs) (that provided employment services for people not eligible for EI-funded programs). Likewise, Aboriginal labour market arrangements were designed to enhance Aboriginal control and flexibility.

We now have twenty years to assess how Canada's public employment service is performing under predominately provincial, territorial, and Aboriginal – as opposed to federal – management. The OECD has been critical of our post-devolution arrangements, noting that the "system-oriented" institutional framework in place fragments PES services such that they are not only difficult for clients to navigate and access, but are also challenging to monitor and evaluate (OECD 2015b, 68–9). There is also disquiet among other commentators. Reflecting on devolution in 2015, Gunderson and Gomez (2016, 544) wondered whether a stronger provincial role was even desirable, as compared to a more pan-Canadian approach.

This book takes on the debate through a systematic assessment of provincial, Aboriginal, and federal policymaking and governance post-devolution. The inquiry is framed around four questions:

1. What governance choices did each province make in taking on the federal programming? Why did they make these choices? How do they compare? What outcomes have been achieved, and how do they compare across provinces?
2. Considered collectively, how do PES services – since 1996 mostly under the control of provincial governments and Aboriginal organizations – compare to when they were delivered by the Government of Canada?

3. How is the Government of Canada managing its role post-devolution? This includes federal-provincial and federal-Aboriginal accountability, direct responsibility for services that were not devolved, and pan-Canadian coordination.
4. How does Canada's PES work together as a whole? Is the current division of responsibility optimal? What challenges remain as Canada moves its public employment service into the twenty-first century?

My investigation of these questions begins in this opening chapter by first considering the priority Canada places on the PES. Drawing on International Labour Office (ILO) Convention No. 88 on the PES, I describe the role of a public employment service and consider how it is nested within and connected to a country's workforce development system. This is a broader term that includes measures to attract and retain talent, solve skills deficiencies, integrate immigrants, incorporate the disadvantaged, improve the quality of the workplace, and enhance the competitiveness of local firms (OECD 2008a). Next I assess why the PES matters and identify the stakeholders that are particularly interested in its success. The chapter concludes with a brief discussion of devolution as well as a look ahead at the other ten chapters of this book.

How Much Priority Does Canada Place on the PES?

PES activities in Canada have always been overshadowed by the big ticket and expensive unemployment insurance benefits scheme. The 1940 Unemployment Insurance Act had a twofold purpose of income protection and labour market adjustment. However, other than a historical volume written by John Hunter in 1993, most books, studies, and analysis of labour market policy in Canada have focused on unemployment insurance, rather than employment services.[2] Yet in 2013/14 1,168,627 Canadians used provincial and Aboriginal-run employment services (at a cost of over $3.1 billion to the Government of Canada), many of them in receipt of federal Employment Insurance or provincial social assistance benefits.

---

2 Hunter's book (1993) was a history of Employment and Immigration Canada's employment programs and services from 1900 to 1990. For information on unemployment insurance, see in particular the Gill and Forget Commissions (Canada 1962, 1986); Dingledine (1981); Struthers (1983); Pal (1988a); Campeau (2005); McBride (1992); and Banting and Medow (2012).

Compared to other countries, Canada is not a big spender on what the OECD calls active labour market policy, active employment measures, or ALMP. This calculation includes spending on the public employment service. The OECD's average of country spending as a proportion of GDP in 2011 was 0.6 per cent. In 2011 Canada's proportion was 0.3 per cent, which was well below the OECD average and in twenty-sixth position among OECD countries. By 2013 it had decreased even further to 0.23 per cent. This compares with Canadian expenditures on education (including postsecondary education), estimated by the OECD in 2011 to be 5.6 per cent of GDP, which was close to the OECD average (OECD 2014a).

While 4 per cent of the labour force in OECD countries participated in active measures, Canada's rate was one of the lowest at less than 1 per cent (Martin 2014, 7). Between 2002 and 2012 Canada's total expenditures on active measures decreased by 34 per cent. The OECD attributed part of the decrease to the devolution of labour market programs to provinces and territories (OECD 2015b, 146, 147, and 148). Recent OECD reports suggested that Canada needs to spend more on active measures than it does (OECD 2010, 2015a).

As a liberal welfare state, Canada underinvests in *public* employment services, because the vast majority of job transitions are done without government assistance. Workers and employers generally rely on personal networks or job search sites. When extra help is needed, they look first to the *private* sector to fill their labour market needs. Commercial employment agencies that match unemployed workers with employers seeking staff earn their revenues mainly through fees charged to employers, not unemployed workers. In 2013 Statistics Canada reported that the operating revenue for the employment services industry in Canada was $12.5 billion, which far exceeded government spending. Regulated by provincial governments, the business sector is the primary client for employment agencies in Canada, accounting for 87 per cent of sales (Statistics Canada 2015).

In contrast, *public* employment services are free and available to anyone. The PES role has been characterized as being the "chef d'orchestre" or "conductor," or being the "gateway" or "gatekeeper" to labour market adjustment programs. It sits at the heart of any workforce development system as the main institutional structure used to tackle unemployment and underemployment. It is like hospitals in the health-care system – it is not the only part but one of the most important parts. The breadth and reach of the PES role is interpreted differently in different countries.[3] Although international organizations such as the OECD and the International Labour Organization (ILO) use the PES term all the time, other than in Quebec it is rarely heard in Canada.

Instead we think of the programs and policies managed and delivered by the PES. This basket of programs has gone by different names over the years, adding to the opacity of the policy domain in Canada. In the 1900s until the end of the Second World War the focus was primarily on labour exchange. During the 1960s and 1970s this switched to manpower training and technical/vocational education. In the 1980s it became labour force development, skills development, and employment and training. The 1990s saw the widespread use of several terms: *active labour market policy, activation,* and *labour force adjustment*. At the start of the twenty-first-century workplace learning, human resource development, and human capital development came into vogue. The term *workforce development* is commonly used in Canada today, especially since our closest neighbour, the United States, uses it to describe its system.

What Is the Role of a Public Employment Service?

ILO Employment Services Convention (1948, no. 88) – which was ratified by Canada on 24 August 1950 – committed Canada to "maintain or ensure the maintenance of a free public employment service … as an integral part of the national programmme for the achievement and maintenance of full employment and the development and use of productive resources" (ILO 1950). It requires the establishment of a national authority, as well as a network of local offices, and regional ones where appropriate. It also prescribes that suitable arrangements, through advisory committees, are made for the cooperation of representatives of employers and workers in the organization and operation of the employment service and in the development of employment services policies. This includes providing for one or more national advisory committees and, where necessary, regional and local committees. In addition to the convention, the ILO passed Recommendation No. 83, providing additional details on the organization of the employment

3 For example, in Germany and Austria the PES is the central institution that organizes, administers, and implements both UI benefits and activation. In Australia, the United States, and Canada it is a subpart of a broader and more fragmented benefit and workforce development system.

service. Unlike conventions, ILO recommendations are not binding on member states.

The 1948 International Labour Organization Convention outlined five duties of a public employment service. First is to assist workers to find suitable employment and to assist employers in finding suitable workers. The labour exchange and job brokerage portion of this role can certainly be shared with the private sector and has increasingly been automated through electronic jobs banks. However, the labour market adjustment part is an essential public service for unemployed people who are vulnerable in the labour market, such as Aboriginal people, youth, older workers, immigrants, and disabled people, or for those who depend on government income support benefits such as EI or social assistance.

As identified by the ILO, labour market adjustment includes job search assistance programs, training and education programs, and direct job creation programs (Thuy, Hansen, and Price 2001). When people lack the skills needed to get a job, the access point for such "second chance" opportunities is through the PES. The private sector does not see this as its role. An evaluation of Canada's PES in 1989 concluded that the rationale for maintaining a publicly funded employment service lies more with its employment equity objectives than with its brokerage functions. It also noted the role of the PES in Canada as a focal point for delivering other programs such as job creation and training (EIC 1989).

The second duty of a PES is to facilitate occupational and geographic mobility so that workers in declining regions can move to expanding regions, or even commute to a job and return to their home community where living costs are lower. One of the most important parts of this duty is to facilitate the removal of barriers to occupational certification, whether across provinces or between countries when new immigrants try to secure work in Canada.

The third duty of the PES is to collect and analyse information on the employment market and its evolution – in different industries, occupations, and areas (national, provincial, and local) – and make this information available systematically and promptly to employer and worker organizations, along with the general public. In this regard the PES is both a producer of labour market information (LMI), as well as a user and interpreter of data.

The fourth duty of a PES is to cooperate in the administration of unemployment insurance and other measures for the relief of the unemployed. Increasing the proportion of the labour force that is employed not only increases social cohesion (and reduces social exclusion), it also ensures greater equality of opportunity in the world of work. The PES is the main instrument for governments to bring long-term unemployed and inactive people into the labour supply, enhance their employability, and prevent long spells on government benefits. The term used to describe this process is *activation*. Most strategies enforce mutual obligation requirements in which benefit recipients are expected to engage in job search and improve their employability, in exchange for receiving employment services and benefit payments (OECD 2013a).

The final duty of a PES – as identified in the ILO Convention – is to assist other public and private bodies as necessary in social and economic planning in order to ensure a favourable employment situation. In particular, the convention noted the need for a country's PES to focus on meeting the needs of persons with disabilities and youth (ILO 1950).

Over time, Canada's PES has taken on other responsibilities that go beyond these basic ILO requirements in Convention 88. Most significant was the provision starting in the 1970s and 1980s to provide a range of labour market development services to help industries, workers, and employers adapt to changing labour market conditions, including providing advice and support to employed workers. Enhancing the skills of the entire workforce through "lifelong learning" has also been actively promoted and in some countries is seen as a core PES activity. The breadth of the role the PES was expected to play in Canada was outlined in a 1989 purpose statement that was made when it was still operating under direct federal control: "The role of the public employment service is to enhance the functioning of the labour market by effecting more timely and beneficial labour market adjustments than would otherwise occur, thereby ensuring a more efficient and more equitable labour market" (EIC 1989, 1).

Why Does Investing in the PES and Workforce Development Matter?

Investing in workforce development – including the PES – matters because it contributes to a country's labour market performance. A strengthened PES is the key policy lever to tackle unemployment and boost job creation and economic development in any country (OECD 2015c). While the demand for workers in Canada in 2015 was – in

Figure 1. Employment Rate, 1999–2014

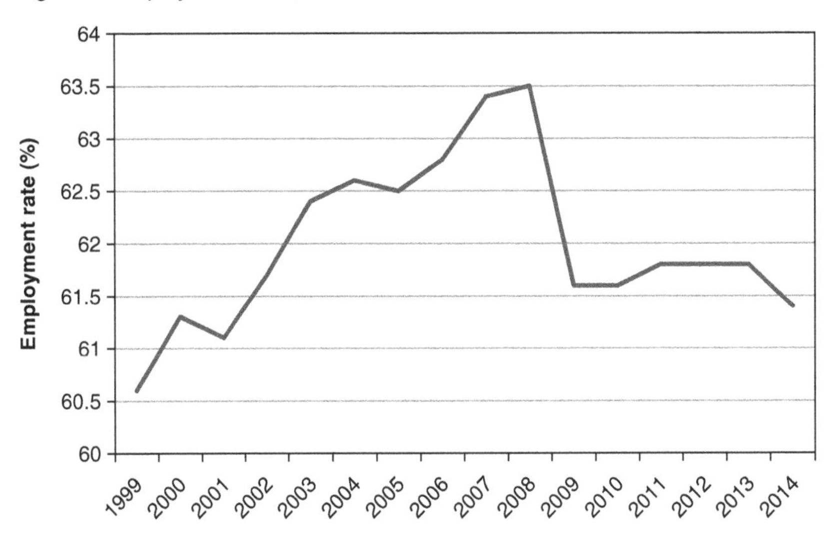

Source: Statistics Canada, table 282-0002.

general terms – far below the supply of job seekers, paradoxically there were jobs going unfilled because there was a lack of workers with the skills that employers need. Not only does the PES help develop these skills; also by facilitating job matching, it provides incentives for jobless individuals to take up jobs and helps employers fill vacancies more efficiently.

Since the 2008 economic downturn, Canada's labour market performance has been weak. While traditionally most attention is paid to the unemployment rate, a better way to measure labour market performance is to measure the employment rate: people in employment as a proportion of the working-age population. The unemployment rate excludes individuals who are not sufficiently active in their job search to qualify as being truly in the labour market. In 2013, while officially the number of unemployed in Canada stood at 1,400,000 and the unemployment rate was 7.1 per cent, "discouraged workers" corresponded to nearly 400,000 more invisible workers, pushing the true unemployment rate above 12 per cent (Stanford 2013).

Measured by the employment rate, Canada's labour market took a substantial hit with the financial crisis and subsequent recession of

2008–9. From a high of 63.5 per cent in 2008, employment declined to 61.6 per cent in 2009, which was the fastest fall-off in employment since the 1930s. For the past four years the employment rate has stayed at around this same level, and in 2014 it was even lower at 61.4 per cent. Without jobs, millions of Canadian workers live at high risk of prolonged unemployment, erratic income, and poverty. Those most at risk are people without a degree or other postsecondary credential, workers whose skills are obsolete or are no longer valuable to employers, adults with gaps in literacy and numeracy, and groups who face challenges in accessing the labour market. This includes older workers, young people, persons with disabilities, immigrants, and Aboriginal Canadians. For example, the employment rate for Aboriginal people in 2015 was 9.1 percentage points lower than the non-Aboriginal rate (NAEDB 2015).

In the absence of sufficient employment income, many Canadians have had to rely on government income support benefits such as Employment Insurance and social assistance. In March 2014 there were 652,840 regular EI benefit cases and 1,335,789 social assistance cases (provincial caseloads and income support on reserve) for a total of 1,988,629 Canadian households who depended on government income support (author's calculation).

In the 1990s Canada made dramatic changes to reduce its social safety net. In 1990 83 per cent of the unemployed received federal EI benefits; by 2013 the proportion had dropped significantly to 38.4 per cent (CEIC 2013/14). EI payments to individual claimants became smaller as the wage-replacement rate was decreased from 60 per cent in the 1990s to 55 per cent. During the same period many provinces reduced social assistance benefit levels. The conditions under which benefits were provided tightened considerably, resulting in fewer people being deemed eligible. Cumulatively these changes have increased homelessness and the use of food banks. This is fraying social cohesion across the country.

Without an adequate workforce development policy – including a vibrant PES – Canada faces the prospect of an increasingly two-tiered economy in which some people prosper while others are left behind with little hope for self-sufficiency. While the tax-transfer system in Canada offset rising inequality in market incomes of families throughout the 1980s and the recession of the early 1990s, Canadian society since then has become much more unequal. The redistributive fade in Canada was among the most dramatic in the OECD world (Banting and Myles 2013). Both the PES and related workforce development programs play a key role in reducing demand on government benefits.

Figure 2. Total Income Support Cases Canada (Social Assistance and Employment Insurance), 1997–2014

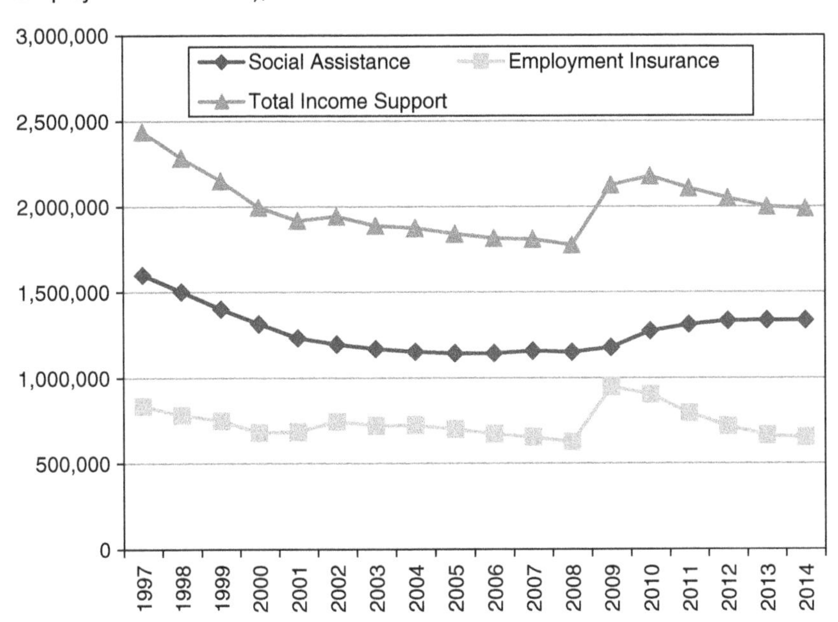

Source: for Employment Insurance, Statistics Canada, table 276-0020, March data on regular beneficiaries. For social assistance, Makhoul (2015) and income support on reserve calculated from Aboriginal Affairs and Northern Development Canada (2014a).

Without adequate and timely employment supports, millions of Canadians will miss out on opportunities for productive work and remain either unemployed or underemployed.

Labour market problems are not focused only on vulnerable workers. In 2015 the parliamentary budget officer (PBO) estimated that, on the basis of educational credentials, the proportion of workers aged twenty-five to thirty-four with a university degree who were overqualified in their current position had been on an upward trend since the 1990s, reaching 40 per cent in 2014. Labour utilization remained above its pre-recession level, indicating that there was more slack in the Canadian economy than was measured by the official unemployment rate. Compared to other advanced economies, Canada's labour market underperformed in 2015. Problems were particularly pronounced in the oil-producing provinces of Alberta and Saskatchewan (PBO 2015).

Who Needs to Be Involved?

Given the scope of PES and workforce development, a large number of individuals, groups, and organizations need to work alongside government in developing and managing the programs to ensure that they are as effective and efficient as possible. At the top of the list are the social partners, whose contributions to the EI account pay for most PES costs. Involving organizations that represent business and unions in PES decision making instils a sense of ownership that is necessary for the effective implementation of policies, as well as an opportunity to benefit from their experience and views. In some European countries the PES is actually managed and delivered by the social partners. A European colleague noted in 2015 that the German PES was so committed to its social partner principles that it would be wrong to view it as an agent of government.

Many other actors also need to be involved in planning, designing, and delivering the PES. They include organizations representing non-unionized, vulnerable, and unemployed workers; community-based training and employment service providers; national, regional, and local Aboriginal organizations; public colleges, training centres, and postsecondary institutions, and organizations that represent them; private employment service providers and agencies; and organizations representing career-development practitioners and other professionals who deliver PES services. Experts, academics, and think tank personnel who provide information and intelligence on the PES and support those who work in it also play an important role in the PES.

What Does *Devolution* Mean?

This book is about the *devolution* of Canada's public employment service, a transformation that started in the winter of 1995. Outside of academics, it is not a term that many people are familiar with, other than, perhaps, in the context of the establishment of parliaments and legislative assemblies in Scotland, Wales, and Northern Ireland in the late 1990s. Unlike a constitutional division of power, under devolution the central authority maintains control, as any legislation that it creates to transfer powers can be repealed or amended in the same way as any statute.

This is exactly what happened in Canada through the Labour Market Development Agreements. There was no constitutional realignment of labour market powers. Authorized through the federal EI Act, the LMDAs can be changed by the Government of Canada in the same way as the powers of the Scottish Parliament can be altered by the Westminster Parliament in the United Kingdom. However, just because they *can* be changed does not mean that they *will* be changed. Giving sub-state politicians increased authority typically unleashes strong political forces that can become deeply institutionalized over time.

Devolution is a particular kind of decentralization: that is, the process of redistributing or dispersing functions, powers, people, or things away from a central location or authority. Depending upon the constitutional make-up of a country, it can take the form of either (1) managerial or administrative decentralization, or (2) political decentralization or devolution. Managerial decentralization usually takes the form of management by objectives (MBO) within a national PES organization. This is what happened in Australia in the late 1990s and was how Canada's PES operated pre-devolution. In political decentralization or devolution, which occurred in Canada and the United States, the subnational tiers of government play a central role in implementation, and sometimes in policy as well. The implementing agencies are not subordinate departments of a central administration, but instead they are autonomous political entities in their own right. In these complex multilevel governance arrangements the relationship between central and regional authorities is inherently less hierarchical than in a national PES organization. By 2011 political decentralization of the PES was evident in twelve European countries, while managerial decentralization was evident in eighteen (Mosely 2012, 9).

A Look Ahead at the Rest of This Book

The opening chapter of this book has provided preliminary information on the devolution of Canada's PES, starting in 1995, and identified key questions to guide this inquiry. It has also outlined the role and place of a public employment service, how Canada fits internationally, why it is important, and who might be interested in its success.

Chapter 2 sets the stage for the remaining chapters of the book. As federal and provincial governments in Canada have squabbled for over a hundred years about who is responsible for labour market programs, history matters, as it defines the parameters of the debate. This chapter walks through developments over four time periods and under the direction of four different federal government departments to arrive at the devolution offer made by the Liberals in 1995. I then describe in general terms how provinces, territories, and Aboriginal organizations took on federal PES and related labour market programming – one step at a time – between 1996 and 2010. I finish off the historical section of the book by outlining the broad parameters of the federal-provincial agreements and the accountability requirements that were agreed to. This set the institutional architecture under which Canada's PES operated between 1996 and 2015.

Chapter 3 reviews the international and Canadian literature on federalism and activation. The federalism literature provides insight into the importance of the balance of power between the centre and sub-national governments in a federation. I am particularly interested in the autonomy of provinces, the notion of "political culture," and how they shaped provincial PES choices. A primary purpose of the PES is to activate the unemployed. Reviewing the international activation literature provided the information needed to develop an analytical framework to compare provincial governance approaches, and compare Canada with other federal political systems. As a preview, the following governance themes were distilled from the literature and are subsequently used to assess provincial approaches: (1) single gateways or one-stop shops, (2) decentralization, (3) outsourcing and contracting out, and (4) partnerships and networks. The literature was also used to help define the concepts of efficiency, effectiveness, and democracy, which are then used to assess and compare provincial performance.

Chapters 4 through *7* are similar, as they organize provincial comparisons into four geographic groupings: the Far West (British Columbia and Alberta), the Midwest (Saskatchewan and Manitoba), the Middle (Ontario and Quebec), and the East (New Brunswick, Nova Scotia, Prince Edward Island, and Newfoundland and Labrador). I chose these particular groupings on the basis of Nelson Wiseman's (2007) book on Canadian political culture. To someone who has lived in different parts of the country, not only did the groupings make sense, I also thought they would be useful, as it is within these groupings that direct governance and outcome comparisons are made. In my experience, people are more interested in knowing about their immediate neighbours (with relatively similar economic conditions), as opposed to other provinces where labour market conditions may be very different.

Each chapter is set up in a similar way. First, the province's political culture – the landscape that provides the values and attitudinal context in which government decisions are made – is examined in terms of how and why it has developed since Confederation. Then I look at historical developments around employment services and how provincial involvement pre-devolution interacted with what the Government of Canada was already doing through the local Canada Employment Centres. This includes a review of devolution events as they played out in that province. Then I look at the different choices made post-devolution around the four governance themes, comparing and assessing why these choices were made and what accounted for the differences between provinces. Next I compare performance, drawing on results in federal and provincial reports as well as other literature. All of these chapters conclude with brief thoughts on how the PES was being managed in each province compared to its neighbour.

Chapter 8 looks at Aboriginal employment programs, where the Government of Canada retains both constitutional and fiduciary responsibility. These federal-Aboriginal agreements are very different from the provincial arrangements. I start with the political context, where I examine the colonial legacy and the impact it has had on Aboriginal labour market participation and employment success. Next, I look at the history of Aboriginal labour market programs, walk through the five periods in their development, and conclude with an overview of how the programs were being managed in 2015, primarily under the banner of the Aboriginal Skills and Employment Training Strategy, or ASETS. Then I examine relationships: Aboriginal–federal, Aboriginal–Aboriginal, Aboriginal–provincial, and Aboriginal–private sector. Subsequently I look at results, using data extracted from government sources.

Chapter 9 looks at the role of the Government of Canada post-devolution. First I consider the federal-provincial accountability arrangements. Then I look at the programming that the federal government did not devolve. In addition to Aboriginal labour market programs, it retained direct responsibility for immigrant, youth, and disability programming, along with the pan-Canadian aspects of labour market development. As the national government, it also plays a part in coordination: between governments, between social partners and other organizations involved with direct PES delivery, and between Canada and international organizations. This chapter also looks at the state of research in labour market matters in 2015, as well as national advisory structures that provided input from non-government stakeholders. This includes an examination of the role of the EI commissioners for employers and workers.

Chapter 10 compares Canada's PES arrangements to three other large and dispersed federal political systems that have made very different choices in the public employment service: the United States, Australia, and the European Union. These are good comparators to Canada as there are two constitutionally defined orders of government in each that operate across a large geographic area. Canada's unemployment insurance program in the 1930s was derived from the European experience, not the American one. Regardless, lessons that might be transferable to the Canadian context from these three political systems are identified and assessed.

Bringing all this together is *chapter 11*. Here I return to the four questions detailed in this first chapter that guided the inquiry and answer them directly. In doing so I knit the strands of the PES devolution story into a coherent pan-Canadian assessment of where PES programming stands in Canada twenty years post-devolution. The book concludes with reflections on how an examination of the PES provides a way to understand the workings of Canadian federalism following our failure to amend the Constitution in the late 1980s and early 1990s. It also looks at what might be ahead over the next decade as the Trudeau Liberals take back the reins of power in 2016. In their 2015 election platform, they made very specific funding commitments that, in my view, will go a long ways towards the revitalization and renewal of Canada's PES programming for the twenty-first century.

Chapter Two

Historical Developments and Devolution Parameters

Canada's unique constitutional arrangements and the lack of clarity in the British North America Act (BNA) over which order of government is responsible for employment and training supports has made labour market policy a uniquely contested domain. Responsibility – along with its accompanying assets, resources, contractual commitments, and government staff – has shifted back and forth between federal and provincial governments three times over the past 100 years. Along the way municipal governments also moved in and out. To make things even more complex, for a period of time Canada's public employment service, or PES, was managed at arm's length from government.

This chapter charts these developments, with most information taken from the historical record, government reports, and books and articles written that describe and analyse the events. It begins with an overview of the development of Canada's PES up to 1996. Then I look at devolution, highlighting in particular how a broader turn towards decentralization, fiscal restraint, and Quebec's drive for autonomy came together to contextualize the federal decision made in 1995 to offer provinces responsibility for the design and delivery of active labour market programs.

Negotiating the deal and political developments post-devolution are examined next, including how subsequent federal decisions to allocate additional funding for groups not well-served by Employment Insurance (EI) funding consolidated and affirmed provincial primacy in the policy area. The chapter concludes by examining the parameters of the four federal-provincial agreements that governed the PES in 2014, including programming and accountability arrangements.

Historical Developments to 1996

Deciding Jurisdictional Responsibility, 1900s–1940s

In the early 1900s, private agencies across Canada were operating employment services, as well as some provinces and municipalities. Since the policy area was not identified in the BNA Act, responsibility for such local institutions was considered as clearly provincial. Given abuse by the private agencies and the need to respond to concerns about unemployment and the potential for social unrest following demobilization after the First World War, in 1918 the federal government enacted – with provincial approval – the Employment Offices Coordination Act. This provided for the establishment of what became known as the Employment Service of Canada (ESC): a national network of provincially operated employment services funded in part by the federal government through conditional grants.[1] This was the first federal involvement in manpower issues (Campeau 2005). However, the fact that the offices were provincially run reinforced the provinces' jurisdictional claim over the labour field (Pal 1988a).

ESC services were managed and delivered across Canada by federal and provincial civil servants, with a National Employment Service Council (consisting of national and provincial administrators as well as business and labour representatives) providing advice and guidance. By the 1930s there were seventy-six ESC offices operating across Canada. Its main focus was on labour exchange (Hunter 1993). While provinces retained complete authority over the establishment and operation of the employment offices, the federal government supervised the system through a national headquarters in Ottawa and four regional clearing houses (Struthers 1983).

Like employment services, education was also a provincial constitutional responsibility. At the same time as the Employment Service of Canada was being developed, the Technical Education Act of 1919 and the Vocational Education Act of 1931 provided conditional federal funding as a way for Ottawa to encourage provinces to expand technical and vocational education under their control. The urgent manpower needs of the Second World War compelled the passage in 1942

---

1 Ottawa subsidized the provincial offices though an annual grant of $150,000 and 50–50 cost-sharing of expanding the provincial systems. They also coordinated provincial activities on a national basis (Pal 1988a).

of the federal Vocational Training Coordination Act, providing funds to provinces on a matching basis to expand this kind of training.

While responsibility for education has always been closely guarded by provinces, the vocational and technical component has strong federal-provincial roots, as it is here that federal jurisdiction in economic matters overlaps with provincial jurisdiction in education. The federal government's economic responsibilities give it an interest in increasing the employment potential of the unemployed through basic or technical training. It also has an interest in ensuring that young people have the education needed for productive entry into the labour force (Dupré et al. 1973, 38). Given constitutional constraints, it was felt that these federal interests could be expressed only through the federal spending power, with provinces free to accept conditional federal funding to expand their programming or not, dependent upon their internal priorities.

Alongside implementation of the Employment Service of Canada, increased focus and attention was also being given to the need for an unemployment insurance benefits scheme. Starting in the fall of 1920 the Canadian economy began a steep slide into depression that it recovered from only by entering the war in 1939. At its depth in 1933, 30 per cent of the Canadian population were unemployed and one fifth of the population was dependent upon last-resort municipal relief, today called social assistance. The ESC could only find jobs, not create them.

As the larger issue of relief came to dominate the federal-provincial agenda, the ESC fell victim to Prime Minister Mackenzie King's dislike of conditional grants, as well as business desires to establish their own employment services to place farm workers. Federal funding to both their own ESC offices and the provincial offices was substantially reduced between 1923 and 1924, and provinces consequently froze their own allocations. There were increasing complaints about the quality of the provincial services, as many of the staff were patronage appointments. Given joint jurisdiction and control, it was difficult for the federal government to hold provinces to account through the conditional grants. In his assessment of the ESC, Struthers (1983, 40) concluded, "After 1924 the ESC was little more than a patronage-ridden clearing house for casual help."

The history of how Canada's unemployment insurance (UI) system came about – the change in social attitude away from unemployment being considered an individual failure to a system failure; the Rowell-Sirois Commission on dominion-provincial relations recommending a national social insurance program to deal with unemployment; the rationale for UI (but not relief) becoming a federal responsibility; the process of disallowance of early federal legislation by the Judicial Committee of the Privy Council, followed by unanimous provincial consent for a constitutional amendment transferring unemployment insurance responsibility from the provinces to Ottawa – has been described in detail in Dingledine (1981), Struthers (1983), Pal (1988b), and Campeau (2005) and will not be repeated here, other than one key element.

All involved in the development of the unemployment insurance scheme – including federal political parties – were convinced that a *national* UI scheme could not be successful without a *national* public employment service. The Canadian scheme drew upon the British experience with unemployment insurance, in which it had been concluded that an efficient employment service was "the very foundation of an unemployment insurance scheme" (Hunter 1993, 66). Those developing the new federal UI program concluded that nationalization of the provincially run ESC would eliminate the problems of joint federal-provincial administration, including the inability of Ottawa to influence the way in which the service was operated. In addition, a federally run employment service was seen to be essential if Ottawa was to take on an enhanced training role to make the jobless "employable."

Under the shadow of the beginning of the Second World War, a new paragraph 91 (2A) was inserted in the BNA Act, authorizing unemployment insurance as a federal responsibility.[2] All nine provinces consented. By June 1940 the federal-provincial wrangling that had gone on for a dozen or more years on the topic was seen as unpatriotic. In addition, provinces were keen to reduce their relief expenditures; by making Ottawa responsible for some of the unemployed[3] the burden could be

2 The 1940 constitutional amendment did not explicitly include employment services. Struthers (1983, 187) suggests that a reference to the PES was dropped by Mackenzie King because he feared that federal responsibility for finding jobs might be used by provinces and municipalities as an argument for the dominion assuming responsibility for relief. Despite the lack of a direct reference, employment services have always been considered as an integral part of UI. Through *Confédération des syndicats nationaux v Canada (Attorney General)*, 2008, SCC 68, the Supreme Court of Canada reaffirmed that the scope of the federal UI program includes employment services.

3 Marsh (1943) noted that, at the time, many provinces interpreted the UI amendments as conferring upon Parliament responsibility and jurisdiction for all unemployed.

shared more equally, contributing to national unity. Previously reluctant premiers had lost elections, providing a window of opportunity for Prime Minister Mackenzie King to secure unanimous constitutional agreement to act (Struthers 1983).

In his view the war – not the depression – had created a compelling new reason for a federal unemployment insurance scheme, supported by a national employment service to ensure a claimant's rapid return to work (Dingledine 1981). Not only would it help with demobilization, a program of compulsory savings would create a pool of money available for government use and a way for people to save in case they became unemployed. A well-staffed and competent federal employment service would provide the dominion government with expert knowledge on the changes and conditions of employment.

Expanding Direct Federal Programming and Reach into Provincial Programs, 1940s–1960s

With the passage of the 1940 Unemployment Insurance Act, in one stroke 3,000 new civil-service jobs were created and 1,600 federal offices were opened in cities and towns across the country (Struthers 1983, 200 and 202). Work began immediately to implement the new Unemployment Insurance (UI) Act. Both parts of the system (UI income support and employment services) were to be run by an Unemployment Insurance Commission (UIC) – a statutory agency reporting to the minister of labour – made up of three commissioners, two of whom were appointed after consultations with organizations representing employers and workers. The third represented government.

In addition to the commission, an Unemployment Insurance Advisory Committee was established to review premium rates, adequacy of coverage, and the benefit structure. A National Employment Committee – consisting of eight members, three each from business and labour, in addition to one from the Canadian Legion and one from the League of Women's Rights – was set up to provide advice to the UI Commission on employment matters (Hunter 1993). While the advisory committees were independent from the UIC, the entire scheme was seen as a cooperative enterprise between employers and workers under government supervision. This cooperative tripartite principle involving government, employers, and workers was embedded in all parts of the program, including the commission, the advisory committees, and the Courts of Referees (Dingledine 1981).

Under the commission, actuarial and insurance concerns dominated, focused on ensuring financial self-sufficiency of the scheme and receptivity to privatization. Not only should UI not be funded by government, the philosophy at its initiation was that its administration had to be kept as far away from government as possible to prevent political leaders from expanding coverage under pressure from their voters (Campeau 2005).

The provincial ESC offices as well as responsible staff in the federal Department of Labour were moved into the newly formed Unemployment Insurance Commission and rebranded as the National Employment Service, or NES. Pal's 1988 analysis of Unemployment Insurance outlines in some detail the bureaucratic challenges in setting up the Unemployment Insurance Commission, especially in relation to its arm's length status and relationship with the federal Department of Labour. In his view, this had to do with the tension at the heart of UI between income security and labour market goals. A UI program must do more than offer benefits: it must also ensure that claimants are available for work and seek employment. It should also provide positive assistance to help them secure stable work (Pal 1988b, 120). These labour market or manpower policy functions were hard to square with a UI system operating under a philosophy of actuarial control.

As a result of this tension, during the post-war era the NES limped along, "severely hampered by lack of adequate staff and facilities" (as reported in Dupré et al. 1973, 47). As a subordinate agency, the NES was diverted from its job placement role to processing Unemployment Insurance claims. It acted more as an unemployment service than an employment service, dealing with no more than 10 per cent of the working population. As a result, few citizens wanted to take advantage of the service for fear of being associated with the indigent proportion of the population (McDonald 1966). Still, the NES expanded, setting up several youth employment offices as well as services for immigrants and women. Between 1958 and 1968 a federal winter works program was implemented at a cost of $267 million over ten years (Hunter 1993).

Over time the UI Advisory Committee, with its labour and business representatives, was largely pushed to the side; instead discussions and decisions took place mainly at the level of the executive and within the federal bureaucracy (Porter 2003, 103). In 1951 a new National Advisory Council on Manpower with more than thirty members was established to consider a number of issues, including the labour stresses emerging from the Korean War, the role of the NES, the need for vocational training, and measures to ameliorate seasonal employment. However, by 1955 the council had been disbanded.

In 1960 the NES was given an increased role in making referrals of UI claimants to training (EIC 1989). However, by 1962 the full shortcomings of the NES as delivered by the Unemployment Insurance Commission (UIC) had been outlined in detail in the *Report of the Committee of Inquiry into the Unemployment Insurance Act*, known as the Gill Report (Canada 1962). Drawing on ILO convention 88 on the functions of a public employment service – that Canada had agreed to in 1950 – the Gill Report recommended that a thoroughly revamped employment service be divorced from the Unemployment Insurance Commission and made a direct responsibility of an operating department of the federal government.

Even though the Unemployment Insurance Commission disagreed with this recommendation – as UI required that recipients demonstrate that they were looking for work – the Government of Canada moved quickly to transfer the NES from the commission to a federal operating department. After first moving it to the Department of Labour, in 1965 Ottawa transferred the NES along with a host of other activities into a newly created Department of Manpower[4] and Immigration. The NES was the major arm of the new department, with 5,049 field personnel (McDonald 1966). Association of the NES with federal immigration responsibilities made sense, as Canada had historically used immigration policies to address skills shortages and inadequacies of the labour force (Klassen 2000a).

Within the NES, responsibility for the placement and settlement of immigrants was consolidated with services for unemployment insurance claimants. The old NES offices were transformed into Canada Manpower Centres (CMCs) as part of a "grand design" for the federal government to assume full responsibility for manpower policy (Pal 1983). The title *National Employment Service* disappeared as employment officers became manpower counsellors (Hunter 1993). The CMCs were to be viewed as a "vital point in the life of each community," with every effort exerted to make them attractive to Canadians and local communities through trained local staff and access to a sophisticated

---

4 The choice of the word *manpower* reflected labelling in the early 1960s. The department name was subsequently changed in 1977 to the more gender-neutral Employment and Immigration.

national network providing economic intelligence and analysis (Dupré et al. 1973).

Changes to the NES were accompanied by increased funding from Ottawa to the provinces to help them cover the costs of training and other income support programs and expand the Canadian welfare state. After the war, Ottawa consolidated its funding to provinces to cover the costs of relief – now called social assistance – especially for single parents and the disabled. This culminated in the Canada Assistance Plan in 1966, with federal funding covering 50 per cent of provincial costs for not just last-resort income support, but also the cost of "work activity" projects to help people on assistance get jobs. Some provinces used the federal money to start specialized employment programs. However, these were relatively small. In 1961 the Vocational Rehabilitation for Disabled Persons (VRDP) Act was passed, authorizing the federal government to share 50 per cent of the cost provinces incurred in providing a range of vocational services to assist people with mental or physical disabilities become capable of pursuing a gainful occupation (Rice and Prince 2013).

The federal government also raised its grants to provinces for training unemployed and marginally employed workers, and in 1960 passed a new and comprehensive piece of legislation known as the Technical and Vocational Training Assistance Act (TVTA), which provided "massive" federal assistance to the provinces for capital, operating, and training costs incurred in vocational and technical guidance and education. Ottawa was motivated to expand its support by the growing realization that immigration could no longer be relied on for a skilled workforce and that the great bulk of unemployment in the 1959–60 economic recession was secular and chronic (Doern 1969). The additional federal funding associated with TVTA enabled provincial governments to bring vocational and technical education into its own in relation to K–12 and postsecondary education (Dupré et al. 1973).

While TVTA funding focused additional resources on training the unemployed (by reimbursing 75 per cent and then 100 per cent of provincial costs), it also included programming intended to assist employed workers to upgrade their skills. However, there were problems with expanding the services, as some provinces – especially Atlantic Canada – lacked the capacity to match the federal funding. Other provinces like Quebec and Alberta were concerned that federal grants were directing provincial policy in their area of competence and were an invasion of provincial jurisdiction over education. These issues meant that the supply of adult occupational training was unevenly distributed across the country. Provincial operational control of adult training provided little recognition for the Government of Canada, even though it was paying much of the costs. While applicants for training were processed through the NES, selection and counselling were firmly in the hands of provincial institutions and local school boards.

Training was the missing link in a comprehensive federal manpower policy. Influenced by the Economic Council of Canada reports, in 1966 the federal Liberal government under Prime Minister Pearson asserted that employment was above all a federal responsibility, and announced that it was going to expand its activities in adult training, using the newly created Canada Manpower Centres as the delivery agent. In this new world the federal government would withdraw from providing conditional grants like the TVTA to provinces, and instead would be free to shop around to purchase training among all potential suppliers – provincial institutions, school boards, industry, and private schools. The federal grants would be made to individual adults, rather than to provincial governments. Where previously provincial institutions did the counselling and training and the federal government provided the placement service, federal officials would now take over the counselling role as well (Dupré et al. 1973).

Dupré and his co-authors describe this "clash of great designs" between the federal and provincial governments in some detail in their 1973 book on adult occupational training in Ontario, with frequent references to the role of the Canada Manpower Centres and how the three functions under adult occupational training – placement, counselling, and training – were carried out by the CMCs, compared to provincial institutions. They were highly sceptical of the potential for the federal CMCs to become a "vital point in the life of each community," given their isolation from the community they served and ignorance of provincial services, including the courses to which they were expected to refer clients. In their view the federal government and the local Canada Manpower Centres should focus their efforts on labour market information, and a provincial placement service should be established in its place, available to provinces that were interested in taking it on. This perspective, expressed in the early 1970s, was certainly prescient about what would actually happen twenty years later with the 1995 federal devolution offer.

Provinces were very concerned over the federal manpower training plans. As a counterbalance to the federal government's assertion of competence over employment, in 1967 they came together to set up the Council of Ministers of Education Canada (CMEC) in order to provide an institutional structure to assert provincial jurisdiction over education. Since that time provincial governments – Quebec and Alberta in particular – have patrolled the boundaries and guarded provincial jurisdiction over education. Despite its direct involvement in supporting students (through the Canada Student Loans program) and universities (through research grants), the federal government is invited to engage with CMEC only on very specific matters, mostly on an ad hoc basis. CMEC is highly institutionalized, with work driven at the level of ministers and deputy ministers, who have held face-to-face meetings two or three times per year every year since its establishment. There is a large permanent secretariat with over sixty staff located in Toronto. In July 2014, ministers from across Canada celebrated their 103rd CMEC meeting (Wood 2014).

The Activation Turn in the 1960s to the 1980s

During the 1960s the Organisation for Economic Cooperation and Development (OECD) started to promote an "activation turn" in employment policy, and in 1964 the International Labour Office (ILO) approved Convention 122 Employment Policy calling for an "active policy designed to promote full, productive and freely chosen employment" (ILO 1964). In 1966 Canada ratified ILO convention 122, shifting the emphasis of employment programs from placement to training, counselling, and job creation (EIC 1989). Moving responsibility for the NES in 1965 from the Unemployment Insurance Commission to a new federal Department of Manpower and Immigration was all part of the new federal focus on activation.

Dramatic changes to Unemployment Insurance after 1971 enlarged the scheme to cover a range of jobs not formerly covered. The reforms also changed UI financing, broadened the range of benefits, and linked payments to national and regional labour market conditions. By 1983 UI had become the largest operating program of the federal government (Royal Commission 1985). The year 1974 saw the first acknowledged "developmental" uses of the Unemployment Insurance fund, referred to as UIDU: paying for training, work sharing, and job creation out of funds contributed by employers and workers to the Unemployment Insurance account. Not only did the idea stem from a desire to enhance the effects of UI on labour market efficiency – primarily on work incentives and job search activity – in 1976 the UI account had a surplus, presenting an opportunity to fund new employment programs without raiding other programs or raising taxes (Pal 1983).

However, not all thought that this was a good idea, particularly employers and unions concerned that the developmental use of UI fragmented the purpose of a UI scheme. Despite these concerns, in 1977 "active measures" became a formal part of the UI program, allowing claimants to continue to collect benefits if they participated in training or job creation programs. Unemployment Insurance soon became the main source of income for people participating in adult training programs (Campeau 2005).

On the administrative front, by 1972 the now separate Unemployment Insurance Commission sought to improve liaison with the Canada Manpower Centres (CMCs), and in 1977 the UI Commission was amalgamated with a newly created Department of Employment and Immigration Canada (EIC). This was accomplished by making the deputy and associate deputy ministers of the federal department the chairman and vice-chairman of the commission, while still retaining the commissioners for employers and workers. According to Pal (1988a) this change was of historic importance, as it "finally buried the 1940 principles that UI should be insulated from political pressure through management by an autonomous Commission and that employers and employees had a proprietary right to the program ... in placing the deputy minister in the chair and reducing private sector representation on the Commission from two out of three to two out of four ... the government in effect expropriated the UI program" (132).

In 1976 the Advisory Committee established under the 1940 UI legislation was disbanded and replaced by the Canada Employment and Immigration Advisory Council (CEIAC). Council activities and scope were much broader than those of the UI Advisory Committee, encompassing all activities under the responsibility of the minister of manpower and immigration. The council was also much larger, consisting of fifteen to twenty-one people, with one third representing employers, another third representing workers, and the final third representing other constituencies such as persons with disabilities, women, etc. While the council was prolific (between 1981 and 1990 it produced twenty-six reports on a wide variety of topics), some considered it to be weaker than the UI Advisory Committee that it replaced (Pal 1988a).

In the 1970s employment equity issues emerged as a concern, and EIC expanded the reach of employment programs beyond UI recipients through what was known as the "designated group policy" to include employment services for four groups: women, the disabled, visible minorities, and Natives. Given concerns about youth unemployment as thousands of young people flooded into the labour market, EIC also established an "opportunities for youth" program. Under an umbrella term called "outreach," many of the services for these new client groups were contracted out to local, community-based training organizations and paid for from government general revenues – not the UI account – as participants did not qualify for UI benefits.

In conjunction with the departmental name change in 1977, Canada Manpower Centres became Canada Employment Centres, or CECs. An internal task force assessment in 1981 – known as the Dodge Report – examined all federal labour market programming, noting the poor image of the service and that over 50 per cent of users found that it did a "poor" or "only fair" job in helping people find work. Employers generally preferred to use informal hiring channels over the PES, even for low-skilled workers (EIC 1981, 77). A number of suggestions for reform were made by the task force, including an increased focus on special needs groups as well as enhanced labour market information and intelligence.

In 1982 Ottawa replaced the 1967 Adult Occupational Training Act with the National Training Act in order to give more emphasis to high-demand skills. In 1983 it revitalized the National Employment Service by dividing it into (1) labour market information, (2) labour exchange, and (3) adjustment services. The traditional job-placement role was de-emphasized, and resources were moved into intake/assessment (Virtuosity Consulting 2003). In 1986 the federal government determined that literacy was another priority and by 1988 had staked out a pan-Canadian coordination role by establishing the National Literacy Secretariat. Federal youth programming expanded, including initiatives for students, work-study, stay-in-school, apprenticeship, youth-at-risk, and summer youth employment programs.

Alongside these federal-only initiatives, some provinces started to fill in the gaps in federal labour market programming, particularly for youth and employed workers. In 1983 governments established the Forum of Labour Market Ministers (FLMM) as a federal/provincial/territorial forum to promote inter-jurisdictional cooperation on labour market issues. Some of the early issues were unemployment insurance, youth programming, and training for women. However, unlike the Council of Ministers of Education Canada (CMEC), little concerted effort was made to institutionalize the FLMM.

As part of a broader Task Force on Program Review (known as the Neilson Report), another review of the PES was undertaken in 1985. A mixed study team – consisting of government officials as well as private sector representatives – looked at sixty-five federal job creation, training, and employment services programs. The private-sector representatives were particularly critical of the federal role in job placement. The report noted that there was a "high level of dissatisfaction with the quality of the screening and referral service by CEC's" (Canada 1985, 78). The task force recommended that the PES should either be improved or withdrawn.

In 1986 the Canadian Jobs Strategy (CJS) was introduced under the newly elected Mulroney Progressive Conservatives. As the economy began to recover following the 1982–3 recession, the view grew that the market itself should look after the high-demand skills, and federal programs should focus principally on disadvantaged and vulnerable groups (Informetrica 1993). As a result, federal public employment services started to focus more on those most in need, while still retaining some "high-end" on-the-job training focused on employer needs. Ottawa also started to extricate itself from direct block purchases of training from provincial governments. These unilateral actions caused federal-provincial tensions to increase, as provinces were concerned about protecting their federal funding and community college systems.

Through this shift, EIC local offices increasingly entered into agreements with community-based delivery agents – not provincial governments – for programs that combined work experience and on-the-job training. Committed to equity and with a non-profit orientation, these organizations focused primarily on serving marginalized groups. Federal evaluation results had shown that these kinds of delivery agents were more effective for clients, "as they strengthened the community non-governmental fabric and avoided federal-provincial-territorial tensions over education/training and seat-purchases" (Virtuosity Consulting 2003, 14). There was no competitive bidding for these contracts, which were regularly renewed from one year to the next.

In 1986 the Forget Commission – set up to review the broader UI program – noted how the earlier Dodge and Neilson Reports had identified concerns over the ineffectiveness of the placement services and employment programs being run by the CECs. While there was no agreement among the Forget commissioners on many aspects of the employment service, they did agree that unemployed workers should go to one federal office for both UI and employment services, and that these services should be available to all the unemployed, not just UI recipients. The commission recommended that the CEC placement services should either be revitalized or cancelled (Canada 1986, 279). Another key message from the review of UI was the need for greater involvement by labour market partners in employment policies and programs. The Forget commissioners concluded that solutions had to come from government in partnership with other groups and organizations in society (Virtuosity Consulting 2003). The work of the commission was discounted when the labour representatives disagreed with the final report (Pal 1988a).

At the same time as this was happening on the federal side, provinces started to experiment with welfare-to-work programs. Part of the imperative was increased social assistance caseloads and costs as a result of the economic downturn in the early 1980s. Another was a growing societal expectation that single parents and disabled people should work, as opposed to being passively supported on government welfare benefits. As part of the Canadian Jobs Strategy, the federal government undertook new cooperative initiatives with provincial governments to reallocate federal employment funds managed by EIC as well as diverted federal funds managed by Health and Welfare Canada through the Canada Assistance Plan (CAP) to a "four-cornered strategy" to provide new employment opportunities for social assistance recipients.

As these federal dollars would normally have gone to provide a 50 per cent share of social assistance benefit costs through CAP – the rationale was to shift "passive" spending (on social assistance) to "active" measures (on employment services, labour market training, subsidized employment, etc.) by providing more flexibility under federal CAP cost-sharing rules. The shift in focus was informed by OECD comparisons showing that Canada ranked fairly low among OECD countries in the proportion of resources going to "active measures" (Virtuosity Consulting 2003, 11). The activation bent was therefore applied not just to federal Unemployment Insurance recipients, but also to provincial last-resort social assistance.

In 1987 the federal government initiated a cost-shared pilot project with the provinces – called the Program for Older Worker Adjustment – to provide support to unemployed older workers affected by major layoffs after their UI benefits expired. The activation turn was further reinforced through the increased use of UIDU, where federal training expenditures were being more and more shifted from being paid out of general revenues to the UI account (Campeau 2005). Some provinces started to co-locate their social assistance and employment services with federal CEC offices so that "one-stop" access to employment supports could be provided to all citizens, regardless of their source of income support. Federal and provincial officials in some provinces also started to meet more regularly, developing a better understanding of each other's programming. This work emphasized the importance of removing work disincentives embedded in the unemployment insurance and social assistance systems, as well as the tax system.

The Corporatist Turn of the Late 1980s and Early 1990s

One requirement of ILO convention 88 on a public employment service was that the signatories would maintain national, regional, and local advisory committees to seek the views of employers and workers in the organization and operation of the PES. In 1984 business and labour – through the Canadian Labour Congress and the Business Council on National Issues – came together to form a bipartite independent national organization, the Canadian Labour Market and Productivity Centre (CLMPC), to develop joint approaches to improve the operation of the labour market and Canada's productivity performance.

In 1985 CECs began to establish Local Advisory Councils (LACs) as a counterpart to the national Canada Employment and Immigration Advisory Council, which provided advice to the Employment Insurance Commission. In 1989 the Mulroney Progressive Conservatives introduced the Labour Force Development Strategy, the cornerstone of which was to use up to 15 per cent of Unemployment Insurance Funds for developmental uses, including work sharing, job creation, support for self-employment, and apprentices (Informetrica 1993). The new strategy also proposed a different model for securing the involvement of the labour market partners. As a result, many of the LACs subsequently closed (Hunter 1993).

One approach pursued by Ottawa focused on business and labour partnerships in specific industry sectors, such as aerospace, steel, automotive repair, and electronics. In 1992 EIC expanded federal funding support for the Sectoral Partnership Initiative; by mid-1997 there were twenty-two National Sector Councils operating with federal funding support (Gunderson and Sharpe 1998). Another approach focused on the establishment of broad-based labour force development boards in defined geographic areas. Following extensive consultations undertaken by the CLMPC, in 1991 the minister of employment and immigration announced the establishment of the Canadian Labour Force Development Board (CLFDB), with twenty-two members drawn from business, labour, social action groups, and training organizations, as well as governments as ex-officio members. The EI commissioners for workers and employers were instrumental in nominating representatives from their constituency.

In the context of a new free trade agreement between Canada and the United States, the Mulroney Progressive Conservatives were motivated to establish labour market advisory boards as a way to increase the training efforts of Canada's private sector. The national board was to be supplemented wherever possible by provincial and local boards that would make local skills training decisions. Federal officials across the country led in creating the boards. Ultimately provincial boards were established in Newfoundland, Nova Scotia, New Brunswick, Quebec, Ontario, Saskatchewan, and British Columbia. For various reasons that are explored in more detail in later chapters of this book, Alberta, Prince Edward Island, and Manitoba never established provincial labour market boards. Ontario and Quebec also established local boards (Haddow and Sharpe 1997).

While the national board was meant to provide leadership, there was no intent that the provincial boards would report to it. The CLFDB was to be concerned mainly with making recommendations to the federal government on training policies and programs and funding levels from the UI account. The emphasis was on partnership. It did indeed do that; in 1993 the CLFDB voiced reservations about the cuts to general revenue financing of training and employment programs and the use of the UI account to finance actions other than income support. By 1994 support for active measures out of general revenue was only $1.4 billion, whereas the UI fund paid out $1.9 billion (as reported in Campeau 2005, 209).

At the same time as these partnership developments were underway, in the early 1990s the Progressive Conservatives passed an Employment Equity Act, set up a House of Commons Standing Committee on Persons with Disabilities, and announced a five-year national strategy for the integration of persons with disabilities. They also reassessed how employment services for Aboriginal people were being managed. Targeted programs were already being delivered through Aboriginal outreach initiatives and by Indigenous people recruited by the CECs as

Native employment counsellors. Nevertheless, many Aboriginal people did not feel that their unique needs were being met.

In 1989 an Aboriginal Employment and Training Working Group was established, made up of representatives from six national Aboriginal organizations as well as federal EIC staff from the regions and headquarters. Out of this initiative and in the shadow of the Aboriginal self-government movement, complementary national, regional, and local Aboriginal Management Boards were established starting in 1991 to set training priorities for Aboriginal communities and develop partnership and co-management practices. Ultimately one national board, 12 regional or territorial, and 100 local Aboriginal labour market boards were established.

None of the labour market boards lasted long. They were easy to disband, as they were not established in legislation. By 1996 the pan-Aboriginal Management Board had disappeared, fractured among the different Aboriginal constituencies, to be replaced by national framework agreements between the federal government and each of the First Nations, Metis, Inuit, and off-reserve groups. For various reasons (discussed in subsequent chapters of this book) all the provincial boards closed down. The national labour market board (CLFDB) struggled for relevance in a changing labour market policy landscape, and its demise was finalized in 1998 when representatives of the Business Council on National Issues and the Canadian Federation of Independent Business announced that they were pulling out (Virtuosity Consulting 2003).

In a conflicted jurisdictional area such as labour market policy, federal-provincial tension and dominance by government executives tended to push aside the views of other stakeholders. At the CLFDB table it was difficult for business and labour to cooperate with each other, let alone with the equity groups that also had a seat at the table. Probably the most important dynamic was political commitment, given that politicians do not willingly give away their decision-making authority to non-government players. With a change in government from the Progressive Conservatives to the Liberals in 1993, the diminished support of the new minister and departmental officials was evident by 1994, when the board's advice on UIDU was overturned. The negotiation of the federal-provincial Labour Market Development Agreements in 1996 and the increased role of provincial governments in EI-funded employment programming ultimately reduced the relevance of a national advisory body (Virtuosity Consulting 2003, 25).

The Devolution Context

So far nothing in this story suggests a willingness of the federal government to offer PES responsibilities to provincial governments, nor was any evidence provided that provinces aspired to it. Federal efforts in the late 1980s to extricate themselves from direct block purchases of training in provincial institutions and Ottawa's decision to use community organizations as delivery agents for training over provincial institutions certainly heightened federal-provincial conflict and tension, as did federal action to set up labour force development boards and national sector councils. As provinces increasingly started to provide employment services to social assistance recipients and become players in the "activation game," perceptions of overlap and duplication grew and magnified. This also spilled over into youth programming, where some federal and provincial governments operated parallel initiatives.

None of these issues were particularly new. However, three additional factors came to the surface in the early 1990s – decentralization, a federal social security review followed by fiscal restraint, and Quebec autonomy – that, taken together, resulted in the dramatic realignment of federal-provincial PES responsibilities starting in 1995.

The Decentralization Turn

By the late 1980s Ottawa was operating 509 Canada Employment Centres across the country, with approximately five thousand employees delivering both UI and employment services (EIC 1990b, 21). It was also responsible for twenty-five specialized offices, 187 itinerant points of service, and over one hundred centres located on campus across the country (Canada 1986, 278). At the same time, provinces were extensively involved in managing a system of social services and postsecondary institutions for their citizens as well as – to varying degrees – employment support services. In the provinces that offered them, these services focused primarily on social assistance recipients and youth.

In 1994 the OECD released its landmark *Jobs Study* and made a series of policy recommendations to correct labour market deficiencies in member countries. Its research also focused on governance, demonstrating how regional and local control and flexibility in employment services were necessary to keep a country's unemployment rate low and employment rate high. Unlike income support payments, in employment services there is a need to "facilitate tailor-made policies in co-operation with other local actors to ensure a regional and local fit" (Mosely 2012, 5). This calls for decentralization of the PES: transferring responsibility for public policies from the national to the regional, subregional, or local level.

This OECD research caused federal and provincial officials to question the appropriateness of the current arrangements, given that all labour market programs across the country were controlled by the federal government out of Ottawa. However, their views were different. Federal officials maintained that Canada's PES was already administratively decentralized. In the mid-1980s the PES had been restructured to give the local managers of the federal CEC offices increased authority in deciding the program mix for their area. They were provided with a global budget and had authority to shift this between interventions (OECD 2001). Employment and Immigration Canada regional director generals operating in the provincial capitals had high status and authority within their organization.

However, most service delivery contracts with local organizations required approvals from Ottawa. Local members of Parliament were also actively involved with employment generation projects, requiring local CEC staff to coordinate these actions with the centre (Bakvis 1996). Given these dynamics, provincial civil servants viewed EIC as highly centralized, especially officials working in the smaller provinces who had many connections with provincial politicians able to make decisions on the spot. Commenting on federal flexibility, one Alberta civil servant interviewed through this research noted that "every morning [her federal counterpart] would look to the east before starting his day." While cooperation was possible, it was significantly constrained by permissions needed from Ottawa on the most mundane matters.

Social Security Review, Program Review, and Unemployment Insurance Reform

In 1993 the Department of Human Resources Development Canada (HRDC) was created as a single integrated ministry with the capacity to address interrelated issues ranging from pensions to unemployment insurance to postsecondary education to labour market development. Immigration issues (including employment services offered as a subcomponent of the settlement services program) were severed and sent off to a new Citizenship and Immigration Department, and welfare issues were moved in from the old Health and Welfare Department.

As part of these changes, in 1995 the Canada Employment and Immigration Advisory Council was discontinued.

When the Liberals took power from the Progressive Conservatives in 1993 they maintained the departmental HRDC structure and also embarked on two major initiatives: "social security review" (as a way to redesign Canada's social safety net) and "program review" (to deal with concerns over the federal debt and deficit). Worries about how federal employment services were managed and delivered were noted in the green paper "Improving Social Security in Canada: A Discussion Paper" (HRDC 1994). "The system is too hit and miss. That's why the results have been inadequate … There is an urgent need to rethink employment development services so that they focus squarely on one simple objective: helping people to find good jobs" (30). The paper also noted that the Vocational Rehabilitation for Disabled Persons Agreement was outdated and required renewal, and that improved linkages to mainstream employment development services were necessary.

Torjman (1995) noted how the HRDC-led social security review was stopped dead by the Finance Canada–led program review, where reducing the deficit and national unity became higher priorities than reform of Canada's social security system. Program review required federal officials to question every area that Ottawa was involved with and suggest ways to engage in partnerships with the provinces as well as the private and voluntary sector. As a result, the 1995 federal budget contained the most significant program and spending cuts in Canada's history involving $29 billion in program expenditure reductions and the elimination of 45,000 public service positions (Virtuosity Consulting 2003, 39). This included the end of the Canada Assistance Plan and 50:50 cost sharing of social assistance by consolidating federal contributions to social assistance, social services, health, and postsecondary education into a new Canada Health and Social Transfer or CHST.

While VRDP was kept as a separate program, an informant interviewed through this research noted that finance officials initially wanted to integrate it into the broader health and social transfer. HRDC officials had it retained as a separate allocation. However, the trade-off was that funding was capped, then frozen, and the type of programming eligible for the federal matching was to be changed. In 1997 the name of the transfer was changed to Employability Assistance for Persons with Disabilities (EAPD), and in 2003 to the Labour Market Agreement for Persons with Disabilities (LMAPD).

As part of a plan to realize a 10 per cent reduction in unemployment insurance costs, the program was renamed Employment Insurance, or EI. The name was changed to reflect its primary objective of promoting employment in the modern economy and labour force, and to move away from the image of supporting unemployment (Haddow 2004). A new EI Act was introduced to replace the previous Unemployment Insurance (UI) Act and the National Training Act, tightening eligibility and access to benefits. Employment Insurance was split into EI Part I (focusing on income benefits) and EI Part II (focused on employment benefits and support measures). EI Part II replaced what had previously been called "active measures" or unemployment insurance development uses (UIDU).

The EI Part II reforms were meant to "transform today's labyrinth of 39 different employment programs into five flexible and effective back to work benefits ... a modernized National Employment Service ... will work with community organizations to provide employment assistance services to unemployed persons" (HRDC 1995, 19 and 20). Subsequent EI legislation detailed five newly designed employment benefits and three support measures (collectively called EBSMs) intended to ensure rapid return to work and savings to the EI account. It also expanded eligibility to longer-term EI funded programming to what were called "reach-back"[5] clients.

In addition to the EI reforms, over $1 billion in reductions were made in expenditures on employment development programs for non-EI clients funded through the Consolidated Revenue Fund. Federal support for social assistance, women, older workers, and visible minority employment programming was terminated, and there was an increased focus on EI clients, including the establishment of a $300 million Transitional Jobs Fund for regions of the country most affected by EI reform. HRDC lost over 20 per cent of its staff (more than five thousand), exceeding its downsizing target but greatly eroding its corporate memory. Youth, Aboriginal, and labour market partnership programming were protected from the cutbacks (Virtuosity Consulting 2003, 37 and 40). Given this focus on downsizing, budget reductions, and the need for a smaller federal government, the idea of transferring federal staff and responsibility to the provinces for employment services made a lot of sense.

5 Reach-back clients had an active EI claim within the past three years, or for parental or maternity benefits within the past five years.

Failed Constitutional Reform and the Quebec Referendum

Quebec in particular had long wanted to take on these federal responsibilities. As described in more detail in chapter 6 of this book, concerned over federal action in areas viewed as provincial competence, in 1966 the Quebec government demanded full control of unemployment insurance and manpower training, as well as a variety of other policy areas. If this was not possible it would leave the Canadian federation. A referendum on a proposal to pursue secession was defeated by a 59.56 to 40.44 per cent margin in 1980. In 1990 the Quebec National Assembly passed a unanimous resolution affirming Quebec's sole jurisdiction over all aspects of labour market development, not only training (Bakvis and Aucoin 2000). In 1991 the Quebec government approached Ottawa to undertake discussions on setting up "one-stop" shops under a single manpower network by gaining control of all the tools related to labour adjustment and skills development. Ottawa refused to engage in discussions on federal withdrawal or the possible transfer of responsibilities through an administrative agreement (Quebec 1993a).

These labour market issues moved onto the broader constitutional agenda involving first ministers in the late 1980s and early 1990s. The Meech Lake Constitutional Accord in 1990 had explicitly tried to recognize Quebec's distinction within the federation. When it failed, the more extensive second round through the Charlottetown Accord (1992) detailed constitutional reform actions specifically related to the PES. While the accord reaffirmed exclusive federal jurisdiction for UI (including income support and its related services, and job creation programs), it called for labour market development and training to be identified in the constitution as a matter of exclusive provincial jurisdiction, with provincial authority to constrain federal spending. At the request of a province, the federal government would withdraw from any and all training activities, except UI, and provide reasonable compensation. Provinces negotiating agreements would be accorded equality of treatment (Virtuosity Consulting 2003). It is noteworthy that the Charlottetown Accord did not call for the transfer of the federal PES.

The failure of the Charlottetown Accord to secure approval in a nationwide referendum in 1992 left these long-standing federal-provincial issues unresolved. Quebec continued to pursue administrative reform, outlining its position at a 1993 FLMM meeting. Its submission described in detail how the whole area of labour force development "has become an example of the inefficiency and complexity that can result when two networks operate on the same territory with the same clientele" (Quebec 1993b, 1–2). Quebec affirmed its desire to develop its own labour market policies with the support of employers and worker representatives contributing to the EI fund. Not only did Quebec want to take on responsibility for active measures so that a single administrative network could be established, it also wanted to negotiate an agreement to manage the income support part of the EI program. Its argument outlined how this could be done within the current constitutional context and in a way that would not affect other provinces.

When the Chrétien Liberals assumed power in 1993 from the Conservatives they also wanted to stay away from further attempts at constitutional reform. The 1994 social security discussion paper noted, "The federal government is prepared to consider an expanded role for provinces and the private sector in managing and delivering federal employment development services, where this makes sense in the interests of individual Canadians" (HRDC 1994, 39–40). Many other provinces – for example, Alberta – supported Quebec's position on provincial responsibility for labour market policy. A provincial consensus on the need to clarify roles and responsibilities in this domain was outlined in a 1995 report to premiers from the Ministerial Council on Social Policy Reform and Renewal (Bakvis and Aucoin 2000).

The crucial development was the election of a Parti Québécois (PQ) government in Quebec in 1994, followed a year later by a referendum on sovereignty as promised in the PQ election platform. In the lead up to the referendum, Liberal Prime Minister Jean Chrétien explicitly recognized that not only Quebec but all provinces had primary jurisdiction in the field of labour market training. When the referendum was defeated in October 1995 by 50.58 per cent of the Quebec population, the federal government aggressively pursued administrative-political federalism, as opposed to the legal-constitutional federalism that characterized the Meech and Charlottetown processes (Virtuosity Consulting 2003, 37).

Negotiating the Deal with the Liberals in Charge, 1996–2006

The federal EI legislation tabled in December 1995 – while focused primarily on changes to the income support side of the scheme – opened up the potential for new partnerships whereby Ottawa could contract with provincial authorities for the delivery of federal employment measures or agree to substitute similar provincial programs. Regardless of the arrangements, cooperation with the provinces was required. For the first time the Act also outlined the responsibilities of the National Employment Service. The EI Act was the starting point for the negotiations with provinces, with new arrangements to be determined bilaterally and considered as administrative – not constitutional – reform.

The process undertaken to negotiate the Labour Market Development Agreements, or LMDAs, as well as the results achieved by 2000 are outlined in considerable detail in Bakvis and Aucoin (2000), Klassen (2000a), OECD (2001), and Bakvis (2002). Only key parts from this analysis are highlighted in the next section of this chapter.

Quebec acted quickly to submit a proposal that would see it take over from Ottawa all labour market development measures. Taking into account Quebec's desires, on 30 May 1996 the federal government put to all provinces and territories a broad-based offer on labour market development intended to meet Quebec's minimum demands. This went beyond training to also include the National Employment Service. Not only were federal employment services resources available to provinces, federal NES employees involved in screening and counselling were also available for transfer.[6] Each province was free to choose the arrangements that suited it best. However, there were certain areas that Ottawa was not willing to hand over, in particular responsibility for EI income support, labour mobility, labour market information, pan-Canadian initiatives, and employment services for Aboriginal people and youth. In addition, Ottawa was firm on the amount of money to be transferred, where it came from (that is, the EI account), how it was to be distributed between jurisdictions, who could be served, and the type of interventions to be provided.

Given the federal offer, every province and territory had to assess its capacity to absorb the federal employees and deliver the array of federal labour market development services on offer. More information on each province's objective in responding to the federal offer is outlined in subsequent chapters in this book. Suffice it to say that, by December 1996, Alberta and New Brunswick had agreed to fully devolved LMDA Agreements. In Quebec it took until April 1997 to come to an agreement in principle. By 2000 Saskatchewan, Manitoba, the Northwest Territories, and Nunavut had also agreed to largely similar

6 Initially this was identified as $1.5 billion in program resources, in addition to $190 million in administrative resources, including 3,620 federal staff positions (OECD 2001, 401).

devolved arrangements, while British Columbia, Nova Scotia, Prince Edward Island, Newfoundland and Labrador, and the Yukon decided on co-managed arrangements. In these jurisdictions, employment and training resources – as well as NES responsibilities – remained with the regional HRDC offices and the local CECs. However, provincial governments had a new and more defined role in influencing federal spending through joint federal-provincial management committees.

The agreements were negotiated one jurisdiction at a time, using the 30 May 1996 federal offer as the basis for all. The inclusion of the "equality of treatment" or "me too" clause in the first agreement negotiated in Alberta assured provinces of similar treatment in order to alleviate fears that those who signed later might get a better deal. In all provinces – except for Quebec – the regional executive heads of HRDC located in provincial capitals led the negotiations, as it was their staff and programming being handed over to the provinces. Given the transfer of federal staff, the agreements were considered as indeterminate in length, with three years of firm funding committed. They could, however, be terminated with notice as well as amended.

Negotiations with Ontario got bogged down by a number of issues, including the reluctance of federal Liberal members of Parliament from Ontario to see funding, programs, and federal staff transferred to a newly elected Conservative provincial government that was in the throes of downsizing, laying off provincial staff, and dismantling the provincial welfare state. Ontario was also concerned that the federal money on offer was inadequate, given Ontario's share of the unemployed. It took until 2005 and the presence of Liberal governments in place in both Ottawa and Toronto for Ontario to come on board with a devolved LMDA agreement. By that time most of the five co-managed jurisdictions had also decided that they wanted devolved agreements, as opposed to co-managed arrangements; however, the federal Liberals balked.

In terms of programming that it continued to control directly, on the youth front Ottawa expanded the federal Youth Employment Strategy (YES). However, an attempt to create a national youth employment strategy through the Forum of Labour Market Ministers failed. In 1996 the Government of Canada established Regional Bilateral Agreements that effectively devolved responsibility for Aboriginal employment programming from the Government of Canada to designated Aboriginal labour market organizations. In 1999 the federal government consolidated and increased federal spending on these programs through a new Aboriginal Human Resource Development Strategy (AHRDS).

As the budget got balanced and the threat of Quebec secession eased, by the late 1990s Ottawa had come to regret its lost capacity to intervene directly in the labour market. As one way to regain control, in June 1996 it established the Federal Task Force on Disability Issues, chaired by Andy Scott, a prominent Liberal MP. Rather than increasing provincial funding through what was now called the Employability Assistance for Disabled Persons Agreements (EAPD), in 1997 a new $30-million HRDC-controlled Opportunities Fund for disabled people was launched. In 1998 federal-provincial-territorial (except Quebec) agreement was reached through the ministers of social services on In Unison: A Canadian Approach to Disability Issues. While consensus was achieved on the employment problems being faced by disabled persons, no agreement was reached on how to move forward with suitable programming.

In 2002 the Government of Canada launched a national Skills and Learning Agenda that included a number of federal-only initiatives: the Canadian Millennium Scholarship Foundation (1998), the Workplace Skills Initiative (2004), the Canadian Council on Learning (2004), and the Foreign Credential Recognition Program (2004). National Sector Councils grew to more than thirty bodies. In 1995 the CLMPC transformed itself into the Canadian Labour and Business Centre (CLBC) and became known as a centre of expertise on labour market and skills issues, especially through its work with the Canadian Council on Learning and the Workplace Partners' Panel.

To deal with federal activism at the same time as provincial transfers had been cut, in 1999 a new accountability regime built around public reporting was articulated in a Social Union Framework Agreement (SUFA). This was agreed to by all governments, with the exception of Quebec. Under SUFA, provinces were no longer bound to report the outcomes of programs funded by Ottawa to the federal government, but rather committed to (1) working jointly on common indicators, (2) transparency in reporting to their public on these indicators, (3) monitoring and measuring outcomes, (4) sharing information and best practices, and (5) using third-parties (as appropriate) to assist in assessing progress on social priorities. SUFA developments significantly influenced subsequent federal-provincial labour market agreements.

By the early 2000s HRDC was reeling from a scandal in how its regions had managed the Transitional Jobs Fund, resulting in undermined confidence in the department and the addition of complex accountability provisions for contractors under its control. While this did not affect the provincial LMDA arrangements, AHRDS and YES contractors found themselves having to divert resources from serving youth and Aboriginal people to program administration. In 2005 Service Canada was set up, intended to focus on "citizen-centred" services by bringing a number of service delivery channels into the same organization. This severed HRDC's policy and operational wings. Contracting out employment services delivery by Service Canada officials in the co-managed LMDA jurisdictions increased significantly.

The focus of Service Canada was on providing Canadians with a single point of access to a wide range of *federal* government services and benefits: by 2007 fifty programs (e.g., EI benefits, social insurance, and old age security) had been included. This significantly undermined the federal-provincial co-location initiatives undertaken pre-devolution that had been aimed at providing Canadians with coordinated access to income support and employment support services offered by both orders of government.

During this period the pilot projects for older workers continued, offering provinces a small amount of additional funding to help unemployed older workers reintegrate into employment. By this time it had become evident that many of those most in need of employment services – immigrants, persons with disabilities, social assistance recipients, youth, and Aboriginal people – were not being adequately served through the LMDA arrangements. Funding restrictions prevented provinces from offering longer-term interventions like training to anyone other than active EI recipients and reach-back clients. As a result of the EI reform that started in 1996, fewer people (about 48.5 per cent of the unemployed in 2006, down from 83 per cent in 1990) qualified for EI benefits (Wood 2015a). Provinces pressed Ottawa to provide additional funding for employment services so that more Canadians could be served (Provincial-Territorial Labour Market Ministers 2002). Quebec evaluations on their success in serving social assistance recipients were particularly persuasive (Noel 2012).

When the Martin Liberal government fell to the Harper Conservatives in 2006, supplementary agreements to the LMDAs to meet these requests had been negotiated in three provinces. As these new agreements would have sanctioned the reinsertion of federal staff into the direct delivery and management of labour market services, Alberta and Quebec with devolved LMDAs saw this federal action as a threat to the coherent provincially managed system they had built post-devolution. Although they wanted the additional federal funding, they vehemently objected to the federal Liberal plan.

A Change in Government in 2006 and Developments to 2015

The 2006 Conservative campaign platform under Stephen Harper articulated a new approach to intergovernmental relations called "open federalism": the notion of strong provinces; restoring the constitutional balance; clarifying federal-provincial roles and responsibilities; working cooperatively with the provinces; limiting the federal spending power; and addressing the fiscal imbalance. Upon assuming power, one of its first actions to implement this vision was in labour market issues. The older worker pilot projects were reaffirmed as the Targeted Initiative for Older Workers (TIOW). The 2007 federal budget outlined "a new labour market training architecture that ... clarified roles and responsibilities and recognized that provinces were best placed to design and deliver this programming" (Finance Canada 2007).

Not only were the five co-managed jurisdictions offered devolved LMDAs, the Conservatives also responded positively to provincial requests for additional money to serve non-EI clients. An additional $500 million annually was allocated – $3 billion over six years – so that all thirteen jurisdictions could enhance the services on offer to unemployed social assistance recipients, persons with disabilities, Aboriginal people, older workers, and immigrants – as well as low income earners – through Labour Market Agreements, or LMAs. The time-limited (to March 2014) but highly flexible LMAs allowed provinces to prioritize whom to serve, the interventions on offer, and how to manage and organize the services. There was to be no intrusive direct federal oversight or control. This new funding – basically a partial replacement for the designated group programming that the Liberals had cut in the 1990s – came from the Consolidated Revenue Fund, not the EI account. As a result, it was not subject to EI's legislative restrictions.

LMAs were also introduced for a very practical reason. LMDA allocations to each province had not changed since 1996. As it was impossible to increase these allocations to the five remaining jurisdictions with co-managed LMDAs – as well as Ontario – without opening up the eight devolved agreements, additional funding through a top-up agreement was essential to get devolved LMDAs all around.

Like all of the other labour market transfer agreements, the LMAs were negotiated and signed bilaterally, starting with British Columbia on 20 February 2008 and ending with Nunavut on 16 July 2009. Provinces could choose the interventions and delivery model that suited them best. They were not constrained by federal legislation such as the

EI Act. However, in keeping with the key objectives of the LMA – meant to be incremental and serve clients excluded under the LMDA – there was a detailed list of clients eligible for the programming that provinces were expected to track and report on. In the 2008 budget Ottawa increased the provincial allocations under the LMDA and LMA agreements for two years as a way to deal with the economic downturn. By 2011 the allocations had returned to their original levels.

For the seven jurisdictions that had negotiated devolved LMDAs in the late 1990s/early 2000s (Alberta, New Brunswick, Quebec, Manitoba, Saskatchewan, the Northwest Territories, and Nunavut), implementing LMAs during 2008 and 2009 was fairly straightforward, involving an expansion of the employment services already in place to new client groups. However, it was much more complicated for the other six. Although Ontario had agreed to take on a devolved LMDA in 2005, implementation did not start until 2007. British Columbia, Nova Scotia, Prince Edward Island, Newfoundland and Labrador, and the Yukon were even further behind, not taking on their devolved LMDAs until 2009. Expanding the programming on offer – at the same time as they developed and implemented a delivery platform for a brand new business line and took on federal staff and contracts – was extremely challenging.

With these changes, by 2010/11 provincial governments were in control of over three quarters of Canada's labour market programming. Ultimately over 2,600 federal staff, more than one thousand service delivery contracts, and about $2 billion annually in program funding transferred to the provinces through the LMDAs. Ottawa's role was now confined to the direct management of contracts that provided employment services for defined groups (youth, the disabled, immigrants, and Aboriginal people) and pan-Canadian initiatives as deemed appropriate.

In 2010 the Conservatives rolled out a successor agreement to the Aboriginal employment programming inherited from the Liberals, recasting it as the Aboriginal Skills and Employment Training Strategy, or ASETS. While the Aboriginal organizations delivering the services remained the same, the principles behind the program were refocused on demand-driven skills development, partnerships, and accountability and results. ASETS and associated Aboriginal labour market programming account for about 12 per cent of Canada's federally funded labour market programming.

In 2013 the Harper Conservatives determined that they wished to transform the Labour Market Agreements into Canada Job Grants in order to increase employer involvement in training. While provinces unanimously rejected the federal changes – concerned over the loss of programming for the most disadvantaged – by the fall of 2014 all (except Quebec) had come to agreement on new Canada Job Fund Agreements (CJFAs) for six years. In recognition of Quebec's greater employer engagement in its PES system, the Quebec LMA was rolled over and extended to 2020. While the CJFAs changed how federal funds could be used, like the LMAs provincial governance choices remained unconstrained.

On the Employment Insurance front, in 2012 EI access was tightened with changes that required program recipients to take any job deemed "suitable" and to use "reasonable and customary measures" to obtain employment, even if the job was unrelated to their career, paid less money, and involved a long commute. A comparative analysis by Venn (2012) had illustrated that, compared to other OECD countries, Canada's job search requirements and monitoring of individual obligations as well as sanctions for EI clients appeared to be particularly weak, undermining the effectiveness of activation measures.

As the Harper Conservative government acknowledged that provinces were now in charge, it did not see a reason to support the institutions that the Liberals had put in place to provide national leadership on labour market issues. In 2007 the Canadian Labour and Business Centre closed. Next up was the Canadian Millennium Scholarship Foundation and its research arm in 2008. The Canadian Policy Research Networks was disbanded in 2009, the Workplace Skills Initiative in 2010, and the Canadian Council on Learning in 2013. The thirty-six national sector councils lost their core federal funding in 2013. Budget 2013 also unilaterally announced that the Government of Canada planned to renegotiate the LMDAs to "reorient training towards labour market demand." Consultations on LMDA "retooling" were undertaken in 2014 through cross-Canada roundtables and hearings of the House of Commons Standing Committee on Human Resources, Skills and Social Development and the Status of Persons with Disabilities (HUMA).

Labour Market Transfer Agreement Funding Arrangements in 2013/14

Appendix C outlines federal funding allocations to each province and territory through the four labour market transfer agreements. It is through these arrangements that provinces have assumed responsibility for Canada's PES. In 2013/14 (the last year of the LMA) it totalled about $2.7 billion, out of about $3.6 billion allocated by the Government of Canada to labour market programming (Wood 2015a). Other than increases in 2009/10 and 2010/11 to deal with the economic downturn, overall LMDA and LMA allocations have not changed since these funding instruments were introduced in 1996 and 2008 respectively. There has also been no increase to LMAPD funding since the early 2000s. This means that the federal contribution to employment programming under these three agreements has declined in real terms. In contrast, funding for TIOW programming has varied from one year to another. While in 2011/12 the allocation was $48 million, in 2013/14 it was only $25 million.

How the money was distributed among provinces also varied under each agreement. While LMA allocations (and now Canada Job Grant Agreements) are per capita, LMDA allocations are distributed between provinces on the basis of a formula chosen in 1996 to mitigate the impact of the EI reforms. This means that the eastern provinces are favoured over the west. No changes have been made in the allocation formula to adjust to changes in unemployment rates in different regions over time. LMAPD allocations are also historical and have not changed in over twenty years. TIOW money gets distributed based on each jurisdiction's share of unemployed older workers.

The amount of provincial-only money allocated to active employment measures is not known; however, before devolution, few provinces were heavily involved in the employment services business. Provincial/territorial labour market ministers noted in 2013 that they invested about $22 billion annually in postsecondary education and skills development programs. At one time 50 per cent of provincial postsecondary education costs were covered by the federal government. After 2010/11 the federal contribution was estimated to be about 10 per cent (PBO 2011, 16; 2012, 2).

As identified in appendix C, 72 per cent of Canada's PES funding comes through the Labour Market Development Agreements. These arrangements are funded by employer and worker contributions to the EI fund. The federal role is one of stewardship and management; although they design and deliver the programs, provinces have no decision-making role. Unions and business can influence decision making only through their role on the Employment Insurance Commission. Unlike the Canada Pension Plan – under joint federal-provincial management – there is no separate EI account; however, there is separate reporting.

Section 78 of the federal EI Act sets out the means for establishing the maximum amount to be made available from EI contributions to pay for employment programs and services. It is not to exceed 0.8 per cent of the insurable earnings of all insured workers for the year in question. In every year since the LMDAs were implemented – now twenty years – there has been excess capacity in the EI account that could have allowed for an increase in funding allocated to active measures through the LMDAs. Ottawa took advantage of this provision only during the economic downturn between 2008 and 2010.

Federal-Provincial Accountability under the Labour Market Transfer Agreements

Each of the four labour market transfer agreements has different accountability parameters. These requirements spell out public reporting and therefore influence the degree to which provincial outcomes can be compared. The provincial chapters of this book focus on provincial programming under the two largest transfers – the Labour Market Development Agreement (LMDA) and the Labour Market Agreement (LMA).

Labour Market Development Agreements

According to Section 56 of Part II of the Employment Insurance Act, the objectives of the program are "to help maintain a sustainable employment insurance system through the establishment of employment benefits for insured participants and the maintenance of a national employment service." Duties under the EI Act are assigned to the Canada Employment Insurance Commission (CEIC), established under the authority of the Department of Employment and Social Development (ESDC) Act.[7] The commission is expected to work in concert with the government of each province to design and deliver the benefits and measures needed to achieve the goals of the EI Act. It is also expected to maintain the National Employment Service (NES), established to "provide information on employment opportunities across Canada and to help workers find suitable employment and help employers find suitable workers" (EI Act).

---

7 Employment and Social Development Canada is the successor department to Human Resources Development Canada.

It is through the Labour Market Development Agreements that NES duties are defined and delegated. Each federal-provincial agreement has a clause that delegates the functions of the NES. These are then described in more detail in an annex to each agreement titled "National Employment Service Functions." While there are small differences between provinces, most LMDAs detail the following NES functions assigned to the provinces: employment counselling, service needs determination, labour exchange, labour market information, labour market adjustment and management, and support to the above functions.

The primary goal of the Employment Benefits and Support Measures (EBSMs) designed in 1995 was to reduce EI expenditures and costs. They consist of five employment benefits (targeted wage subsidies, targeted earnings supplements, self-employment initiatives, job creation partnerships, and skills development assistance) and three support measures (employment assistance services, labour market partnerships, and research and innovation). These are described in appendix D. When they were designed, federal officials thought that the Government of Canada would be responsible for program delivery. In light of devolution, provinces were able to develop different interventions; however, they have to demonstrate to federal officials that their services and supports meet a "test of similarity" to the federal EBSMs. Only insured EI beneficiaries can be provided with employment benefits; support measures are available to anyone. By expanding eligibility to reach-back clients, the intent of the 1995 EI Act was to extend eligibility beyond current EI claimants to also include some of the longer-term unemployed.

The LMDAs provide wide latitude to provinces in the programs and services that they can design with the federal funds, provided they meet several objectives: (1) are broadly similar to the EBSMs outlined in the EI Act; (2) are results based and incorporate an evaluation of outcomes; (3) reduce individual dependency on passive income support; (4) promote cooperation and partnership with labour market partners; (5) involve local decision making; (6) eliminate unnecessary overlap and duplication; (7) encourage individuals to take personal responsibility for finding employment; and (8) ensure service to the public in either official language where there is significant demand (Virtuosity Consulting 2003, 45–6).

Each LMDA has an accountability framework that includes four components: (1) annual negotiation and review of results indicators and joint federal-provincial setting of targets for the upcoming year;

(2) financial probity and integrity through audits; (3) defined processes to undertake program evaluations; and (4) monitoring and evaluation through annual reports. In order to ensure that provinces focus on the objectives of EI reform, every provincial agreement has the same three indicators for measuring the results of the provincial EBSMs:

1. the number of active EI claimants that access provincial benefits and measures;
2. returns to employment of EI clients, with an emphasis on active EI claimants; and
3. savings to the EI Account.

The Canada Employment Insurance Commission reports annually through a Monitoring and Assessment Report (MAR) on the results achieved in each province using LMDA funding. This requirement to report is detailed in Section 3(1) of the EI Act. Using data provided directly to Ottawa by provincial governments – as well as other information available exclusively to the Government of Canada – federal officials draft the text of the *MAR* in cooperation with the EI commissioners for workers and employees, then provincial officials approve the section that applies to their jurisdiction. Once the report is finalized by the commission, it is tabled in Parliament and publicly released.

Labour Market Agreements

While provinces did not play much of a role in identifying LMDA indicators – as they had been developed by Ottawa as part of the 1995 EI reform objectives – they were more engaged in developing the LMA accountability framework, to ensure that it met their objectives of providing enhanced services to non-EI clients, including social assistance recipients, persons with disabilities, Aboriginal people, older workers, youth, and immigrants, as well as low-income earners. While these client groups are mentioned in the accountability framework, each province was free to choose the interventions on offer, which were then described in the respective LMA agreement. There was no prescribed federal list.

The LMA accountability framework consisted of five components: (1) planning, (2) financial reporting, (3) performance measurement, (4) public reporting, and (5) evaluation. Each province agreed to collect and compile information on ten areas of performance. This information was to be provided to Ottawa by a defined timeframe each year, and also publicly released by each province to its citizens in a format of the province's choosing.

In addition to provincial commitments, Ottawa agreed to develop and publicly release a national LMA report every year. Every bilateral LMA agreement had the same clause: "Following the end of each Fiscal Year during the Period of the Agreement, Canada will report annually to Canadians on the aggregate results of the labour market agreements with provinces and territories."

Labour Market Agreement for Persons with Disabilities

Over the twenty-year period covered by this book, federal-provincial agreements covering employment services for persons with disabilities have changed names three times: from Vocational Rehabilitation for Disabled People (VRDP), to Employability Assistance for Persons with Disabilities (EAPD), to the Labour Market Agreement for Persons with Disabilities (LMAPD). Other than the name change, very little has changed in programming or federal funding available. However, the Government of Canada has sought to focus its funding on job preparation and employment services and move away from funding of sheltered workshops, mental health services, or addictions treatment that were seen as unrelated to the labour market. The 2014 federal budget announced a new generation of LMAPDs with the provinces, with stronger accountability measures but little in new federal dollars (Prince 2016).

The LMAPD is cost-shared 50:50 between provinces and Ottawa, subject to certain conditions and a cap on the annual federal commitment. Each province is expected to release an annual report to its citizens every year on 3 December, the International Day for Disabled Persons. Recent provincial reports demonstrated that provincial spending generally far exceeded the federal allocation. Provincial priorities varied considerably and included education and training initiatives, workplace disability supports, and awareness campaigns. Many provinces continued to use LMAPD funding for mental health and addiction services. Given the wide variety of activities funded under the LMAPDs and the difficulties provinces experienced in data collection – where they reported numbers "where possible" – comparing and assessing provincial outcomes in any kind of systematic fashion was not possible.

Targeted Initiative for Older Workers

This is a cost-shared program, where Ottawa puts in up to 70 per cent and the provinces fund 30 per cent of program costs. Unlike the other three labour market transfer agreements, under the TIOW there is almost no public reporting at all. The program parameters used in 2015 have developed over time on the basis of various pilot projects since the earlier Program for Older Worker Adjustment was implemented in 1987. Unlike the LMAs, the TIOW program is highly targeted to eligible participants, eligible communities, and eligible project activities. These can range from employment assistance to employability improvement (e.g., skills upgrading, work experience, and mentorships).

ESDC officials set the TIOW program parameters, oversee implementation, manage the allocations, and conduct the evaluations. Under Conservative oversight between 2006 and 2015 the federal minister approved each application. There was a standardized intake form that all participants completed that fed a federal database. The federal-provincial agreements are highly prescriptive on what provinces can do with the federal funding and what and how they must report to the Government of Canada. There is no obligation to report to citizens. The only public information available on program results was federal evaluations, which did not compare provincial outcomes.

Conclusion

Canada's public employment service is highly complex, decentralized, and generally opaque. Nevertheless, it is the key means used to help people who are disadvantaged in the labour market – Aboriginal people, immigrants, disabled people, older workers, and youth – find and keep jobs. In 2015 the PES still is – like in 1940 – "the very foundation of an unemployment insurance scheme" (Hunter 1993, 66). While in 1996 almost all programs were under direct federal control, by 2010 87 per cent of the programs were under provincial, territorial, or Aboriginal control. The next stage of our inquiry is to find a way to compare their approaches.

Chapter Three

Using the Federalism and Activation Literature

In Canada, provinces matter as they play a large role in developing, implementing, and managing public policy. However, their choices are largely contextualized by the complex relationship they have with the federal government, with each other, as well as with other actors such as Aboriginal governments, local governments, and members of civil society. The beginning part of this chapter reviews some of the scholarship on Canadian federalism, with a particular focus on the concepts of "province-building" and provincial "political culture." These are important, as they form the explanatory backdrop for understanding choices made by individual provincial governments before (but mostly after) the federal devolution offer.

The second part of this chapter reviews the literature on the governance of activation. A movement towards activation – meant to bring the long-term unemployed and inactive into the labour market – was significantly influenced by the rise of neoliberalism in the 1970s and 1980s. Unlike federalism, there is almost no literature on activation developments in Canada, either federally or provincially. However, there is a rich literature from other countries. Reviewing this literature was instrumental in developing an analytical framework to compare provincial governance choices (chapters 4–7), as well as to compare Canada with other places (chapter 10).

Using the Federalism Literature

A "federal political system" is one in which – in contrast to the single central authority in unitary systems – two (or more) levels of government combine elements of shared rule through common institutions, and regional self-rule for governments of the constituent units. How powers are shared or divided varies considerably from one federal political system to another. It can take many forms, including federations like Canada, where neither the federal nor constituent units are constitutionally subordinate to the other; each is empowered to deal directly with its citizens in the exercise of its legislative, executive, and taxing powers, and each is directly elected by its citizens (Watts 1999, 7). Federations are a particular form of multilevel governance, where the unit of analysis extends beyond governments to also include non-government players. The term became particularly popular in the 1980s in the context of studies of the European Union, where there was great reluctance to use the *f* or federal word to describe their developing political system.

Province Building

After the Second World War Canada went through a period of "nation building" in order to develop the Canadian welfare state. As part of this process, provinces significantly expanded their social services, healthcare, and postsecondary education systems, using federal money that was conditional on somewhat similar, federally prescribed programming choices. This led to a period of "province building" in the 1960s, a process through which provinces (with federal dollars) developed the political sophistication, civil service expertise, and financial power to begin challenging the federal government in a more assertive way (Elkins and Simeon 1980). Nowhere was this more evident than in the Province of Quebec, when, after the 1960 election of the Jean Lesage government, nationalist forces started to grow, and protecting provincial jurisdiction and upholding the division of powers became an article of faith of all Quebec provincial governments.

Canadian scholars following these developments – especially Black and Cairns (1966) – posited that the provinces were now the primary actors responsible for the formulation, implementation, and financing of policy programs in Canada and that the provincial role in "country building" deserved closer inquiry. In their view, up to that point in Canada's history, there had been a disproportionate emphasis on the federal government and an exaggeration of its ability to accommodate social integration and promote economic development. The significance of the "province-building" scholarship lay in its argument that provinces were at least equal to the Government of Canada. While cooperation between levels of government was common, researchers argued that provincial policymakers could be expected to prioritize provincial interests whenever they possessed the means to do so. Two variables of government strength – needed to press provincial interests – were policy capacity (measured by personnel numbers, bureaucratic professionalism, and financial resources) and policy action (measured as targeted expenditures) (Wilder and Howlett 2016).

When the province-building hypothesis came in for considerable criticism in the 1980s – with some scholars suggesting instead that the gradual blurring of jurisdictional barriers had resulted in a system of "fused federalism" – there was a decline in studies focused on Canadian provinces. However, Atkinson et al. (2013) note that trends since 1980 demonstrate that – across many key metrics – provinces have indeed become increasingly significant actors. They encouraged scholars to undertake work to increase our knowledge of governance and policymaking in Canada's provinces, especially from a comparative point of view.

The benefits of comparative provincial studies are many. For governments it provides an opportunity to recognize their relative position as a way to search for new ideas to use in their own arena. For the political scientist, comparisons provide social laboratories for the study of policy determinants. For the publicly minded citizen, they offer a rough set of policy indicators to situate the progress of her or her province in matters institutional, administrative, or policy-related (Dunn 2016, xv). Comparative interprovincial studies are precisely what this book is about.

Provincial Political Culture

Another policy concept from the federalism literature that is relevant to this book is the idea of provincial "political culture." While surveys suggest that Canadians outside Quebec have remarkably similar *popular* culture, they have very different regional *political* preferences. Wiseman (2016) identifies regionalism as a predominant characteristic of Canadian politics, one of its axes and fault lines. *Political culture* refers to deeply rooted, popularly held beliefs, values, and attitudes about politics. The term sums up many factors that are unique to each province: the historical baggage accumulated as a result of immigration and settlement patterns; the political effects of resource exploitation and economic development; historical voting trends and parties in power;

and the attitudes of citizens towards government, including their political identification (Gibbons 2001).

Canada's political traditions and institutions are old and firmly implanted, and they continue to shape and resonate in today's politics. Wiseman (2007, 11) notes, "The Canadian political cultural tradition is one of evolutionary change: gradual, incrementalist, and iterative. Certainly the past is no infallible guide to the future, but neither is it simply over and done with. Grievances will persist and fissures may widen in Canadian political life, but acceptance of working with what is feasible or practical will probably prevail among leaders and followers."

Combining the "province-building" literature with the provincial "political culture" literature provides a way to understand why provinces make different policy choices when confronted with the same opportunities and challenges. Every provincial chapter of this book provides insight into the province's respective "political culture." As will be seen in chapters 4–7, differences in political culture and provincial government strength were clearly evident, given the different reactions to the 1995 federal devolution offer and the choices they ultimately made in developing their provincial PES.

Using the Activation Literature

A neoliberal ideological paradigm has dominated policymaking in most Western countries since the 1970s. Replacing the Keynesian welfare state paradigm that arose out of the Depression and the Second World War, the neoliberal agenda rests on two planks. The first plank is increased competition achieved through deregulation and the opening up of domestic markets, including financial markets, to foreign competition. This means that markets in capital, goods, information, culture, and even labour are now international and global. Everything that can be traded moves across national borders, and government policies have been deliberately adjusted to smooth the way (Pivan 2015).

The second plank is a smaller role for the state, achieved through privatization and limits on the ability of governments to run fiscal deficits and accumulate debt (Ostry, Loungani, and Furceri 2016). Neoliberalism is often blamed for rising inequality, the weakening of welfare state policies, the decline of wages, the rolling back of workers' rights, and the weakening of unions (Pivan 2015). Applied to social policy, neoliberalism is defined by measures promoting individual responsibility (including user-pay), private delivery of services, attachment of strict conditions and obligations to receipt of benefits (workfare), tougher qualification requirements, and lower benefit levels for recipients of government income support (McBride, Mahon, and Boychuk 2015, 6).

To align with the new neoliberal paradigm required reform of a country's public employment service from entitlement towards activation. Canada was no exception. As identified in chapter 2, provincial governments had been activating social assistance claimants since the 1970s and 1980s. The first federal "developmental" uses of the unemployment insurance account occurred in 1974. This was expanded in the 1980s and early 1990s. The key focus of the Employment Insurance reforms in 1995 was to reinforce a focus on activation by officially recognizing it in the EI legislation and differentiating income benefits from employment benefits. Activation was further reinforced on the federal side in 2012 when Ottawa began to impose more stringent work search and employment obligations on EI claimants. In that year it also started to place new work expectations on First Nations recipients of on-reserve social assistance benefits.

While many reforms to the PES have emphasized changes in program design and content (e.g., eligibility, benefits, conditions, programming instruments), there has also been a growing recognition that a precondition for changing the substance of employment policies in a neoliberal direction is reforms to the steering and implementation structure: that is, changes to the *governance* of the PES. Governance focuses on who has power, who makes the decisions, at what level, how other players make their voice heard, and how account is rendered (Institute on Governance 2011). A focus on steering and implementation in activation matters cannot be divorced from policy content. The two components are interrelated and connected.

What Is Activation?

The term *activation* was coined after the *active society* ideal (Carcillo and Grubb 2006; Martin and Pearson 2005). Active measures (ALMPs) – such as vocational training, wage subsidies to employers, career development, and job matching services – are designed to improve access to the labour market and jobs, develop employment-related skills, and promote more efficient labour markets. Passive measures (PLMPs) – such as unemployment insurance and social assistance – are designed to mitigate financial hardship for the unemployed by providing income support (OECD 1994). Some authors note that the line between passive and active measures is not always clear-cut, as the structure of PLMPs inciting workers to join the labour force sometimes exerts "activation effects" (Huo 2009).

Activation strategies first emerged in the 1960s, 1970s, and 1980s and were further reinforced through the OECD Jobs Strategy in 1994. Over the past twenty years most developed countries have aimed to make an explicit linkage between social protection and labour market participation in order to bring long-term unemployed and inactive people into the labour supply, enhance their employability, and prevent long spells on government benefits. They have also moved to directly coordinate their ALMPs with the administration of benefits and make-work-pay policies, and transformed their tax and other social policies (Barbier and Ludwig-Mayerhofer 2004).

Most activation strategies enforce mutual obligation requirements where benefit recipients are expected to engage in active job search and improve their employability, in exchange for receiving employment services and benefit payments (OECD 2013a). This creates deep connections between the PES and income benefit schemes. There are two parts: an expectation imposed by the benefit provider that those receiving benefits will engage in activities to prepare for and accept work, and the offer of employment services including, where necessary, access to training. Eichhorst and Konle-Seidl (2008) and Kenworthy (2010) describe these as *enabling* (e.g., financial incentives and training) and *demanding* (conditionality and coercion) elements. Activation is aimed at changing people's situation, behaviour, or attitudes. For many groups – such as disabled persons, single parents, Aboriginals, and immigrants – successful activation depends on the availability of a range of services suited to their needs in health care, housing, language training, and child care.

What International Literature Has Looked at Activation?

There has been extensive research undertaken in the last ten years on the governance of activation in the European Union, the United States, and Australia, resulting in dedicated books and journal special issues comparing approaches in different places. Canadian scholars and practitioners have participated in only a few of these international undertakings. The only material identified that provided insight into the governance of activation in Canada post-devolution was Wood (2010) focused on Alberta and New Brunswick; Palameta, Myers, and

Conte (2013), Gold and Mendelsohn (2014), and the BC Centre for Employment Excellence (2014), all focused on British Columbia; and OECD (2014b and 2015b), Noel (2012), and Bramwell (2012) focused on Ontario and Quebec. There was very little comparison between provinces in this material.

Over the past twenty years European countries have carried out extensive reforms to their public employment service (PES). Funded by the European Commission, in 2006 a European Network of Excellence called Reconciling Work and Welfare in Europe or RECWOWE was created to consistently describe, analyse, and compare the impact of reforms in nine European countries (France, Germany, the United Kingdom, Italy, the Netherlands, Switzerland, Czech Republic, Sweden, and Finland). The research results were published as an edited book with twelve chapters entitled *The Governance of Active Welfare States in Europe* (van Berkel, de Graaf, and Sirovátka, 2011). There was also a special themed issue from this research with eight articles in the *International Journal of Sociology and Social Policy* (2012).

The OECD Directorate for Employment, Labour and Social Affairs has also carried out detailed reviews of activation in seven countries (Ireland, Norway, Finland, Switzerland, Japan, Australia, and the United Kingdom). Included in its *Employment Outlook 2013* was chapter 3, "Activating Jobseekers: Lessons from Seven OECD Countries" (OECD 2013a). European, American, and Australian scholars studying activation came together in 2009 through a network called Reform of Employment Services Quorum to gain a deeper understanding of the policies of workfare (as practised in the United States and Australia) and the policies of activation (as practised in Europe). The exchange started through a symposium held at the University of Chicago and resulted in fifteen researchers publishing their findings in an edited book called *Work and the Welfare State: Street-Level Organizations and Workfare Politics* (Brodkin and Marston 2013). Like in this book, public bureaucracies and private and not-for-profit organizations that deliver policies and services directly to individuals were placed at the heart of the analysis.

The final collaborative activity identified through the literature review was initiated in Australia. The University of Melbourne hosted a roundtable titled "Markets and the New Welfare: Buying and Selling the Poor," in February 2013. This attracted ten papers from researchers in seven countries, including Australia, Germany, Italy, the United Kingdom, the Netherlands, Belgium, and Israel. Their work was published as a special issue of *Social Policy and Administration* 48, no. 2, in

April 2014. It focused on a single governance element: the purchasing of employment services through the outsourcing or marketization of service delivery.

What Governance Themes Emerge from the Activation Literature?

This international research in sixteen different countries provided a way to develop a framework for comparing provincial approaches in Canada, as well as a method to compare Canadian approaches to those of other countries. Four governance themes emerged from a review of the literature.

1. DECENTRALIZATION AND DEVOLUTION

The OECD has been promoting decentralization of active labour market programs for many years, as a way to ensure that local labour market offices have enough flexibility to ensure program effectiveness (OECD 1998). Local labour markets vary in their business base, skills of the local workforce, and needs and circumstances of those who are unemployed. Problems are complex, requiring multifaceted solutions that work across income support, economic development, and skills-training policy areas. Decentralized arrangements are a way to ensure policy flexibility, adaptability, and responsiveness to local needs, and that local partners have the capacity to develop integrated services suited to individual and local needs.

Decentralization of active measures is therefore one of the strongest trends in almost all developed countries, as employment services to reintegrate the unemployed cannot be implemented according to standardized national rules in the same way as can the payment of income support benefits (Mosely 2012). As detailed in chapter 1, decentralization can be either managerial or political. While in the 1980s and 1990s the federal government in Canada chose managerial decentralization (giving regional and local Canada Employment Centre managers more authority), this direction was overtaken by political events in 1996 that transformed managerial decentralization into political decentralization and devolution. But Canada was not alone. For example, in the Netherlands and Denmark, responsibility for active measures has been devolved to municipal governments that are also responsible for the delivery of social assistance (ibid.).

Van Berkel, de Graaf, and Sirovátka (2012) noted the complexity of assessing decentralization reforms in Europe. The United Kingdom represented a highly centralized system, as activation was the responsibility of Jobcentre Plus – a U.K.-wide agency – rather than the municipalities. Recent government reforms have not changed that picture, as the program is still managed directly from London. In the Netherlands and Sweden the trend towards lower-level autonomy at the regional or municipal level has been accompanied by higher-level direct control in monitoring and supervision. The researchers also noted additional complexity in those countries when activating unemployment insurance recipients was managed by an agency different from the one responsible for social assistance claimants. They concluded that, in Europe, the activation of social assistance recipients was more decentralized than the activation of recipients of unemployment insurance.

The OECD's work in assessing decentralized labour market arrangements in different countries has compared Canada (focusing on Alberta and New Brunswick) to Denmark, the Netherlands, and Belgium (Flanders) (Froy et al. 2011; Wood 2010). A number of indicators were developed to assess the flexibility available to regional and local offices: Do they have input into the design of policies and programs? Do they have global budgets or line item budgeting requirements? To what extent are performance measures and targets centrally determined? Can regional and local offices choose whom they serve? Can they hire, recruit, and outsource at their discretion? Can they decide whom they will partner and collaborate with, or is this prescribed by national government?

By means of this OECD research, Canada's decentralized arrangements through the LMDAs were assessed as providing Alberta and New Brunswick – as well as their regional and local offices – with more flexibility than had been the case under the previous federally managed regime; however, considerable authority was retained at the provincial (as opposed to the regional or local) level (Wood 2010). In this same study Denmark was considered to have arrangements that allowed for the most flexibility at the local level in labour market programming, followed by Alberta and New Brunswick (in Canada). The Netherlands and Flanders (in Belgium) were considered as more centralized (Froy et al. 2011).

2. SINGLE GATEWAYS OR ONE-STOP SHOPS

While labour ministries play an important central role in setting activation policies, the division of responsibilities for benefits and employment support services are not always straightforward, and other ministries – especially those with education, social development, and economic development responsibilities – also have significant roles. The research results from the RECWOWE project demonstrated that, at the country level, problems with coordination, institutional fragmentation, and incompatible objectives prompted several countries to draw together their delivery agencies involved with activation. "One stop" or "single gateway" access to employment services, benefits, and employer supports under one management structure was seen as a way to increase convenience for clients and employers, reduce duplication, facilitate information sharing, and improve overall program effectiveness.

This theme examines the scope of the public employment service, and the extent to which three of the main functions of the PES (job brokering, benefit administration, and referral to active measures) are integrated. It also considers how the PES relates to employers. The OECD (1994 and 2013a) believes that the first three functions should be managed within a single organizational structure. They identified three reasons. First, monitoring job-search enforces benefit eligibility. To ensure a rapid return to work, the PES should be able to administer benefit sanctions. Second, training services and job-creation projects can more easily accept referrals of clients who are disadvantaged, poorly motivated, or otherwise at risk of long-term unemployment if they are in the same organization. Third, matching benefits paid to unemployed workers (including incentives and withdrawal rates) and employment support services are more effective when a single organization is responsible.

While many countries have embraced the notion of "one-stop models," they often mean only the integration of the job brokering and active measures dimension, and do not include benefit administration. One-stop Career Centres have existed in the United States since the 1998 Workforce Investment Act (WIA) mandated that all states must provide a range of services for all job seekers. Likewise Australia integrates all employment services through a single network. However, benefit administration in these two countries is managed by different players.

The most notable example of one-stop shops that integrated all three key PES functions was in the United Kingdom, where the introduction of JobCentre Plus in 2002 involved a merger between the U.K.-wide agencies providing cash benefits and activation services. The development of single gateways to benefits and employment services was also a central feature of the reforms in Norway, Finland, and the Netherlands. In Germany and the Czech Republic the PES was responsible for activation as well as for administering unemployment benefits. In Denmark municipal job centres provided information, advice, social work, and casework to the unemployed via a single entrance (van Berkel, de Graaf and Sirovátka 2012).

Terpstra's (2002) review of the Dutch Centres for Work and Income showed that promoting cooperation and service integration was a long-term process during which many problems needed to be solved (e.g., different cultures and histories, different management styles, and different ways of servicing clients). In their comparison of the U.K., Norwegian, and Danish experience of "one-stop shops," Askim et al. (2011) outlined a variety of important dimensions to be determined, including the breadth and depth of the task portfolio; whether there were one or few agencies that came together; whether agency participation was voluntary or compulsory; and the management devices used to facilitate integration. In their analysis they noted many challenges and the problems of coordination and specialization that persisted, even with "one stop" centres.

Despite its promotion of the idea, the OECD has been ambivalent about the success of the "one-stop shops" that it examined through its activation research: "In the case of Norway it is too early to tell whether the ambitious reform effort has been successful. The UK experience suggests that merging the public employment service and benefit agency has improved employment outcomes and services for clients and has been cost effective" (OECD 2013a, 7).

3. OUTSOURCING AND CONTRACTING OUT

Of all the new forms of governance, outsourcing (also referred to as contracting out or marketization) of active measures is the theme area that has generated the highest volume of research. Many authors noted that activation services had traditionally been provided by government staff working in the PES. A drive for outsourcing often came from outside the PES, from higher levels of government, wishing to use markets and incentives in employment support services in order to save public money and improve efficiency. Outsourcing is a key component of New Public Management, which also includes hands-off professional management, performance standards, output controls, decentralization, competition, and reduction (Hood 1991). Considine and O'Sullivan (2014) suggest that the willingness of policymakers to take radical steps in welfare-to-work may be because those most in need of the services are poor and disenfranchised.

Outsourcing divides up the roles of service purchaser (e.g., the PES or a local welfare agency) and service provider (e.g., a private reintegration company or non-government organization, or NGO). The idea is to promote competition and have a positive impact on the efficiency and effectiveness of services, on their quality, their flexibility and responsiveness to local and individual needs, and their price. Outsourcing is also expected to promote more innovation and quality, compared to the traditional bureaucratic provision, and increase the "voice" and "choice" of service consumers. Not only does it multiply the range of actors involved in service provision, it also means that actors find themselves in different relationships with each other (as competitors) or with the main agency (agents vs principal) (OECD 2013a).

In activation, outsourcing arrangements are "quasi-markets," as purchasing power does not come from consumers of services (unemployed people), but from the state. These quasi-markets can look very different in different places, depending upon the nature of the service providers (e.g., private vs not-for profit), the number of service providers and how they are organized and secured (e.g., through competitive contracting and the use of prime versus sub-contractors), and the nature of the contracting arrangements (e.g., whether funding is performance and outcome based or allocated on the basis of calculations of costs) (van Berkel, de Graaf, and Sirovátka 2011). Governments are increasingly tying service providers' compensation to their performance, offering service delivery organizations a share of the savings that accrue when program recipients get and keep a job and leave income assistance (Gold and Mendelsohn 2014).

In their research on nine European countries van Berkel, de Graaf, and Sirovátka, (2012) found that outsourcing had been introduced in all. However, they distinguished three families: "committed marketizers" (the United Kingdom, the Netherlands, Germany and Switzerland), "modernizers" (Sweden, Finland, and France), and "slow modernizers" (Italy and the Czech Republic). In the Netherlands private, for-profit companies played an important role, while in Germany it was not-for-profit organizations. In the United Kingdom there was a mix, while in Italy, France, and Germany temporary agencies played a role. In most countries the purchasers – the PES – also acted as a provider, thus the split between purchaser and provider was not complete. In several countries service provision for unemployment insurance recipients was more marketized than that provided to social assistance claimants. Market competition seemed to be fiercer in some countries than in others. Depending on their constitutional make-up, there were also differences in where the purchasing decision was made: in the United

Kingdom, Sweden, and Switzerland decisions were made at a national level, whereas in Germany and the Czech Republic decision making was decentralized.

Outsourcing has been pursued most vigorously in liberal welfare regimes, especially in the United States, Australia, and the United Kingdom. Australia fully replaced the Commonwealth Employment Service with privatized service provision in 1998. In 2014 there were roughly a hundred for-profit and non-profit provider organizations delivering 650 contracts in 116 Employment Services areas under the Job Services Australia banner. The contracts were let by the commonwealth (not state) government. To ensure competition there were at least two service providers in each Employment Service area (BC Centre for Employment Excellence 2014).

Although the primary emphasis in the early days of contracting out in Australia was on "work-first," a change in 2009 brought more emphasis on human capital development, including skills development and workforce training. There was mandatory participation for most benefit recipients, including those with greater levels of disadvantage (Palameta, Myers, and Conte 2013).

In 2014 performance in Australia was managed through a Star Rating system, where outcome measures were used for paid placements. Providers were given an overall rating of five stars for performance of 40 per cent or more above average. These ratings played an important role when the government awarded the three-year contracts. The OECD (2012) noted that it was a challenge to ensure that targets and indicators were well designed and did not include perverse incentives. They also noted the importance of transparency and the need for a significant investment of organizational resources in management information and reporting systems.

In 2014 in the United Kingdom all work-to-welfare programs were managed by the national government (not regional or local governments) and let by the London-based Department of Work and Pensions (DWP), the parent organization to JobCentre Plus. DWP has been outsourcing for many years, leading to the development of the U.K. employment-related services industry that includes large multinational companies, small specialist organizations, local authorities, housing associations, health institutions, and others.

The Work Program – rolled out by the U.K. government in 2011 – was considered as a radical departure from past practice, using large-scale "prime providers" who could both deliver services themselves and/or sub-contract to other providers. Contracting was considered only in terms of inputs and outputs, with no attention paid to its internal workings (otherwise known as "black-box") in order to give providers greater flexibility in how they secured job outcomes. Of the forty contracts that were initially let, in 2011 eighteen were awarded to prime providers, mostly in the private sector. Under each prime was a supply chain of organizations recruited to provide geographical coverage, for a total of some 800 organizations (BC Centre for Employment Excellence 2014). The program operated on a payment-for-results basis. There were differential payments by claimant group as part of the performance-based system.

Many researchers have identified problems with "creaming" and "parking" in the U.K. system – either skimming off clients closest to the labour market or de-prioritizing the least employable (Rees, Whitworth, and Carter 2013). The OECD (2013a) noted that the 2012 U.K. performance results were disappointing, requiring prime contractors to rapidly reorganize service delivery and make adjustments to their "supply-chain" (i.e., their subcontractors). Maddock (2012) suggested that there were an increasing number of cases of companies with huge public contracts unable to deliver the services they had contracted for. She identified the DWP commissioning model and a poor alignment with locality partnerships as key problems.

Finn (2011) reviewed a large body of research findings on subcontracting in public employment services and concluded that the evaluations demonstrated mixed results, with the most positive found in the United Kingdom and more negative findings in Germany, France, and Sweden. He noted, "The findings suggest that private providers can, under certain contractual arrangements, improve outcomes for particular groups and bring innovation to service delivery. The competitive pressure they bring may also prompt improved PES performance" (4).

The RECWOWE studies on outsourcing were likewise ambivalent, concluding that typical market failures were emerging – most evidently with advanced marketizers – and that de-marketization was emerging in some countries (e.g., Sweden and the Netherlands) (van Berkel, de Graaf, and Sirovátka, 2012). Considine and O'Sullivan (2014, 122) noted that, while Australia was the first country to introduce a fully privatized delivery model, arrangements were continually being restructured. They characterized them as "the reform that never ends."

4. PARTNERSHIPS AND NETWORKS

The final theme in the international literature on activation focuses on partnerships and networks. This theme takes into account the presence of a large range of public and private actors beyond government involved in designing, directing, influencing, and managing the PES. This includes business associations and unions; private and not-for-profit (NGO) employment agencies for vulnerable workers; universities and community colleges; individual employers; employer, employee, and NGO associations; and experts who study the PES.

A "partnership" implies the sharing of resources, work, risk, responsibility, decision making, power, benefits, and burdens. Operating along a spectrum, it goes beyond the notion of "cooperation" (which by its very nature is informal, loose, without joint goals, and often mostly about information sharing) to include "coordination" (some joint planning and a close working relationship) and sometimes even "collaboration" (intense communication, sharing of resources and commitment, joint decision making, and risk) (Wood 2010).

The term *multilevel governance*, or MLG, is often invoked when considering partnerships and networks. This looks at integration (1) vertically between different tiers of government (supranational, national, regional, and local), (2) horizontally between different spheres of society (public, private, voluntary, and civil), and (3) across sectors (social, economic, environmental). In a federation such as Canada, MLG takes a particular form that privileges the federal and provincial levels over all other partners as a result of their roles being identified in the Constitution. Within a Westminster parliamentary system, our MLG system is also unique in that it is dominated by executives (politicians and senior bureaucrats) as opposed to other actors.

Irrespective of its form, the benefits of partnerships for the PES are considerable. They supply important knowledge about the labour market and the issues involved, and create legitimacy for the goals and strategies selected. The presence of different partners provides an opportunity for creativity and innovation. Sharing resources among different partners can increase efficiency and allow measures to take place that would not otherwise be possible, given the resources of one partner alone. If all important stakeholders take ownership of the goals and strategies in an employment plan, the opportunities for good results are increased when the measures are implemented in practice (Froy et al. 2011). While partnerships are considered as a positive feature, van Berkel and Borghi (2008) noted that they often required adaption in response to diverging objectives or cultures.

Partnerships surrounding the PES are strong in the United States, where the 1998 Workforce Investment Act (WIA) required that local Workforce Investment Boards be established to support the American Job Centers. In 2015 there were about 550 such boards across the United States; private employers must comprise a majority of each board and the chair must be elected from the private sector membership. The U.S. government recently reinforced this direction through a new Workforce Innovation and Opportunity Act (WIOA). States and regional authorities were required to carry out long-term planning with employers to understand which skills and occupational training programs the boards should concentrate on, and to continuously improve programs over the long term in light of evaluations.

In a paper released in 2013 the European Commission highlighted the importance of PES partnerships in Europe. Mandated by a separate chapter in the Amsterdam Treaty, the European Employment Strategy (EES) required the involvement of social partners (business and labour) and civil society organizations to work alongside governments at both the EU and member-state level. The EES has also tied European Social Fund money to partner involvement, thus facilitating the development of networks in some countries that would not otherwise have occurred (Wood 2013b).

Given their different traditions, EU member states had various models of partnerships and networked governance. One variety was corporatist governance, in which social partners – that is, organized interests of employers and employees – were strongly involved in policymaking and policy implementation. Corporatist governance has traditionally been weak in the United Kingdom and the Czech Republic. Van Berkel, de Graaf, and Sirovátka (2011) noted than in one group of EU countries (Italy, Switzerland, Sweden, and Finland) no major changes in the involvement of social partners took place as a result of the activation reforms. However, in France, Germany, and the Netherlands corporatist governance had clearly weakened, although to varying degrees. In the Netherlands social partners were completely removed from social insurance and PES institutions. The Danish reforms to dissolve the public employment service were also carried out with the express intent of reducing the influence of social partners.

What Difference Do the Governance Arrangements Make?

The international literature suggests that three themes be used to assess and compare PES performance: *effectiveness*, *efficiency*, and *democracy*.

As identified in the preface to this book, the Employment Insurance Monitoring and Assessment Reports, the provincial Labour Market Agreement Performance Reports, and information from interviews and other studies were used to compare provincial results along these themes.

Effectiveness refers to how useful the programming is: that is, the degree to which outcomes benefit unemployed workers and society. Effectiveness is basically about doing the right task, completing activities, and achieving goals. Typically PES resources focus on integrating the most disadvantaged. Information was reviewed to try to answer several questions: What employment services were being provided and to whom? Were the most vulnerable being served? Were more low-cost measures being used at the expense of more costly training that might be more effective? Was a greater variety of clients able to be served? Were they completing their programs? Were they getting jobs? Were they making enough money to be independent of government income support? Did the training they received help? What kind of research and evaluation was taking place to assess performance, and did best practice information get exchanged?

Efficiency refers to how well the programs are being provided to maximize returns. It is about doing things in an optimal way, such as doing it fastest or in the least expensive way. It could be the wrong thing, but done optimally. Relevant questions include: What was the cost per client ratio? What was the return on investment? How coherent was the programming across provincial departments and with federal programming? Had economies of scale been realized? Were clients satisfied with the services being provided? What kind of policy capacity had the province developed? Did those working for the PES have access to training to improve their skills and professional associations to facilitate certification if they desired?

Democracy refers to the ability of legislators, business, labour, community organizations, researchers, program users, and citizens to be involved in the PES to ensure that initiatives are taken in accordance with society's needs. Transparency is essential to democracy, as stakeholders – because they command specific knowledge – can act as a "transmission belt" to inform citizens about executive behaviour. Relevant questions to assess democracy include: What kind of information was available on the employment programs and services being provided, and how easy was it to access? Were accountability reports written and released and tabled with legislators? Were the indicators and benchmarks used easy to understand? Were there consultative structures for views from outside the bureaucracy to be heard?

Conclusion

This chapter has considered the federalism and activation literature as a way to explain and understand PES governance choices made by provinces post-devolution, why they made these choices, the outcomes they achieved, and how they compared across provinces. The chapter also reviewed the international activation literature, as a way to develop an analytical framework to *compare* the choices provinces made following the 1995 devolution offer.

Using this literature, provincial governance arrangements post-devolution will be described according to the four governance themes identified from the literature: (1) single gateways or one-stop shops, (2) decentralization, (3) outsourcing and contracting out, and (4) partnerships and networks. Then provinces will be compared in groups (Far West, Midwest, Middle, and East), assessing the strengths and weaknesses of the provincial models chosen. Then results will be compared, using the concepts of *effectiveness*, *efficiency*, and *democracy*, drawing on data in federal and provincial reports and other material.

The analysis begins on the West Coast through an exploration and comparison of the Alberta and British Columbia PES arrangements.

Chapter Four

The Far West: Alberta and British Columbia

Alberta was the first province to agree to take on a devolved Labour Market Development Agreement (LMDA) in 1996, while in British Columbia this did not happen until 2008, over a decade later. As each province negotiated bilaterally with the federal government to take on responsibility for the National Employment Service and Employment Benefits and Support Measures (EBSMs) – as authorized in the federal Employment Insurance (EI) legislation – the key questions provincial politicians and officials ultimately faced after the deal was signed were: (1) Which provincial department would hold prime responsibility for managing and organizing the services? (2) To what extent would work and welfare programs be managed as integrated or separate responsibilities? (3) How much flexibility would regional and local offices within the province be given in implementing program objectives? (4) Would the services be contracted out or delivered by provincial civil servants? (5) To what degree and how would external partnerships and networks influence provincial policymaking and service delivery choices?

The answers to these questions built upon the legacy of the province's long-standing social assistance, training, and active measures programming responsibilities, as well as their individual political cultures. Despite sharing a single geographic space and, since 1867, a political union, there are a diversity of provincial landscapes in Canada, each shaped by distinct socio-economic environments, political cultures, and institutional legacies (Atkinson et al. 2013). These political landscapes provide the values and attitudinal context in which provincial choices in assuming the federal responsibilities were made.

This chapter compares how Alberta and British Columbia took on federal PES responsibilities and the governance choices they made up to 2014. It starts with a reflection on each province's political culture, followed by a brief historical overview of work and welfare in each province, focusing in particular on the circumstances in the years surrounding the federal devolution negotiations. Developments in the two provinces post-devolution are assessed, drawing on the themes in the analytical framework outlined in chapter 3 of this book. Similarities and differences in the two provinces are summarized, followed by a discussion of what accounts for the differences. The chapter concludes with an assessment of the impact the different governance arrangements have had on the performance of the provincial PES, using data and information from federal and provincial reports as described in the preface to this book.

The Political Context

Wiseman (2007) characterizes Alberta and British Columbia as sharing a "parvenu" political culture – a lack of tradition and an upstart and recalcitrant political character. The interaction between them is evident in interprovincial migration, where in the last quarter of the twentieth century more than four of five Albertans and British Columbians who relocated did so to each other's province. Attitudes to federal powers have been more stridently critical in these two provinces than in any other region other than Quebec, posing a common front in resisting what is often considered as a federal assault on provincial autonomy. This resistance has its roots in old grievances: in BC the delay in building the railway promised by Confederation and the disallowance of provincial legislation related to the Chinese; in Alberta by the delay in giving the province control over its natural resources and land, Ottawa-determined freight rates, financial controls from eastern bankers, and the Ottawa-imposed National Energy Program (Whitcomb 2005a, 2006).

Both provinces were hit hard by the Depression in the 1930s, as neither could cope with having more than 25 per cent of its workforce unemployed. Unfortunately their collective lobbying did not result in adequate federal support to cover municipal relief costs, and it took until the Second World War for their citizens and economies to fully recover. Alberta's perceived exclusion from national decision making is a foundational element in the province's political culture, resulting in a conscious strategy of inter-governmentalism to ensure that the province's views are heard on the national stage (Gibbons 1998).

Conservative ideas emanate from and are well received in both Alberta and BC: over the past decade this mindset has expressed itself federally as electorate support for the Reform/Alliance and Conservative political parties. Both provinces have had long-serving Social Credit governments (Alberta starting in 1935 and BC in 1953), determined to protect their citizens from the perils of socialism (Whitcomb 2005a). Other than somewhat brief New Democratic Party interludes in BC,[1] for fourteen years post-devolution Alberta and BC were governed by business-friendly right-wing regimes – Liberals in BC and Progressive Conservatives in Alberta. This changed when the NDP under Rachel Notley took over the reins of power in Alberta in 2015 and John Horgan's NDP assumed power in BC in 2017. BC and Alberta's shared tradition of neoliberalism has driven their public policies, as each has sought private-sector solutions to public-policy challenges. Both have a firm-centred industry culture and a highly competitive liberal market economy that makes enterprises reluctant to cooperate with each other, let alone with unions or government (Haddow and Klassen 2006).

However, there are also many significant differences. The American immigrant influence during Alberta's formative years has resulted in a form of "moral conservatism" that places much more emphasis on individual than collective responsibility. Since becoming a province in 1905 Alberta has had a strong executive government, one that as a result of windfall natural resource revenues expanded significantly between 1971 and 1985, when public spending increased tenfold and the size of the civil service tripled (Nikiforuk 1987, 118). Polarization in Alberta is external (against Ottawa or the rest of Canada) as opposed to internal, evidenced by the consistency of one-party rule, with only six premiers over the seventy-year span from 1935 to 2005 (Gibbons 2001).

The energy sector dominates the Alberta economy, with many companies controlled out of the United States. The presence of unreliable natural resource revenues has produced a "boom and bust" economic characteristic. More than in any other province in Canada, there has been a melding of party and state in Alberta, with relations between the government and the energy sector characterized by a high degree of mutual dependence (Patten 2015). The 2013 Global Entrepreneurial Monitor ranked Alberta as Canada's most entrepreneurial province and one of the most entrepreneurial places in the world (Toneguzz 2015).

1 The NDP formed the government in British Columbia between 1972 and 1975 and again between 1991 and 2001.

The agriculture sector based upon the family farm and the lack of a significant manufacturing base has resulted in a low unionization rate in Alberta, compared to other places in Canada.

In contrast, British working-class immigrants who came to British Columbia in the early twentieth century bred strong labour leaders who felt a vigorous class consciousness influenced by the British trade union movement. As the mining, lumbering, and fishing industries dominated the province's economy in its early years, unions established a substantial toehold. The presence of the Rocky Mountains isolates BC from its eastern neighbour; its long coastline orientates it towards Asia and the sea, as opposed to the rest of Canada. Ever since becoming a province in 1870, the political culture in BC has "pit leftists against rightists; one that is more riven and conflicted than in Alberta where the left is marginalized and there is more of a societal consensus about political values" (Wiseman 2007, 239). Organized business and labour in BC are frequently at loggerheads, in a conflict that is exacerbated as the province's party system has labour supporting the left-leaning NDP, with business supporting the party of the right (Haddow 2000b).

As a result of this internal polarization, BC had seven premiers in the ten years between 1991 and 2001 alone, and considerable swings between parties in power. As provincial politicians and citizens are unable to mobilize around decisive action, long-standing traditions and consistent approaches to intergovernmental relations have not formed (Gibbons 2001). In contrast, political stability and continuity in Alberta have resulted in relatively consistent mandates among line departments delivering government services, as well as a consistent approach to increasing Alberta's influence within the federation (Gibbons 1998).

Since provincial governments have a mandate to protect and promote the economic interests of their specific province, on many issues – for example, gas investment in the northern parts of the province, attracting immigrants and business investors – British Columbia and Alberta are competitors, and cooperation has been a challenge. To overcome some of these problems, formal ties between the western provinces started to develop in the 1960s and 1970s, evolving in the 1990s with the addition of the three northern territories into the Western Premiers Council. This has now become an annual event and an opportunity for substantial interprovincial consultation; however, unlike the Council of Atlantic Premiers, the WPC has no permanent organization to support it. Starting in 2003 Alberta and British Columbia forged even stronger ties, signing a Trade, Investment, and Labour Mobility Agreement and holding joint Cabinet meetings. In 2009 this expanded to include Saskatchewan. The renamed New West Partnership is intended to reduce non-tariff internal trade barriers among the three provinces. There are also procurement, innovation, and research elements to the agreement (Berdahl and Gibbons 2014).

Ever since Confederation, the Government of Canada has made transfer payments to the less wealthy provinces to equalize their "fiscal capacity" and ensure that every Canadian citizen has access to comparable public services while bearing roughly the same tax burden. Formally enacted in 1957, the right of poorer provinces to equalization payments was placed into the 1982 Constitution Act. Although Alberta received payments during the early years of the program, ever since natural resources were included in the formula it has been considered as a "have province," with a fiscal capacity "that is easily quintuple that of resource-poor provinces on a per-capita basis" (Bakvis 2014, 55). While British Columbia received equalization payments between 2001 and 2007, since 2008 it too has been considered as a net contributor to Canada (Bernard 2012).

Historical Developments around Activation

Alberta

Until 2015, Alberta had been run by one political party – the Progressive Conservatives – for forty-four years. Starting under Social Credit rule, in 1969 Alberta's social assistance department began providing employment supports to help welfare recipients access work. These included a civil-servant run Employment Opportunities Program and the Northern Alberta Job Corps (Reichwin 2002). In 1975 responsibility for employable social assistance recipients was transferred from municipal governments, integrating all last-resort benefits and employment support services for social assistance recipients under provincial control. During the 1980s Alberta actively participated with the federal government in initiatives under the "four-cornered strategy" that realigned federal Canada Assistance Program (CAP) dollars from passive welfare to active employment programming.

Parallel to these developments, in the 1980s the career development department also became involved in employment programming, with rising oil revenues used to fund a network of Career Development Centres across the province, available to all citizens. These supports were put in place as the provincial government viewed the services being provided by the Canada Employment Centres as inadequate. As a result of these initiatives Alberta developed significant capacity among its civil servants for career development and employment services programming, and became known as a leader among provinces in labour market information (Wood 2010). Alberta has also long been considered a leader in apprenticeship matters, producing certified trades people at double the proportion of its general population, compared to other provinces (BC Construction Association et al. 2007).

In response to a steadily rising welfare caseload, a provincial desire to eliminate the deficit without raising taxes, and political direction to move from an entitlement to an activation paradigm, in 1990 and 1993 the social services department in Alberta undertook major reforms to its social assistance program. A new administrative culture was introduced, benefits were reduced, and some financial benefit worker roles were realigned into employment counsellor roles as new work experience and training programs were mounted in collaboration with the provincial career development department. These employment programs were shielded from budget cutbacks undertaken by the Klein government in the early 1990s, demonstrating the high priority placed on active measures by the province (Wood 2015b).

At the beginning of the 1990s Ottawa encouraged all provinces to establish corporatist labour market development boards. Alberta declined, seeing the tripartite model promoted by Ottawa as one that would unduly privilege labour and as interfering with government actions in labour market policy. It was also viewed as redundant, given the province's historical use of employer advisory boards for its apprenticeship system. Instead the province used a mostly informal mechanism – the Alberta Congress Board – as a way for business, labour, and government to discuss workplace and labour market issues (Haddow and Klassen 2006). In its fortieth year in 2014, the congress annual conference continued to provide a mechanism for labour market actors in Alberta to engage in a degree of dialogue.

To support welfare reform, in 1994 a tripartite agreement was signed between the provincial social services and career development departments and Human Resources Development Canada (HRDC) to pilot the integration of labour market and income support programs and services in four Canada-Alberta Service Centres. "The experience gained as a result of [federal-provincial staff co-location] contributed to the trust, flexibility and positive working relationships required for the successful integration of former federal staff into the provincial operation" (Alberta Strategic Planning and Research Branch n.d., 12). In establishing this trust, it became important for the federal government to recognize some important values held by the Alberta government, namely that Alberta did not want to be treated as a contractor delivering federal programs, but rather as a government exercising its legitimate jurisdiction (Bakvis and Aucoin 2000).

When in May 1996 Ottawa made all provinces a formal broad-based offer on labour market training and development (including the National Employment Service), there was little doubt that Alberta would opt to negotiate to the limit of the federal offer, building upon the long-standing federal-provincial collaborative initiatives established through the Canada-Alberta Service Centres. While the provincial career development department took the lead, officials from the social services department were directly involved in the negotiations.

Alberta was motivated to negotiate a devolved agreement in 1996, because it provided an opportunity to have full control, with federal funding, over the design, management, and delivery of most active measures within the province, allowing for a more integrated and strategic set of programs for EI recipients, those on social assistance, as well as the general public. Not only did the agreement remove a jurisdictional irritant (because the Government of Canada officially recognized labour market training as a provincial responsibility), it also enabled Alberta to assume an expanded role and align federal programs with provincial priorities and programs.

The LMDA agreement involved the transfer of $97.5 million in federal funds and 156 staff to Alberta (Haddow and Klassen 2006). Alberta officials were confident that they could deliver the federal programs, given their policy expertise and regional delivery networks in the two separate departments. They viewed a transfer of federal responsibilities as a way to improve services to the public, eliminate overlap and duplication, and increase flexibility by allowing more decisions to be taken at the provincial and local level.

As the first province off the mark, Alberta was keen to demonstrate its capacity to assume the new labour market responsibilities and integrate federal programming and staff into the provincial system (Wood 2008). Federal programs were modified to ensure a provincial stamp. One primary change was the contracting process. Previously the federal government rolled its employment services contracts over from one year to the next, whereas Alberta insisted on issuing requests for proposals. This introduced a competitive element not previously present. Establishing a management system to support the new contracting process resulted in delays and underspending in the early years after Alberta took on the federal labour market responsibilities.

When in 2008 the Harper Government offered to expand labour market funding available to provinces to provide enhanced programs for non-EI clients through Labour Market Agreements (LMAs), Alberta was pleased to sign on to this agreement, as it provided new resources for underserved groups. Rolling out this new federally funded programming was relatively seamless, given the regional infrastructure Alberta already had in place to deliver employment programming.

British Columbia

Unlike the relative political stability seen in Alberta, work and welfare programming in BC over the past forty-five years has been buffeted by changing political direction – from NDP in 1972 to Social Credit in 1975, back to NDP in 1991, to Liberal in 2001 to NDP in 2017. By the mid-1970s, social assistance had become a full provincial responsibility, as the remaining municipal programs were consolidated under provincial control. Social Credit undertook no signature policies to help social assistance clients get work; however, the NDP reign in the 1990s signalled a new emphasis on getting people off social assistance and into work. The training and employability budget in the social services department was doubled, new staff employment counselling positions were introduced, and contracts with community-based training organizations were let.

One informant noted a growing realization in BC that civil servants should not be used to do this kind of work. As provincial efforts increased to reduce social assistance caseloads, a new model of performance-based contracts for employment services – based on a fee-for-service model – was developed. In 2000 the Job Partnership Pilot Project directly awarded large-scale contracts to two private-sector employment service-delivery agencies. The contracts were severely criticized – especially by community-based training agencies delivering similar programming under both federal and provincial contracts – for the short notice and the requirement for community agencies to provide free services to the larger contractors. The provincial contracts were later opened to competitive bidding.

In the early 1990s the province also established Bladerunners to match construction industry needs with opportunities for inner city disadvantaged "street-involved" youth. Even with these initiatives, active measures in the province remained small. The NDP's main efforts in employment matters focused on the establishment of the British Columbia Labour Force Development Board, launched in 1994. The board closed in 1996, brought down by a plethora of interests,[2] reluctance of senior bureaucrats and politicians to let the board influence provincial decision making, and lack of senior-level business and union involvement (Haddow 2000a). When in the early 2000s the BC Liberals ended business subsidies, all active measures were terminated, other than industrial training and programs for social assistance recipients (Haddow and Klassen 2006).

During this period BC was also responding to the 1996 federal LMDA offer. Fearful of downloading and being blamed for federal funding cutbacks already underway, BC NDP politicians were reluctant to take on the federal responsibilities, and in 1997 the province signed a co-managed LMDA arrangement whereby federal civil servants working in BC continued to be directly responsible for active measures funded under the EI legislation. However, BC kept its options open by invoking the reopener clause on the same day that it signed the co-managed LMDA. Even with this option to transition to a devolved arrangement, by the time that BC politicians warmed to the idea of taking on the federal responsibilities, the federal Liberals had cooled. While the provincial Liberals, elected in 2001, promised to expand job training and skills development, Premier Campbell was unwilling to pick a fight with his Ottawa cousins to gain control of the federal programming.

For eleven years under the co-managed LMDA, there were, in effect, two parallel active employment measures delivery systems operating in British Columbia, one federal and another provincial. The provincial system – mostly focused on social assistance recipients – was significantly contracted out to third-party organizations. Likewise, the federal government also outsourced to third-party community-based organizations; this practice accelerated in the 2000s under Service Canada, as HRDC staff were downsized and those remaining focused on contract management. While federal and provincial officials working in British Columbia tried to coordinate programming through the joint LMDA management committee, provincial informants interviewed through

2 In addition to business and labour, representatives of "equity" communities were appointed to the board.

this research noted that the meetings provided limited opportunities for the province to influence federal programming. BC requests to reopen the co-managed LMDA and transform it into a devolved arrangement, as Alberta had negotiated, were ignored.

When Ontario finally negotiated a devolved LMDA with the federal government in 2005, this opened up the potential for similar arrangements in British Columbia. However, it took the Harper Conservatives coming to power in 2006 before devolved agreements were offered to those jurisdictions that had initially signed co-managed arrangements (British Columbia, Nova Scotia, Prince Edward Island, Newfoundland and Labrador, and Yukon).

BC was the first province to step up to the plate, and negotiations began right away, not only on a devolved LMDA focused on EI clients, but also on a Labour Market Agreement (LMA) that would provide additional funding for employment services for non-EI clients. For BC, signing the two agreements as a package was essential, as – despite the passage of ten years – Ottawa refused to increase the BC LMDA funding allocation, for that would have necessitated opening all the devolved agreements already in place across the country.

In the view of BC officials, there was a significant shortfall in LMDA funding available to the province for administration. Without the extra LMA funding, BC would have refused to take on a devolved LMDA, a key objective of the new Harper Conservative government. Given that signing a devolved LMDA was now a priority on both sides, the negotiations were completed quickly and successfully, and in February 2008 British Columbia and Ottawa announced that they had agreed to a devolved Labour Market Development Agreement as well as a Labour Market Agreement. The BC agreements were almost identical to what had been signed in the other provinces.

Post-LMDA Governance Reforms

Single Gateways or One-Stop Shops

When Alberta implemented its devolved LMDA in 1997, responsibility was initially assigned to the career development department, including the federal staff positions transferred to the province. By 1999 not only had federal staff and contracts been integrated into the provincial system, but key parts of the two provincial departments responsible (social services and career development) were also amalgamated into a single department, Alberta Human Resources and Employment.

While the department and the programs it operates have changed names over the years, the organizational integration of provincial work and welfare programs in Alberta remained consistent for over fifteen years. In 2012 the department was renamed Alberta Human Services (AHS) and also became responsible for programs for children and the disabled. Respondents viewed the change in departmental structure as a signal that Alberta's work and welfare programs were moving from an economic development orientation to one focused on social development. Post-devolution, all federal labour market transfer agreements ($192.7 million as identified in appendix C) were under the responsibility of Alberta Human Services. In 2013 the "strategic" component of the AHS department that was related to employment, training, and skills was transferred to a newly formed Ministry of Jobs, Skills, Training and Labour (AJSTL), created according to one informant, "to create a job for [politician X]."

With approximately fifteen hundred provincial government staff working in fifty-three service access sites across the province, in 2014, within one organization, the AHS-operated Alberta Works Centres provided access to a broad spectrum of activities related to employment, welfare, and the workplace. For many years post-devolution, the provincial sites were co-located with federal Employment Insurance (EI) offices, in order to ensure easy access for EI clients. However, most co-located sites have since closed, as Service Canada moved to reorient federal service delivery. In 2007 the scope of provincial services on offer expanded, as AHS created new staff positions called business and industry liaison (BIL) officers to reach out to business and industry and bring employers into the Alberta Works Centres. All Albertans seeking these services went in the same door; however, Alberta Works Centres were most heavily utilized by federal EI and provincial social assistance recipients. AHS staff – working out of Alberta Works offices – also provided access to social assistance benefits. In 2013 responsibility for employer supports through the BIL positions was transferred out of the Alberta Works offices to the AJSTL department.

British Columbia has seen more churning of responsibility for employment matters between provincial ministries than Alberta. This reflected the divergent views of the provincial NDP vs Liberal parties on whether labour market programs were social or economic development tools. The 2008 LMDA negotiations were led by the economic development department; however, when the devolved LMDA agreement was signed under the provincial Liberals, the Ministry of Social Development (in 2014 called Social Development and Social Innovation, or BCSDSI) was assigned responsibility ($280.6 million, 250 federal staff positions, and 350 federal contracts), given its historic role in active measures for social assistance recipients and the fact that it had a regional delivery system in place. BCSDSI was also responsible for the Labour Market Agreement for Persons with Disabilities.

Between 2008 and 2011 BCSDSI undertook a major business transformation project to integrate the more than four hundred federal and provincial contracts into one streamlined program and service delivery mechanism. In the meantime, the federal employment services contracts continued, to ensure continuity in programming. In 2012 BCSDSI launched the Employment Program of British Columbia (EPBC), funded primarily through the federal-provincial LMDA.

Federal funding that came through the LMA agreement ($66.3 million) was assigned to the economic development ministry, in 2014 called BC Jobs, Tourism and Skills Training (BCJTST). More than one person interviewed through this research suggested that the federal LMDA and LMA funding was split between two provincial ministries on the basis of personal political and bureaucratic preferences, as opposed to government efficiency. BCJTST also carried prime responsibility for labour market services for immigrants, youth, and older workers, including the federal-provincial Targeted Initiative for Older Workers Agreement. BC Advanced Education was also involved in employment programming, as it held lead responsibility for Aboriginal employment programming.

As a result of the split in programming, in 2014 BC had one of the more complex PES systems in the country, with two separate and parallel provincially managed tracks for employment programming and active measures (Coward 2013). Given the need to set up a new infrastructure in BCJTST for the LMA funding starting in 2008, implementation was delayed and BC underspent LMA money in the early years. However, the province was allowed to carry the funds over to later years. Efforts to improve provincial coordination were enhanced in 2014 through an interdepartmental committee called the Labour Market Priorities Board, established to implement BC's Skills for Jobs Blueprint. While the EPBC presented itself as a single door for the province's PES (replacing the previous client-segmented contracts), with BCJTST contractors offering separate opportunities for non-EI clients and those with low skills, BC's delivery system was more fragmented than Alberta's single door.

Decentralization

By devolving labour market responsibility to the thirteen provinces and territories, Canada clearly embraced the OECD's decentralization ideas. Given our federal system, decentralization has focused on the provincial level, as opposed to the local level. The 2010 OECD study that looked at Alberta and New Brunswick concluded, "Considerable power and authority for strategic direction, policy and programme design has been retained at the provincial/territorial level and has not been passed down to the regional and local level ... However, in both Alberta and New Brunswick regional and local managers did not see the retention of policy and performance control at the provincial level as a big concern ... as they have ample opportunity to influence overall programme direction and design" (Froy et al. 2011, 25).

Organizationally, Alberta separated the policy development function from the program delivery function. Six powerful regional directors and their area and local managers – responsible for employment, social assistance, and workforce development – made most PES decisions. AHS regional directors were free to adjust staff allocations between different departmental activities (e.g., social assistance vs employment programming vs supports to employers) and between offices within their individual region, subject to the overall government classification system and an ability to meet the measures and targets in the departmental business plan. Although policy was clearly determined at a provincial level, there was regular and ongoing delivery staff involvement in internal processes to AHS policy development, as well as those that involved larger consultations with industry. This was both formal and ad hoc. The department was small enough to allow for short lines of command and intensive communications between staff involved with both delivery and policy (Wood 2010).

In contrast, decision making on active measures in British Columbia in 2014 was more centralized. Within BCSDSI, social assistance and employment programming were managed in two separate business lines that did not cross at the regional level. Policy and service delivery staff in each stream reported to their respective head office assistant deputy ministers. Social assistance recipients accessed services through a welfare door, as well as an employment services door. On social assistance matters there were five regions, with government staff in over a hundred Employment and Income Assistance Offices responsible for paying client benefits, developing a personalized employment plan, and making a referral to an appropriate employment services provider. PES services were delivered by for-profit and not-for-profit contractors operating under the centrally let and directed EPBC. Although the contracting framework was centrally determined, regional office staff were involved in selecting the contractors and managing the contracts. Many of these officials were former federal employees.

The ministry assigned responsibility for managing the federal LMA money (BCJTST) did not have a regional network. These contracts were centrally let through province-wide programs that involved the Industry Training Authority, or ITA (responsible for apprenticeship), public postsecondary colleges, private and not for-profit contractors, and Aboriginal organizations. The framework and the contracting decisions were made in the provincial capital.

Outsourcing and Contracting Out

By 2014 Alberta had developed a mixed model of government staff and contractors providing the provincial public employment service. Government staff delivered the following active labour market services: information and resources; online job search and career planning resources; and assessment and referral. They also provided social assistance benefit delivery, as well as liaison with employers and training support. Career and employment counselling, training assessment, résumé writing, training, placement services, work experience programs, self-employment assistance, and access to more intensive interventions for those with barriers to employment were contracted to for-profit and not-for-profit service providers and to postsecondary institutions.

At least forty contractors received AHS funding (some providing services in more than one location), as well as twenty-six public postsecondary institutions in 2014. Post-devolution the Alberta government invested in training its career development practitioner employees, and provided them with routes to certification. Initially these same opportunities were provided to staff employed by third-party contractors who provided similar services. However, this changed over time, such that by 2014 it was up to each organization to train its staff according to its own resources and capacity. Most contracts funded through the LMDA and LMA in Alberta included an allocation for staff development.

Regional directors in Alberta could decide what they wanted to outsource (with the exception of union jobs), when, and to whom, as long as they followed the overall departmental guidelines and were within the identified budget. There was a centrally determined accountability and financial management framework for each AHS tuition-based and contract-based service. The tuition-based providers (that is, post-secondary institutions) provided training. They did not respond to a request for proposal but signed a standard accountability agreement that allowed them to assess and approve learners in their programs. Smaller providers required approval from AHS staff. In contrast, employment services contracts were let through a standardized request for proposal (RFP) process, ensuring openness and transparency. There was no province-wide process for letting any of these contracts, nor central oversight. All was determined in the Alberta Works regions, where the directors had highly delegated financial authorities.

In Edmonton and Calgary contracted employment services were managed at the regional level; in the other regions it was a mix of regional and local office contract management. Each region had a contract manager handling the arrangements, where conditions were highly prescribed by provincial policy and tightly controlled at the regional (not local) level. All contracts had defined outcomes, indicators, and targets and were let for a period of between one to three years. There was very competitive and open bidding for securing the AHS contracts; however, there was some ability to negotiate targets as part of the contracting process (Wood 2010).

In Alberta the driver of performance for both civil servants and contractors was the departmental business plan, renewed annually. This was derived from strategic framework documents, the most important of which was Building and Educating Tomorrow's Workforce: Alberta's Ten-Year Strategy (2006). Indicators and targets were set at a provincial level, with delivery services input; locally determined measures and targets could also be set. AHS local offices were not benchmarked one against another; in fact senior AHS regional staff interviewed through this research suggested that they were not looking for consistency but for innovation. Inconsistency was encouraged so that innovation could be fostered. However, a stricter approach was taken with contracted services. If service providers did not meet their targets, the sanction was that their contract might not be renewed. Having targets and measures in the contracts was accepted as the way that business was done in Alberta (Wood 2010).

The situation in British Columbia in 2014 was quite different. Before taking on the federal services in 2009, all provincial employment services (mostly for social assistance clients) were contracted out to not-for-profit and for-profit organizations on the basis of open bidding and payment for outcomes. Unlike in Alberta, there were no provincial government staff providing these services. Pre-devolution, federal Service Canada officials used a mixed delivery model of federal staff plus third-party contractors – usually not-for-profit (NGO) community-based training organizations – with funding awarded through non-tendered contribution agreements. This was a contracting model very different from the one being used by the province. When BC took on a devolved LMDA in 2009, this meant that service delivery providers who had previously provided employment programming under federal contracts were now subject to a very different and highly competitive contracting environment.

As a result of this historical legacy, BC took a much more aggressive approach to outsourcing than occurred in Alberta. Following an intensive two-year consultation with more than seven hundred stakeholders and fourteen to fifteen community roundtables, BCSDSI replaced the province's 400 "legacy programs" with an integrated employment services model for all residents seeking an employment attachment and eligible to work in BC. In March 2011 the province issued a request for proposal (RFP), and in October 2011 the successful contractors were announced, consisting in 2014 of forty-seven prime contractors, seventy-three catchment areas, and 101 WorkBC Employment Services Centres. The program became fully operational 1 April 2012. The entire model was outlined in a 100-page prospectus placed on BC Bid, the province's main procurement website.

A "prime contractor" model was chosen in order to reduce the number of contracts and government administration. Each contractor has responsibility in a defined geographic area, including coordination and integration of activities of a number of subcontractors (up to seven or eight in some areas).[3] The EPBC was based on a detailed business model, including program outcomes and objectives, service contract requirements, defined client tiers, specialized populations, business processes, payment structures, a control framework, evaluation and audit criteria, and a detailed governance structure.

3 In 2013 400 contracts were counted, but many of these subcontractors operate in more than one location.

Payment-for-performance uses a mixed funding model, according to the tier that the client was assigned to. Alongside outcome payments, service delivery organizations were also eligible to receive a "fixed operating fee" to cover overhead, a "variable service fee" for case management, and reimbursements for any additional "financial supports and purchased services" given to job seekers (Palameta, Myers, and Conte 2013, 10). Each WorkBC contractor was expected to hire qualified staff and train them as needed. The province provided resource material (e.g., documents, videos, etc.) on how the program was to be implemented, and any changes to program delivery.

This highly defined EPBC framework was intended to ensure a consistent model across the province, so that all BC citizens would have access to the same services, with the same signage, regardless of where they lived. During development of the EPBC, consistency was valued over flexibility or local innovation. A centralized province-wide business model was also required for the parallel development of a new computer system to track client inputs, outputs, and outcomes. In 2014 the integrated case management system was shared between BCSDSI and four other provincial ministries. BC has promoted the EPBC as a "one-stop" model, as information needed to be entered into the shared computer system only once.

Many challenges were encountered while operationalizing the EPBC program after it was launched in April 2012. The integrated case management system created obstacles with privacy, as information was shared across a wide range of government programming. The "forced partnering" arrangements as required in the contracts created tensions between service delivery agencies, and some with a long history of providing employment programming closed. The distinction between "prime" contractors and "subcontractors" introduced a hierarchy. Most contracts ended up with the community-based agencies that had previously been involved in providing employment supports, so in fact many things did not change; however, one informant from the community sector interviewed through this research described the process as "taking the system apart and then putting it back together again."

The ministry responsible for the LMA agreement (BCJTST) did not have the same approach to contracting, and funds were open to bids through a formal tendering system, depending upon the availability and constraints of federal funding. Ultimately, twenty-seven programs were funded in BC using federal LMA funding up to 2013/14. The separation of the LMA funding stream from the LMDA funding stream created an additional competitive dynamic within the BC employment services community that did not occur in Alberta, where only one provincial government department was involved in employment services contracting, with most decisions taken at the regional or local (as opposed to provincial) level.

Partnerships and Networks

WITH BUSINESS AND LABOUR

Both Alberta and British Columbia have industry associations – organized by sector – to facilitate business, labour, training providers, and other stakeholder input into training and employment matters. Between 2005 and 2007 BC's Industry Training Authority (ITA) – a Crown agency responsible for trades training and apprenticeship – established and funded six Industry Training Organizations (ITOs) as independent not-for-profit societies to consult with industry on training needs for their sector (automotive, construction, horticulture, resource, tourism, and transportation).

As part of an independent review of the ITA carried out in 2013/14, in 2014 the ITOs were closed and replaced by ten Sector Advisory Groups made up of employers, contractors, labour, and the Aboriginal community. Support is provided directly by ITA staff (McDonald 2014). In 2012, using LMDA funding, BC also established eight Regional Workforce Tables as part of Canada Starts Here: The BC Jobs Plan. The development of a Regional Skills Training Plan was a key deliverable. The northeast and northwest regions of the province were the first to establish Regional Workforce Tables, followed by the Kootenay region. Projects were also funded under the Labour Market Partnerships program in seven high-growth sectors (forestry, mining, natural gas, agrifoods, technology, tourism, and transportation).

In Alberta the long-standing Apprenticeship and Industry Training Board provides advice and recommendations to government on trades and apprenticeship matters. Starting in 2006 – as part of a larger provincial workforce development strategy – Alberta began to develop sector-specific workforce strategies through Industry Contributor Groups consisting of business, labour, professional organizations, volunteer and community agencies, education and training providers, Aboriginal groups, and governments. By 2014 five Industry Contributor Groups were active in tourism and hospitality/retail; energy; construction; manufacturing/forest; and supply chain logistics. Industry – not government – led the implementation of strategy actions. In 2013 Alberta also set up two separate advisory councils (private and public) to identify solutions to help more people with disabilities enter the workforce. The BC Partners in Workforce Innovation Pilot Project has similar objectives. In Alberta, special efforts were also underway in 2013/14 on a youth engagement strategy as well as a provincial social policy framework.

WITH COMMUNITY ASSOCIATIONS RESPONSIBLE FOR EMPLOYMENT SERVICES

To implement the EPBC, Social Development and Social Innovation (BCSDSI) set up a formal partnership structure consisting of (1) a ministry program steering committee, (2) a corporate program advisory committee that included representatives from the ministry and the forty-seven WorkBC prime contractors, (3) an external advisory panel, and (4) an external advisory committee on specialized populations. In 2014 all information on the EPBC governance structure was available on a public website. Also established as part of the EPBC governance structure was the BC Centre for Employment Excellence (BCCfEE),[4] which provided a single provincial contact point for research, best practices, and resources on employment and training programs. The BC Ministry of Jobs, Tourism and Skills Training was not part of the EPBC governance structure.

An important stakeholder in PES programming in BC is the Association of Service Providers for Employability and Career Training (ASPECT)[5] – a non-profit organization that has represented community-based training agencies across BC for over twenty-two years. Funded by its membership, ASPECT provides leadership, education, advocacy, and public awareness through regular meetings with provincial government staff and politicians. It also hosts an annual conference that brings most of the players in the employment services business in BC together. In 2014 the executive director of ASPECT chaired the BC external advisory committee for the EPBC.

Since Alberta delivered much of its employment services through government staff (managed through the normal hierarchical controls), it did not need as formal a governance structure as BC with its contracted

---

4 See http://www.cfeebc.org/.
5 See https://www.aspect.bc.ca/.

employment services agencies. AHS regional directors met informally to secure input from stakeholders in their respective regions. There was also consultation on service delivery through a province-wide group that met regularly with government called the Training Provider Advisory Committee, involving public and private colleges as well as contracted training providers. The Alberta Association of Colleges and Technical Institutes, the Alberta Association of Career Colleges, and the Private Career Development Contractors Association of Alberta[6] were all influential within this context. Unlike in BC, none of these groups organized events that brought all the key players together on a provincial basis.

Other organizations also partnered in the provincial PES in each province, including the BC Career Development Association (that in 2014 supported professional development for 650 members and 859 certified career development practitioners in the province). Likewise, the Career Development Association of Alberta supported more than three hundred career development professionals in the province by setting professional standards and offering learning opportunities.[7]

WITH THE GOVERNMENT OF CANADA

Relationships with the Government of Canada – the prime funder of the employment programs delivered by the two provinces – were defined mostly through federal-provincial management committees established under the agreements. After 1996, in BC the federal-provincial LMDA/LMA Management Committee met twice a year, often through teleconference. A provincial informant characterized discussions as "high level, polite, and professional," serving mostly for information exchange. A federal government official noted that Ottawa was mostly "hands-off" in determining provincial programming; however, a senior federal official was seconded to the province to assist with the LMDA transition and participated in all the EPBC consultations carried out by the province between 2009 and 2011.

There were fewer formal federal-provincial connections in Alberta. When the province initially negotiated its devolved LMDA in 1996, as a way to diminish federal control, it deliberately did not establish a federal-provincial LMDA management committee. It did, however,

---

6 See http://pcdcalberta.ca/influencing-government-policy-changes/.

7 See https://www.bccda.org/ and http://www.careerdevelopment.ab.ca/.

agree to an Alberta-based LMA committee in 2009. In general, the bilateral federal–provincial working relationship was viewed as productive and positive. However, Alberta policy officials interviewed through this research advised that Ottawa rarely consulted with them on employment insurance or immigration matters. Likewise, AHS regional directors noted that coordinating youth, disabled, and homelessness strategies within Alberta was challenging when local federal officials did not come to the table.

WITH ABORIGINAL LABOUR MARKET ORGANIZATIONS

With an Aboriginal population of 5.8 per cent in Alberta and 4.8 per cent in British Columbia, both provinces place a high priority on engaging Aboriginal people in the provincial workforce. Chapter 8 in this book provides detailed information on Aboriginal employment programs – including the Aboriginal Skills and Employment Training Strategy, or ASETS, as overseen by the Government of Canada. This chapter (as well as chapters 5, 6, and 7) provides insight on partnerships between ASETS holders and their respective provincial government.

In 2014 BC had sixteen Aboriginal Skills and Employment Training Strategy (ASETS) agreement holders, with employment programming funded directly by the Government of Canada. For many years First Nations ASETS holders had come together to form the BC First Nations Human Resource Labour Council.[8] BC's Industry Training Authority (ITA) developed a formal relationship with the council, and ASETS holders frequently partnered on LMA initiatives managed by the ITA as well as the Ministry of Advanced Education. Over time this relationship had demonstrated positive results for Aboriginal learners; however, there was not a similar relationship with the WorkBC contractors funded through the EPBC.

BC ASETS holders interviewed in 2012 noted how implementation of the EPBC had created resentment among their members, for a number of reasons. First, historically when federal Service Canada officials could not spend their national allocation on EI clients, they routinely topped up ASETS allocations. With devolution this practice ended, leaving many ASETS holders resentful over the loss of "their" money to the provincial government. Second, ASETS holders viewed devolution

---

8 In 2015 the organization changed its name to the British Columbia Aboriginal Training Employment Alliance.

as being imposed without their input. Third, they did not consider that EPBC consultation took their concerns into account. The gap between the EPBC and the ASETS holders in BC was characterized by more than one respondent as "huge," with few efforts underway to bridge it. ASETS holders testifying at the federal HUMA parliamentary hearing in 2014 delivered the same message.

While Aboriginal employment partnerships in Alberta did not carry as much negative baggage, an Aboriginal informant interviewed through this research suggested that an important relationship dynamic was whether provincial officials regarded ASETS agreement holders as service delivery providers or as partners. This varied from one region in Alberta to another. Most relationships between provincial officials and the thirteen ASETS holders in Alberta were usually worked out at the regional level. Where it made sense, money was pooled and projects were worked on together. In some cases formal framework agreements had been put in place; in other cases the relationship was more informal.

Starting in 2002, AHS regional offices began to actively extend provincial employment services to Aboriginal Albertans living on reserve through the First Nations Training to Employment Program. This involved partnerships between First Nations, ASETS holders, the private sector, as well as the responsible federal government departments, all facilitated through Alberta Works staff and seeded with provincial training funding as well as federal LMA money. In 2009 Alberta established an Aboriginal Best Practice Table between ASETS holders and provincial and federal officials that met quarterly. In 2013 it had expanded through political involvement into an Aboriginal Workforce Strategy whose work carried over into 2014.

Comparing Alberta and British Columbia

Table A summarizes Alberta and British Columbia approaches to the governance of the PES, using the four themes identified in chapter 3 of this book.

What Accounted for the Differences between the Two Far West Provinces?

The different approaches to governance seen in Alberta's and BC's public employment service had mostly to do with differences in historical

Table A. Comparing Governance Features in Alberta's and BC's Public Employment Service, 2014

	Alberta	British Columbia
Single gateways or one-stop shops	53 Alberta Works Centres under Alberta Human Services provided single door access to employment services and social assistance (SA).	101 WorkBC Employment Services Centres under BC Social Development and Social Innovation (BCSDSI) provided employment services. 100 separate SA offices. BC Jobs, Tourism and Skills Training also contracted for employment services.
	Employer supports provided under Jobs, Skills, Training and Labour.	Employer supports scattered across government.
	All federal labour market transfer funding managed by same provincial department.	Federal funding divided between two provincial departments based on client and agreement focus.
Decentralization	Decision making decentralized to 6 AHS regional directors. Work and welfare fused at regional level.	Policy control centralized at provincial level under BCSDSI. More limited regional coordination across business lines within BCSDSI.
	Key priority was innovation at regional and local level.	Key priority was to ensure similar services across province.
Outsourcing and contracting out	PES was a mix of government staff and contracted agencies.	Extensive outsourcing. PES provided exclusively by contracted service providers.
	Regions chose whether to outsource and to whom, and facilitated coordination between all contractors. Most contracts let through RFP process.	BCSDSI contractors chosen on basis of province-wide RFP. Prime contractor model ensured coordination with subcontractors but not with other contractors.
	All contracts let by single department had defined outcomes, indicators, and targets to match business plan.	2 departments had different contracting and outsourcing models.
Partnerships and networks	5 Industry Contributor Groups	10 Sector Advisory Groups, plus 8 Regional Workforce Tables
	Training Provider Advisory Committee facilitated relationships.	Formalized relationship with WorkBC contractors. ASPECT ensured coordination among community-based agencies.
	Aboriginal partnerships with ASETS were an important priority.	ASETS holders not fully coordinated with WorkBC Centres.

arrangements pre-devolution, and the timing of when the province took on devolved LMDAs. However, they also reflected subtle differences in political culture between the two provinces.

Until 2013 in Alberta, single door access to a broad spectrum of activities related to work, welfare, and the workplace was provided through fifty-three Alberta Works Centres across the province. These arrangements grew out of the mid-1990s Canada-Alberta Service Centre experiments that integrated services between not just two provincial government departments, but also with the federal government. The fourteen-year provincial integration of all strategic and operational activities related to the PES (until departmental changes in 2014 that moved the strategic component and employer supports to a new ministry) ensured a consistent and strong Alberta response to workforce development in the province.

BC's public employment service was predominately built on its platform of active measures for social assistance recipients. While the Ministry of Social Development and Social Innovation established a single door for Employment Insurance and social assistance clients through 101 WorkBC Employment Services Centres, there was another door for other target groups (e.g., Aboriginal people, immigrants, older workers) through the provincial Ministry of Jobs, Tourism and Skills Training, and still another door to access social assistance benefits. Over the years shifting political direction in BC has created more competition between politicians and bureaucrats over departmental mandates. Given the split in delivery services by client group, in 2014 BC had two provincial ministries with prime responsibility for the PES (three if Advanced Education with prime responsibility for Aboriginal people was included), each with its own delivery system to implement the federal programs.

Alberta's PES was much more decentralized than was BC's. When in 1999 Alberta reorganized provincial government departments in order to integrate work and welfare programming within a single human resources department, the delivery and policy role were separated, resulting in a significant delegation of authority to an assistant deputy minister and six regional offices with responsibility for managing and integrating staff and contractors across business lines. Services to employers were added later as another business line, all under regional control.

In contrast, BCSDSI's five regional offices managed "templated" programs on both the work and welfare side, with little operative flexibility to adjust across programs or vary from the provincially determined model. The different approaches in the two provinces lie in the coming together of parts of three large departments in Alberta in 1999 (provincial social services and career development officials as well as federal PES staff), each of which historically had regional delivery systems managed by government staff. For more than thirteen years a powerful and stable assistant deputy minister of regional delivery services in AHS – with a wide span of responsibilities – protected regional autonomy and flexibility in Alberta. With mostly contracted PES arrangements in BC, there was a need for more government control, hence centralization in the provincial capital.

In both provinces social assistance is provided by government employees, and there has been no outsourcing or contracting out. This approach reflects a desire to retain government control, as well as a preference for consistent province-wide benefit levels and eligibility conditions in each province. Employment supports, however, are not the same, with extensive outsourcing in BC, compared to Alberta. The roots of the different approaches lie in history. Alberta came to the employment support business earlier than BC, using provincial civil servants. While BC had some government staff early on, with reorganization and cutbacks government positions disappeared.

When helping social assistance recipients access employment became a political priority in BC, expertise needed to be purchased, hence the decision to enter into arrangements with external contractors, and the choice of "brokering models" consisting of prime contractors and subcontractors. In addition, the organizational strength of the community based employment sector in BC expanded under Service Canada after 1996, as the federal government increasingly moved employment services from government staff to contractors. BC's employment program governance structure in 2014 was dominated by province-wide contracting and parameters determined by staff from central office, not the regions. In Alberta regional delivery-level civil servants controlled the system to a much greater degree.

The differences in external partnerships and networks were an outcome of the different approaches to outsourcing. Since the contracted WorkBC Centres were, in effect, delivering the same front door service as the government-run Alberta Works Centres, a more formal partnership was required, hence the defined governance model for the EPBC. The long-term organizational presence of ASPECT in BC that brings together community-based employment and training contractors resulted in a more structured relationship between these groups and the province than occurred in Alberta. Without public reporting, it was difficult to know the impact the external advisory committees were having on the EPBC. Informants interviewed through this research suggested that by 2015 the committees had essentially closed down.

Unlike Manitoba and Quebec (explored in later chapters of this book), neither BC nor Alberta had institutionalized industry-run boards with broad responsibility for labour market matters. Instead, sector-council-type organizations have developed, particularly in occupations closely tied closely to the provincial apprenticeship and trades training systems. None of these sector-council-type activities were codified in legislation, making them subject to changing political winds. In BC there has been considerable churning and change in how industry input was secured, with four different organizational structures put in place over the past twenty years. The 2014 changes in BC that set up "Sector Advisory Groups" were specifically meant to avoid "the former interest-based model which led to dysfunctional gridlock and win/loss decisions that did not reflect the outcomes needed by employers" (McDonald 2014, 6). While Alberta's arrangements seemed stable, they were also open to changing political priorities, especially with three premiers in the space of three years. Differences in industry engagement in Alberta and BC were clear examples of differences in political culture, including stronger unions in BC than in Alberta.

How Alberta and British Columbia related to their respective ASETS holders could be partially attributed to timing. With seventeen years' experience in running an integrated PES system (compared to BC's five), Alberta has had more time and resources to put steps in place to productively manage the government–Aboriginal relationship. In BC the long-standing presence of two provincial government departments in the employment services game has made building relationships that much more challenging. As of 2015, few steps had been taken by the provincial government to overcome the lack of coordination between the EPBC and the BC ASETS holders.

How Did PES Performance in the Two Provinces Compare?

In exchange for the federal money, all provinces committed to prepare annual LMDA and LMA plans, as well as LMA performance reports. All (except Quebec with respect to the LMA) used the same indicators. In addition, the Employment Insurance Commission publishes an annual EI Monitoring and Assessment Report (MAR) that contains detailed information on provincial activities funded through the LMDA.

Drawing on this information, the performance of British Columbia's and Alberta's public employment service – using effectiveness, efficiency, and democracy as described in chapter 3 as key indicators – were compared. Appendices E and F summarize performance data for British Columbia's and Alberta's PES for the fifteen years between 1999 and 2014. All of Alberta's results reported in appendix F were under provincial control, whereas in BC the LMDA results reported until 2011/12 in appendix E were under the responsibility of Service Canada. All BC LMA activities were under provincial control.

Demographic and Economic Conditions

There are many demographic and economic similarities between the two provinces. British Columbia's population in 2014 was 4,631,000 people, whereas Alberta's was slightly less at 4,121,700. Alberta's population was growing faster than BC's (25 per cent growth since 2000 vs 11 per cent) as people moved to the province from the rest of Canada and overseas to take advantage of the jobs available. Landlocked Alberta covers 661,848 square kilometres vs coastal BC at 944,735 square kilometres. Between 1996 and 2014 the Alberta unemployment rate (ranging between 3 and 6 per cent) was consistently lower than BC's by about 2 percentage points, and the employment rate at around 70 per cent was higher by about 10 points. Until the economic downturn that started in 2014 due to the drop in the price of oil, Alberta had the tightest labour market in the country, with investment in the oil sands a key driver of its economy. In the 2000s both provinces were dealing with significant skills and labour shortages in some areas.

British Columbia's social assistance caseload (134,591 in 2014) as well as the number of regular Employment Insurance recipients (58,000) was considerably higher than in Alberta (at around 80,000 vs 33,000 respectively). The 2012 social assistance dependency rate in Alberta at 3.2 per cent was the lowest in the country, compared to BC's at 4.7 per cent (Kneebone and White 2014). In both provinces there were almost twice as many people dependent upon social assistance than Employment Insurance, reflecting tighter EI eligibility rules in these two provinces compared to other regions in Canada, as well as stronger labour markets.

Effectiveness

LMDA expenditures in each province reflected the allocations provided by the Government of Canada. They had not fundamentally changed since the 1996 devolution offer and were rooted in the historical LMDA allocations coming out of the 1996 EI reforms.[9] Despite populations of relatively similar size today, Alberta's LMDA allocation of $109,143,000 in 2013/14 was less than half of BC's at $276,402,000. In 2013/14 there was actually *less* money spent in Alberta than thirteen years earlier, whereas in BC spending has grown somewhat. In neither place did expenditures grow with inflation; if that had occurred, Alberta would have been allocated $158,146,000 and British Columbia $313,921,000 in 2013/14, an increase of 31 per cent.[10]

With the overall federal LMDA allocations relatively fixed, each province could decide whether to spend the federal funds on longer-term employment benefits (like training and wage subsidy) vs shorter-term employment assistance services vs other support measures like labour market partnerships and research and innovation. When the federal government was in charge in 2005/6, BC allocated 62 per cent of all expenditures to long-term activities, 38 per cent to short-term, and less than 1 per cent to labour market partnerships and research. By 2013/14 under provincial control, long-term and short-term expenditures had declined somewhat to 57 and 35 per cent respectively, while allocations to labour market partnerships and research had increased to 8 per cent of all expenditures. This reflects the priority BC has placed on the BC Centre for Employment Excellence and the Labour Market Partnerships program. Under consistent provincial government control, the proportion of expenditures allocated to long-term activities in Alberta has risen slightly over the years from about 65 per cent in 2005/6 to 73 per cent in 2013/14. Alberta has been remarkably consistent over the years in its allocation to labour market partnerships and research at about 1 per cent of all expenditures.

---

9 The only time LMDA allocations grew was in 2009/10 and 2010/11, as a result of extra federal money allocated to fight the Great Recession. By 2011/12 the funding allocations were back to normal.

10 Calculation based on Alberta and BC LMDA expenditures in 1999/2000. Data Source: Statistics Canada, Consumer Price Indexes for Canada, Monthly (V41690973 series).

Using LMDA funding, Alberta served considerably more clients than BC, averaging 123,317 per year (over the period 1999/2000 to 2013/14) compared to BC, where 88,604 people were served on average per year. It is hard to identify why the numbers were so divergent, other than that Alberta's larger apprenticeship program may have had an impact.[11] Compared over time, the number of clients served with LMDA funding in Alberta remained relatively stable each year, growing somewhat since 2008/9. In BC it was fairly stable under Service Canada control and then dropped considerably once the province took the programs on, starting in 2011/12. This can be explained by the shock to the delivery system as a result of the implementation of the EPBC, and time needed to bring new contractors on board.

About half of Alberta's LMDA clients were receiving EI benefits, and half were non-insured, whereas in BC there were consistently more EI clients being served (e.g., in Alberta in 2013/14, 48 per cent were EI attached vs 56 per cent in BC). LMA funding in both provinces was used to serve those without an EI attachment (immigrants, Aboriginal people, disabled persons, older workers, and youth). With this LMA funding Alberta served an average of 28,574 clients per year, compared to BC's 12,107 clients. Again, BC's lower number of clients served may be due to delays encountered in implementing a new delivery system. When it did become operational, in BC the program emphasis was on skills development for the employed, whereas in Alberta most funding was allocated to lower cost employment and training services.

Alberta's total LMDA interventions[12] increased significantly over time, effectively doubling over the period, yet using the same amount of money. Given that they cost more money, less than 9 per cent of Alberta's interventions in 2014 were long-term interventions[13] (e.g., training or work experience); the rest were short-term employment assistance services (EAS). BC's interventions showed the same trend, increasing in total over time, with long-term interventions a small portion (8 per cent) of the total in 2014. In the early LMDA days (1999/2000) Alberta's long-term interventions were 14 per cent of the total, while

11 When apprentices attend their short-term technical training, they can draw on LMDA funding to cover their costs.

12 Interventions count the number of activities provided to a single client; for example, Employment Support Services (EAS) followed by a work experience program. Many clients receive only one intervention.

13 In 2013/14 73 per cent of Alberta's expenditures were on employment benefits.

BC's were 32 per cent. Post-devolution, both Alberta's and BC's PES programming has moved away from longer-term training towards low-cost EAS services. This is why more clients can be served with the same amount of money. The emphasis in both provinces on short-term inventions through the LMDA was mitigated to some degree through LMA programming, as many of these interventions involved more than short-term EAS.

In both provinces LMDA programming results vs targets (in relation to EI returns to employment as well as EI unpaid benefits) were generally met and sometimes exceeded. Alberta's targets were more aggressive than those in BC (e.g., in 2013/14 Alberta sought to return 22,000 EI clients out of 33,170 to work, while BC sought to return 24,000 EI clients out of 58,000). In LMA programming, the proportion of clients who completed programming in Alberta (ranging from 74 to 89 per cent) was consistently higher than those who were employed (from 57 per cent in 2008/9 to 39 per cent in 2013/14). In BC, while over 78 per cent completed training in 2013/14, the number employed was identified at 70 per cent. Information on earlier years in BC was not available, making the comparison more unreliable. Between 70 and 85 per cent of LMA program recipients in Alberta reported that the training provided helped. In BC the data were available only for 2013/14, where the proportion was 94 per cent. It appeared that substantially more people received credentials in BC than in Alberta; however, whether this statistic is directly comparable is open to question.

While each province was required through the federal-provincial agreements to report on results, it was up to each to decide whether it wished to undertake additional reporting and research to improve the effectiveness of the provincial PES.[14] British Columbia's public reports and information on PES programming were much more extensive than Alberta's. Both provinces provided annual ministry departmental reports; however, BC also released a monthly report on the EPBC, as well as reports on related programming. Even upcoming activities (e.g., information on BC's EPBC evaluation) were posted on the provincial website. The BC Centre for Employment Excellence (BCCfEE) offered a website, articles, training, and other opportunities to enhance knowledge and practice among key stakeholders in BC, including the

14 The Government of Canada also undertakes formal program evaluations, done in collaboration with provincial governments.

WorkBC employment contractors. Alberta may have undertaken similar additional reporting and research; however, this information was not shared publicly. This limited the capacity of external researchers and stakeholders from gaining a better understanding of Alberta's programs.

Efficiency

There were virtually no differences in satisfaction expressed in either province by clients who took part in LMA programming, with scores in BC consistently exceeding 90 per cent and Alberta's in the high 80s. However, with less than half the money, Alberta consistently served twice the number of clients using LMDA funding than BC did. Between 1999/2000 and 2013/14 Alberta served an average of 123,317 clients per year with an average allocation of $118,877,000, vs 88,604 clients with an annual allocation of $277,991,000 in BC.[15] Using simple mathematics, this worked out to a cost per client of $963 in Alberta vs $3,137 in BC over the entire period. In terms of return on investment, for the $109,143,000 allocation of funds through the EI account in 2013/14, Alberta returned $249,300,000 in EI unpaid benefits, whereas BC's $276,402,000 investment saved only $121,800,000 in EI unpaid benefits. Using these measures, Alberta's PES programming was more efficient than BC's. Efficiency measures can and should be debated. Doing the calculation and comparing the two provinces allows this debate to begin.

Alberta's greater efficiency may have been because of one-stop shops managed (until 2014) under one provincial government department. During the same period there was much more turmoil in BC, including the transition of responsibility from federal to provincial and then two different BC departments taking on elements of the federal programming. The more positive Alberta relationship with ASETS holders vs BC's more adversarial relationship may have been because BC ASETS holders were dealing with actors under the authority of a variety of provincial departments, whereas in Alberta it was generally just one. It was also important that Alberta had been delivering the PES for much longer than BC and – under stable political direction – put management structures and processes in place that endured. BC's interdepartmental

15 For half of this time, BC's services were being managed and delivered by the Government of Canada.

Labour Market Priorities Board put in place in 2014 may – over time – achieve the same efficiency outcomes in programming as Alberta's single window did.

In terms of the training given to individuals who provided public employment services, both provinces had professional associations that career development practitioners (CDP) working in each province could join. Post-devolution, Alberta took leadership on a pan-Canadian basis through the Forum of Labour Market Ministers (FLMM) to establish a career development practitioners' working group.[16] Alberta government officials were supported in this work through key contacts at the University of Calgary and Athabasca University. This also ensured an investment in training of CDPs who worked for government. The province also provided funding so that contracted service delivery agencies could provide staff development. As a result of these factors, a large proportion of the Alberta PES workforce has had access to professional career development training. For many years the province was considered as a leader in career development. This work was done in cooperation with the Career Development Association of Alberta and the Canadian Career Development Foundation, who support career development practitioners from across Canada.

In contrast, BC expected its WorkBC contractors and their subcontractors to undertake staff training and development as they deemed necessary. While funding for these supports could be built into the contracting arrangements, it was up to each contractor to decide whether and how its staff would be trained. In 2014 the provincial government did not focus special efforts on the training of career development practitioners, leaving this to the BC Career Development Association. In recent years this organization has started to work with the BC Centre for Employment Excellence to build stronger linkages with the WorkBC contractors. Given this history and investment in career development matters, Alberta's PES workforce was considered as better trained than BC's.

Democracy

Transparency is essential to democracy, as a way for stakeholders to inform citizens about executive behaviour. While both Alberta and BC released LMA plans and reports as required in the agreements, neither

16 The FLMM Career Development Practitioners' Working Group was disbanded in 2010, as some provinces did not think the work was of value.

province had this information easily accessible on a provincial website, and the links on the federal site were often broken. Alberta's LMA reports were short (six pages) and direct, and contained information that was consistent from one year to the next. Constructing appendix F from the Alberta data was relatively easy. In contrast, BC's reports were much longer (about forty pages). While informative, the report layout made extracting information for BC's appendix E more challenging. In addition, not all the indicators were reported on in BC. However, in both provinces information was released, and most of the indicators were reported on as outlined in their respective Labour Market Agreements.

Democracy also requires engagement, and both provinces outlined their engagement strategies in their annual LMA plans. While Alberta's information in the LMA plans was extensive and more detailed than British Columbia's, BC also provided additional information on public websites relating to the EPBC, their sectoral advisory committees, and regional workforce roundtables, including the names of people directly involved. As a result of this additional information, democratic engagement in BC was stronger than in Alberta. Neither province had stakeholder engagement institutionalized through legislation, providing much greater potential for practices to be abandoned when governments and leadership changed.

Conclusion

Having an effective public employment service is essential to ensuring the development of a highly educated and skilled workforce. British Columbia and Alberta are respectively Canada's third- and fourth-largest provinces, and both are growing faster than other provinces in Canada. This chapter has demonstrated that the two provinces do indeed share a "parvenu" political culture – a lack of tradition and an upstart and recalcitrant political character. However, despite being close neighbours, Alberta and BC made very different governance choices for their PES.

Alberta was the first province to implement a devolved LMDA in 1997, while BC was one of the last in 2009; given upheaval to the system in BC, it has really only been since the launch of the Employment Program of BC (EPBC) in 2012 that the province started to play the lead PES role. In contrast, by 2014 the provincial government in Alberta had played that role for more than fifteen years. During that period

Alberta implemented a single-window, decentralized, PES delivery system – providing income support, employment services, and workforce development – with the front door managed by government staff. Specialized contractors provided a supporting role. In contrast, BC's PES delivery system used third-party contractors operating under a common brand as the front door, with contracts centrally managed out of the provincial capital. The EPBC focused only on employment services, with related income support and employer support services accessed through other doors and sometimes operated by different provincial government departments.

It was in the area of partnerships and engagement beyond government where there were more similarities between the two provinces, notwithstanding the fact that the governance structure of the EPBC was more formal than that found in Alberta. Both provinces brought industry into decision making through sector initiatives; however, in neither province had these partnerships been formalized through legislation. Both reached out to their Aboriginal partners, who were managing services under the federal ASETS program; however, BC's greater fragmentation of responsibility for the PES across provincial government departments resulted in more relationship difficulties than were evident in Alberta.

On the basis of performance data contained in federal and provincial reports, Alberta's PES was considered as both more effective and more efficient than BC's, consistently serving more clients at a lower cost. This may improve in BC over time, especially given the province's additional investment in research and evaluation, compared to Alberta. Democratic engagement and a commitment to transparency in BC were better than in Alberta, where government control and a lack of public information were more dominant features.

Chapter Five

The Midwest: Saskatchewan and Manitoba

Many people from eastern and central Canada think of the "west" – consisting of the three prairie provinces and British Columbia – as a distinct and coherent political community with a shared set of issues and values. The evidence suggests otherwise, as illustrated by the different reactions of the four western provinces to the federal offer in 1996 to devolve responsibility for the public employment service (PES) and related workforce development measures. As has already been identified, three provinces (Alberta, Saskatchewan, and Manitoba) said yes, and one (British Columbia) said no. Manitoba was the third province to agree to take on responsibility for the PES from Canada, in April 1997, and Saskatchewan signed on less than a year later, in February 1998.

These two provinces were also the first in 2005 (along with Ontario) to agree to a federal Liberal proposal to enhance the labour market services on offer to their citizens through Labour Market Partnership Agreements, or LMPAs. While Saskatchewan and Manitoba were comfortable with a delivery arrangement that would have sanctioned the reinsertion of federal government staff into the management and delivery of labour market programming within their province, Alberta saw these new developments as a threat to the coherent provincially managed system they had put in place post-devolution. The disagreement became moot when the Martin Liberal government fell to the Harper Conservatives in 2006. All three LMPA agreements were cancelled, to be replaced in 2008 with much more "province-friendly" Labour Market Agreements, or LMAs, which were readily accepted by all provinces and territories.

These responses demonstrate that, in labour market matters, Saskatchewan and Manitoba – labelled here as the midwest – share many common traits. This chapter explores this similarity in greater detail, starting with a reflection on political culture in the two provinces. This is followed by a brief historical overview of work and welfare in each province, focusing in particular on the circumstances in the years leading up to the federal devolution negotiations. Developments post-devolution are assessed next, drawing on the themes in the analytical framework as outlined in chapter 3 of this book. Similarities and differences are summarized, followed by a discussion of what accounts for the differences. The chapter concludes by assessing the performance of the provincial PES, using data and information from federal and provincial reports.

The Political Context

The provinces of Saskatchewan and Manitoba – like their neighbour Alberta – were carved out of Rupert's Land, involving the transfer of a vast swathe of land in 1869 from the British-controlled Hudson's Bay Company to the newly formed Dominion of Canada. Given its earlier settlement patterns, Manitoba was up first, becoming a province in 1870 following the Louis Riel–led Red River rebellion, where the Metis, First Nations, and white inhabitants of the area fought for some kind of say over how they would be governed. The establishment of Alberta and Saskatchewan as provinces followed in 1905. Many historians have noted that the three jurisdictions were treated at the time as "second-class" provinces or as "colonies" to be exploited for the benefit of central Canada. While British Columbia and Prince Edward Island got to control their natural resources as soon as they became provinces (in 1870 and 1873 respectively), this privilege was not extended to the three prairie provinces until 1930. Creating three provinces in the west (rather than one) was also seen by some as a deliberate attempt by the federal government to ensure a weak region unable to rival and overtake Ontario and Quebec in wealth and power (Whitcomb 1982).

The involvement of Louis Riel in preserving Metis rights and culture also played a part in Saskatchewan's development through the North-West Rebellion in 1885. Native self-rule ended when the Metis were defeated at Batoche, Saskatchewan, and Louis Riel was hanged for his role in the uprising. The consequences of assigning control of Natives and lands reserved for Natives to the federal government through the BNA Act is felt much more keenly in Saskatchewan and Manitoba than anywhere else in Canada, as a result of the high proportion of the population with Aboriginal ancestry (14 per cent compared to about 3 per cent in the rest of Canada). By 2045 persons of Aboriginal descent are projected to make up 32 per cent of the population of these provinces (Wiseman 2007, 215). By all quality-of-life measures, Aboriginal people are significantly disadvantaged in Canada; for example, in 2012 the general unemployment rate was 7.2 per cent, while the Aboriginal rate was 12.8 per cent (HRSDC 2013a, 8). Problems are even greater for First Nations people living on reserve, where 34 per cent of the population are dependent on band-delivered social assistance (AANDC 2014b).

In addition to similar grievances about the lack of control over natural resources and railways, Manitoba's borders were restricted and did not reach the 60th parallel like its sister provinces until 1912. The building of the railway in the 1880s and 1890s opened up both Saskatchewan and Manitoba to settlement, with most people coming from Ontario, Britain, continental Europe, and the United States. Manitoba is often referred to as the Ontario of the prairies, with many of the province's governing institutions imported from its eastern neighbour. Between 1881 and 1921 the prairie population went from 100,000 people to 2 million. Most immigrants became farmers and agriculture became a defining feature of the economy in both provinces. Subsequently, a tradition of government-assisted cooperatives developed – viewed as a way to cope with large amounts of land and distance, the dramatic range of weather, and the demands on resources and trade. The large Aboriginal population is also deeply invested in collective practices. Today Saskatchewan is home to the highest number of cooperatives (in child care, recreation, and economic activities) compared to other provinces in Canada (Holden et al. 2009).

Wiseman (2007) characterizes the political culture of Saskatchewan and Manitoba as populist and progressive. Women's suffrage originated in the prairies, with women getting the vote in 1917. The depression of the 1930s hit both provinces very hard. As a result, many citizens abandoned the traditional Conservative/Liberal party system – perceived to serve central Canada interests – to form protest parties. Unlike Alberta and British Columbia, which gravitated towards the more individualistic and conservative Social Credit movement, in Manitoba and Saskatchewan social-democratic parties emerged – committed to collectivist values, government planning, and the welfare state.

J.S. Woodsworth, from Manitoba, was instrumental in joining workers and farmers to found a new western-based socialist party, the Commonwealth Cooperative Party in 1932 – the forerunner of the present

New Democratic Party (NDP). The NDP came to power in Saskatchewan under Tommy Douglas in 1944 and introduced pensions, minimum wages, and Crown corporations to the province. These ideas spilled over into the national arena, and Douglas is credited as the father of Canada's most-loved and important social program, medicare (Whitcomb 2005b). Over the past seventy years, citizens of these two midwest provinces have had considerable experience with social-democratic, activist, provincial governments. Saskatchewan was under NDP control for forty-seven of the past seventy years and Manitoba for thirty.

After the Second World War Saskatchewan boomed while Manitoba's fortunes declined, as Winnipeg – where half of the province's population lives – lost its "gateway to the west" advantage to other western cities. During and after the Great Depression Manitoba was instrumental in championing the need for a strong federal government, able to provide leadership and financial support in order to equalize public services across the country. Provincial politicians and civil servants were not averse to abandoning provincial rights for federal grants and – unlike Alberta and Quebec – not offended by federal intrusions into policy fields under exclusive or prime provincial responsibility. Over the years Manitoba's approach to intergovernmental relations has been pragmatic, problem-specific, cautious, and driven by the issues at hand as opposed to overarching federalism political objectives. With 34.7 per cent of provincial revenue in 2007 coming from federal transfers (Bakvis et al. 2009, 52), Manitoba governments – stuck in the middle of the country looking both east and west – have traditionally adopted a conciliatory and constructive approach when dealing with the federal government and the other provinces (Thomas 2008).

With similar constrained financial resources – subject to volatile swings based on the province's agriculture and natural resources economy – Saskatchewan's intergovernmental views are seldom different from Manitoba's. With relatively small populations, both provinces lack political power through federal House of Commons seats. In 2007, only 17 per cent of Saskatchewan's revenues came from federal transfers and in 2014 the province received no equalization payments. However, it was not always this way. In addition to the difficult times of the Great Depression, Saskatchewan's crushing debt of more than $15 billion in 1993 brought the province to the brink of bankruptcy. It was only through quiet intervention and back-room assistance that a federal bail-out was arranged and a crisis averted.

This incident clearly illustrated to Saskatchewan elites – especially the NDP under Premier Romanow, who took power in 1991 after nine years of Conservative reign – the value of being part of a larger federal political union. Saskatchewan's willingness to see the federal government actively involved in programs and projects is evident in the principle of "constructive entanglement" articulated by Romanow during the Social Union Framework Agreement (SUFA) negotiations. Saskatchewan's preference is to engage, rather than exclude the federal government, especially if money is available (Garcea and Pontikes 2004).

By accommodating a business-first agenda and successfully positioning itself as a fiscally responsible and pragmatic government (Sheldrick 2015), the Manitoba NDP was able to dominate the political landscape for seventeen years, until it was replaced in 2016 by the Progressive Conservatives. The NDP in Saskatchewan was less successful, losing power after sixteen years to the conservative-oriented Saskatchewan Party in 2007. Winning a third term in 2016, the Saskatchewan Party has now replaced the NDP as the natural governing party in Saskatchewan, serving as the stronghold for neoliberalism in Canada (Conway and Conway 2015). While Manitoba has consistently received equalization payments from the federal government, as of 2008 Saskatchewan moved from being a "have-not" to a "have" province (Bernard 2012). It is lauded for its "comeback" story: from being a province of declining population and prospects, in recent years it has had above-average growth and below-average unemployment (OECD 2016).

Given the differences in the economies of the four western provinces, there is less regional thinking and action and more competition as each seeks to attract investment to its province. Although western premiers have met annually since 1973, the level of activity and willingness to take joint action has dissipated over time (Thomas 2008). This contrasts with the institutionalized cooperation in eastern Canada through the Council of Atlantic Premiers. The most noteworthy western cooperation in recent years has been a 2010 New West Partnership agreement between Alberta, British Columbia, and Saskatchewan to expand trade and investment opportunities and reduce labour mobility impediments. There are also procurement, research and development, and international cooperation elements. Under the NDP, Manitoba was not invited to join, in part for lack of ideological congruence between the Manitoba party and the more conservative leanings of the political parties in charge in the other western provinces (Berdahl and Gibbons 2014).

Negotiations to join were opened up after the election of the Manitoba Progressive Conservatives in 2016.

Historical Developments around Activation

Saskatchewan

Like many other provinces in Canada, Saskatchewan moved control of social assistance from municipalities to the province in the 1960s, triggered by the availability of federal cost-sharing. The Saskatchewan Assistance Plan of 1966 embodied clear social democratic values, noting in its promotional material that "the welfare of each individual is essential to the total welfare of the community" (August 2015). While firmly on the "entitlement" – as opposed to the "obligation" – end of the spectrum, by the late 1970s the provincial social assistance department had started to offer employment services to multi-barriered clients. These government-run services were transformed in the mid-1980s into community-based contractual arrangements.

Other than these services to social assistance recipients, pre-devolution Saskatchewan had very limited capacity in employment programming. Provincial postsecondary education programs relied on federal training monies over which the province had very limited control. This caused resentment among Saskatchewan officials, who also viewed Ottawa's desire to establish provincial labour force development boards as a way to extend federal dominance over the policy area. Saskatchewan was a reluctant player in this national undertaking, although it eventually did agree in 1994 to set up a provincial board aligned with the federal model. However, the province refused to invest its own funding and give control over policy to the business, unions, and equity partners on the board. The Saskatchewan Labour Force Development Board lasted for only two years, until 1996 when the federal money was withdrawn (Haddow 1997a).

By the mid-1990s Saskatchewan's dire financial situation had been stabilized with federal support. While the province had investigated alternatives to welfare – especially for the working poor – and was keen to move forward with its ideas, it had no money. This was the era when all provinces (except Quebec) and the federal government worked together to develop the National Child Benefit to reduce child poverty across the nation, involving increased payments for children's income support provided by the federal government and complementary provincial investments using savings accrued from reduced social assistance payments. Saskatchewan was a leader in the NCB initiative, and ended up developing an array of companion provincial programs under the Building Independence label. These included separate and defined employment and rental supplement programs, as well as a child benefit and a family health benefits programs.

Taking on federal active measures through the Labour Market Development Agreement (LMDA) in 1996 was viewed in Saskatchewan as just another piece of these larger changes, as a way to stop people from moving back and forth between social assistance and unemployment insurance, and help them get into work. The transfer of ninety-seven federal staff and $33.5 million in funding (Klassen 2000a) provided an opportunity for Saskatchewan to build a coordinated delivery system to ensure that social assistance claimants got the same services as those receiving Employment Insurance (EI). It also facilitated reform of the provincial college and training system, including the development of enhanced connections with Saskatchewan employers and a way to improve the quality of labour market information and job matching services. Through the LMDA, Canada-Saskatchewan Career and Employment Services Centres were opened across the province, providing deliberate linkages for federal EI clients and provincially offered active measures.

Despite these early reforms, post-devolution there has been considerable churning in responsibility for employment programming in Saskatchewan and, according to informants interviewed for this research, little progress in the PES. When the LMDA was signed in 1998, responsibility was assigned to the provincial postsecondary education department; shortly afterwards an integrated Saskatchewan Community Resources and Employment Ministry was put in place. The provincial integration of employment and welfare services did not last long and was ultimately viewed as a failure, dismantled by differences in culture between provincial social services administrators vs provincial educators and federal officials who did not want to serve multi-barriered social assistance clients. Saskatchewan employers were also reluctant to deal with a social services ministry. By 2006 social assistance had been sent back to the social services ministry, and employment programs were reintegrated with the postsecondary education department. This was the department that was responsible for rolling out Labour Market Agreement (LMA) programming starting in 2008.

Dismantling administrative linkages between the social assistance and employment services functions also affected the work orientation of the welfare department. The Building Independence initiatives focused on the working poor became devalued and undersubscribed. The emphasis on active measures for social assistance clients was further reduced when the Saskatchewan Party took control of government in 2007, anxious to improve benefits for the severely disabled, a key concern of welfare lobby groups. Even though accessing employment was mandatory for certain elements of the social assistance caseload, there were limited consequences for non-participation. In 2012 the basket of LMDA- and LMA-funded employment programs run by the postsecondary education department were moved to a new Ministry of the Economy and integrated with immigration, energy, natural resources, and tourism programs. The overall direction for labour market programming became a component of Saskatchewan's broader economic development policy, as articulated in Saskatchewan's Plan for Growth: Vision 2020 and Beyond.

Manitoba

Manitoba is well known for its involvement in MINCOME, an experiment undertaken in the 1970s between the provincial government and Ottawa that tested whether a guaranteed, unconditional annual income caused disincentives to work for social assistance recipients. The MINCOME experiment was never expanded beyond the pilot phase, as centre-left governments were replaced by centre-right governments less interested in poverty. At the time Manitoba had a two-tiered welfare system, with municipalities responsible for employable welfare recipients and the province responsible for single mothers and the disabled. Manitoba did not give up its two-tiered welfare system – moving all responsibility to the provincial level – until 2004.

Even with an orientation to benefits and administrative responsibility split between two levels of government, by the mid-1990s Manitoba had started to develop active measures, with provincial welfare reform requiring employability plans for those expected to work (Simpson 2015). Most of the money for Manitoba's employment programs came from Ottawa through the "four-cornered strategy," using Canada Assistance Plan funding. The programming was offered through Employment Development Centres run by the provincial education and training department. Pre-devolution, Manitoba offered services to youth through a program called Mb4Youth, adult literacy programs, in addition to an array of services for people receiving income assistance benefits (labour market training, employment connections, industry-based training, community-based employability, and community partnerships).

Unlike Saskatchewan, Manitoba was not willing to establish a provincial labour force development board, as promoted by Ottawa in the early 1990s. Provincial officials saw this as federal meddling in an area of provincial responsibility (Haddow 1997a). In 1989 the province established the Skills Training Advisory Committee; in its final report the committee recommended that the province set up sector councils – business-labour organizations focused on training and human resources development within a specific industrial sector. This happened at the same time as Ottawa was expanding the national sector council network.

Launched in 1991 as Workforce 2000, Manitoba sector councils were seen as a way to leverage limited resources, focus training efforts, and undertake long-term human resources planning to meet changing business requirements. Pre-devolution, nine sector councils had been established with Ottawa support; post-devolution Manitoba assumed full responsibility. Supported through provincial funding as well as some federal project funding, by 2014 seventeen sector councils had been developed, with activities coordinated through the Manitoba Alliance of Sector Councils. On the basis of advice from the sector councils, since 2008 a variety of industry workforce development initiatives have been put in place to support Manitoba employers with human resources planning, essential skills training, and customized training for their staff.

Developing and ramping up sector councils formed part of the provincial adjustments undertaken when the postsecondary education department assumed responsibility for a devolved LMDA in 1997. The province was interested in assuming federal active measures, as it did not want Manitoba programming to be dictated by Ottawa; in addition, provincial officials were worried that if it did not take on the programming, federal money would leave the province. Manitoba also recognized devolution as an opportunity to reduce overlap and duplication between governments and a way to provide a closer link between provincial programs and services and available jobs (Manitoba Department of Education and Training 1997). It was also around this time that Manitoba identified immigration as a source of building the province's population and sought more responsibility from the federal government. Only Manitoba and British Columbia were interested in Ottawa's 1995 offer to devolve immigrant settlement services. Manitoba was also the first to sign onto the Provincial Nominee Program in 1998 (Paquet 2014).

Pre-devolution, the working relationship between Manitoba and Canada Employment Centre officials was not close, with the systems operating as two solitudes. According to an informant interviewed for this research, implementation of the LMDA – including the transfer of 118 federal staff and $46.3 million to the province (mostly for third-party service delivery contracts) – did not go smoothly, and many federal officials were highly resistant to the change. Following a brief consultation with individuals, organizations, and training providers, the first step was to establish Employment Centres in thirteen locations across the province, and co-locate federal and provincial offices to ensure that EI clients could get all their services from the same place. This did not work well, as office walls were erected and referrals of EI clients to the province started to diminish. Then the federal government started to pull out of the shared locations as Ottawa became more focused on the integration of federal – not federal-provincial – services through the development of Service Canada. By 2014, the only Canada-Manitoba co-located arrangements remaining were in rural Manitoba.

Relationships post-devolution between the postsecondary education department and the social services ministry – responsible for welfare reform – were also rocky, as the attitudes of the two provincial ministries towards active measures started to diverge. There was also considerable upheaval in the early 2000s as municipal social assistance was transferred to the provincial government and caseloads became over-burdened. With the end of the Canada Assistance Plan, specialized employment services for social assistance clients started to close, but then were later rebuilt through third-party contract arrangements administered by the social services ministry separate from the mainstream employment services system run by the postsecondary education department.

The availability of federal money through the Labour Market Agreement starting in 2008 provided new opportunities for Manitoba to focus on the employment programming needs of social assistance clients, and new cooperative arrangements developed between the social services and the postsecondary education departments. With politicians concerned that social assistance caseloads were too high, parallel employment services systems within the provincial bureaucracy, and mixed messages when the programs were managed by two different departments, in 2012 the economic development department was assigned responsibility for all social assistance programming (benefits as well as active measures). In 2013 Manitoba's Strategy for Sustainable Employment and a Stronger Labour Market was released, focused on modernizing the provincial social assistance program. As part of this reform the province started to offer new opportunities for skills assessment and training to single parents, who had previously not been expected to work until their youngest child was six years old. However, participation remained voluntary.

Post-LMDA Governance Reforms

Single Gateways or One-Stop Shops

In 2014, neither Manitoba nor Saskatchewan provided access to employment services, welfare, and employer supports in one-stop shops. Managed by the Ministry of Jobs and the Economy (MJE), sixteen Manitoba Jobs and Skills Development Centres (MJSD) provided front-door access to two of these functions: employment services (including skills training for individuals) and industry workforce development. Access to apprenticeship was also provided through this door. A new service delivery model developed in 2013 was meant to "streamline business and employment services and provide common client centred experiences regardless of the channel of entry" (Manitoba 2013). The three activities were previously in silos and available at different locations; the change created a single door for individuals and employers to come through.

Although part of the MJE, social assistance benefits were still accessed through thirty-five dedicated Family Services offices. Government staff in these offices undertook employability assessments and provided personalized employment planning for recipients who were employment-destined, using common assessment tools developed with their MJE colleagues. There was a defined referral protocol, and social assistance recipients accessed employment supports through the MJSD offices, many of which were co-located with the Family Services offices. Those accepted for training left social assistance and started to draw training allowances. While integrating social assistance and employment services through a common front door was considered, Manitoba rejected this option on the basis that most people receiving social assistance benefits were not suited for immediate employment.

The Manitoba MJDS Centres are separate from dedicated services available for Aboriginal people, immigrants, and youth, who each go to different doors for their employment services. In 2014 Aboriginal services were provided through four federally funded ASETS providers, and youth through forty Manitoba Youth Job Centres, funded by the Children and Youth Opportunities Department. Immigrant services were provided through Manitoba Start. The province significantly expanded newcomer services (including employment supports) when it took on a devolved settlement agreement with the Government of Canada in the mid-1990s. Manitoba Start used to be under provincial control; however, this was realigned as a result of the 2012 Government of Canada decision to take back control of immigrant settlement services and cancel the Manitoba Settlement Agreement.

In 2014 Saskatchewan had a somewhat more concentrated delivery system than Manitoba as it did not have dedicated immigrant or youth services centres. There were, however, two Aboriginal Skills and Employment Training Strategy (ASETS) holders that provided parallel access to employment services for Aboriginal persons. Social assistance and related employment support services were delivered through twenty income assistance offices under the Social Services Ministry. Under the Ministry of the Economy (ME), nineteen Canada-Saskatchewan Career and Employment Services (CSCES) offices provided career and employment services to unemployed and under-employed individuals, as well as training and/or education options that enabled participation in the provincial labour market. Jobs First was a long-standing CSCES initiative specifically targeted for social assistance recipients. Those who were accepted for training were moved onto a provincial training allowance. Labour Market Services – intended to assist employers to find the workers they need – were provided out of six Ministry of the Economy regional offices.

In Manitoba all federal transfer agreement funding was managed by Jobs and the Economy and in Saskatchewan by the Ministry of the Economy. As detailed in appendix C, allocations in 2013/14 in Saskatchewan were $63,681,000 and $71,700,000 in Manitoba. Rolling out the additional federal LMA funding in both provinces in 2008 was relatively easy, with each province using the employment services network already in place.

Decentralization

Both Saskatchewan and Manitoba managed their employment services offices within their respective economic development departments through regional networks – six in Saskatchewan and three in

Manitoba. Budgets were assigned to the regional level and allocation decisions were generally made in the regions, not in the provincial capital, based upon the provincially developed framework. On paper, both systems seemed relatively decentralized. However, a Manitoba respondent interviewed through this research noted that decision making was becoming increasingly centralized, and the authorities that regions used to have now required Winnipeg's approval.

The social assistance offices in the two provinces also had regional networks, but these were different from the employment services networks. Without overarching authority over the full basket of employment, welfare, and workplace programs, regional directors in the two provinces could manage only within their defined basket of services. The only place where the full array of services came together was in the provincial capital, thereby confining regional discretion and the flexibility to meet local needs. Having the flexibility to move resources across three business lines at the regional level, as had occurred in Alberta, was fundamentally impossible in Manitoba and Saskatchewan because of how responsibility for the services was assigned and organized by the provincial government.

Also noteworthy in these two provinces was the high degree of reorganization since the federal employment services were devolved almost twenty years ago. Responsibility was bounced between postsecondary education, social services, and economic development departments as provincial Cabinets were made and then remade. Respondents in both Manitoba and Saskatchewan interviewed through this research noted that moving the programs around like puzzle pieces had diminished the capacity of key actors to form firm anchors and relationships, both within the province and with their intergovernmental colleagues from across Canada. When governments keep shifting program boundaries for Cabinet-making expediency, the consequence is poorly conceptualized and implemented labour market programs.

Outsourcing and Contracting Out

Both Saskatchewan and Manitoba had a "mixed model" of PES services in 2014, where the employment services front door (Manitoba Jobs and Skills Development Centres, or MJSD, and Canada-Saskatchewan Career and Employment Services, or CSCES) was staffed and managed by provincial government employees, with more specialized employment support services provided by third-party contractors. Industry workforce development consultants in Manitoba who work with employers to provide human resources planning assistance were also government employees. Social assistance in both provinces was delivered exclusively by civil servants.

In 2014 Manitoba had four tiers of employment service, where government employees provided tier one and the rest were contracted through defined funding arrangements. Funding was provided to around 150 community-based organizations that delivered a combination of services: employment plan development; case management; assessment and employment counselling; self-service labour market information; job search assistance; job-finding clubs; job referral and placement; diagnostic and testing services; and brokered access to other services (Manitoba 2013). Some of these contracts were transferred over from the federal government in the late 1990s.

Traditionally, Manitoba did not use requests for proposal, and contracts were rolled over from one year to the next; however, in 2013 a new funding model was built, in order to reduce the number of agencies and improve consistency in contracting between the two employment services branches within MJE. As part of the process some of the social services contracts transferred over from one branch to another. A request for proposal, or RFP, bidding process may emerge out of this work, with contracts that were more performance-related. Most Manitoba community organizations received money from a wide variety of funders, including provincial and federal governments as well as charitable organizations.

Saskatchewan's contracting arrangements were similar, with staff at the CSCES making referrals to a variety of community-based organizations for defined employment services. While Saskatchewan had an RFP process in place, preferred contractors received long-term funding through the LMDA. When the LMA money came available an RFP was let, so that the province could secure additional services in line with the program objectives of serving under-represented groups. The Social Services Ministry also contracted directly for training and employment support services for people receiving social assistance benefits. In 2015 CSCES began to shift to outcomes-based contracting based on retention in employment (OECD 2016).

Partnerships and Networks

WITH BUSINESS AND LABOUR

Manitoba's partnerships with business and labour were among the most developed and formalized in Canada. In addition to individual sector councils covering areas like aerospace, arts and cultural industries, food processors, etc., in 2014 Manitoba had an Alliance of Sector Councils to bind the seventeen provincial councils together. The alliance also undertook defined activities on its own. Some of the individual sector councils had connections with their national counterparts and colleagues in other provinces, others did not. Pan-Canadian connections became much more diminished when federal funding to national sector councils ended in 2013.

Manitoba officials described the sector councils as an important business arm of government and as "co-creators" of policy. Government funded the core infrastructure, consisting of a CEO and a training coordinator; the rest of the funding came from industry. Sector councils were created as a way to help industries in Manitoba's diversified economy organize themselves and also ensure that the key partners – labour, business, and the education sector – were all at the table when government training decisions were being made. Provincial officials felt that it was more effective for training decisions to be made at the sector – as opposed to the company – level. Sector councils in Manitoba focused considerable attention on the training and upgrading needs of the current workforce; this placed the province in an ideal position to deliver the new Canada Job Grant.

To ensure continuity, sector council activities were placed into legislation. In 2008 the Manitoba Advisory Council on Workforce Development Act was passed, and its membership was announced a year later. In 2014 the role of the council was meant to "encourage the cooperative participation of employers, employees and labour organizations in the development of government policies and strategies for development of Manitoba's workforce" (Manitoba 2008). The council was made up of a majority of members recommended by the sector councils, as well as key Manitoba deputy ministers. Administrative support was provided by government staff. The Act prescribed that the council must have balanced representation from northern, urban, and rural areas, and reflect the perspectives of employers, employees, and labour organizations.

While Saskatchewan had councils involving business, they were industry driven and industry funded. For example, in 2014 there were councils in tourism, construction, and agriculture. Unlike in Manitoba, they were not organized by government, provided with funding, covered by legislation, nor considered as "co-creators" of government workforce development policy. Some of them did, however, relate to Saskatchewan's Apprenticeship and Trade Certification Commission, established in 1999 as a corporation and agent of the Crown. This commission – comprising industry (equally representing employers and employees), the provincial college system, the provincial government, and equity groups – managed the apprenticeship and trade certification system. However, the scope was limited to the designated trades.

In a review undertaken in 2016 the OECD noted the lack of mechanisms in Regina for bringing together local employment and training actors, including business, unions, postsecondary institutions, and Aboriginal organizations. Noting the success of labour market boards in other places, the OECD recommended that the province consider setting up local labour market boards as a way to improve coordination in Saskatchewan's larger cities.

WITH COMMUNITY ASSOCIATIONS RESPONSIBLE FOR EMPLOYMENT SERVICES

Beyond individual contractual agreements, relationships between the provincial government and community organizations involved in employment programming in both provinces were mostly ad hoc. Neither Manitoba nor Saskatchewan had an association like ASPECT in BC that tied the community-based employment sector together. In Manitoba the Federation of Non-Profit Organizations Inc. was the main connecting glue, as most of the community employment organizations delivering LMDA and LMA programming belonged to this sector council. There is also a provincial organization that supports immigrant-serving agencies. In Saskatchewan most employment services agencies had few provincial or pan-Canadian connections.

Saskatchewan and Manitoba established provincial career development associations only in 2013. Both provinces provided training to provincial employees working in the employment services system. Through a partnership with the University of Winnipeg, Manitoba extended this training to non-government service providers.

WITH THE GOVERNMENT OF CANADA

The relationship that Service Canada officials had with provincial officials within each province was identified by provincial officials as cordial but distant. In both provinces there was a formal federal-provincial LMDA/LMA management committee that had existed since the LMDAs were implemented almost twenty years ago. This committee met twice a year, with federal officials from both Ottawa and either Manitoba or Saskatchewan respectively directly involved.

In its review of Saskatchewan labour market services the OECD (2016, 91) noted that "contact between Service Canada and [provincial] Labour Market Services is sporadic." This was because supervision was provided in another province. Some respondents interviewed through this research thought that Service Canada officials working within the province could be doing more to facilitate the provincial-ASETS relationship, but had taken no initiative to do so.

WITH ABORIGINAL LABOUR MARKET ORGANIZATIONS

Aboriginal organizations are critical players in employment programming in both provinces, especially federally funded ASETS holders. Manitoba has four ASETS organizations (two First Nations, one Metis, and one in Winnipeg serving all Aboriginal groups), while Saskatchewan has only two (a First Nations and a Metis organization). With Aboriginal programming so concentrated in these provinces compared to Alberta and BC (where the federal money is divided between thirteen and sixteen different Aboriginal organizations respectively), Aboriginal employment and training organizations in Saskatchewan and Manitoba are large and powerful. Some of them were providing employment services before provincial governments took on this role through the LMDAs.

For example, the Saskatchewan Indian Training Association Group was created in 1987 and serves all First Nations people across the province through fourteen points of service. With an annual budget of over $24 million in 2014 it was the largest ASETS holder in the country. This was almost double the amount of LMA funding ($15 million) that Saskatchewan received each year from Ottawa. Manitoba Keewatinowi Okimakanak Inc. is another large agency, serving First Nations people in northern Manitoba with an annual budget of around $12 million. The Centre for Aboriginal Resource Development in downtown Manitoba has been around for thirty-seven years. Serving all Aboriginal groups, programs are run out of the former Canadian Pacific Railway Station.

While relationships between the federally funded ASETS providers and the provincial government were cordial, in neither province in 2014 were they strong. The Manitoba Education and Employment Action Plan provided some structure for Aboriginal issues in the province; however an update beyond the 2008–11 provincial plan could not be located. A Manitoba provincial official characterized the siloed ASETS/provincial delivery systems as a turf issue – between the Aboriginal organizations themselves as well as with the province. In seeking and protecting their own federal funding, the Aboriginal leadership decided not to engage in a formal way with the provincial government.

Relationships at the working level were better, and Manitoba started to provide training for First Nations youth on reserve that also brought in industry, supported by LMA funding. In many areas of rural and northern Manitoba provincial ministry officials could be found working side-by-side with their First Nations counterparts to achieve common employment goals. Relationships in the cities were more strained. An ASETS holder in Winnipeg interviewed through this research observed that their weakest link was with the provincial Ministry of Jobs and the Economy. Intermediary researchers and the Aboriginal Council of Winnipeg provided some interconnections. All parties agreed that the Aboriginal–provincial relationship in Manitoba could be strengthened. Under the ad hoc relationship in place in 2014, client services suffered, as different parties had different understandings.

A similar message was heard in Saskatchewan, even though there was a March 2011 tripartite memorandum of understanding to increase labour force participation of First Nations people through active measures between the five Saskatchewan Tribal Council chiefs (representing more than half of Saskatchewan's seventy First Nations) and the federal and provincial governments. The initiative was cost shared between the federal and provincial governments and focused in particular on First Nations youth on reserve. The province and the Federation of Saskatchewan Indian Nations also convened a task force on improving education and employment outcomes for First Nations and Metis people that reported in 2013.

In 2014 Saskatchewan provincial officials described the provincial–Aboriginal relationship as cordial and respectful and, like in Manitoba, new initiatives focusing on youth on reserve were being implemented with the support of Saskatchewan's Ministry of the Economy. However, officials as well as ASETS holders acknowledged that employment programming in Saskatchewan was siloed and could be better coordinated. Like in Manitoba, it was noted that while there was no active collaboration or process to do province-wide planning, there was good cooperation on the delivery side, where individuals and projects were often co-funded.

Comparing Saskatchewan and Manitoba

Table B summarizes Saskatchewan and Manitoba approaches to the governance of the PES, using the four themes identified in chapter 2.

Table B. Comparing Governance Features in Saskatchewan and Manitoba's Public Employment Service, 2014

	Saskatchewan	Manitoba
Single gateways or one-stop shops	19 Canada-Saskatchewan Career and Employment Services Centres provided access to employment services for individuals and support services for employers. Social assistance (SA) through 20 social services offices. SA workers did case management and referral. All federal labour market transfer money managed by Ministry of the Economy (ME).	16 Manitoba Jobs and Skills Development Centres (MJSD) provided access to employment services for individuals and industry workforce development for employers. SA through 35 Family Services offices; separate immigration and youth offices. Defined protocols for SA referrals to MJSD. All federal labour market transfer money managed by Ministry of Jobs and the Economy (MJE).
Decentralization	Policy control decentralized to 6 ME regional offices. Different department for SA and employment services.	Policy control decentralized to 3 MJE regional offices. SA within same department but not same business line at regional level.
Outsourcing and contracting out	PES was mixture of government staff and contracted agencies. Some RFP contracting but mostly stable relationships and no performance contracting.	PES was mixture of government staff and contracted agencies. Four defined service delivery tiers. RFP for contracting and performance measures being considered.
Partnerships and networks	Mostly informal relationships with industry. Sector councils were industry-initiated. Few linkages among community-based employment organizations. No formal coordination with ASETS holders.	17 formal, government-supported sector councils plus Minister's Advisory Council on Workforce Development. All in legislation. Non-profit sector council linked employment services agencies. No formal coordination with ASETS holders.

What Accounted for the Similarities and Differences between the Two Midwest Provinces?

Given their shared social-democratic origins and similar trajectories – as responsibility for the PES moved from a postsecondary education department to an economic development department – there were more similarities than differences between the two midwest provinces in the management of their provincial PES post-devolution. This similarity was reinforced by the fact that both provinces took on devolved LMDAs at around the same time in the late 1990s.

Although they have both toyed with the idea, neither province had, like Alberta, implemented and sustained a fully integrated one-stop access to employment services, social assistance, and employer supports. In both Manitoba and Saskatchewan the transferred federal employment services were initially assigned to the postsecondary education department; in recent years both provinces realigned them with an economic development department. While connections have been built, social assistance has consistently been managed by another provincial government department, with both provinces experiencing difficulty in coordinating employment services on offer to their citizens. Manitoba took significant action to fix the linkage problem in 2012 by moving social assistance responsibility to the Ministry of Jobs and the Economy; in Saskatchewan in 2014 the linkage problems remained.

The requirement for social assistance recipients to seek work has been more muted in Saskatchewan and Manitoba than in other western provinces; indeed, it was only recently that Manitoba started to impose more stringent work obligations on single parents. This relative lack of political concern about work obligations for social assistance recipients (compared to Alberta and British Columbia) has its roots in the social democratic heritage of Manitoba and Saskatchewan, but was also a result of the fact that neither province experienced such dramatic increases in their welfare caseloads as Alberta and British Columbia did in the early 1990s (Kneebone and White 2014). Unlike Alberta, the economies of Manitoba and Saskatchewan are less cyclical, with fewer booms and busts. Growth in the Alberta caseload that peaked in 1993 drove the pre-devolution cooperative federal-provincial arrangements to integrate employment services for both EI and SA recipients (as well as the public at large) through one-stop shops. As its caseload did not rise so dramatically, neither Saskatchewan nor Manitoba had the same cost-saving imperative.

At the time of the LMDA transfer in the late 1990s, many of the federal employment services in Manitoba and Saskatchewan were being delivered by civil servants, supported by specialized third-party contracts. Both provinces maintained this model with few changes, thus accounting for the more limited outsourcing or contracting-out models that existed in 2014. Most of the third-party contractors involved had been providing similar employment services for years, and the contracts were usually rolled over from one year to the next. In 2014 Manitoba started to consider doing things differently by implementing an RFP process.

Both provinces had fairly traditional organizational arrangements within the provincial government department responsible for managing the PES, and both operated under relatively decentralized service delivery arrangements. Managers of the local employment centres reported through to regional offices (six in Saskatchewan and three in Manitoba) responsible for supervising government staff as well as letting and managing the employment services contracts. In both provinces an assistant deputy minister was responsible for both policy and service delivery, with regular internal mechanisms in place for service delivery officials to provide input into central office decision making.

The greatest differences between Saskatchewan and Manitoba were in partnerships and networks. Manitoba's social partnerships with business and labour through the sector councils, and the services they had on offer to employers through the sixteen MJSD centres, were much more extensive than those found in Saskatchewan. These may be a result of Manitoba's social democratic roots being stronger than those found in Saskatchewan, as well as the consistency in government approaches due to seventeen years of rule by the New Democratic party in Manitoba that continued until 2016.

In contrast, Saskatchewan has been through more political churning, with the Saskatchewan Party taking control of government in 2007 from the NDP. It may also be a result of Manitoba having a more diversified economy, hence a need to formalize relationships with a wider variety of industries. Many of Saskatchewan's institutions used to interact with labour and business mirror those of Alberta and British Columbia, where there is no real tradition of ongoing government financial support provided to industry associations, nor legislation guaranteeing a place at the table as "co-creators" of government policy.

Relationships between provincial officials in Manitoba and Saskatchewan with their Aboriginal ASETS holders were similar, with neither province having strong coordinated and collaborative partnerships. Much of this was the result of long-standing federal-provincial disagreements over who was responsible for providing services to Aboriginal persons on reserve, with provincial governments historically maintaining that this was a federal responsibility. Some of the tension also related to competitiveness among the ASETS holders themselves and their privileging of federal over provincial engagement. In the early days of the devolved LMDAs, Manitoba and Saskatchewan officials were told by their federal colleagues not to worry about Aboriginal programming, as it was provided through the ASETS agreements, with the federal government retaining oversight responsibility. Over time, provincial governments and the ASETS holders have had no choice but to develop relationships in order to ensure that provincial citizens have access to needed services. Relationship-building between them was further complicated by the presence of the federal government, which funded employment services for each through separate programming streams.

How Did PES Performance in the Two Provinces Compare?

To assess performance of the provincial PES, each province's LMA and LMDA annual plans, their LMA performance reports, and provincial information detailed in the annual Employment Insurance Monitoring and Assessment Reports (MAR) were reviewed and analysed. Appendices G and H summarize performance data for Manitoba and Saskatchewan's PES between 1999 and 2014 from these data sources. Until 2014 both provinces had had over fifteen years to implement the provincial PES; all of the performance data reported occurred under provincial control.

Demographic and Economic Conditions

There are many demographic and economic similarities between the two provinces. They are about the same size, at about 650,000 square kilometres each, with Manitoba's population in 2014 at 1,282,000 people and Saskatchewan's slightly less at 1,125,400 (Statistics Canada 2014). Both have large Aboriginal populations (15.5 per cent in Manitoba and 14.9 per cent in Saskatchewan). The unemployment rate in Manitoba over the period 1999 to 2014 had been around 5 per cent, while Saskatchewan's had been somewhat lower. It also had a slightly higher employment rate, reaching over 67 per cent in 2015. The number of social assistance cases was relatively similar (25,000–35,000), with Saskatchewan's dependency rate at 5.1 per cent in 2012 somewhat below Manitoba's at 5.8 per cent (Kneebone and White 2014). In both provinces there were twice as many people receiving social assistance as those receiving regular Employment Insurance benefits. Reflective of their relatively low unemployment rates and therefore more restrictive federal rules for accessing benefits, EI caseloads in both Manitoba and Saskatchewan had fallen over the period from 1999 to 2013.

Effectiveness

As detailed in appendices G and H, LMDA expenditures in Manitoba and Saskatchewan remained fairly steady over the 1999 to 2004 period. Like in other provinces, the only time when expenditures grew in Manitoba and Saskatchewan was in 2009/10 and 2010/11 as a result of increased federal allocations during the economic downturn. By 2011/12 the allocations and expenditures were back to around the 1996 levels. More funding in Saskatchewan (around 80 per cent) went to employment benefits (for training, wage subsidy, etc.) than in Manitoba, where the proportion over the years was around 69 per cent. It is noteworthy that Manitoba expenditures on labour market partnerships (which contributed to its sector council program) were much higher at around 12 per cent of the total spending, compared to Saskatchewan's at around 8 per cent.

With this relatively fixed pot of money Manitoba served significantly more clients over the years, averaging just under thirty thousand per year, whereas Saskatchewan's numbers were about half this at just over thirteen thousand people. These numbers remained relatively steady over the years. While Manitoba served slightly more clients with an EI attachment than the non-insured (ranging from 60 per cent in 1999 to 53 per cent today), over 90 per cent of Saskatchewan LMDA clients had an EI attachment (meaning that they were either receiving EI benefits or were a reach-back client). Very little LMDA money in Saskatchewan was being spent on social assistance recipients or others with a marginal attachment to the labour market.

This was where the LMA funding came in, with clear evidence from a review of the LMA reports that both provinces focused this funding on Aboriginal people, social assistance recipients, immigrants, older workers, and youth. The number served in Saskatchewan with this money increased each year to reach over nine thousand people in 2014; this was mirrored in Manitoba where more people were served every year reaching over eleven thousand in 2014. Manitoba focused most of this funding on wage subsidies to employers, while Saskatchewan focused on employment assistance services.

Given that in real dollars the Saskatchewan and Manitoba LMDA allocations have fallen over time, the interventions selected also changed – from long-term interventions such as training and work experience to short-term interventions such as employment assistance services – as these cost less. In Saskatchewan in 1999 long-term interventions made up 64 per cent of the total; by 2013 this figure had decreased to 43 per cent. Manitoba did not place as much emphasis as Saskatchewan on long-term interventions under the LMDA, with only 28 per cent of interventions in 1999 being long-term. Its focus and programming choices have been relatively consistent over the years; by 2014 only 12 per cent of LMDA interventions in the province were considered as long term.

In both provinces LMDA targets on returns to employment and unpaid benefits for EI clients were largely met and sometimes exceeded substantially. The targets in the two provinces (where each sought to return roughly 50 per cent of those receiving EI benefits to work) seemed reasonable, given the buoyancy of the provincial economies. Using federal LMA money, more people were employed in Manitoba after the programming, averaging around 70 per cent over the period, compared to Saskatchewan at 54 per cent. However, more people in Saskatchewan considered that the training helped (averaging 87 per cent) compared to Manitoba at 70 per cent. In both provinces average earnings after the LMA programming was completed were between $15 and $19 per hour.

Evidence of provincial research, analysis, and information – beyond reports required by the federal government – was also sought. By 2015 neither province had established a dedicated centre like the BC Centre for Employment Excellence to undertake research, best practices exchange, and information sharing. In 2012 Manitoba participated in an OECD project focused on leveraging training in small and medium-sized businesses. Its sector councils were heavily involved. In 2014 Saskatchewan undertook a provincial needs assessment on employment programming; the study was posted on the departmental website. In 2016 it participated in an OECD project on employment and skills strategies. Other than this, neither province had information available on the provincial PES beyond their departmental annual reports.

Efficiency

In Saskatchewan, with average annual LMDA expenditures of $41,183,000 over the period from 1999/2000 to 2013/14 and an average of 13,233 clients served each year, the cost per case was calculated at $3,112 vs $1,740 in Manitoba (with average annual expenditures of $49,443,000 and 28,409 clients served). Performing the same calculation in regards to the LMA revealed a more similar cost per case of $2,159 in Saskatchewan vs $2,312 in Manitoba. On these measures Manitoba's programming was considered to be more efficient than Saskatchewan's. However, when one looks at return on investment, Saskatchewan's performance seemed better: for LMDA expenditures of $36 million in 2014, Saskatchewan had $61 million in unpaid EI benefits vs Manitoba's cost of $44 million and $44 million in unpaid EI benefits. Efficiency measures can and should be debated. Doing the calculation and comparing the two provinces allows this debate to begin.

In both provinces LMA clients seemed quite satisfied with the services they had received, with Saskatchewan ratings ranging from 84 to 97 per cent and Manitoba from 93 to 96 per cent. In terms of coherence *within* the provincial government, civil servants in both provinces interviewed through this research described long-standing difficulties in ensuring that employment services for social assistance clients were coordinated with the mainstream services provided to the general public and those in receipt of EI benefits. Manitoba appeared to have reduced the problem by placing responsibility for social assistance within the purview of the economic development ministry. In Saskatchewan the problem continued into 2015, with some respondents suggesting that social assistance clients were not well served by the current arrangements. A Saskatchewan respondent noted that, in his view, reorganization was rarely a panacea to a problem with more far-reaching causes.

In neither Manitoba nor Saskatchewan were relationships strong with ASETS holders who managed employment services for Aboriginal clients, and provincial civil servants as well as ASETS holders interviewed through this research acknowledged that improvements could be made. Manitoba's support for its contracted employment service providers (through the non-profit sector council) was stronger than in Saskatchewan, where service providers found themselves in a more competitive environment with no organized access to peers other that through voluntary organizations such as the United Way.

While both Manitoba and Saskatchewan provided training for career development practitioners working for government, only Manitoba extended this opportunity to individuals working in contracted service delivery organizations. On this measure Manitoba's PES could be considered as better trained than Saskatchewan's. It was only recently that career development practitioners seeking professional development with their colleagues could get it in Saskatchewan. Employment services managers working in Saskatchewan and Manitoba organizations did not have the advantage of their counterparts in BC, where ASPECT brings employment organizations and their staff from across the province together through an annual conference.

Democracy

Democracy requires transparency as well as engagement. On transparency, both Saskatchewan and Manitoba had produced and published stand-alone and complete LMA annual plans and performance reports, as prescribed in the Labour Market Agreements. Manitoba's reports were easily accessible on the departmental website, complete for all years, and available earlier than in any other province.[1] Saskatchewan's reports were harder to find, and not completely up to date, with 2012/13 and 2013/14 reports not posted by the fall of 2015. However, reports in both provinces were generally complete in terms of reporting on all the indicators as outlined in the LMA agreements.

Both provinces outlined their engagement and consultation practices in their annual LMA/LMDA plans and made this information publicly available. Manitoba reported a higher degree of democratic engagement in matters relating to the PES than Saskatchewan. For example, in addition to highlighting the roles of the sector councils and the Advisory Council on Workforce Development, over the years several additional engagement initiatives were detailed in their LMA plans: Manitoba employer survey; Apprenticeship Future's Commission; Immigrant Settlement Strategy; Adult Literacy Strategy; Community Organization Strategy; ALL Aboard: Manitoba's Poverty Reduction and Social Inclusion Strategy; Opening Doors: Disability Strategy Consultation; and Employment and Income Assistance Related Consultations.

---

1 For example, the 2013/14 LMA report that covers results up to March 2014 had been posted by October 2014.

Given its profile, structure, and level of government support, information on Manitoba's sector council program was easily accessible online; however, there was limited information on the operation of the Minister's Council on Workforce Development. As this was how Manitoba secured input from business, labour, colleges, and community organizations on the province's workforce development system, it was surprising that so little information was in the public domain, including who was on the council, the work currently underway, and past successes and challenges.

Saskatchewan also engaged in consultation, highlighting in its LMA plan the roles played by the five Career and Employment Services regions; the Saskatchewan Institute of Applied Science and Technology; Aboriginal training institutions and Aboriginal organizations; the Saskatchewan Apprenticeship and Trades Certification Commission; employment service community organizations; immigrant serving organizations; employer organizations; and industry sectors. However, unlike Manitoba there was no mention of specific engagement initiatives or strategies in their LMA reports.

Conclusion

Saskatchewan and Manitoba's political culture was described earlier in this chapter as populist, progressive, pragmatic, and federal-friendly. The detailed analysis in this chapter on how each has implemented the provincial PES since assuming these responsibilities from the federal government in the late 1990s supports this characterization. There were more similarities than differences in the two provincial approaches.

Both provinces took on the federal PES responsibilities at around the same time, eventually moving them through a postsecondary education department to arrive by 2014 under the responsibility of an economic development department. Neither had a full "single window" where access to social assistance was available along with employment services for individuals and employer supports. Responsibility for the PES has been subject to churn in both provinces, as it bounced between provincial government departments. Both Manitoba and Saskatchewan have had difficulties in providing seamless coordinated services for social assistance recipients and Aboriginal people. In 2014 each had mixed, regionally based, service delivery models in place, consisting of civil servants operating the "front door" supported by specialized employment services agencies working under third-party contracts.

Neither province had defined and structured RFP contracting arrangements in place or hard performance contracting.

It was in the area of partnerships and networks and democratic engagement where the differences between the two provinces were most pronounced. Manitoba's engagement process was more extensive and structured than Saskatchewan's, especially through its seventeen defined sector councils and the Minister's Advisory Council on Workforce Development. As these were detailed in provincial legislation and supported by ongoing provincial government funding, they were highly institutionalized and unlikely to change without defined political effort. Manitoba also provided more support to its community-based employment service providers through staff training and opportunities for networking than did Saskatchewan.

While both provided effective employment services, Manitoba's were considered as more efficient and democratic. Based on past programming choices that privileged employer-based wage subsides, Manitoba was better positioned than Saskatchewan to implement the new "supply-side" labour market directions prescribed by the federal government in 2014 through the Canada Job Grant.

Chapter Six

The Middle: Quebec and Ontario

Quebec and Ontario are Canada's two largest provinces – in both geography and population – yet they took on responsibility for federal labour market programs at very different times and under very different circumstances. Quebec was the fourth province to sign on to a devolved Labour Market Development Agreement, or LMDA, in April 1997, while it took Ontario another eight years, until November 2005, to do the same. For both provinces, coming to agreement with the Government of Canada on labour market arrangements was equivalent to the high politics of constitutional reform, involving provincial premiers as well as the prime minister of Canada.

The near-death experience of the October 1995 referendum on whether Quebec should become an independent country was the main reason that Ottawa made the devolution offer to provinces in the first place: to demonstrate flexible federalism and to recognize Quebec's long-standing position that education and labour market training were a provincial responsibility. While Ontario may have shared Quebec's constitutional interpretation of who was responsible for labour market training, this did not mean that it was prepared to upend provincial priorities to take on federal programs, staff, contracts, and assets.

In 1996 the Ontario Progressive Conservatives under Premier Mike Harris – back in power after ten years of Liberal and NDP rule – were interested in divesting the province of responsibilities, not taking more on. For Ontario to come to agreement with the federal government on a devolved LMDA happened in response to a brief window of opportunity in 2005 when Liberals were in charge in both Ottawa and Queen's Park. Coming to agreement also required a promise of extra federal money through what eventually became known as the

Labour Market Agreements to assuage Ontario's long-standing grievance that its share of Employment Insurance funds available for training was inadequate.

These provincial responses to the federal labour market offer demonstrate that Ontario and Quebec's priorities are very different. Unlike other groupings of provinces in this book, each sees itself as a separate region; there is no monolithic "middle" Canada. This chapter compares how the two provinces governed their public employment service (PES) post-devolution, and the results they have achieved.

As all decisions in any policy area come from values, historical legacies, and the provincial socio-economic environment, this chapter begins with a reflection on political culture. It is followed by an overview of employment services in each province, focusing in particular on the years leading up to the devolution negotiations. Developments post-devolution are assessed next, drawing on the themes in the analytical framework outlined in chapter 3. Similarities and differences are summarized, followed by an analysis of what accounts for the differences. The chapter concludes by assessing the impact the different arrangements have had on the performance of the provincial PES post-devolution, using data and information from public reports.

The Political Context

Quebec and Ontario are located in the middle of Canada, and also contain the National Capital Region of Ottawa/Gatineau. Together they represent the manufacturing heartland of the country. In 2014 six in ten Canadian citizens (almost 22 million people) lived in these two central Canadian provinces. As a result, their residents do not suffer from the historic grievances of Canadians in other provinces who live far from the levers of power, often described as the Toronto, Montreal, and Ottawa triangle.

Following Britain's victory over France on the Plains of Abraham in 1759, the Canada Act of 1791 established "Canada" as a legal, political, and constitutional entity divided into the English-speaking province of Upper Canada (present-day Ontario) and the French-speaking province of Lower Canada (present-day Quebec). After the conquest Quebec was cut off from Europe. Under British rule, its societal leaders were the Catholic clergy who served as the guardians of French-Canadian identity, religion, and language. Living in a North American sea of English-speakers, Quebec's population grew only through high birth rates (Wiseman 2016).

Ontario's initial non-Aboriginal residents were British loyalists who no longer wished to live in the United States after the American Revolution; they subsequently fought a war in 1812 to defend this position. Ontario was a by-product of the American revolution. While it has always been inextricably connected to the United States, the war reinforced a determination to keep American ideas and institutions at bay. Its next large wave of immigrants came from the British Isles. This reinforced Ontario's attachment to the United Kingdom (Wiseman 2016).

The 1839 Durham report that precipitated political integration of the two provinces disparagingly noted that French Canadians were "a people with no literature or history." For the next twenty-five years the two Canadas found it almost impossible to establish a stable government. Through Confederation in 1867 both Ontario and Quebec got what they wanted. Attaching more importance to economic issues (including expansion to the west), Ontario wanted a strong federal government. Quebec attached more importance to preserving its culture and so wanted strong provincial governments. For the Quebec Fathers of Confederation, control of culture and education was essential to the survival of the French-Canadian nation (Whitcomb 2007, 2012).

Since Sections 92 and 93 of the British North America Act deliberately spelled out federal and provincial powers, Quebec interpreted that the two orders of government were equally sovereign in their respective spheres and provinces were not inferior or subordinate to Ottawa. However, it was Ontario Premier Oliver Mowat in the late 1800s who solidified provincial rights against a centralizing Prime Minister John A. Macdonald through a series of judgments from the U.K.-based Judicial Committee of the Privy Council. In 1887 Quebec Premier Mercier hosted the first interprovincial conference in Canadian history, demanding increased federal subsidies, as well as the abolition of Ottawa's residual powers and right to veto provincial legislation. Over time all of these provincial demands have been realized.

Protecting provincial sovereignty was taken up after the Depression and Second World War by Quebec Premier Maurice Duplessis, who resisted Ottawa leadership in developing the Canadian welfare state as an incursion into provincial jurisdiction. Holding power for almost two decades, his Union Nationale party had a low regard for unions and a strong business and laissez-faire orientation. Quebec's agreement in 1940 to a constitutional amendment transferring responsibility for unemployment insurance to the federal government occurred during the brief period when Duplessis was out of office. Ontario was also a reluctant participant in Ottawa's post-war plans to build a Canadian welfare state, proposing private sector solutions instead. However, they stopped short of blocking it (Haddow 2015). The winning federal strategy consisted of designing programs for the provinces, allocating funds, and offering to share costs 50:50. Politically, provinces could not refuse.

In the 1960s Ontario Premier Robarts believed that, as Canada's richest province, Ontario had a particularly important role to play in promoting unity and solving national problems. As a result, Quebec and Ontario solidarity on protecting provincial jurisdiction began to waiver. Ontario and Quebec increasingly started to go their separate ways on issues such as the appropriate federal/provincial split of tax revenues, pensions, postsecondary education, hospital insurance, and immigration. By refusing to participate in national projects – or by participating in a separate way such as through the Quebec Pension Plan – Quebec was becoming increasingly distinct (Whitcomb 2007, 61).

Quebec's political class was convinced of the province's national distinctiveness and the responsibility of the provincial government to conserve it (Haddow 2015). After Maurice Duplessis's death in 1959, Quebec underwent a "Quiet Revolution" in which responsibilities for health, education, and social services were transferred from the Roman Catholic Church to the Quebec government, significantly enhancing citizen loyalty to their provincial government as it became the repository of the growing Quebec welfare state. What was unique was the delivery agent. In Ontario – and in other provinces – most of these welfare state responsibilities were delivered (and partially funded) by municipal governments and other local organizations. While the province provided oversight, for the most part it did not deliver the programs.

After 1960, state intervention in Quebec's economy increased significantly, marking a radical departure from the previous laissez-faire approach. Asserting its uniqueness, in 1966 the Quebec government demanded full control of unemployment insurance, manpower training, pensions, housing, family allowance, and social policy from the federal government. It also took action to promote the French language, including Bill 101, which alienated many English-speakers and forced newcomers to send their children to French schools. As the church's political influence declined, language replaced religion as the defining characteristic that united Quebeckers. Concerned with responses from the rest of Canada to their actions, by 1976 many citizens became convinced that Quebec should become an independent country and the

Parti Québécois (PQ) assumed power to work towards this goal (Whitcomb 2012).

"The national struggle has always been at the heart of Québec politics and in the soul of its culture" (Wiseman 2007, 166). Stéphane Dion (1992) identified three conflicting reasons for this struggle: fear (of losing their language); confidence (that they have the capacity to govern themselves); and rejection (three constitutional rounds in 1982, 1987, and 1992 where the rest of Canada refused to accommodate Quebec's aspirations). A failed sovereignty referendum in 1980 precipitated these three constitutional rounds, with Ontario Premier Davis abandoning in 1982 a long tradition of Ontario leadership in the protection of provincial rights. These constitutional failures subsequently led to the 1995 referendum, which also failed to secure the necessary support of the Quebec people.

Province-level nationalism in Canada is clearly evident in only one province: Quebec. Survey evidence gathered between 1998 and 2010 found that the proportion of residents that identified with their province first, rather than Canada as a whole, is highest in Quebec, where about 50 per cent of respondents express this view. It was lowest in Ontario at only 4 per cent in 2010, illustrating that most Ontarians do not strive for a provincial identity separate from being Canadian (Mendelsohn and Matthews 2010). They neither have the same sense of collective identity as Quebeckers, nor do they, in general, harbour the grievances of other provinces of being ignored or shunted aside. Ontarians are the most likely of all Canadians to articulate a pan-Canadian position and are less knowledgeable about provincial politics when compared to citizens in the rest of Canada (Wiseman 2007). Many pan-Canadian organizations are housed either in Toronto or Ottawa and often believe that the interests of Ontario and Canada are the same.

Part of this belief was due to the stability, moderation, and continuity of the political order as the Progressive Conservatives were continuously in charge of Ontario's provincial government between 1943 and 1985. "During their 44 year dynasty, the longest of any party in the twentieth century, the Conservatives successfully bridged the Old Ontario – agrarian, rural, small town, white Protestant, and conservative – with the New Ontario – an increasingly urban, cosmopolitan, polyethnic, multiracial, and liberal society" (Wiseman 2016, 31). Ontario is Canada's most multicultural province, with one in three residents not born in the province. Most new immigrants reside in Toronto or one of its suburbs.

This political stability in Ontario changed dramatically between 1987 and 1995 when three majority governments – led by three different parties with different ideological roots – gained power. The sense of "what is good for Canada is good for Ontario" started to change in 1990 when the federal government unilaterally altered the 50:50 sharing of social assistance by imposing an upper limit on Canada Assistance Plan (CAP) funding to the three provinces not receiving federal equalization payments. Between 1991 and 1994 the "cap on CAP" cost British Columbia $1.5 billion, Alberta $241 million, and Ontario $6.8 billion (as reported in Starr 2014, 161). Ontario costs were higher than other provinces as the result of welfare rate increases and higher caseloads following the recessions of the early 1980s and 1990s.

In response to the federal action, in the early 1990s the NDP government under Premier Bob Rae launched a "fair-share" campaign questioning the entire system of federal-provincial transfers. It commissioned ten separate studies to bolster its claim that Ontario was receiving much less federal money than it should, while bearing a disproportionate burden of the federal spending in other provinces. The campaign changed provincial attitudes. In 1998 just 37 per cent of Ontarians felt that the province received less than it deserved in federal spending, indicating a greater level of satisfaction than the other provinces. By 2010 the situation had changed, with 63 per cent dissatisfied, above the national average of 59 per cent (Mendelsohn and Matthews 2010). The province continues to focus considerable attention on this issue through the work of the Mowat Centre for Policy Innovation (Zon 2014). Discrimination against Ontario as it applied to the Canada Assistance Plan became a moot point when in 1995 federal funding to all provinces was reduced and the Canada Assistance Plan was rolled into the larger Canada Health and Social Transfer.

The distinctive development of the Quebec welfare state (in pensions, day care, family allowances, income support, employment policy, immigration, tax policy, and economic development), as well as a desire to be "masters in their own house" has led to growing the size, competence, and capacity of the Quebec civil service when compared to other provinces, including Ontario. The size of the Quebec provincial civil service exploded in the 1960s and 1970s, growing from 7 per 100 citizens in 1960 to 23 per 100 in 1985. It is the most powerful subnational government in the OECD world (Dion 1992). When governments in Canada came together in 1963 to discuss a Canada pension plan, the Quebec proposal was better than what Ottawa had proposed.

Premier Robarts realized how superior the Quebec civil service was to Ontario's and launched an overhaul, expansion, and modernization of his bureaucracy (Whitcomb 2012).

Unlike other provinces, Quebec is never willing to substitute federal research or expertise for provincial views, resulting in independent research agendas and extensive linkages between Quebec civil servants and the academic community within the province. On research matters Quebeckers view themselves as more advanced, competent, and knowledgeable than the other Canadian provinces. It often chooses to compare itself to other countries rather than other provinces in Canada, most of them in Europe. While Quebec looks to France, Belgium, Scandinavia, and the United Kingdom for inspiration, Ontario looks to the United States.

The "Quebec social model" is based on a notion of solidarity and a commitment to redistribution that closely resembles European social-democratic regimes. In 2007 public expenditures at the provincial and local level in Quebec accounted for 32 per cent of GDP, compared to 23 per cent in Ontario (Saint-Martin 2009). Quebec's social investment focus has accelerated since 2000, particularly in family policy and the fight against poverty, social exclusion, and inequality. In 2002 Quebec's Bill 112 put into law a "national strategy" to fight against poverty. The social policies that have emerged have played a major part in moving the province from the typical "liberal" welfare state found in the rest of Canada to more closely resemble the Swedish social democratic system (Raiq, Bernard, and van den Berg 2012). These policies include low-cost day care, enhanced parental leave,[1] increased provincial family allowances, working income tax credits, minimum wage stabilization, as well as income tax adjustments (Fortin 2010).

One of the most striking differences between Ontario and Quebec is the power of non-government actors. As part of the Quiet Revolution, Quebec business and unions became hugely involved in "catching up" with the rest of Canada by nurturing a French-speaking business class through a provincial economic development strategy and the expansion of state-owned corporations. The more progressive social values and interventionist approaches that developed were a significant

1 Quebec is unique among Canadian provinces in having a distinct parental insurance plan, financed by Quebecker contributions to the Employment Insurance account supplemented by Quebec funding. In 2005 the Canada-Quebec Final Agreement on the Quebec Parental Insurance Plan (QPIP) came into effect (Noel 2012).

contrast to the Duplessis era that had insisted on low taxes, low wages, and weak unions. Quebec's economic crisis in the 1980s forced business and labour to find ways to work together. The Parti Québécois (PQ) social democratic model that emerged after its 1976 election win saw state policy arising from the coordinated, consensual, and cooperative efforts of elite decision makers representing primarily business and unions.

Between 1976 and 1983 more than thirty tripartite economic summits were held to develop a social consensus. The Quebec women's movement was also powerful, with a 1995 Bread and Roses march against poverty and violence fuelling demands that the Quebec economy be organized around the principles of need and social utility rather than the principles of profit (Graefe 2015a). As a result, socially oriented community based enterprises also became involved, as part of building a Quebec-based "social economy" (Haddow 2015). These enterprises – funded by the Quebec state – are an outgrowth of when the church used to be in charge of social welfare programs. Their mandate includes advocacy as well as service delivery.

The Quiet Revolution also resulted in substantial growth for organized labour, with Quebec's unionization rate at 39.9 per cent in 2012, much higher than Ontario's at 28.2 per cent. In 1983 the Quebec Federation of Labour started a capital development fund that called on the savings and solidarity of Quebeckers. By 2003 more than $5 billion in investments had been accumulated, making it a major player in the economy (Wiseman 2007); ten years later the fund had grown to $9.3 billion. The PQ strategy of holding referendums on sovereignty made it particularly supportive towards social movements, in order to portray the nation as united and standing above the normal social divisions. This spurred the development of representative structures that included social partnerships in decision making (Graefe 2014).

These partnerships have endured through changes in government from PQ to the Liberals, who have held power since 2014. Haddow (2015) views Quebec's political economy as a "hybrid model," where coordinative elements are aligned with the traditional North American market-based liberal model. While bargaining occurs, it is episodic and much of it happens in specific sectors, not at the macro level. In his view, Quebec concertation owes much to the national identity shared among its participants.

The rise to power of the Harris Conservatives in 1995 – on a platform promising to shrink welfare rates and rolls, cut taxes, and downsize government – dramatically altered the orientation of the Ontario welfare state and caused considerable change and upheaval. Even under the Liberals – who regained power in 2003 and continued to lead government in 2016 – Ontario's political economy remains market oriented and non-interventionist. Where once its party system was brokerage, it is now competitive. There is limited mediation across interest groups, and the state's economic role continues to be limited (Haddow 2015).

With this kind of orientation it was surprising to some when, in 2007, Ontario launched a poverty reduction initiative. What is particularly noteworthy is the choice of agents, compared to Quebec. Ontario has deeply entrenched municipal delivery of social programs, with social assistance, child care, and housing closely aligned. The City of Toronto is particularly powerful and progressive. "If social policy ideas in Ontario came from anywhere, chances are that place is Toronto and quite likely in advocacy networks reaching back to the Toronto municipal government" (Hudson and Graefe 2011, 14). In contrast, Quebec uses the provincial government to deliver its major social programs, not municipalities.

In Ontario the traditional approach of business and unions has been to compete, not cooperate. The prime objective is the creation of a favourable investment climate, in order to facilitate capital accumulation. As a result, the underlying criterion for social or labour policy in Ontario is that measures be "economically practicable" (Evans and Smith 2015). Efforts to coordinate business and labour interests undertaken by the Liberals and NDP in the decade between 1985 and 1995 were largely abandoned by the Harris Progressive Conservatives. It consulted only with interests it saw as supportive, especially the business community (Haddow 2015).

The Ontario business community is highly fragmented and overlaps with national communities more than in other parts of Canada. Ontario's style involves the premier, Cabinet ministers, and senior bureaucrats meeting quietly behind closed doors with either business or labour leaders, depending upon the current government's power base and the issue at hand. This "informal bargaining" style often leaves other players like community organizations on the sidelines (Haddow 2015). Regardless of access, the settings for non-government involvement in policymaking in Ontario are significantly under-institutionalized when compared to Quebec. In power since 2003, the Liberals have avoided formalized bargaining with business, labour, and other interests.

This Ontario policymaking style holds even though both provinces now share something in common: receipt of federal equalization payments. Quebec has been a long-term recipient, but Ontario joined the club starting only in 2009 as a result of the economic downturn (Bernard 2012). Historically federal transfers as a share of personal income have been much higher in Quebec than in Ontario; for example, in 2006 they were $2,240 per capita in Quebec vs $1,870 in Ontario (Vaillancourt and Laberge 2010). Quebeckers are also more reliant on Employment Insurance (EI) than most other Canadians, as Quebec is home to the largest proportion of seasonal workers in Canada. In contrast, many out-of-work Ontarians find themselves ineligible for EI as the result of long-standing entrance rules that disadvantage residents of the province (Banting 2012). This only adds fire to Ontario's "fair-share" grievance.

Historical Developments around Activation

Quebec

Before the Quiet Revolution, last-resort social assistance was considered to be a responsibility first of the family, then of the parish. The 1963 Boucher report went against this view, asserting that only the state had the capacity to meet such needs. With this direction – as well as the availability of federal cost-sharing under the Canada Assistance Plan – Quebec significantly expanded its last-resort welfare programs. However, unlike Ontario, Quebec did not distinguish between "expected to work" and "not expected to work" income support recipients. In 1981 the Quebec government combined the "welfare" component from the social services ministry with the labour and manpower ministry, becoming the first province to formally associate welfare with workforce development. The province's first substantial movement towards activation came through the establishment of a separate Work and Employment Incentive category within the welfare program in 1989; however, there was little money available to fund programs to help people on social assistance back to work. Unlike other provinces, participation in activation measures in Quebec was considered voluntary; however, extra financial incentives were provided for participation (Noel 2015).

Ever since the Quiet Revolution Quebec has maintained that social and economic development are closely linked. Starting in 1969, a network of regional Commissions de formation professionnelle had provided private sector advice on the delivery of provincial training measures. In the mid-1980s Diane Bellemare, a Université du Québec à Montréal economist, published an influential study on full employment that recommended the province take over leadership on active employment measures from the Government of Canada. In her view, for labour market programs to be effective, provincial, regional, and local management – not federal – was required. An economic summit in 1989 involving more than two thousand people brought unions, business, community organizations, school boards, churches, educational groups, and cooperatives together; from this the idea of establishing a Quebec-based forum for employment began to build. In December 1990 Quebec's National Assembly passed a unanimous resolution affirming Quebec's jurisdiction over all aspects of labour market training (Bakvis 2002).

The provincial Liberals followed this affirmation of Quebec competence by creating a labour market board, the Société Québécoise de développement de la main-d'oeuvre (SQDM) to (among other things) advise government on labour market policies, to secure this jurisdiction from Ottawa, and to receive the federal programs. Diane Bellemare was appointed as SQDM president in 1993, and prominent business and labour leaders joined the board. Community organizations representing people excluded from the workforce (e.g., women's, poverty, and immigrant groups) struggled to join the SQDM board. By coming together to create a formal strategic partnership called the La Coalition des organismes communautaires pour le développement de la main-d'oeuvre (COCDMO), these organizations eventually secured a place on the board.[2]

The SQDM – an independent organization run by employers and unions – was instrumental in facilitating the development of the "Quebec consensus" on labour market policy: that Quebec must be exclusively responsible for labour market and professional training programs and that federal funds allocated to such programs – including passive unemployment insurance benefits – must be handed over to Quebec (Johnson 1997). A commitment to activation, decentralization, one-stop shops, equal access (for unemployment insurance, social assistance, and "sans chèque" individuals), and social partner leadership were all part of the developing Quebec consensus.

The SQDM managed and coordinated federal and provincial training dollars through forty-eight service outlets. Focused on training in the

2 The mission of COCDMO covers employment integration, education and training, promotion and human rights, and local and community development.

workplace as well as the unemployed, SQDM found siloed programs, too many restrictions, and conditions around the federal money, and initiatives that did not meet Quebec's priorities (Johnson 1997). It also discovered that the separate Ottawa- and Quebec-funded employment networks and contractors hired to provide employment services did not interact with each other. The City of Montreal was also involved. With over one hundred programs, there was duplication, overlap, gaps in service, little coordination, and lots of tension between those who worked in the system. Depending upon their source of income support, people were eligible for different types of employment services and supports, including training.

While Quebec's demands on active (not passive) measures were acceded to in the 1992 Charlottetown Accord, the defeat of the accord left the matter unresolved until after the 1995 Quebec referendum on sovereignty when Prime Minister Chrétien committed to withdraw the federal government from training. In January 1996 Quebec sent a proposal to the federal human resources minister, which sparked further work by federal officials to deal with this issue (Klassen 2000a). In May of that year Ottawa made a formal offer to all provinces on new labour market arrangements that reflected many of Quebec's demands. The negotiation of Quebec's LMDA required two steps: first an agreement in principle in 1997 announced by Premier Bouchard and Prime Minister Chrétien and – following seven months of "very tense" negotiations – an implementation agreement signed in 1998 (Bakvis and Aucoin 2000).

The negotiations were complex and detailed, as there were a number of issues to be worked through that were unique to Quebec. For example, there was a strong aversion to there being any reference in the agreement to federal legislation (notably the Employment Insurance Act), as that would imply that Quebec was subject to federal laws on training. Given that the agreement involved a permanent transfer of federal staff, Quebec also pressed for an indeterminate, rather than a fixed length agreement. They also wanted no mention of "joint" evaluations or monitoring as had occurred in the agreements already negotiated in the other provinces. References to language issues were carefully crafted by both sides. However, Ottawa refused to budge on the amount of money to be transferred or the inclusion of federal programs for youth or disabled people (Bakvis and Aucoin 2000).

Negotiations on both sides were led by the respective deputy minister, supported by a variety of senior officials. In 1999/2000 the transfer of 1,022 federal civil servants to Quebec and about $561.1 million in funding became a reality (Klassen 2000a). Many of the former federal employees welcomed the opportunity to join the provincial government as Quebec pay scales were higher than Ottawa's. Federal officials who transferred over became intimately involved in building and implementing the new Quebec organization being developed to run the integrated provincial and federal programs (Bakvis and Aucoin 2000).

To prepare for the transfer, the Quebec government decided that the SDQM should be replaced by a consultative body, and by 1998 most SDQM employees and offices had transferred back to the provincial employment ministry, to be joined by staff from 130 social assistance offices in the Ministry of Social Development. Integration of the functions was meant to focus the minds of all involved on ensuring that the provincially run employment programming would suit the needs of social assistance clients, Employment Insurance recipients, as well as those who were "sans chèque." In 1999 a new provincial government department, the Ministère du Travail, de l'Emploi et de la Solidarité sociale (MTESS) was created, as well as a separate business line called Emploi-Québec (EQ), responsible for program delivery.

The partnership part of SDQM was transitioned into the Commission des partenaires du marché du travail (Labour Market Partners Commission), or CPMT. Its role was not to manage the employment services and training – as that was to be handled by EQ – but to steer and provide advice. In the transition from SDQM to CPMT those previously in charge lost their jobs. Initially the social partners were reluctant to take on responsibility for long-term clients in receipt in social assistance. Having community organizations responsible for employment services on the CPMT board eased the process and enhanced understanding for both business and unions; in time there was a growing realization that these individuals would be workers and union members as well. The CPMT was also made responsible for the Act to Foster the Development of Manpower Training, known as the 1 per cent law. Inspired by a similar law in France, this sought to close the gap between Quebec's low investments in workforce training compared to the other provinces. At the same time, regional labour market boards and sector councils were also established, reporting to the CPMT.

By the time that the Harper Conservatives offered provinces additional funding in 2008 through Labour Market Agreements to serve non-EI clients, Quebec's labour market services and organizational structure were fully mature. The province received an additional federal allocation of about $115 million per year through the LMAs, allowing it to expand the services on offer, especially for those who were "sans chèque." This effectively doubled the number of people that Emploi-Québec could serve. While its LMA agreement was largely similar to that signed in the other provinces, reporting and planning used Emploi-Québec's existing processes. This included the use of federal funding provided to Quebec through the Labour Market Agreement for Persons with Disabilities and the Targeted Initiative for Older Workers.

Ontario

While a Premier's Council established by the Peterson Liberals in 1986 had highlighted problems with duplication, overlap, and gaps between federal and provincial employment programming, in the late 1980s and early 1990s Ontario (unlike Quebec) was relatively content for Ottawa to lead in employment matters. Federal programs were delivered through Canada Employment Centres located across the province; by the mid-1990s program delivery through federal civil servants had given way to Employment Resource Centres managed by third-party agencies, many of them connected with social welfare charities (OECD 2015b). Contracting decisions were influenced by local federal politicians. After Unemployment Insurance became Employment Insurance in 1995, community organizations in Ontario started to notice that longer-term skills-training programs for EI recipients and other vulnerable workers became much harder to access as funds were cut from the federal budget and services were re-prioritized.

The provincial postsecondary education department was also involved in providing employment services. In 1986, the Ontario government announced the new Ontario Training Strategy, focused primarily on upgrading and modernizing the skills of the employed workforce. In its 1992 budget the Ontario government announced the establishment of the JOBS ONTARIO training fund, a three-year program focused on the long-term unemployed (Informetrica 1993). Klassen (2000b) estimated that in the early 1990s the province spent in excess of $400 million annually on a range of training and labour market adjustment programs. For example, for about twenty-five years the Ontario government – in partnership with the Ontario Association of Youth Employment Centres – had operated Job Connect, a "light-touch" job placement and wage subsidy program for youth and others who fell into the gaps between Employment Insurance and social assistance. Like the federal employment programs, this provincial service was also contracted out to third-party organizations. Provincially run literacy and apprenticeship programs, federal-provincial partnerships to deal with large industry layoffs, and immigrant settlement services were also part of the mix.

Unlike Quebec, which wanted to take on responsibility for the federal labour market programing, Ontario officials were more concerned that federal management was short-changing provincial citizens. As part of Ontario's broader "fair-share" concerns, one of Informetrica's commissioned papers focused on labour market development and training. This paper provided considerable information on Ontario's circumstances pre-devolution. While the 1991 Canada-Ontario Labour Force Development Agreement committed Canada to spending $846 million for labour force development in Ontario, the paper demonstrated that in 1993/4 actual expenditures were short by between $255 million and $395 million. It noted how federal Canada Job Strategy expenditures had been steadily declining, and that the shortfall in Ontario was inhibiting provincial efforts to get social assistance recipients into employment. Had Ottawa kept to its commitment, as many as 150,000 additional Ontario workers would have received training (Informetrica 1993).

However, the main focus of the Informetrica paper was to demonstrate that, year after year, Ontario had come out on the short end of the federal funding allocations. The analysis demonstrated that – while Ontario accounted for 37 per cent of both employment and unemployment in Canada, for 43 per cent of general revenues, and for 41 per cent of unemployment insurance funds – it received less than 30 per cent of UI developmental uses (UIDU) funds and 22 per cent of Consolidated Revenue funding. The paper was critical of federal choices to increase the use of UI funds for training, noting that funds derived from a payroll tax were more regressive than funds derived from the personal income tax. In Informetrica's view, the federal government was offloading the largest share of its labour force development expenditure onto workers and employers. The paper's authors also noted how the Atlantic provinces and Quebec were being over-funded, even when the likelihood of the training outcome being a success was greater in Ontario. For them, this made little sense in terms of value for money (Informetrica 1993).

This research provided a backdrop to all federal-Ontario discussions on labour force development in the early 1990s. As the new federal strategy announced by the Mulroney Progressive Conservatives played out across Canada, the Ontario Training and Adjustment Board, or OTAB, was established by the province in 1993 as a bipartite management and labour authority to oversee most provincially run workplace training and adjustment activities. Social equity groups were later added to the board. OTAB was deliberately designed with the idea that it would take over funding and delivery responsibility for about forty-eight programs in ten provincial ministries. If the Charlottetown Constitutional Accord had passed in 1992 – recognizing provincial competence for labour market training – OTAB would have been the logical place to receive the federal labour market programs (Klassen 2000b).

However, the political instability that resulted from changes in the provincial government from Liberal to NDP to Conservative control within the space of ten short years – as well as precarious cooperation between labour, business, and equity groups on the OTAB board – meant that the organization lived for only three short years (Klassen 2000b). While the process of establishing local boards continued (about twenty-five boards were set up, cost shared between Ontario and Ottawa), OTAB and the sector councils were closed down in 1996 when the Harris Conservatives took control of government (Wolfe 1997). In its place the government created the business-dominated Ontario Jobs and Investment Board. It did not last long and was dissolved in 1999 (Haddow and Klassen 2006).

Ontario is unique in Canada for having retained municipal delivery of social assistance,[3] with municipalities providing benefits to people who are "expected to work" through what is now called Ontario Works, or OW, and provincial government offices responsible for disabled people through the Ontario Disability Support Program, or ODSP. Over the years there have been many changes in the names and configuration of these programs (including uploading and downloading between municipalities and the province in the groups to be served, who delivers, and who pays). Until the late 1980s the entire focus of the program was on passive income assistance. Ontario turned towards activation when a program review in 1988 called Transitions recommended "opportunity planning" to help social assistance recipients back to work. Before this time there had been only small-scale employability

3 Quebec moved responsibility from the municipal to the provincial level in 1975. The City of Montreal still had some residual involvement pre-devolution. The change happened at different times in other provinces: Nova Scotia, 2001; Manitoba, 2004; British Columbia, 1978; Alberta, 1975; Saskatchewan, 1966; New Brunswick, 1967; Prince Edward Island, 1972; and Newfoundland and Labrador, 1977.

pilots in Ontario, and single mothers were actually discouraged by policy from taking full-time work (Graefe 2015b).

It took the Harris government's Common Sense Revolution and the introduction of what many called "workfare" in 1995 before employment services for social assistance recipients started to be rolled out across the province, under the overall direction of the Ministry of Community and Social Services (MCSS), also responsible for disability employment services using federal funding through what at the time was called the Vocational Rehabilitation of Disabled Persons Agreement. Elected in 1995 on a mandate of welfare reform (about 12 per cent of the Ontario population were receiving benefits at the time), new legislation creating OW and ODSP specifically prescribed either mandatory (OW) or voluntary (ODSP) participation in employment support services, with service responsibility assigned to the organization responsible for benefit administration.

In the City of Toronto alone, between 1997 and 2008 municipal employment program budgets grew from virtually nothing to about $55 million, and staff roles were adjusted as case planning and assessment was added to benefit administration duties. Many municipalities decided to contract the required employment services out to specialized agencies; others (especially those in the northern part of the province) provided the services with internal staff. Employment services for ODSP recipients were not managed by municipalities, but were contracted out directly by MCSS.

As a result of these historical developments, by the mid-1990s, four large government funders – the federal human resources department (through the Canada Employment Centres), the provincial postsecondary education ministry, the provincial social services ministry, and municipal social services departments – were each responsible for the design and delivery of employment support services for their respective client group. Coordination was disjointed and generally ineffective. Since most of the services were contracted out, third-party employment services agencies proliferated, with some receiving funding from all three levels of government as well as different departments of the same government. One respondent from a community-based organization interviewed through this research described the period from the mid-1990s to 2005 in Ontario as "like the Wild West. For example, at the corner of Kipling and Bloor in Toronto four different agencies competed using three different government funding sources. Arguments over signage and flags prevailed over the quality of client services."

This was the environment in which the 1995 offer to devolve federal labour market programs fell. Not only were the Harris Conservatives in the throes of cutting provincial staff in the postsecondary education department that might have received the federal programming, there was a fraught relationship between provincial Conservative politicians and their federal Liberal counterparts, including Premier Harris and Prime Minister Chrétien. As provincial employees were being let go, taking on over a thousand federal staff through a devolved LMDA and offering them a three-year job guarantee was extremely problematic. As already identified, Ontario was also very concerned with a federal offer that gave them only 28 per cent of the funding while Ontarians contributed more than 42 per cent to the EI account. Getting its "fair share" would have required about $145 million more than the $600 million on offer (Ontario 2003). In response, Ottawa contended that the offer to Ontario – like the one made to every other province – reflected what it was already spending to deliver the services in the province, and no more money would be made available.

By 1998 all provinces had accepted the federal funding allocations and terms, and had negotiated LMDAs, either full devolution or co-managed, while Ontario had not come to any agreement at all. As the 101 Ontario federal Liberal politicians became increasingly aware that devolving federal programs to Ontario would limit their opportunities to connect with constituents and mean handing over federal programs to a provincial government that was the antithesis of what the Liberal party stood for, federal positioning about the inadvisability of signing a devolved LMDA with Ontario began to harden (Bakvis and Aucoin 2000). When in May 2001 Ontario indicated that it would accept all the federal terms and conditions for a devolved LMDA without amendment, Ottawa refused to come to the table. In 2003 an Ontario deputy minister testified at a public hearing, "It just doesn't seem to be going anywhere." Another official noted that under federal delivery the budget allocated to Ontario was being underspent, further depriving the province (Ontario 2003).

A breakthrough on the federal-Ontario impasse finally came in 2005 when Liberal Prime Minister Paul Martin and Liberal Premier Dalton McGinty signed a devolved LMDA worth approximately $525 million annually, and the province accepted the transfer of about six hundred federal staff and over four hundred third-party contracts. The provincial Ministry of Training, Colleges and Universities (MTCU) was designated as lead for the negotiations and ultimately became responsible for integrating the federal programming into the provincial service delivery system through what was to become known as Employment Ontario, or EO. Ontario's LMDA terms and conditions were very similar to what had already been agreed to in the late 1990s with Alberta, New Brunswick, Manitoba, and Saskatchewan. MTCU was also responsible for the federal-provincial pilot projects for older workers.

Also signed was what was known at the time as a Labour Market Partnership Agreement (LMPA), which provided additional money to deal with the Ontario "fair-share" issue and assist other groups who were ineligible for EI. When the Harper Conservatives came to power in 2006, they agreed to proceed with the LMDA but not the LMPA. In 2007 the conditions in the LMPA were changed to be more province-friendly (a key demand of Alberta and Quebec), and all jurisdictions agreed to Labour Market Agreements, or LMAs, in 2008, involving an additional federal allocation of about $193 million annually for Ontario. That same year Ontario created its high-profile Second Careers program, a grant providing technical training for laid-off workers affected by the economic downturn. Federal money through the LMDA and LMA agreements provided key financial resources to the province for this undertaking.

Post LMDA Governance Reforms

Single Gateways or One-Stop Shops

One of the first choices that each province had to consider when it took on the federal employment services was how they would be aligned within the provincial government structure and the degree to which other provincial programming would change. Quebec's public employment service was aligned with provincial social solidarity programs, while Ontario's was aligned with the postsecondary education system. Emploi-Québec's "one-stop shop" approach that integrates all employment services in Quebec under a single brand is very different from Employment Ontario's "no wrong door."

In 2014 Emploi-Québec (EQ) provided a broad range of labour market services for people receiving government income support benefits (Employment Insurance and social assistance), as well as the public at large. Employment support services, training, social assistance benefits, and services for employers were accessed through one of Emploi-Québec's 158 centres locaux d'emploi (CLEs), staffed by provincial civil servants. Many people think that Emploi-Québec is a separate organization or agency, but in reality it is the delivery arm of the Ministère du Travail, de l'Emploi et de la Solidarité sociale (MTESS). EQ has a performance and accountability agreement with MTESS as well as with the Commission des partenaires du marché du travail (CPMT). Over three thousand EQ staff reported through a local and regional management structure.

Establishing Emploi-Québec as a single network involved integrating government staff from three different organizations as well as reducing the number of contractors in 256 service outlets to 153 and the number of services provided from sixty-five to a dozen. Initially employment services and social assistance staff within MTESS merely cohabited and continued to maintain their separate business lines; it took ten years for them to be merged and integrated offices to be established across the province. It also took time to manage the culture change between the top-down control-oriented management of social assistance and the more collaborative labour market orientation (Noel 2012). Like the other provinces, MTESS was also challenged in its efforts to integrate all of the "external resource" contracts inherited from the previous three entities. Initial efforts led to overspending, followed by funding cutbacks, and resulted in major political demonstrations. This triggered considerable efforts to formalize and improve the relationship between Emploi-Québec and its third-party contractors. As a result of these efforts, complaints and glitches soon settled down (Bourque, as referenced in Lazar 2002, 21).

In 2014, Quebec's CLE offices provided all who walk through the door (social assistance claimants, EI recipients, and the general public) with access to job banks, screening, service needs assessment, case management, and job placement services. While benefits and employment services were offered at the same site, it was not mandatory for social assistance recipients to take advantage of employment supports. Each CLE also had a team dedicated to business services that provided outreach to employers in human resources and training. Informal relationships were forged between the CLE and employers to help promote sustainable employment placements for the unemployed. More in-depth services were contracted out to third-party, non-profit organizations, local school boards, or colleges, which provided both basic skills and technical training. In 2014 Emploi-Québec drew on over 350 external employability resources, including 110 Youth Employment Centres. While EQ generally acted as the gatekeeper, people could also access the external resources directly, without a referral (OECD 2014b).

Ontario's employment services delivery system in 2014 was much more complex than Quebec's. Although the federal government was no longer the major player, a number of provincial and municipal players funded different public access sites. Most programs were managed by the Ministry of Training, Colleges and Universities (MTCU) through Employment Ontario (EO), a separate business line created in 2010 to receive the transferred federal staff and third-party contracts and combine them with the pre-existing provincial Ontario Employment Assistance Service, Targeted Wage Subsidies, Job Connect program, apprenticeship services, and literacy and essential skills programs.

MTCU's first job post-devolution was to create a provincial architecture for employment services and stabilize the system. With the assistance of a service-delivery reference group, between 2010 and 2012 it researched, consulted on, and then implemented EO Service Transformation (Ontario 2014). Pre-devolution, MTCU did not have a regional delivery system (other than in apprenticeship), and any provincial employment programming on offer was centrally managed out of Toronto. In contrast, Quebec built Emploi-Québec upon its pre-existing local and regional social assistance delivery structure.

Employment Ontario in 2014 consisted of a network of 170 third-party employment service providers in over four hundred locations, over two hundred literacy service-provider organizations at over three hundred sites, and seventy apprenticeship-training delivery offices, supported by about nine hundred provincial civil servants, most of whom used to be federal civil servants. Like in Quebec, integrating the federal staff was relatively easy, as Ontario salaries were higher than the federal compensation. Provincial civil servants were responsible for contract management, training approval (including access to Ontario's Second Career program), apprenticeship, and some centralized delivery.

The contracted EO employment service providers are the public front door of Ontario's PES. They offered information and referral, career planning, job search, job development, job placement, and job retention services, all directed at the unemployed. They were not responsible for outreach to employers in the area of human resources and training.[4] A quantitative profiling tool – the Employment Service

4 This changed in 2015 with the implementation of the Canada Job Grant, in which EO employment service providers were expected to support smaller employers.

suitability indicator – considered twelve potential barriers to employment to determine the intensity of client services. While the third-party employment service-providers had considerable latitude in organizing counselling and placement services, recommendations for training went to a MTCU consultant, who reviewed and approved the application (OECD 2014b).

Most EO employment service providers used to be either provincial Job Connect agencies or federal service providers. With input received through the consultation process, it was decided to build EO on the province's successful Job Connect model and try to fit the existing service delivery network into the new model. The federal contracts that transferred in were a combination of specialized and generic services, and many contracts were split between assessment and delivery. Ontario wanted to ensure a full suite of employment programs and decided to go to a "no wrong door" model. This meant that all specialized services (e.g., for immigrants, youth) were transitioned into generic service providers offering similar services to whoever walked in the door. Previously people had to navigate between specialized service providers on their own.

A single branded point of access to employment and training programs and services ensured integrated service delivery whether in person, over the phone, or through the Internet, all supported by the Employment Ontario Information System. "People in our community will be able to go to only one provider and be referred from there to all the necessary services they need. It will greatly simplify the process of getting training and will also help employers get the skills they need" (Ontario MTCU 2006).

Approximately 400 federal and 130 provincial contracts were replaced by fewer and larger third-party service delivery agents, primarily through a "capacity assessment," not through a large province-wide request for proposal, as was used in British Columbia. There were winners and losers through the process and considerable angst as some organizations worried about losing their contract. Approximately eighty agencies left the system. The specialized federal contracts for disabled persons were retained by MTCU and by 2015 had still not been mainstreamed into the broader EO network. The consensus among those interviewed for this research was that the transition was smooth, especially given the lack of political will to terminate some contracts. This view was confirmed by the formative evaluation undertaken by both governments (HRSDC 2012). Each EO employment service provider maintained its own identity but was also branded as part of the larger Employment Ontario network. EO is clearly nested within and marketed as part of the province's broader postsecondary education system.

Despite setting up Employment Ontario, employment services controlled by other provincial Ministries in Ontario were maintained. One of the largest array of programs was overseen by the Ministry of Community and Social Services (MCSS), delivered in 2014 by forty-seven consolidated municipalities (using third-party contracts or municipal civil servants) for Ontario Works (OW) clients, by MCSS directly (using over 150 third-party service providers) for Ontario Disability Support Program (ODSP) clients, and by 101 First Nations for income assistance recipients living on reserve. For some social assistance recipients, participation in employment support services is compulsory: to receive OW benefits, recipients must sign a participation agreement setting out the employment activities they will undertake to find work or improve their skills. In 2010 MCSS spent over $200 million on employment supports for social assistance claimants.

Most OW individuals who participated in employment activities engaged in independent job search (70.1 per cent), basic education and training (28.5 per cent), and structured job search (13.9 per cent) (Ontario, MESS 2013). Municipal capacity to provide employment supports varied from one place to another. For example, in 2014 the City of Toronto operated nineteen Employment and Social Services Centres and had service contracts with forty-three agencies. Many of their employment services agencies also held EO contracts. The city also provided services to employers – including an employer help line – and has undertaken the development of a Toronto Workforce Development Strategy. The focus of Ontario Works in Toronto has shifted completely from a welfare program to an employment service (Toronto 2012).

The Commission for the Review of Social Assistance in Ontario (Ontario, MESS 2012) noted that separating social assistance recipients from other job seekers reinforces the stigma of receiving assistance and makes it more difficult for people to access a wider range of services. The separation also resulted in service duplication and gaps, confusion for job seekers and employers, and administrative inefficiencies. At the time that the federal LMDA contracts transferred over, there was no serious discussion of integrating employment services for social assistance recipients into the EO network, as it was felt that this was too large a task. In 2014 there were no province-wide or regional protocols to coordinate employment services for OW and ODSP recipients with EO services; however, in some places there were local arrangements. As part of its performance management system, EO employment service providers were expected to be responsive to service coordination in their community. In 2012 only 17 per cent of people using EO employment services were social assistance claimants, as most preferred to use the specialized services provided through OW or ODSP (Ontario MESS 2013).

In 2012 the Commission on the Reform of Ontario's Public Services – known as the Drummond Report – highlighted the large variety of provincial players in the employment services business in Ontario (including also the Ministry of Citizenship and Immigration and other smaller provincial programs) and recommended that programs be streamlined and integrated with Employment Ontario (Ontario Finance 2012). A business respondent interviewed through this research also noted that the Ontario system was fragmented and hard for employers to navigate. In his view, the employment services market in Ontario needed to be redesigned so good providers could thrive and bad ones disappear. By 2015 this redesign was underway through an initiative called Employment and Training Services Integration or ETSI under the leadership of MTCU.

Decentralization

Both Quebec and Ontario have taken up OECD recommendations to embed a decentralized approach into their public employment service. In each province a mix of civil servants working out of regional and local offices located across the province,[5] contracted service delivery organizations, and formal local/regional labour market boards planned, designed, and delivered the provincial PES. Ontario also has municipalities and First Nations bands delivering employment services for social assistance recipients, ensuring local input. Despite the fact that these approaches seem similar, respondents interviewed through this research suggested otherwise. In Ontario the MTCU local offices were tightly controlled, with regional office and headquarters making most of the decisions. Quebec was much more decentralized, about 75–80 per cent of EQ's budget decisions were made at the regional and local levels.

5 In 2014 Employment Ontario had four regions with forty-three MTCU offices; MCSS had five regions with forty-five offices. In Quebec there were seventeen EQ regional offices and 158 local offices.

Quebec and Ontario's local or regional workforce planning boards are unique in Canada, with no other province institutionalizing social partner input in this way. Ontario's twenty-six Workforce Planning Boards are meant to identify local workforce issues and provide collaborative solutions by engaging stakeholders and other partners. With representation from business and labour as well as education and community groups, the Ontario boards were jointly set up by the province and the federal government pre-devolution and surprisingly survived the demise of OTAB and the Ontario sector councils. In 2014 the local boards did not report to a provincial board, nor did they collectively come together on a province-wide basis. The province did not produce a cumulative report on all of their activities. The boards were accountable to their community and – only recently – to their respective MTCU regional director.

The shift in 2012 from provincial to regional oversight of the planning boards was meant to provide autonomy, promote stronger linkages, and broaden community involvement (OECD 2104b). However, these MTCU-funded boards were only one actor among many that did workforce planning at the local level in Ontario; many communities also had other "workforce intermediaries" who contributed to matching the supply and demand sides of the labour market. For example, in Kitchener-Waterloo in 2014 there was a Waterloo Region Immigrant Employment Network, a Prosperity Council of Waterloo Region, and a Community Employment Linkages Group that also represented different subsets of local workforce development actors (Bramwell 2008). In Toronto, the municipal social services department developed a workforce development strategy that sat alongside that of the MTCU-funded Toronto Workforce Innovation Group. There were separate regional networks for literacy and basic skills across the province, which also did community planning.

Given the plethora of groups, there was considerable variation in local workforce development in Ontario, with governance failures more common than successes. In Bramwell's view, the Ontario MTCU boards were mostly ignored and functioned "under the radar" of provincial policymakers. "The policy hierarchy is clear: policy is made at the provincial level by the Ministry of Training, Colleges and Universities; translated and negotiated through the regional offices, and implemented at the local level by service delivery organizations … Beyond consultation, information sharing and service delivery, there does not appear to be a formal process for local involvement in this policy area in Ontario" (Bramwell 2010, 64–5).

Tom Zizys (2014) reached a similar conclusion, noting that the Ontario workforce planning boards had not been used anywhere near their full potential. He saw no cohesive vision guiding the boards and concluded that their work was too small-scale, operating on too short a time horizon. The OECD (2014b) also concluded that Ontario's local boards played a limited role in the design and delivery of employment and training. It recommended that their mandate be reviewed and strengthened. In 2015 this was underway through the MTCU piloting of Local Employment Planning Councils, viewed as the next generation of local boards.

In contrast, Quebec's seventeen labour market councils (CRPMTs) provided significant leadership in ensuring that the needs of local labour markets were heard. Matched to support each of EQ's regional offices, the councils brought together representatives from business, labour, educational institutions, the community sector, and government to identify labour market issues particular to their region, help develop a regional action plan, and suggest target results and how EQ money should be spent in the region. They also had a defined reporting relationship to the provincial Commission des partenaires du marché du travail, or CPMT.

As the leading instruments for coordination in Quebec, not only did the CRPMTs identify challenges in the regional labour market, they also helped formulate and approve a regional action plan for employment measures to address these challenges, including recommending programs and initiatives to the CPMT (OECD 2014b). To ensure control, EQ instituted a results-based management system using indicators, targets, and annual reports as tools. Information was collected and shared so that regions could compare themselves with each other.

Outsourcing and Contracting Out

In 2014 the Employment Ontario service delivery system was almost completely outsourced, while Emploi-Québec offered a more "mixed" system of provincial civil servants delivering "front door" services, supported by specialized third-party agencies that provided more in-depth and individualized services.

Ontario's network of 170 Employment Ontario contracted employment providers all operated under relatively similar arrangements, with provincial staff responsible for allocating and monitoring the contracts. The contracts were normally for one year and open for renewal.

There was no flexibility in the contracts to adjust client eligibility or program design features, nor could service providers set performance targets or make adjustments to take local conditions into account. All were subject to the same Service Provider Guidelines (Ontario MTCU 2014), which detailed the components of the employment service to be provided, program delivery arrangements, the performance management system, and administrative controls. While performance targets were not negotiated, changing local conditions could be considered in the evaluation of a service provider's performance (OECD 2014b).

Despite this lack of flexibility, many respondents interviewed through this research noted that the contracting conditions under Employment Ontario were a significant improvement over what they had experienced when the federal government was in charge. Performance expectations changed significantly once the province took control: the federal programs were based on counts, not outcomes, and were very accountability heavy, with expenditures scrutinized in detail by federal officials. Post-devolution, performance was based on outcomes.

In 2014 EO employment service-provider budgets had three components: infrastructure, incentives to employers, and client supports. Contractors were paid in lump sums and were expected to report back. They were free to spend as they deemed necessary, as long as they met the outcomes and targets identified. However, there were no financial incentives for performance, and contractors were not compared with each other in a way that would facilitate best-practice learning. The performance management framework was intended to serve as a "balanced score card" for service providers, creating a Service Quality Standard that incorporated measures for customer satisfaction, employment outcomes, and service coordination with other types of education, training, and other services (SRDC 2013). Most provincial EO service providers were not-for-profit organizations, as opposed to for-profit firms.[6] MTCU facilitated information sharing with their contractors through an Employment Ontario partners gateway that provided regular updates on a wide range of issues. Updates often related to implementation of the EO case management system, as well as stakeholder consultation on the next stage of service delivery integration.

---

6 International employment services agencies were interested in becoming more involved in delivering employment services in Ontario, as they already did in British Columbia.

The Ministry of Community and Social Services also used about 150 third-party contracts in 2014 to provide employment services to ODSP recipients, as did municipalities under OW. ODSP service providers received payment based on their success in placing and retaining people in employment. Respondents noted that there was resistance to integrating MCSS-funded employment services with EO, as disability advocates were keen to preserve their specialized services. It was not uncommon for the same agency to have multiple contracts – each with different provisions – to provide employment services for EO, OW, and ODSP clients. Many of the municipal contracts covered a range of services that went beyond just employment supports. Like Employment Ontario, most of the third-party organizations delivering employment programs under OW or ODSP were not-for-profit organizations.

To support the PES "front door" managed by Quebec civil servants, Emploi-Québec also funded a dense network, consisting in 2014 of over 350 community-based organizations (mostly non-profit as well as a few for-profit) that provided specialized supports such as job search workshops, youth, and disability programming. Many of these community organizations were built in the 1960s and 1970s out of the women's movement as well as poverty and immigrant groups. Many were previously funded by the federal government. The network of youth employment agencies in Quebec (Carrefour Jeunesse-Emploi, one in each electoral district) was unique in Canada, as all management responsibilities had been delegated to individuals aged sixteen to thirty-five (OECD 2014b). None of these "external resources" were branded as Emploi-Québec, with each maintaining its separate identity. Their missions were complementary to EQ, and for many it was their sole source of funding.

Emploi-Québec's results-based management relationship with its external contractors has been formalized through publicly available operational and financial guideline documents that detail the shared understanding of accountability and outline results indicators and the methods used to establish targets. In 2014 there was no competitive bidding for these Quebec contracts or requests for proposal, and contracts were regularly renewed each year. While there were province-wide parameters for the contracts, it was up to each EQ region and local office to decide on the nature and organization of its contracts in order to meet province-wide goals. Although targets were included within each contract, it was not a rigorous performance-management system. EQ officials worked with underperforming organizations to improve results and monitor progress. Like in Ontario, the political cost of ending some of these contracts was substantial.

Partnerships and Networks

WITH BUSINESS AND LABOUR

Quebec has the most formal arrangements of any province in Canada to receive business, labour, education, and community input into the direction of the provincial public employment service. In 2014 there was a provincial board, regional boards, sector councils, and a number of advisory committees – all cross-linked with each other and different parts of the Ministère du Travail, de l'Emploi et de la Solidarité sociale (MTESS) as well as Emploi-Québec. In contrast, with the demise of OTAB in 1996, Ontario lost its provincial labour market board and formal sector councils; however, it retained twenty-six local workforce boards. To fill the gap, post-devolution, consultations on labour market matters and related issues in Ontario are done "as needed." For example, social assistance reviews in 1988 and 2012 focused on employability for social assistance recipients. In 2014/15 MTCU undertook consultations on the integration of employment services, as recommended in the Drummond Report on the reform of Ontario's public services. This included dedicated conversations with representatives of Ontario business and labour organizations.

The most influential body in Quebec is the Commission des partenaires du marché du travail, or CPMT. In operation for almost twenty years, CPMT works collaboratively with MTESS to develop Quebec's employment and workforce policies, determine strategies and objectives, and approve Emploi-Québec's annual action plan. It does not advise on social assistance policy. In 2014 CPMT's twenty-five members were made up of six labour, six business, three community, and two academic representatives. There were also four non-voting members designated by Quebec government departments, as well as one guest member representing Quebec's French- and English-language universities. Three ex-officio members represented MTESS, including the associate deputy minister responsible for Emploi-Québec. By having this senior provincial official sit on the CPMT, coordination was ensured. Although each representative was chosen to represent a specific constituency, they were selected on the basis of their individual merits and potential contribution to the work of the CPMT. Not all members could vote; however, decisions were usually taken by consensus.

In addition to its advisory role, the CPMT was also directly responsible for certain elements of Quebec's Act to Foster the Development of Manpower Training, first passed in 1995 and then updated and expanded in 2008 as the Act to Promote Workforce Skills Development and Recognition. This legislation encompasses the "1 per cent law" that requires employers of a certain size to invest in the skills development of their employees. If they fail to do so, they are required to contribute to a training fund administered by the CPMT, available to employers as well as EQ staff to support training in the workplace. In 2014 this fund was worth about $70 million and received an annual contribution of about $25 million. Because of Quebec's long-standing focus on workplace training and employer involvement in decision making, its federal-provincial Labour Market Agreement was rolled over with the same parameters to 2020, as opposed to being transformed in 2014 into Canada Job Fund Agreements, as occurred in all other Canadian provinces and territories.[7]

In 2014 the CPMT had about one hundred staff. In addition to managing the training fund, it financially supported and directed the work of twenty-nine sectoral workforce committees (CSMOs); the seventeen regional labour market councils (CRPMTs); an employment integration and maintenance committee for the disabled; and five advisory committees targeted to youth, women, adults in conflict with the law, workers forty-five and older, and First Nations and Inuit. The CPMT also undertook independent research. The CSMOs expanded significantly as a result of the 1 per cent law. They facilitate coordination between firms and adult learning providers, develop professional standards, and assess labour market needs in their sector. They are similar to Manitoba's sector councils, as described in chapter 5 of this book.

WITH COMMUNITY ORGANIZATIONS INVOLVED IN EMPLOYMENT SERVICES

There were also dedicated processes for Emploi-Québec to coordinate with the more than 350 not-for-profit community employment agencies (with over three thousand employees) that supported it. In 2014 there were eight separate umbrella networks that represented these organizations: Association des Centres de recherche d'emploi du Québec (ACREQ); Collectif des entreprises d'insertion du Québec (CEIQ);

7 The press release accompanying the federal announcement noted that "Quebec already has a long-standing well-functioning system that puts employers at its centre and requires them to invest in training."

Le Regroupement québécois des organismes pour le développement de l'employabilité (RQuODE); Canadian Practice Firms Network (CPFN); Le Réseau des carrefours jeunesse-emploi du Québec (RCJEQ); Le Réseau des services spécialisés de main-d'œuvre (RSSMO); Le Regroupement des organismes spécialisés pour l'emploi des personnes handicapées (ROSEPH) ; and the Collectif autonome des carrefour jeunesse-emploi du Québec (CACJEQ).

Funded by their member agencies, the eight networks managed operational issues between Emploi-Québec and the service providers through what was called the "National Forum." There were also regional forums to facilitate information sharing and search for regional solutions. The forum was put in place in the early 2000s to reset the government–community relationship that had broken down in Emploi-Québec's early days. Its prime goal was to build and sustain partnerships between EQ and the community agencies that supported it, and ensure dialogue on operational issues. An explicit "recognition and partnership protocol" was developed – a sixteen-page document publicly available – to ensure that the specialized services provided by the community organizations working in the employability field are complementary to Emploi-Québec. The protocol defined roles, clarified concepts, and outlined common values and principles (Quebec 2006). In addition to the protocol, an accountability framework and financial reporting documents have been developed and agreed to through the forum.

Quebec's "partnership" arrangement as outlined in this protocol was very different from the "contractual" relationship between the provincial government in Ontario and the community organizations that delivered employability services under Employment Ontario. In 2014 a Service Delivery Advisory Group provided a structured mechanism for dialogue between MTCU and third-party stakeholders in the EO network. This group met regularly to share information on changes to service delivery, clarify government guidelines and expectations, consider new programs and initiatives, and receive feedback from the field. Through this group and the network it has created, community organizations also became involved in MTCU pilot projects, evaluations, and research. Other ad hoc and informal groups were also formed from time to time.

Ontario also has a rich history with long-established networks that support community employability organizations working in the province, including the Ontario Network of Employment Skills Training

Projects (ONESTEP) and First Work.[8] These networks represent agencies both within and beyond the EO network: in 2014 ONESTEP had about seventy-five member agencies delivering services in fifty communities across Ontario, while First Work represented about seventy youth employment agencies. Both were established in the late 1980s, and ONESTEP used to get core funding from the federal government. First Work (originally the Ontario Association of Youth Employment Centres) began as a collective effort to lobby the provincial government and has never received core funding. Post-devolution, neither organization received core funding from any government, and both operate through the support of their membership, foundations, and project activities, and by organizing conferences.

MCSS also had formal advisory structures on service delivery through an ODSP Service Delivery Advisory Group and an Ontario Works Administrators Service Delivery Advisory Group. The Ontario Disability Employment Network – comprising employment service providers and employers – champions the business case for hiring people with disabilities. This work was carried out under the auspices of the Ministry of Community and Social Development, responsible in 2014 for the federal-provincial Labour Market Development Agreement for Persons with Disabilities.

Both provinces have organizations that support training for career development practitioners (CDP). Ontario's professional organization – the Ontario Alliance of Career Development Practitioners – was one of the weakest in Canada. In 2014 registration was on hold, and it did not organize conferences for its membership, one of the key activities of CDP associations in other provinces across Canada. Specialized training for employment counsellors working in Ontario's municipal system was not required; however, the City of Toronto encouraged its staff to complete the Career and Employment Coach Certificate, a joint program with the Winnipeg Transition Centre and Humber College. Although performance expectations were embedded in the broader performance accountability framework, EO guidelines did not prescribe the qualifications or training of agency staff.

Quebec's vocational and guidance counsellors are highly regulated through the L'Ordre des conseillers et conseillères d'orientation du Québec. To practise as a vocational or guidance counsellor in Quebec

8 See http://www.onestep.ca/ and http://www.firstwork.org/.

(which also permits psychotherapy) requires certification. While most of the staff of the 350 community based organizations associated with EQ were not certified, they had a bachelor's degree. Practitioners received support for professional development through their respective parent organization, often through annual conferences. The Quebec associations were also highly involved with the International Association for Educational and Vocational Guidance, hosting their last meeting in 2014 in Quebec City. They also actively promoted the use of the Canadian Standards and Guidelines for Career Development Practitioners among their associations.[9]

WITH THE GOVERNMENT OF CANADA

Bilateral relationships between provincial civil servants responsible for the PES and the federal government (Service Canada officials working in each province as well as Ottawa officials) were guided by formal management committees detailed in the LMDA/LMA agreements. In 1998, a Canada-Quebec Joint LMDA Committee was established to share information and provide a forum for cooperation involving Quebec's MTESS staff and Service Canada officials working in Quebec. It has proven useful as a way to secure Statistics Canada information. Under the LMA, Quebec and Canada agreed to meet in the spring and autumn of each year to share information and ensure effective implementation of the agreement. A Quebec official interviewed through this research noted that these meetings have not been able to bridge differences on issues such as the presence of parallel federal and provincial youth programming.

In Ontario the joint LMDA committee initially focused on transition issues such as the sharing of client information and facilitating service delivery. An ongoing Operations Working Group committee has ensured that staff from each government are aware of each other's programs and services, including the importance of referring Employment Insurance claimants to EO programs. Post-devolution, officials also acted together on a Joint Rapid Response Action plan to ensure coordinated services were available to employees of companies facing major layoffs (HRSDC 2012). By 2014 the bilateral federal-provincial committee encompassed coordination of all labour market agreements and met twice a year, co-chaired by federal officials from Ottawa and MTCU officials in Toronto.

---

9 See http://career-dev-guidelines.org/career_dev/.

WITH ABORIGINAL LABOUR MARKET ORGANIZATIONS

Unlike the western provinces, Ontario and Quebec's Aboriginal population is much smaller at 2 and 1 per cent of the population respectively. In 2014 Ontario had seventeen Aboriginal Skills and Employment Strategy (ASETS) holders funded directly by Employment and Social Development Canada, while Quebec had four. The relationship between Quebec's ASETS holders and Emploi-Québec was strong, especially in the urban areas where both organizations operated. It is noteworthy that this relationship did not include the federal government, the primary funder for Quebec's ASETS holders. First Nations ASETS organizations deliberately coordinated their employer outreach activities with EQ offices and often shared resources to support individual clients as they moved off reserve. CPMT had developed an Aboriginal strategy in cooperation with Quebec's four ASETS holders, and in 2010 formalized a CPMT, First Nation, and Inuit Labour Market Advisory Committee.[10] RQuODE (one of Quebec's eight community networks) acted as a service provider in relation to the Kativik Regional Government ASETS holder.

In Ontario relationships between the province, municipalities, EO contractors, and ASETS holders were more informal and unstructured. While Service Canada officials regularly brought Ontario's seventeen ASETS holders together, they had not facilitated relationship building between ASETS holders and provincial officials responsible for the PES. Some ASETS holders thought that a more formal overarching agreement with the province and ASETS holders would be useful. Ontario officials saw the ASETS system as running quite separately from the Employment Ontario system; however, they expected their EO employment service providers to share information and interact on a local basis as necessary. Ontario's ASETS holders were consulted on the initial transformation of the federal programs into Employment Ontario and had also been consulted on the service delivery transformation underway in 2014/15 through a separate Aboriginal engagement. Unlike Quebec, no formal and ongoing consultation mechanisms have been established, nor were ASETS holders considered as an EO partner organization. One respondent noted that this left them on the outside looking in.

10 See http://www.ccpnimt-fnilmac.com/en/index.html.

Comparing Quebec and Ontario

Table C summarizes Ontario and Quebec approaches to the governance of the PES in 2014, using the themes identified in chapter 3 of this book.

What Accounted for the Differences in Governance Approaches between the Two Provinces?

The governance arrangements that Quebec and Ontario chose to manage their provincial public employment service (PES) since taking these responsibilities on from the Government of Canada were dramatically different. These different choices reflected different political cultures, the timing of the devolution decision, and how government was organized in each province before the federal responsibilities transferred in.

Quebec could introduce one-stop shops for employment services because the province was directly responsible for the management and delivery of social assistance, and deliberately chose to incorporate employment services for this group into the provincial PES platform developed post-devolution. The pre-existing province-wide social assistance delivery system was used as the foundation for building a new and broader service delivery system that not only integrated the federal employment programs, but also brought in what was on offer through SQDM, a separate provincial agency responsible for a smaller array of employment services.

As Quebec had been seeking the federal programs for a long time, it had ample time to plan the new structure. The "Quebec consensus" that developed in the late 1980s and 1990s was motivated not only by a desire to take on labour market responsibility from Ottawa, it was also motivated by a desire to ensure that all Quebeckers – whether receiving employment insurance benefits, social assistance, or "sans chèque" – had access to relatively similar employment services. This consensus has held – even through changes in government – as a result of the long-standing involvement of Quebec's social partners and community organizations in the policy field.

In Ontario, social assistance responsibility has historically been split between municipalities and the province. Unlike every other province in Canada that has "uploaded" responsibility for this very large and expensive program from the municipal to the provincial level, Ontario has stayed the course, reflecting a path-dependent political culture that values local decision making over provincial consistency. When

Table C. Comparing Governance Features in Ontario and Quebec's Public Employment Service, 2014

	Quebec	Ontario
Single gateways or one-stop shops	Emploi-Québec's (EQ) 158 Local Employment Centres (CLEs) under the Ministère du Travail, de l'Emploi et de la Solidarité sociale (MTESS) provided one-stop access to employment services, social assistance, and employer supports. Each EQ office was supported by community-based agencies.	170 Employment Ontario (EO) service providers under the Ministry of Training, Colleges and Universities (MTCU) provided no-wrong-door access to employment services. Parallel doors for Ontario Works (OW) clients through 47 municipal entry points and 101 First Nations bands; ODSP clients received services from over 150 Ministry of Community and Social Services (MCSS) employability service providers.
	Each CLE provided employer supports through dedicated staff.	Each agency connected with employers as required.
	All federal labour market transfer agreements managed by EQ.	MTCU managed 3 federal-provincial agreements; MCSS managed the LMAPD.
Decentralization	Decision making decentralized to 17 EQ regional offices and 158 local offices.	Policy control centralized at headquarters and in the regions. There were 4 EO regional offices and 43 local MTCU offices. MCSS had 5 regions and 45 offices.
	Local offices had responsibility for SA, employment services, and employer supports.	Different departments for SA and employment services as well as employer liaison.
	17 labour market councils ensured flexibility and social partner/community input. Central reporting.	26 Workforce Planning Boards not integrated with EO network or other local boards. No central reporting.

Outsourcing and contracting out	PES was a mix of government staff and over 350 contracted agencies called "external resources"; NGOs were considered as EQ partners.	Extensive contracting out. PES provided almost exclusively by contracted service providers (170 in EO employment services, 150 in ODSP plus municipalities), supported by government staff.
	Regions chose contractors and managed relationships with support of regional labour market councils. No competitive bidding or rigorous performance contracting.	Capacity assessment process used to decide on contracts, not broad-based RFP. Contracts outcome based with some ODSP contracts paying for success.
	All contracts managed by EQ under same rules.	Different rules for EO, ODSP, and municipal contracts.
Partnerships and networks	Commission des partenaires du marché du travail secured business, labour, and community input. Also managed 1% law, training fund, and other committees. Established in legislation. Met regularly. 17 local labour market councils.	Ontario Training and Adjustment Board closed in 1996. Business, labour, and community input obtained informally and through one-off consultations on defined issues. 26 local Workforce Planning Boards.
	29 sectoral workforce committees, highly integrated with CPMT.	No sector councils.
	National Forum managed relationship between EQ and external resources using defined protocol.	Service Delivery Advisory Group provided ongoing coordination and opportunity for input on EO.
	Eight Quebec networks supported EQ's community agencies.	Two province-wide networks supported community agencies.
	Formal coordination between ASETS holders, EQ, and CPMT.	ASETS holders consulted by EO but no institutionalized connections.

employment services responsibilities were added to social assistance in the form of "workfare" under the Harris Conservatives in 1995, it was municipalities – not the province – that were compelled to add a new employment services business line to their responsibility for social assistance.

All of this was happening quite separately from the employment services run by the provincial postsecondary education department, which was given responsibility for negotiating the transfer of the federal PES programs. By the time that Ontario secured a devolved LMDA in 2005, a strategic decision had been made to *not* incorporate employment services for social assistance recipients in Ontario into the mainstream employment services system. Instead, it was decided to align the incoming federal services to the provincial postsecondary education system.

Given the large number of federal and provincial staff to be incorporated into the Quebec delivery system, establishing a decentralized delivery system through seventeen regional offices and 158 Local Employment Centres was necessary in order to ensure management control over the public servants who directly delivered a large part of Quebec's PES. The decentralized nature of the Quebec system was further reinforced through the later establishment of regional labour market councils for each of the Emploi-Québec's regional offices to relate to. Post-devolution, these councils have influenced the activities to be undertaken and the programs to be offered.

In contrast, Employment Ontario had fewer regions (four) and local offices (forty-three), as most of the Ontario PES was contracted out to 170 Employment Ontario third-party service providers, not delivered by public servants directly. Contracting out, by its very nature, means more centralized control, as the conditions for the exchange of money are delineated in individual contracts. In 2014 Ontario's twenty-six Workforce Planning Boards were not geographically aligned with how Employment Ontario was managed and delivered in four regions and forty-three offices, making their voice advocating for decentralized delivery less effective. But this was only part of the delivery system: by its very nature, delivery of employment services by forty-seven consolidated municipalities under Ontario Works ensured that decisions – at least for OW clients – were in tune with local needs. Decision making on employment services for ODSP clients was much more centralized.

The differences in the degree to which employment services were contracted out was, in large part, a result of the timing of LMDA implementation and the nature of the delivery platform on which it was built. Quebec's LMDA was implemented when the federal government still delivered many employment services directly by public servants, and so these individuals transferred over to the province and continued to provide much of the service. All of the early LMDA jurisdictions – Alberta, New Brunswick, Saskatchewan, and Manitoba – have arrangements similar to those of Quebec, where the front door is managed predominately by public servants, with specialized services provided through third-party contracts generally available by referral.

In contrast, almost all employment programs that were in place predevolution in Ontario – federal, provincial through Job Connect or ODSP, or municipal through social services – were provided through third-party delivery agents. Ontario had no choice but to consolidate the variety of employment services contracts under the single Employment Ontario brand. The only choice was the breadth of the services to be consolidated, and in the initial go-around the services for OW and ODSP clients managed by municipalities and MESS were excluded.

Even though there were differences between the two provinces in the extent of contracting out, it is noteworthy that up until 2014 neither province had implemented vigorous performance contracting through competitive bidding. In both provinces the political ramifications of terminating non-performing service delivery agencies were similar and mostly avoided by politicians if at all possible.

The most significant difference between the two provinces was in partnerships and networks, with Quebec having long-standing institutionalized arrangements and Ontario having almost none. These practices are firmly rooted in the political culture of each province. The Quebec government – under both Liberal and PQ control – used its well-established partnerships with business, labour, and community organizations as a way to secure control of the policy sector from the federal government and build a sense of distinctiveness from the rest of Canada. Business and labour initially came together out of necessity but have stayed together to help build the "Quebec social model," which is closer to the social democratic regimes of European countries than the rest of Canada.

These Quebec partnerships have now been institutionalized in law and continue to be supported by government funding, in an approach that the more business-oriented province of Ontario has avoided. The corporatist OTAB experiment of the early 1990s in Ontario failed badly – not just as a result of political churning as government changed from NDP to Liberal to Conservative to Liberal – but also as a result of the difficulty that business, labour, and equity groups had in overcoming their differences to work together. Even though the local Workforce Planning Boards in Ontario have survived, in 2014 they were not recognized by the community as being the "orchestra conductor," responsible for bringing local actors involved in workforce planning together. Without this role being clearly designated by the provincial government (like the CPMT and Emploi-Québec in their sister province), Ontario's multiple PES systems and the complex relations underpinning each one of them will continue to exist.

How Did PES Performance in the Two Provinces Compare?

By 2014 Quebec had had over seventeen years to put provincial PES arrangements in place post-devolution; in contrast, Ontario had had less than eight. To assess performance of the provincial PES, the annual Employment Insurance Monitoring and Assessment Reports (MAR) were reviewed, and information on Ontario and Quebec results was consolidated. Ontario's LMA annual plans and performance reports were scrutinized, as well as Emploi-Québec's annual reports and evaluation studies, seeking results from federal LMA funding. As Quebec did not differentiate LMA results from total PES results in their Emploi-Québec annual report, the results for under-represented groups in appendix J could be funded through the LMA, Quebec funds, or other federal-provincial agreements like LMAPD or TIOW. As employment services for social assistance clients in Ontario were managed by MCSS, these results are not necessarily included in Ontario's LMA results reported in appendix I.

Additional sources of information on program results in Quebec and Ontario – not available in most other provinces – were OECD reports. Two recent reviews – *Employment and Skills Strategies in Canada* (OECD 2014b) and *Back to Work Canada: Improving the Re-employment Prospects of Displaced Workers* (OECD 2015b) – compared some key elements of PES performance in Ontario and Quebec. Academic and provincial reports examining these two provinces were also helpful.

Demographic and Economic Conditions

Ontario is much larger than Quebec in population (13,678,000 people in 2014 vs 8,214,700 in Quebec) but smaller in size (1,076,395 sq. km vs 1,542,056 sq. km). Quebec's unemployment rate has held relatively steady in the 7–8.5 per cent range over the 1999 to 2014 period, while Ontario's was lower at the start of the period (less than 6 per cent) and rose more sharply (to 9 per cent) as a result of the economic downturn that started in 2009. In 2014 the unemployment rate in the two provinces was about the same, at 7.7 per cent in Quebec vs 7.3 per cent in Ontario. Their employment rates were also similar in the range of 60 per cent; Quebec's improved slightly over the period, while Ontario's slipped somewhat.

Ontario's social assistance caseload at over 566,000 cases in 2014 (a dependency rate of 7.6 per cent in 2012) was higher than Quebec's at around 319,000 (dependency rate of 7.0 per cent in 2012) (Kneebone and White 2014), reflecting its larger population as well as more restricted access by its residents to Employment Insurance benefits. Despite significant differences in population, there were about the same number of people (200,000) dependent on EI benefits in each province in 2014. Those receiving EI benefits in Ontario increased sharply as a result of the recession in 2009, while Quebec's increase was more moderate. In both provinces the number of people receiving EI benefits has dropped steadily every year since 2009. Ontario's EI coverage rate (the proportion of the unemployed who have paid EI premiums) was much lower at 56.6 per cent, compared to Quebec's 70.2 per cent (CEIC 2014). At the height of the recession in 2009, Quebec's EI beneficiaries as a proportion of unemployed workers was calculated at 58.6 per cent compared to Ontario's 41.4 per cent (Jackson and Schetagne 2010). As a result of these EI factors, Ontario's social assistance system has had to support more of the unemployed than Quebec's.

Effectiveness

Despite Ontario's larger population, LMDA funding allocations to the two provinces were relatively similar at between around $550–585 million each, with Quebec's allocation dropping slightly since 1999 and Ontario's increasing slightly as a result of how the LMDA funding formula was applied each year. As noted earlier in this chapter, in the negotiation of the LMDA Ontario felt that it was being short-changed. It is interesting to compare the 2014 federal allocation to Ontario using EI funding with what Informetrica reported the Government of Canada was spending in Ontario in 1993. The 1991/2 Canada-Ontario Agreement allocated $846 million annually, far in excess of the 2013/14 $565 million Ontario allocation. Despite the passage of time, nothing has been done to address this fundamental issue, with no increases to any province since the LMDAs started to be rolled out in 1996. The only exception was a two-year period during the economic downturn (2008–10) when all LMDA allocations were increased. By 2011/12 it was back down to the pre-recession levels.

Every year since taking control of the federal programs, Quebec has spent its funding allocation. In Ontario, when federal officials were in charge of programming, the Ontario budget was underspent by about $100,000 annually. As previously noted, Informetrica identified much larger underspending. Since the province took control in 2007, all funds have been fully spent. For Ontario, this has been the key benefit of devolution: with the programs under its control, there is no slippage in expenditures.

In Quebec the money allocated to long-term employment benefits (like training, wage subsidies, etc.) vs short-term employment assistance declined somewhat from about 64 per cent of expenditures in 2006 to around 60 per cent in 2014. Spending on short-term initiatives increased from about 19 per cent to 24 per cent. In Ontario there was not much difference in spending on short- and long-term measures before and after devolution; about 50–59 per cent of expenditures were for long-term activities and about 40–47 per cent for short-term. Quebec spent more on other support measures (including labour market partnerships and research and innovation) than Ontario did. This has consistently been around 17–18 per cent of all LMDA expenditures, reflecting the value that Quebec placed on such activities. In Ontario the proportion of federal money spent on labour market partnerships and research and innovation remained relatively steady at around 2 per cent under both Ottawa and provincial control.

Since Quebec took control of EI-funded active measures, approximately 200,000 people have been served each year, the vast majority of them in receipt of EI benefits (70–80 per cent). After Ontario took control of programming in 2010, about 160,000 clients were served each year (fewer than in Quebec) using LMDA funding; however, more clients in Ontario were uninsured (47 per cent in 2013/14) – that is, they had no attachment to the EI system.

In Quebec the number of interventions provided through LMDA funding increased steadily each year, and the mix between short-term (e.g., jobs club) and long-term (e.g., training) interventions remained relatively stable with about 20 per cent longer term and 80 per cent short term. The recent trend has been towards more short-term interventions, with 85 per cent of the 284,158 interventions in 2013/14 being short term. The Ontario trend was about the same, with about 83 per cent of the 179,041 interventions in 2013/14 being short term.

On returns to employment using LMDA funds, Quebec has consistently outperformed Ontario. Each year Quebec targeted to return about 55,000 EI recipients to work; sometimes it exceeded the targets (106 per cent) and sometimes it was a bit short (85 per cent). At 25 per cent of the total number of regular EI claimants, these were relatively modest targets. Ontario's targets were more aggressive when the programs were under federal control (35–45 per cent) and were exceeded in 1999/2000 and not achieved in 2005/6. Since the province took control of the programming, the target has been 55,000–60,000 EI claimants returned to employment. While these targets were exceeded in 2008/9–2010/11, in 2011/12 and 2012/13 the success rate was only 59 and 58 per cent. This underperformance on returns to employment was likely a result of the rollout of Employment Ontario and transition issues as the contracts moved from federal to provincial management. There was a similar story in EI unpaid benefits. Every year since 1999/2000 Quebec exceeded its targets, sometimes by a considerable amount. Ontario did not meet its targets in any of the three years between 2010 and 2013.

Quebec has long focused its PES resources on under-represented groups, including social assistance recipients, youth, older workers, disabled people, and immigrants. These groups were served with federal LMA funding, as well as provincial resources. The total number of people served in Quebec rose from 93,880 in 2008/9 to 114,913 in 2013/14. Ontario's LMA report identified that in 2008/9 86,000 clients were served with the federal funding, rising to 196,242 in 2013/14. These numbers were significantly higher than in Quebec. Quebec evaluation reports identified that 57 per cent of clients were employed and 88 per cent were satisfied with the services received. The comparable numbers in Ontario were 91 per cent satisfied and 69 per cent employed. Ontario also reported on infrastructure projects (from 80 to 268) and apprenticeship bonuses (an average of 4,300 per year) put in place with LMA funding over a five-year period.

Ontario also has the separately run OW and ODSP employment services systems. According to an internal MCSS research report, in 2011/12 81 per cent of Ontario Works, or 234,722 adults, participated in employment support services (Ontario, MESS 2013). Internal MCSS reporting using the provincial data system identified that about 22 per cent of clients exited to employment; however, municipal reports from six delivery partners (Toronto, Peel, Hamilton, London, Waterloo, and Ottawa) indicated that this number was much higher. The report also concluded that the earnings of those who exited social assistance for employment was low, with clients finding themselves in low-paying jobs with little stability. Intensive case management, structured job search, and jobs skills training were found to be the most effective interventions.

As an additional measure of PES effectiveness, evidence of provincial research, analysis, and information – beyond reports required by the federal government – was also sought. Quebec has invested in this area through the establishment of the L'Observatoire Compétences-Emplois sur la formation continue et le développement des compétences,[11] in cooperation with the University of Quebec at Montreal. Under the supervision of the CPMT, the Observatory provided intelligence and analysis and served as a place of exchange between researchers, policymakers, and practitioners on employment issues. Its scope and work extended beyond researching the unemployed to also focus on training in the workplace. For example, an area of continuous research was the impact of Quebec's 1 per cent law.[12]

Until 2015 Ontario had not invested in such a research institute; however, in 2016 it launched the Ontario Centre for Workforce Innovation to provide a single coordinated access point for research on evidence-based employment and training approaches. It will operate in partnership with the Ontario Chamber of Commerce, the Workforce Planning Ontario Network, and postsecondary institutions through four provincial hubs.[13] When fully operational, the centre may offer research similar to that done through the Quebec L'Observatoire Compétences-Emplois and the BC Centre for Employment Excellence.

The Ministère du Travail, de l'Emploi et de la Solidarité sociale (MTESS) also invested directly in research, with results publicly available on its website. According to Quebec officials interviewed for this research, Quebec spends money on research, as it will not accept federal

11 See http://www.oce.uqam.ca/.

12 Bélanger and Robitalle's study of work-related learning in Quebec (2008) concluded that Quebec's measures have increased the rate of participation in work-related adult learning and training in Quebec from 21 per cent in 1997 to 33 per cent in 2002, an increase of twelve percentage points.

13 See http://www.ocwi-coie.ca/.

direction in evaluations or research work. Since much of this Quebec research is available only in French, it hampers the efforts of unilingual English researchers in deciphering richer understandings of matters, given their need to translate documents or to hire bilingual research assistants to aid in research.

With funds from the LMDA, Ontario also established an Ontario Human Capital Research and Innovation Fund to support short-term research and projects to improve knowledge in postsecondary education, labour market, and employment and training policy. In 2013/14 twenty-six projects were funded. The province also supports the Mowat Centre – an independent research institute at the University of Toronto – as a non-partisan, evidence-based voice on public policy. In 2010/11 the Mowat Centre invested considerable resources in examining the Employment Insurance program through a dedicated task force.[14] This included an examination of employment programs post-devolution by Bramwell (2012), Noel (2012), and Wood and Klassen (2012).

In 2015 the OECD compared the effectiveness of Quebec's and Ontario's evaluation and monitoring systems to help displaced workers get back to work. In its view, Quebec's MTESS appeared to do a better job of monitoring the effectiveness of the active measures offered than MTCU in Ontario. The OECD noted a lack of evaluation of net impacts of the Ontario programs, given that the quality of job placements was not reported and MTCU did not identify best practices among the EO subcontractors or inefficient practices. It noted that Emploi-Québec was unique among provincial employment services in conducting rigorous evaluations of its services, including those provided by subcontractors. These evaluations demonstrated that EQ had obtained quite positive results for its employment services programming (OECD 2015b, 69–70). Noel (2012) also noted that the evaluation reports done by Quebec assessing the gross and net impacts of the different measures offered by Emploi-Québec went well beyond the scope of other evaluations undertaken in Canada.

As detailed in this chapter, Ontario's twenty-six workforce planning boards must compete for influence with other "workforce intermediaries" established at the municipal level, and were not aligned with the Employment Ontario regional structure and the 170 EO agencies responsible for delivering employment programming. In contrast,

---

14 See http://www.mowateitaskforce.ca/.

Quebec's seventeen CRPMTs or regional labour market councils led in bringing local actors together. They also helped develop the regional plan, suggested target results, and identified how EQ money should be spent in the region.

Comparing the flexibility available to local labour market organizations in Ontario and Quebec, the OECD concluded that Quebec's approach was more effective than Ontario's (OECD 2014b). It noted that the EO agencies in Ontario had very limited flexibility to design strategies outside the terms and conditions of the EO contracts, thus hindering their capacity to respond to local needs. The opposite occurred in Quebec. EQ's regional offices had considerable autonomy in determining how to target employment and training programs to local client groups within a flexible funding pool. They could also design programs to be delivered at the local level, and negotiate and manage outsourced services (OECD 2014b, 68).

Efficiency

Under provincial management (2008/9–2013/14) LMDA expenditures in Ontario averaged $619,426,000 per year, with an average of 160,950 clients served. This worked out to a cost per case of $3,849 over the period in question. The comparable figures for Quebec were average expenditures of $632,000,000 and 202,612 clients served for a cost per case of $3,120. On this measure Quebec was slightly more efficient than Ontario. In neither province was the return on investment high; for LMDA expenditures of $565,471,000 in Ontario in 2013/14 there was $237,600,000 in unpaid EI benefits; the comparable figure for Quebec was $581,242,000 in LMDA expenditures vs $252,400,000 in unpaid EI benefits.

Evidence from two high-profile Ontario reports – the Commission for the Review of Social Assistance in Ontario and the Commission on the Reform of Ontario's Public Services (Ontario, MESS 2012; Ontario, Finance 2012) – have highlighted the inefficiencies involved in having so many provincial players providing employment services (Employment Ontario, Ontario Works, and ODSP). Quebec did not have this same problem, as Emploi-Québec was constructed on a 1981 decision to align social assistance programming with workforce integration, using the district and regional social assistance offices as the platform on which the larger workforce development system was built. As a result, in Quebec in 2014, all workforce development services were managed by a single organization through a well-recognized brand operating across the province.

Since relationships with ASETS holders in Quebec were more structured and formalized than in Ontario, Aboriginal employment services in Quebec were considered as more efficient. The Quebec government provided defined support to ASETS holders working in the province, whereas Ontario considered Aboriginal employment services agencies as outside the provincial system. Coordination in Ontario was more dependent upon local considerations; Quebec's structured relationships ensured similar supports to all ASETS holders across the province.

In 2014 each province had long-standing and active provincial organizations providing networking, conferences, and policy advice to the not-for-profit community organizations delivering employment services in their respective province. Not only did these province-wide organizations support their respective provincial service delivery agents, RQuODE and RCEE (in Quebec) and ONESTEP and First Work (in Ontario) had been leaders for twenty years in pan-Canadian coordination through the Canadian Coalition of Community Based Training (CCCBET). It has been through the efforts of these organizations that career development practitioners working in the provincial PES in both provinces have received most of their training and support. There was no evidence that the quality of career development practitioners providing employment support services in Ontario was any better than in Quebec.

Democracy

While there was information on public websites that described Employment Ontario and the Workforce Planning Boards, there was very little public information available on employment programming results. Ontario LMA reports were posted in a timely fashion on the MTCU and the federal website; however, the only information made publicly available was annual expenditures and the number of clients served each year by program type. Outcome information prescribed in the LMA agreement – clients satisfied, the proportion competed and employed, whether training helped, whether people earned credentials, and their average hourly earnings – was not publicly posted, even though it was collected and provided to the federal government. Concerned over the accuracy of the data, as well as causing confusion among stakeholders, an informant interviewed through this research noted that Ontario decided to do "high-level" reporting only. When Ontario MTCU officials were contacted seeking access to the full data set (outlined in appendix I), the information was readily released.

Ontario's stand on information contrasts sharply with almost all other provinces that reported publicly on *all* the indicators identified in the LMA agreements. Representatives of Ontario community employment organizations interviewed through this research were not even aware of the existence of these Ontario LMA reports, the federal reporting requirements, or that the Ontario reports were significantly less informative when compared to those of other Canadian provinces.

The annual LMA plans from Ontario also neglected to outline the provincial stakeholder engagement strategy, with the exception of 2009/10, where the published report noted collaboration with its third-party delivery network (through the Service Delivery Advisory Group), employers, labour groups, literacy groups, francophone organizations, community agencies, and representatives of those with particular barriers. This lack of information in the LMA report was surprising, given evidence readily available on stakeholder engagement on the Employment Ontario partner's gateway.

The Ministry of Training, Colleges and Universities did not release an annual report on employment services in Ontario that would provide a reader with detailed information on the numbers of clients served and results achieved, even though this would be relatively easy to do, given the computerized information system that all the EO agencies must feed. The MTCU results-based plan on ministry activities was brief (twenty-nine pages) and covered *all* ministry programs. EO was noted on a few pages only, with most of them focused on postsecondary education. The Ministry of Community and Social Services results-based plan report was equally brief with very little mention of employment services.

In contrast, Quebec reporting on the PES is extensive. Every year there is an almost three hundred–page annual report from the Quebec Ministère du Travail, de l'Emploi et de la Solidarité sociale (MTESS) that includes the CPMT annual report (thirty pages) as well as Emploi-Québec's annual report (fifty pages). There was also extensive information on public websites about Emploi-Québec and its partnership arrangements, many of the documents translated into English to enhance understanding. Quebec reporting on its results using funding provided through the LMA agreement was available through an evaluation, available on the MTESS website.

A second indicator to assess democracy was evidence of mechanisms for those affected by government PES services to have input and influence on how the services are designed and delivered. As described in this chapter, Quebec's partnership arrangements in the public employment services were the most sophisticated, complex, and institutionalized in the country, including a provincial board, regional boards, sector councils, and protocols that defined the relationship between service delivery agents and the provincial government. While Ontario's arrangements provided space for non-government participation, they were more executive dominated, ad hoc, and subject to change dependent upon the government in power. In this respect, they were not significantly different from the arrangements in other provinces.

Conclusion

The choices that Ontario and Quebec made on the organization and delivery of the PES since assuming this responsibility from the Government of Canada were very different. Their responses derived from the political culture in each province, the timing of taking on a LMDA agreement, and the characteristics of the provincial department identified to lead the transformation.

Quebec was one of the earliest movers on this file, in 1997, while Ontario was the last province to come to agreement with the federal government on any kind of Labour Market Development Agreement, in 2005. In 2014 Quebec had one-stop shops; decentralized delivery; a mix of public servants and third-party contractors; and extensive and institutionalized ways for business, labour, and community organizations to influence government policy, all contained within the competence of a single ministry dedicated to employment and social solidarity.

In contrast, Ontario had multiple entry points, with PES responsibilities tagged onto the duties of two large provincial departments (postsecondary education and social services) as well as municipal government delivery; both centralized and decentralized management arrangements; significant outsourcing all around; and weakly institutionalized mechanisms for stakeholders to influence government policy.

About the same number of clients were served in each system using federal LMDA and LMA funding; however, Quebec's returns to employment and unpaid EI benefits were better. Assessed on the basis of performance data examined in this chapter, Quebec's public employment service was more effective, efficient, and democratic than Ontario's.

Chapter Seven

The East: New Brunswick, Nova Scotia, Prince Edward Island, and Newfoundland and Labrador

While Atlantic Canada may have been where the Canadian federation was conceived, only one province of four – New Brunswick – agreed to a devolved Labour Market Development Agreement, or LMDA, when it was initially offered in 1996. New Brunswick was the second province to take this on, signing its devolved agreement just over a week after Alberta on 13 December 1996. In fact, the two provinces competed to see who would sign first. Although civil servants in the other Atlantic Canada provinces were aware of the potential benefits of integrating federal resources and responsibilities into provincial programming, their political masters decided in the spring of 1997 to sign "co-managed" or "partnership" arrangements with Ottawa, leaving the Canada Employment Centres in the region to continue with its long-standing direct responsibility for employment programming.

It took a full eleven years and a change in Ottawa from Liberal to Conservative rule in 2006 for the other three Atlantic provinces to sign onto devolved LMDAs, with Nova Scotia doing so in June 2008, followed by Newfoundland and Labrador and Prince Edward Island in September of that same year. At the same time as the devolved LMDAs were being implemented, all Atlantic provinces also took on Labour Market Agreements, or LMAs, that provided additional federal resources to serve non–Employment Insurance (EI) clients. For Nova Scotia, Prince Edward Island, and Newfoundland and Labrador, implementation of these two related but separate agreements did not get underway until late 2009, and by 2014 many of the new governance arrangements had only just started to settle in.

Why was Atlantic Canada – other than New Brunswick – initially uninterested in taking on responsibility for the public employment service, or PES, when most of the other provinces, especially those in the west, were? That is one of the questions that this chapter considers, along with an analysis of how the four Atlantic provinces governed their PES in 2014. I start with a reflection on political culture, considered from both a regional and provincial perspective. This is followed by a brief historical overview of work and welfare in each province, focusing in particular on circumstances in the years prior to the devolution offer. Governance developments post-devolution are assessed according to the framework outlined in chapter 3, followed by a discussion of what accounted for the similarities and differences. The chapter concludes with an assessment of how the different governance arrangements affected the performance of the provincial PES, using data and information from federal and provincial reports.

The Political Context

Geography is a strong predictor of political culture. Atlantic Canada is close to Europe, and most settlers in the late 1700s and early 1800s came from there – with Scotland, Ireland, England, and France providing the most immigrants. Long-standing grievances and traditions – particularly religious beliefs – were transplanted from the old country to their new home in Atlantic Canada. Also populating the region in those early years were United Empire Loyalists, who moved north to Canada from the New England states seeking free land when they decided not to remain American after the War of Independence. Unlike the rest of Canada, this homogeneity has been retained in Atlantic Canada, as there is neither a large Aboriginal nor visible minority population. A key exception is New Brunswick, where its French-speaking Acadian population makes up one third of the province. Two of the provinces – Prince Edward Island and Newfoundland and Labrador – are islands, reinforcing a sense of solidarity, localism, and community. Since Newfoundland joined Canada later (in 1949), its British and Irish ties are even more enduring than in the rest of Atlantic Canada. One respondent interviewed through this research noted, "Newfoundland is on the edge of the world and largely ignored by Ottawa."

Wiseman (2007) points to the region's traditionalism and conservatism as key features. There is resistance to change, with fewer immigrants and many more people living in rural areas than in other Canadian provinces. For example, although 80 per cent of Canadians live in cities, about half of the people in the Maritimes reside on farms or in small communities (Ibbitson 2015). Outsiders are often characterized as "come from away," or CFAs, and "Who's your father?" opens many conversations. Reinforcing this tradition is a stable and long-established two-party political system with tight linkages to their national counterparts. Until 2009 – when the NDP gained power for a single term in Nova Scotia – only the Liberals and Conservatives had ever ruled in the four provinces. As a result of its more closed political system, for many years post-Confederation, political patronage was considered the normal way of doing business.

With the gradual deterioration of the fishing, agriculture, forestry, and mining sectors, unemployment rates in Atlantic Canada have been chronically higher than in the rest of Canada and incomes persistently lower. As identified in the appendices to this book, unemployment rates in Atlantic Canada since the 2008 recession have generally exceeded 10 per cent, compared to around 5–7 per cent in the western provinces. While median total family income in Canada in 2014 averaged $78,870, this ranged from a low of $69,290 in New Brunswick to $100,750 in Alberta (Statistics Canada 2017b). Out-migration exceeds in-migration. Atlantic Canada also has an older population, further straining government resources. In 2007 about a third of all revenues in each province came from Ottawa, compared to the Canadian average of 18 per cent (Bakvis, Baier, and Brown 2009, 52). As a result of these economic challenges, over time a sense of dependence and servitude in relations between the federal government and the four Atlantic provinces has developed.

But another predictor of political culture is politics. The mid-1800s were a prosperous time in most of Atlantic Canada. Many historians have concluded that the three Maritime provinces were cajoled, bribed, and manipulated by British and Canadian politicians to enter Confederation. By exchanging customs revenue for a federal subsidy and by transferring key decision making to central Canada, they got far less than they gave up (Whitcomb 2010c). Many Maritimers had little desire to join the Canadian federation, until debts and railway obligations and promises – along with pressure from the British – made it inevitable. Nova Scotia even tried unsuccessfully to secede in 1882 (Whitcomb 2009). Newfoundland's decision to join Canada in 1949 took two referendums and was highly controversial, with the promise of a welfare state and Ottawa taking on the province's debts and railway responsibilities as the deciding factors. The vote was very close, with the Confederation with Canada choice receiving just 52.3 per cent (Whitcomb 2010b).

Atlantic Canada grievances post-Confederation have included requests for better freight rates, lower tariffs, and higher federal subsidies. These common interests have resulted in a greater willingness to develop institutions to protect their interests and facilitate more regional integration. The most significant institution is the Council of Atlantic Premiers, established in 1971 to take collective and integrated action on matters under provincial responsibility. Its institutional strength is unique in Canada, with a common legislative base, a permanent secretariat with twenty-eight employees, and a history spanning thirty-five years (Dennison 2005, 7–8). Other Atlantic institutions include the Atlantic Provinces Economic Council, the Maritime Board of Trade, and the Atlantic Institute for Market Studies. In 2012 premiers set up an Atlantic Workforce Partnership, with harmonization of the Atlantic apprenticeship system as a key priority. Although the four provinces comprise less than 7 per cent of the Canadian population (2.3 million people in 2014), Atlantic premiers know that by working together they can collectively thwart the wishes of the rest of Canada. They are generally unwilling to give up the limited constitutional power they do possess (Wiseman 2007).

The traditional approach of Atlantic Canada to managing the federation has been to strive for political power at the federal Cabinet table, protect and enhance equalization and other federal transfers, and advocate for regionally designated federal programs (Wiseman 2007). Given the long-standing domination of the Government of Canada in labour market matters, provincial politicians and civil servants have not been averse to manipulating federal programs in their interest, most notably the Employment Insurance (EI) program. Shortly after joining Canada, Newfoundland persuaded Ottawa to extend the EI program to self-employed fishermen, and has from time to time exploited it through the creation of provincial make-work projects that allowed people to cycle between EI, social assistance, and work (Whitcomb 2010a).

All four Atlantic Canada provinces have been regular recipients of federal equalization payments, with only Newfoundland leaving the club in 2008 as the result of offshore oil revenues (Bernard 2012). With a resource-based and seasonal economy, unemployment is far more prevalent and part of the labour market experience, than in other regions of Canada. In recent years some people have taken to commuting to jobs in western Canada, making remittances a new part of the Atlantic Canada experience. In 2012, Newfoundland and Labrador had the highest unionization rate in the region at 38 per cent, down significantly from

45 per cent in 1981. The other Atlantic provinces had lower rates, with Prince Edward Island at 32 per cent, Nova Scotia at 29 per cent, and New Brunswick at 28 per cent in 2012 (Galarneau and Sohn 2013).

Citizens in the region rely more on the EI program than do other Canadians, with 26.7 per cent of people who worked in 2010 collecting EI benefits. EI benefit payments comprised 4.3 per cent of total income in the Atlantic region, more than double the 1.8 per cent for Canada (Council of Atlantic Premiers Employment Insurance Advisory Council 2014). With the federal government controlling this program, EI issues (and related active measures) are never far from Atlantic Canada political concerns.

Historical Developments around Activation

New Brunswick

New Brunswick's quiet revolution under Liberal Premier Robichaud from 1960 to 1970 modernized and centralized the provincial state apparatus. Control of social assistance was moved from municipalities to the province in 1967 in order to ensure a province-wide, uniform approach (Thériault and LeBreton 2015). However, the program remained largely passive with a primary focus on benefits.

Activation of social assistance recipients through mutual obligation started in the late 1980s, shortly after Frank McKenna became premier. He was determined to create a more adaptable and skilled provincial workforce and reduce social assistance dependency. A Cabinet committee on human resources was established, as well as a dedicated Human Resources Ministry. As Ottawa dominated the labour market policy field financially and constitutionally, next came a direction to cultivate new federal partnerships. The first and foremost joint program established was NB Works in 1992, providing an intensive and expensive program of training and skills upgrading for social assistance recipients. This was followed in 1994 by the NB Jobs Corps for older workers. New Brunswick also participated in the Self-Sufficiency Project, a demonstration project that provided a generous, time-limited earnings supplement to single parents who had been on welfare and subsequently found full-time work (Haddow 1997b).

Much of the cost of these initiatives was born by the Government of Canada through the pan-Canadian "four-cornered agreements" detailed in chapter 2. Despite its smaller population, New Brunswick received more money for its labour market initiatives than its neighbour Nova Scotia. Haddow (1997a) noted that in 1993/4 the province received $80 million in funds from Ottawa, whereas Nova Scotia received only $67 million. In his view New Brunswick's favoured position came about, in part, as the result of good relations between the federal and provincial training bureaucracies, as well as the presence of Bernard Valcourt, a New Brunswicker who served as employment minister in the Mulroney Progressive Conservative government.

Premier McKenna wanted to ensure that the province – not Ottawa – controlled the labour market agenda in New Brunswick. In early 1989 Ottawa announced a new national Labour Force Development Strategy, involving the establishment of labour force development boards. These corporatist boards were meant to bring business, unions, and equity organizations into decision making on a pan-Canadian, provincial, and local basis. While New Brunswick was prepared to set up a provincial board, it wanted to ensure that it maintained control. In 1990 the province created a Human Resources Council that was later transformed into the New Brunswick Labour Force Development Board. Costs were shared with Ottawa, and provincial staff were seconded to manage the joint federal-provincial initiative (Haddow 1997b).

This investment in provincial capacity-building paid off when the federal offer to devolve programming came in 1995. Building on its long-standing federal-provincial collaboration, New Brunswick was keen to take on a devolved LMDA, as it saw this as an important tool in the province's economic development, and as a way to ensure a consistent approach to labour market programming across the province (Bakvis and Aucoin 2000). The full devolution agreement involved a transfer of 124 staff and $66.4 million in funding (Haddow and Klassen 2006) and was implemented in the spring of 1997. The process was characterized by one what New Brunswick respondent interviewed through this research described as "devolution and then revolution" as the provincial government came to grips with its new responsibilities as well as the opportunities presented (Wood 2010).

Nova Scotia

In contrast to New Brunswick, Nova Scotia demonstrated little interest in setting up a provincial board under the federal Labour Force Development Strategy in 1989, nor was it interested in taking on responsibility for active measures for EI clients through the LMDA offer in 1995.

During the 1980s and 1990s no fewer than seven government reports had proposed substantial reforms to active labour market policy in the province, yet little action materialized. Haddow (2000b) noted a lack of focus as mandates and responsibility became divided and shifted among provincial departments. A lot of this was a result of political churning, with the Liberals in charge from 1993 to 1999 and the Conservatives from 1999 to 2009.

Adding to the fragmentation was the fact that, until 2001, Nova Scotia had a two-tiered welfare system, with municipalities responsible for employable clients, and the province running the family benefits program (for single mothers and the disabled). While some federally funded activation initiatives were undertaken by municipalities in the 1990s, participation for most social assistance recipients was considered as voluntary (Lord 2015). But the most significant barrier to a consolidated focus on active measures was limited provincial resources to cost-share with Ottawa. With federal policies and money dominating the field, it was very difficult for the province to challenge federal authority, even when its action had direct impact on the provincial community college system (Haddow, Schneider, and Klassen 2006).

The Nova Scotia government was therefore a reluctant player in the federal labour market game. It had limited interest in setting up an Ottawa-driven initiative, the Nova Scotia Labour Force Development Board, in the early 1990s. Not only was it suspicious about the ability of non-government actors to make a constructive contribution to training policy beyond general advice, it was also concerned that the board would reinforce federal dominance over the province's training system. Federal appointments to the provincial board were made without sensitivity to provincial traditions of selecting people considered "government friendly." The province was unwilling to contribute financially and, in the end, the provincial board folded, once the federal funding dried up (Haddow 1997b).

This was the intergovernmental environment in which the 1996 federal offer to devolve federal labour market programming landed. Within the province, management of labour market policy was highly centralized and there was no regional delivery system. At the same time that the LMDA offer was unveiled (funded from contributions to the Employment Insurance account), Ottawa was curtailing its own spending on training for designated groups such as women and persons with disabilities, funded out of the Consolidated Revenue account. Haddow

(1997b, 101) quotes a Nova Scotia official saying, "The devolution of authority is fine, except for the fact that prior to the devolution the federal government is taking somewhere between two and 2.7 billion dollars out of the system."

Given these circumstances, Nova Scotia officials and politicians were quite happy to keep Ottawa as the prime player in active measures in order to avoid blame for problems like high unemployment, lack of jobs, de-skilling, etc. Nova Scotia opted for neither a "devolved" or "co-managed" arrangement, but rather for what was called a "strategic partnership." Effectively Ottawa continued to manage its expenditures as before, with limited oversight by the province. The only requirement of the agreement was that a joint management committee examine areas where cooperation and collaboration might be enhanced (Klassen 2000a, 177).

However, the LMDA strategic partnership provided a new way for the province to influence federal spending in Nova Scotia, especially on active measures for social assistance recipients. A coordinated federal-provincial response to the EI cutbacks in the late 1990s – put in place as a result of the partnership arrangement – built up provincial capacity in the sector. With all social assistance programming consolidated from municipal to provincial control in 2001, the Social Development department started to invest in specialized workers to undertake employability assessments and career planning. It often used federally funded employment service providers to deliver on the provincial plan. On the federal side, in the mid-2000s Ottawa increased the contracting-out of its employment services to third-party organizations. As a result, federal civil servants became contract managers and stopped being service providers. The federally funded community-based service delivery organizations often also got bits of provincial funding.

The Harper Conservative government decision to devolve the federal employment programming in 2007 came as a surprise to Nova Scotia officials; unlike other provinces, it did not seek it out. Federal officials administering employment programs in the province also felt that they had been blindsided. Nova Scotia agreed to take on a devolved LMDA only as the offer was coupled with additional funding through the LMAs to serve non-EI clients whom the province perceived as needing services the most. Devolution in Nova Scotia involved the transfer of $113 million in federal funding, 125 civil servants, and sixty-five service contracts to the province.

Prince Edward Island

With a population in 2014 of 146,300, Prince Edward Island (PEI) is the smallest and most densely populated of Canada's provinces. Travel anywhere by car is easy; after the opening of the Confederation Bridge in 1997 the province became much more connected with the mainland. Social assistance in the province was consolidated under provincial control in 1972; in some cases this involved moving responsibility from churches and religious organizations.

PEI took advantage of federal funding experiments through the "four-cornered approach" in the early 1990s to "activate" its welfare programs, and initiatives called Job Creation and Employment Enhancement were implemented. These were deliberate provincial efforts to divert social assistance recipients to the Employment Insurance program (Flanagan 2015), using specialized staff to manage the provincial employment programming. While Ottawa encouraged PEI to set up a provincial labour force development board in the early 1990s, the business community balked, unwilling to accept equal representation from unions.

The 1996 LMDA offer came just as governments in PEI were changing from Liberal to Conservative. While the Liberals were interested in taking on the federal staff and programming, the Conservatives decided that the safest route was to enter into a co-managed LMDA. This also ensured a continuing presence of federal civil servants who understood PEI labour market conditions. Under the co-management model there was no transfer of resources, but joint federal-provincial management of program design and implementation was put in place.

In the 2000s the federal government was the dominant actor in labour market programming on the island. In 2003 it outsourced the employment services front door; the successful contractor was a for-profit organization called Career Development Services, expected to offer similar services in six locations across the province. Separate agreements for specialized target groups (e.g., women, youth, Aboriginal people, and disabled persons) were retained. The Service Canada regional office initiated these contracts and generally left it to the agencies themselves to decide on the interventions needed. Service Canada officials also took the initiative to set up provincial sector councils.

The province learned a lot over the ten-year LMDA co-management period. When the second offer to devolve came in 2007, PEI was ready and eager to take on the federal responsibilities, involving a transfer of twelve to thirteen contracts, forty federal staff, and $27 million in federal funding. The LMA money offered at the same time made the LMDA transfer possible, given that its restrictive provisions meant that few unemployed could get the services they needed. Through LMA funding the province was able to serve youth and persons with disabilities, key target groups under the provincial skills strategy.

Newfoundland and Labrador

More than in any other Atlantic province, employment in Newfoundland and Labrador was historically tied to one economic activity – fishing – carried out mostly in isolated outport communities. Cut off from mainland wealth and with a common cultural heritage, after Newfoundland entered Confederation in 1949, Employment Insurance (EI) came to play a major role, providing financial support as people could work for about ten weeks and then receive relatively generous EI benefits for the rest of the year. Provincial social assistance also became part of the mix in sustaining people throughout the year, moving from an in-kind to a cash program under provincial management in 1977. Like other provinces, various social assistance make-work projects started in the 1980s and 1990s, funded by the Government of Canada. The low and specialized skill requirements for fishing-related jobs and easy access to government benefits kept many Newfoundlanders from changing their occupation, one of the reasons so many became unemployed by the Atlantic cod moratorium in 1992 (Lysenko 2012).

Between 1990 and 1998 Ottawa implemented a number of adjustment programs to deal with the collapse of the fishery. The 1992 federal attempt to establish a provincial labour force development board was largely unsuccessful, as the result of conflict on business and union representation. This Ottawa-driven board was ultimately suspended in 1995 when the federal funding dried up. However, the province took the initiative in the mid-1990s to develop a Strategic Social Plan, holding extensive consultations across the province. While initially the province was inclined towards a devolution-type agreement, with a change in premier from Brian Tobin to Clyde Wells in 1996, the new premier saw distinct advantages in maintaining a strong federal presence (Bakvis and Aucoin 2000). Not only did he not want to lose the advice and influence of federal officials based in Newfoundland, the province lacked the capacity and expertise to take on the federal responsibilities. Mistrust of Ottawa and – like in Nova Scotia, a fear of downloading and having to take up the slack for federal cutbacks – resulted in the selection of a co-managed LMDA model, giving the province a significant say in federal program design and delivery.

The Strategic Social Plan led in the late 1990s to the development of a stand-alone provincial Human Resources and Employment Ministry that integrated social assistance and labour market programming, as well as new services for youth and the disabled. Welfare benefit staff were realigned to take on duties as career development specialists, and provincial capacity in employment programming grew. The formal commitments in the co-managed LMDA led to considerable strengthening of the federal–provincial relationship and improved coordination of programming for EI-eligible, reach-back, and social assistance clients, using mostly federal LMDA funding. When the Atlantic Groundfish Strategy ended in 1998, Ottawa provided funding to local organizations to run employment assistance offices across the province. Provincial funding also expanded in this period – the Community Youth Network was established in 2000 through the National Child Benefit Reinvestment Fund. Federal-provincial coordination also reached down to the regional level through the establishment of four regional committees.

By early 2000 business and labour had also decided that something needed to be done differently, given the economic problems that the province was experiencing, and came to the provincial government with a proposal on how they could work together. Influenced to a significant degree by the Irish model of social dialogue, the Strategic Partnership Initiative, or SPI, was formally structured in 2002. Supported through a provincial Order in Council, a small permanent secretariat, and government funding to help business and labour organize themselves, the Labour Market Subcommittee of the SPI provided a way to plan and coordinate labour market programming across the province. The committee was chaired by the provincial deputy minister, with senior representation from business, labour, and the federal government.

SPI provided the political and infrastructure support to make the LMDA co-management model a success. Prior to this point, there had been limited formal federal-provincial interaction on labour market issues. During the ten-year co-management period both the federal and provincial governments transformed their respective delivery systems. The federal government moved to third-party contracts for its employment services. The province moved to a decentralized model and transformed its social assistance sites into employment services offices. However, it did not make participation in active measures mandatory.

With the discovery of offshore oil, the provincial economy boomed; in 2008 Newfoundland and Labrador stopped receiving federal equalization payments. It also started to invest in research, analysis, and labour market information. When the second devolution offer came in 2007, Newfoundland and Labrador was much better positioned to take on the federal responsibilities than in 1996 and was keen to have greater influence over employment programming for EI clients. When the devolved LMDA was implemented in 2009, Newfoundland and Labrador took on seventy federal contracts, seventy-five staff, and $132 million in federal funding.

Post–LMDA Governance Reforms

Single Gateways or One-Stop Shops

In New Brunswick LMDA responsibilities and federal staff were initially assigned in 1997 to the social development department, with Employment Insurance and social assistance clients served by the same infrastructure through seamless service delivery. When the provincial Liberals were defeated in 1999, the Conservatives dismantled the McKenna integration of work and welfare, moving responsibility for all labour market programs away from the social development department. Through adjustments and realignments, the programs were eventually absorbed within the Post-Secondary Education, Training and Labour department, or PETL.

PETL's scope includes labour and postsecondary education, but does not include industry liaison or social assistance. In 2014 the provincial PES was offered primarily through about two hundred provincial government staff working in seven regional offices and nineteen provincial Career Information Centres across the province. Support services for employers were provided through a network of fifteen Enterprise Agencies, whose staff included labour market development officer positions. There were defined links with PETL regions. Social assistance was managed by the Ministry of Social Development. Participation in employment services for social assistance recipients in New Brunswick is voluntary. A defined interdepartmental partnership called Transition to Work ensured that those with work potential were case-managed by Social Development staff, and then sent to PETL for employment support. To facilitate this process some Social Development staff transferred to PETL in 2000.

These programming arrangements in New Brunswick have been stable since 1999. Total federal funding for employment programming in New Brunswick through the LMDA and LMA was $100,599,000 in 2013/14, all managed by PETL. It also managed the Labour Market Agreement for Persons with Disabilities and the Targeted Initiative for Older Workers. The province used its existing infrastructure to expand programming and serve more people when the LMA money became available in 2008.

As Nova Scotia had not sought a devolved LMDA, it did not have a pre-existing provincial organization that could easily accept the federal contracts and staff. The NDP decided in 2008 to create a new department (called Labour and Advanced Education, or LAE), integrating skills and adult learning from the Department of Education, provincial labour programming, and the federal programs. Industry liaison was not assigned to LAE but to the economic development department. Moving responsibility for employment services for social assistance recipients into the new department was considered, but not carried out. As a result, specialized employment staff within the Community Development department continued to provide these supports; however, enforcing work obligations for social assistance recipients was not a pressing provincial priority.

By 2014 considerable work had been undertaken by Nova Scotia officials to plan how they might streamline and rationalize the delivery model inherited from the federal government, as well as do a better job of integrating social assistance and employment programming offered by two separate provincial departments. However, actually making changes was stymied by a lack of political will. Employment Nova Scotia (ENS) – with four regional and thirteen local offices and about one hundred provincial government staff – has been built to manage the service delivery system as well as authorize individual programming. The province inherited sixty-five federal employment services contracts. These were brought over "as is," and by 2014 very little had been done to change them, other than collecting the contractors under the Careers Nova Scotia banner. In 2014 there were sixty-eight Careers Nova Scotia Centres (CNSC) operating across the province, all under contract. Each related to a defined ENS office. CNSC contractors maintained their own branding and were a mixture of generic and targeted services.

Implementing the LMA starting in 2008 at the same time as the province took on LMDA programming was challenging in Nova Scotia, given that the province was building an administrative infrastructure at the same time as expanding the programming on offer. An interdepartmental committee was created to allocate the LMA funding, and money was ultimately awarded to almost three hundred organizations, especially literacy groups where there was a long-standing unmet need. Total federal funding for LMA and LMDA programming in Nova Scotia in 2013/14 was $92,613,000, managed by Labour and Advanced Education, also responsible for the Targeted Initiative for Older Worker funding. In 2014 the Labour Market Agreement for Persons with Disabilities was managed by the Community Services department.

Like Nova Scotia, Prince Edward Island also changed its internal departmental structure in 2008 in order to take on the federal labour market programming. Officials first thought about creating a Crown corporation but could not see how they could take on unionized federal civil servants in such an environment. A new alignment was therefore formed among the existing provincial apprenticeship, student loans, literacy, and workplace-based training programs, which were then consolidated with the federal programming. This stand-alone department – with its own legislation – brought together all provincial programs to get islanders back to work. In 2014 SkillsPEI – a division of the Department of Innovation and Advanced Learning – had offices in six locations across the province. Internal protocols defined linkages and referral practices for social assistance recipients who were served by the Community Services department. Those who were expected to work – identified at the social worker's discretion – accessed the SkillsPEI programming. SkillsPEI also offered island businesses assistance to train their employees to increase their skills. Total federal allocations in PEI in 2013/14 for LMDA and LMA programming was $28,178,000.

In 2014 PEI used a combination of government employees and contracted services to deliver the provincial PES. While many of the existing federal contracts were maintained, their budgets were streamlined and a focus on work was emphasized. The generic employment assessment and case management services inherited from the federal government was put out for bidding, but the same contractor, Career Development Services, has continued to offer the service. PEI also had ten employment services agencies that provided specialized services to persons with disabilities, Aboriginal persons, etc. The LMA money that started to flow in 2008 was dispersed using this provincial infrastructure. In PEI federal funding under the Targeted Initiative for Older Workers was managed by SkillsPEI, while the Labour Market Agreement for

Persons with Disabilities was managed by the Community Services department.

As already noted in this chapter, Newfoundland and Labrador spent its time during the 1996–2007 LMDA co-management period developing a provincial infrastructure in order to be ready to take on the federal employment programming. By the time a devolved LMDA was offered in 2007, the Newfoundland Department of Advanced Education and Skills (the successor to the Human Resources department) already had a broad mandate that included employment services, social assistance, postsecondary education, apprenticeship, poverty reduction, immigration, youth engagement, and disability programming. Social assistance recipients were not required to undertake job searches or participate in the active measures.

In 2014 approximately six hundred government staff managed the Newfoundland PES through twenty-seven Advanced Education and Skills Employment Centres that provided services to job seekers and employers, as well as access to income support benefits. There were also specialized contracts (inherited from the Government of Canada) to support designated groups such as disabled persons. Since 2000 the province has also operated a Community Youth Network, with thirty centres across the province. Its goal is to help youth overcome educational and employment barriers. Advanced Education and Skills also managed the federal TIOW and LMAPD funding.

Total federal funding for employment services under the LMDA and LMA in Newfoundland and Labrador in 2013/14 was $136,568,000. Under the LMA under-represented groups got more money, and programming was expanded, including longer-term training not previously available. LMA implementation was relatively smooth, using the provincial infrastructure already in place.

Decentralization

In 2014 New Brunswick's programs and services were centrally developed with considerable input from regional delivery staff who had ample opportunity to influence the provincial programming selected. Respondents in New Brunswick noted the importance in such a small province of having a standard suite of employment programs, to ensure that there was no political favouritism that diverted more services to some areas than others (Wood 2010). The Employment Development Division was relatively small, and connections between central, regional, and local office staff occurred regularly. Regional directors in New Brunswick had the authority to let contracts, select contractors, and assign funding to partnerships in cooperation with their respective Enterprise Agency, all within the context of a province-wide delivery model. As a result of this governance model, the New Brunswick PES in 2014 was relatively decentralized.

Employment Nova Scotia was managed through four regional offices that reported to a single director in Halifax, with their respective Careers Nova Scotia contractors and Employment Nova Scotia offices reporting through this newly developed administrative structure. Nova Scotia has a history of centralized management. Post-devolution, the province implemented a common case management system with a defined set of business processes and accountability requirements to track and account for federal and provincial labour market programming. Community Development ran the social assistance program (including active measures) through a separate business line; the two departments came together in Halifax, not at the regional level. As a result of all of these factors, the management of Nova Scotia's PES in 2014 was relatively centralized.

Similarly, SkillsPEI directed the provincial system out of its Charlottetown office; since the province is so small, centralization or decentralization is not as important a factor as in other provinces where the distance between the capital and the regions is much greater.

In 2014, Newfoundland and Labrador PES services were organized into four regional offices. In an analysis of active measures in the province in 2012, Lysenko concluded that – despite the presence of regional and local offices across the province – decision making in the provincial PES was relatively centralized, noting that local actors had limited authority to approve funding and that every application had to be approved on a regional or provincial level. In Lysenko's view, this lack of flexibility at the local level – coupled with easy access to EI and no requirement for social assistance recipients to participate in active measures – undermined the effectiveness of the province's PES system and its ability to address the needs of local employers.

Outsourcing and Contracting Out

While all Atlantic provinces had both government employees and third-party contractors involved in PES delivery, in 2014 two provinces (Nova Scotia and Prince Edward Island) contracted out almost all front door services, while in the other two (New Brunswick and Newfoundland and Labrador) most services to the public were provided by provincial civil servants. These different models reflect the timing of devolution and provincial preparedness to take on the federal responsibilities.

When New Brunswick took on its devolved LMDA in 1997, most of the employment services were provided directly by federal government staff, and there was limited outsourcing or contracting out. PETL built on this structure, and in 2014 provincial government employees provided employment counselling (case planning, return to work places) as well as career counselling services. Targeted (e.g., youth, disabled) and specialized (e.g., résumé writing, work search groups) services were generally outsourced, as well as activities needed quickly or where the necessary expertise was not available in-house.

Eighty per cent of employment services in New Brunswick were provided directly by departmental staff, with the balance outsourced, primarily to not-for-profit service providers. Given its long-standing involvement in the sector and provincial expertise, New Brunswick invested in training career development practitioners and managers who worked in the sector, using courses developed by the Canadian Career Development Foundation (CCDF). For many years post-devolution PETL's third-party contracts were renewed regularly; in 2013/14 a centrally developed RFP process with open bidding was implemented. While there were defined deliverables, the contracts were not performance based. Open bidding has expanded the process and made it more transparent. Government respondents interviewed for this research did not think that this new RFP process made much difference to the contractors selected. A long-standing contractor disagreed, noting that the competitive dynamic and increased performance monitoring through the RFP process had been difficult to manage.

Newfoundland and Labrador's PES was also run primarily by provincial civil servants. At the time of devolution, responsibility for seventy federal contracts transferred to the province, as well as federal contract management staff. About half of the contracts were for generic employment assistance services (EAS) and half for specialized services (e.g., self-employment, disability, and women's programming). For three years the province continued to manage the federal contracts with no changes; then in March 2013 it announced that it was shutting down forty EAS contracts and taking the services in-house, affecting 226 employees.

Employment Minister Shea noted at the time that the EAS contracts were a duplication of what the province was already providing, and that by shutting them down the province was "levelling the playing field and setting up a one-stop shop" (Robinson 2013). When faced with the need to rationalize and increase accountability for the contracted services that it had inherited, provincial politicians decided that that it was easier to shut all the EAS contracts down than be selective. In 2014 the remaining specialized contracts were managed in the regions, were not performance based, and were regularly renewed. Like New Brunswick, Newfoundland and Labrador had invested in training its career development staff, but in this case training was available only to provincial government staff, not external contractors.

Almost all employment services on offer to individuals in Nova Scotia and PEI in 2014 were provided by third-party contractors, most of them inherited from the federal government and rolled over to provincial management and control. Unlike British Columbia, there was no large procurement process undertaken province-wide to rationalize and streamline the basket of provincial and federal contracts in place pre-devolution. There was no "prime contractor" and "subcontractor" model developed to define services by geographic region, identify different roles, and specify payment for performance.

PEI held a consultation post-LMDA and adjusted the federal EAS service to meet provincial needs and ensure a similar front door across the province. By 2014 protocols had not been developed to link this single EAS contractor with the specialized service delivery organizations. From time to time the province organized training, development, and information sessions for all of their third-party contractors; however, according to a respondent interviewed for this research, these sessions have diminished under SkillsPEI, compared to when Service Canada was in charge. All service delivery contractors were expected to have qualified staff, and there were minimum requirements in the contracts. All were members of the PEI Career Development Association.

While Nova Scotia invested heavily in altering the conditions of the federal contracts, it did not change the contractors or the services to be delivered by putting out requests for proposals. In 2014 there were two contracts for each service provider: one for generic management services and another for specific interventions. These were not performance based. Nova Scotia adapted national standards for career development practitioners and embedded professional association membership fees as well as professional staff development costs in the contracts. While the province supported a career development practitioner certification project with the Nova Scotia Career Development Association, training was done by the association, not the province.

Partnerships and Networks

WITH BUSINESS AND LABOUR

Sector councils bring together business, labour, government, and education stakeholders to share ideas, concerns, and perspectives about human resources and skills, and to find solutions on a sector basis. In 2014 PEI had active sector councils in seven sectors as well as two associations. The sectors included agriculture, trucking, residential construction, health care, and culture. Many of these councils had been set up with federal funding by Service Canada officials. In March 2012 SkillsPEI announced that they were withdrawing core funding and that sector councils would have to apply for money on a project-by-project basis. Nova Scotia had nine sector councils, as well as an overarching association; in 2014 these continued to receive funding support from the province. New Brunswick and Newfoundland and Labrador did not have sector councils, although they had self-organized and self-funded industry associations. The Community Sector Council in Newfoundland and Labrador was particularly strong, established in 1976 as an independent non-profit organization to encourage citizen engagement, to promote the integration of social and economic development, and to provide leadership in shaping public policies.

As outlined earlier in this chapter, all Atlantic Canada federally initiated labour force development boards closed in the late 1990s. Post-devolution, Nova Scotia and PEI did not set up institutional structures to provide an ongoing structured mechanism to receive input from business, unions, government, and the community sector on labour market issues. Instead, input was received on an ad hoc basis. As outlined in its LMA annual plans, PEI held defined stakeholder sessions in early 2011. In 2012 it set up joint tables related to the Acadian and francophone community and postsecondary education students. Nova Scotia undertook an extensive consultation exercise in March 2009, and subsequently established "Employability Tables" charged with developing services for Acadians, African Nova Scotians, Aboriginal Nova Scotians, and persons with disabilities. None of these processes were established in legislation.

In contrast to this more informal and ad hoc approach, post-devolution Newfoundland and Labrador and New Brunswick have set up ongoing, institutionalized, provincially led partnerships that bring people from key organizations together from across the province to work on labour market issues. Newfoundland and Labrador was the first mover in this regard, with the Community Sector Council leading in the mid-1990s to develop a Strategic Social Plan. Not only did this evolve into the Strategic Partnership Initiative (SPI) noted earlier, it also led to the development of a provincial poverty reduction strategy, as well as detailed "community accounts" that report on well-being indicators. The Labour Market Committee of the SPI – a tripartite forum involving business, labour and government – played a significant role after 2002 in identifying and responding to the province's human resource requirements and labour market challenges.

While the community accounts and provincial poverty strategy continued, after nine years in operation the SPI and the Labour Market Committee were "put on pause" in 2014. Secretariat staff were laid off, and responsibility was moved into the Office of Public Engagement. Changes in key players – in the Premier's Office, as well as business and labour representatives – were responsible for the demise of the SPI. Many respondents interviewed through this research found this action to be unfortunate; one noted that while bilateral conversations may be useful, "You get a different sweet spot when all three actors [government, business, and labour] are in the same room together at the same time."

New Brunswick has also engaged extensively in partnerships. Each of PETL's seven regional offices has a committee made up of the business community, educational sector, employer groups, and municipalities that meets at least twice a year to set labour market priorities in response to stakeholder needs. There was also an overarching provincial process that touched on labour market issues. Concerned over the lack of economic integration of low-income people in the province, in 2008 the provincial government passed legislation to create an Economic and Social Inclusion Corporation to develop, oversee, coordinate, and implement initiatives to reduce poverty and help people living in poverty become more self-sufficient.

Access to employment is a key concern of the corporation. In 2014 it had a very broad engagement process, with a twenty-two-member board of directors representing government, business, community non-profit organizations, and persons having experienced poverty. Despite a change in government from Liberal to Conservative and now back to Liberal, momentum had been maintained as the advisory structure was deliberately non-partisan and high level, including the premier.

The latest five-year poverty plan was released in 2014 and New Brunswick's social partnership is now deeply entrenched.

WITH COMMUNITY ASSOCIATIONS INVOLVED WITH EMPLOYMENT PROGRAMMING

Like the other provinces, in 2014 each Atlantic Canada province had an association that supported professional training and certification for career development practitioners, whether they were government employees, worked for a PES contractor, or were an educational institution.[1] Many of the PES contractors also participated in relevant networks within their province; for example, in 2014 Nova Scotia and New Brunswick each had provincial literacy networks, and Newfoundland and Labrador and New Brunswick each had provincial disability networks. Sometimes provincial governments provided financial support for building these provincial networks. Post-devolution, the sixty-eight Career Resources Centre managers in Nova Scotia self-organized and arranged to meet twice a year with each other and the provincial government; however, unlike in British Columbia and Quebec, there was no defined governance relationship with the province to hear their views. The PEI contractors did not meet collectively at all.

WITH THE GOVERNMENT OF CANADA

Officials in all Atlantic provinces engaged bilaterally with their federal counterparts through LMDA/LMA management committees that provided a forum to meet regularly, usually on a quarterly basis. Respondents interviewed through this research noted that productive federal-provincial connections were important in order to coordinate the provincially run PES with labour market programming that was still managed directly by the Government of Canada (e.g., for Aboriginal people and youth). However, some respondents noted that this engagement had become increasingly difficult as Service Canada officials moved out of province and federal offices disengaged with provincial sites. For example, the last of the New Brunswick co-management sites were shut down at Ottawa's initiative in 2010. In 2014

---

1 See http://www.nbcdag-gadcnb.ca/; http://www2.nscda.ca/; http://contactpoint.ca/listing/prince-edward-island-career-development-association/; and http://ccepp.ca/news/newfoundland-labrador-association-career-practitioners.

most intergovernmental relations were coordinated with federal officials working out of Ottawa, not with people working in the province.

WITH ABORIGINAL LABOUR MARKET ORGANIZATIONS

Newfoundland and Labrador's Aboriginal population is the largest in Atlantic Canada at 4.7 per cent, compared to 1.3 per cent in Prince Edward Island, 2.7 per cent in Nova Scotia, and 2.5 per cent in New Brunswick. In 2014 Nova Scotia had two Aboriginal Skills and Employment Strategy (ASETS) holders, PEI had one, New Brunswick had four, and Newfoundland and Labrador had seven. All of Newfoundland's ASETS holders were in rural and remote communities, whereas ASETS holders in the other three provinces served the main centres as well as rural areas of the province.

In New Brunswick, a special Aboriginal Employment Strategy Initiative committee was established to bring the four ASETS holders together on a quarterly basis with the province and key federal departments. The tripartite relationship was described by an Aboriginal informant as well managed, consistent, and effective. In PEI in December 2007, the three governments came together to sign a historic Canada/PEI/Mi'kmaq Partnership Agreement to restore, revitalize, and strengthen the relationship. Employment program coordination took place through this broader structure. Since the single ASETS holder in PEI also received provincial PES funding, it was included when the province held training, development, and information sessions for all of its third-party contractors.

Nova Scotia managed its relationship with ASETS holders through a standing item on the federal-provincial Labour Market Management Committee agenda; there were no separate and dedicated undertakings that also involved the ASETS holders, as in New Brunswick. ASETS holders in Nova Scotia also received provincial funding and were considered like any other third-party contractor in the province. In Newfoundland and Labrador, Service Canada officials tried to bring the seven ASETS holders together annually to share ideas and develop partnerships. Each related separately to its respective provincial Advanced Education and Skills office; there was no broader pan-provincial coordination.

Comparing Atlantic Provinces

Table D summarizes approaches to governance of the PES in the four Atlantic provinces, using the themes identified in chapter 3 of this book.

Table D. Comparing Governance Features in the PES in Atlantic Canada, 2014

	New Brunswick	Nova Scotia	Prince Edward Island	Newfoundland and Labrador
Single gateways or one-stop shops	19 Career Information Centres provided single-door access to similar employment assistance services (EAS).	68 Careers Nova Scotia Centres under Employment Nova Scotia (ENS) provided different EAS services.	6 Career Development Services offices under SkillsPEI provided common front-door access to EAS.	27 Employment Skills Centres provided single-door access to employment services, SA, and employer supports.
	Employer supports through 15 Enterprise Agencies; social assistance (SA) through Social Development.	Employer supports through economic development. SA through Community Development.	SkillsPEI offices provided employer liaison. Separate SA offices for income support only.	30 Community Youth Network Centres supplemented provincial programming.
	All federal funding managed through same provincial department.	LMDA/LMA/TIOW managed by same department. LMAPD by another.	LMDA/LMA/TIOW managed by same department. LMAPD by another.	All federal funding managed through same provincial department.
Decentralization	Decision making decentralized to 7 regional directors.	Policy control centralized through 4 ENS regional offices.	Policy control centralized through 6 SkillsPEI offices.	Policy control centralized at regional and provincial level.
	Separate business lines for employer liaison and SA.	Separate business lines for employer liaison and SA.	Separate business line for SA decision making.	All 3 business lines came together at local and regional level.

Outsourcing and contracting out	Limited outsourcing. PES was mostly government staff supported by specialized contracts.	Extensive outsourcing. PES provided almost exclusively by contracts.	Extensive outsourcing. PES provided almost exclusively by contracts.	Limited outsourcing. PES was mostly government staff supported by specialized contracts.
	Regions decided on outsourcing and facilitated coordination.	All federal contracts rolled over. Mix of EAS and specialized.	EAS contract put out for bid. Rest of contracts rolled over.	Province cancelled all EAS contracts and took services in-house.
	RFP for contracting, with defined outcomes, indicators, and targets.	No RFP process. New accountability requirements were not performance-based.	RFP for some contracts, with new accountability requirements.	Specialized contracts rolled over, no RFP.
Partnerships and networks	No sector councils	9 sector councils	7 sector councils plus 2 industry associations	No sector councils
	Economic and Social Inclusion Corporation for structured engagement.	No formal social partner engagement.	No formal social partner engagement.	Until 2012 Strategic Social Partnership provided structured engagement with business and labour.
	Formal coordination with ASETS holders.	Ad hoc coordination. ASETS holders receive provincial funding.	Ad hoc coordination. ASETS holders receive provincial funding.	Ad hoc coordination between province and each ASETS holder.

What Accounted for the Differences in Governance Approaches between the Four Atlantic Canada Provinces?

In 2014 only one Atlantic province – Newfoundland and Labrador – had a full single-window delivery system like in Quebec, with all work, welfare, and employer supports accessible through the same front door and fully coordinated within a single provincial government department. Post-devolution, New Brunswick started in this direction, but the integration of employment support and social assistance did not last long, as politicians eased work obligations for social assistance recipients and realigned responsibility for the provincially run PES with its postsecondary education portfolio.

Nova Scotia and Prince Edward Island had traditionally had employment supports for social assistance clients managed by a social services department, using internal staff and defined contracts. There was not a need to integrate social assistance and employment programming for the larger population within the same department as no strict work obligation was imposed on social assistance recipients. Newfoundland's decision to bring social assistance and employment supports together into a single human resources department in the early 2000s resulted from a need to protect basic incomes after the fishery collapse. The Strategic Social Plan consultations brought social and economic interconnections into public discourse across the province. Emerging from these consultations, social services such as child protection and seniors programming were transferred to community health boards, while income support, disability, and youth programming were aligned with provincial employment supports, immigration, and economic development activities.

In Atlantic Canada, two basic delivery models have emerged for the PES: one where provincial civil servants manage the front door of the employment service (New Brunswick and Newfoundland and Labrador), and another where it is provided by third-party service delivery organizations (PEI and Nova Scotia). In all models there was a mix of provincial government staff and third-party contracts, but the balance varied.

Almost all employment services in New Brunswick in 2014 were delivered directly by government staff, with only specialized services outsourced. When New Brunswick took on its LMDA, federal employees who provided employment counselling services transferred in, and the province just carried on with this model. By the second devolution offer in 2007, Newfoundland and Labrador had built up its internal staff expertise by transforming benefit administrators into employment counsellors. Facing the 2008 recession and a need to reduce provincial budgets, Newfoundland and Labrador determined that it had the capacity to take some of the services in-house.

Prince Edward Island and Nova Scotia did not have that luxury, as they had no provincial infrastructure capable of providing employment support services. They mostly maintained the inherited federal contracts, and instead built up their provincial management and contracting support through Employment Nova Scotia and SkillsPEI. Provincial capacity is the best explanation for the different provincial approaches.

Until 2014 New Brunswick had had over seventeen years to stabilize its PES system, and put a regional structure in place that, over time, has permitted decision making to become relatively decentralized. Since by 2014 it had been less than five years since the three other Atlantic provinces had taken on the federal programming, decision making was more centralized, especially as decisions were made to build new computer systems to track the federal spending and how it related to provincial programming already in place. Given that most PES services in Prince Edward Island and Nova Scotia were delivered by non-government organizations through contractual arrangements, there was a greater need for government control, hence greater centralization. Newfoundland was also heading in that same centralized direction, with consideration being given to reducing the number of regional offices from four to two.

On the partnership and network front, post-devolution both New Brunswick and Newfoundland and Labrador brought business, labour, and community organizations into government decision making through broad ranging, institutionalized processes involving senior politicians. Newfoundland was influenced by Ireland's experience with social dialogue, and New Brunswick was influenced by Newfoundland, at least as far as dialogue on poverty was concerned. Neither was influenced by Quebec, which – as outlined in chapter 6 of this book – has a long-standing provincial poverty plan and labour market partners board.

In Newfoundland the collapse of the fisheries was one of the motivators behind developing a Strategic Social Plan, coupled with concern over out-migration and an aging population. Consultations were led by a Social Policy Advisory Committee, an independent committee appointed by government representing groups from across the province. Likewise, representation on New Brunswick's Economic and Social Inclusion Corporation comes primarily from outside government, with a twenty-two-member board of directors in place in 2014 representing government, business, community non-profit organizations, and persons having experienced poverty.

Instead of high-profile overarching partnership activities such as these, Prince Edward Island and Nova Scotia focused on sector councils – models inherited from the federal government – as well as ad hoc engagement with community, business, and labour as needed. This fragmented the consultation process and made it much lower profile from a political perspective. Although sector councils were supported, their input was not privileged over other types of input. This reflected the traditional and conservative orientation of these two provinces, and a sense of path dependence. It also reflected the two provinces taking the time to "find their feet" and build internal capacity in labour market matters before striking out on bold engagement processes.

Partnerships with ASETS holders varied from one Atlantic Canada province to another. New Brunswick's model of a regularized quarterly tripartite forum was unique in Canada as a way to engage ASETS holders with the mainstream PES run by the province and coordinate the programming provided by each order of government. While relationships were respectful, Nova Scotia and PEI officials treated the ASETS holders like any other contracted service delivery provider, and there were no separate consultation or coordination arrangements. Since Newfoundland's Aboriginal population was almost exclusively in remote areas of the province, relationships were managed primarily at the local level.

How Did PES Performance in the Four Provinces Compare?

To assess performance of the provincial PES, each province's LMA and LMDA annual plans, its LMA performance reports, and provincial information detailed in the annual Employment Insurance Monitoring and Assessment Reports (MAR) were reviewed and analysed. Appendices K, L, and M, and N summarize PES performance data for New Brunswick, Nova Scotia, Prince Edward Island, and Newfoundland and Labrador respectively between 1999/2000 and 2013/14 from these data sources. New Brunswick has had over seventeen years to implement the provincial PES, whereas Nova Scotia,

Prince Edward Island, and Newfoundland and Labrador had less than five. All of New Brunswick's results reported in appendix K were under provincial control, whereas the LMDA results reported for the other provinces until 2011/12 were under the responsibility of Service Canada. LMA results for all four provinces were under provincial control.

Demographic and Economic Conditions

In 2014 Nova Scotia had the largest population of the four provinces at 942,700 people, followed by New Brunswick at 753,900, Newfoundland and Labrador at 527,000, and Prince Edward Island at 146,300. The Government of Newfoundland and Labrador has by far the most geography to govern at 404,212 square kilometres and Prince Edward Island the least at 5,660 square kilometres; the other two provinces are somewhere in between.

Economic conditions in the four Atlantic provinces are more similar than different. Newfoundland and Labrador's and Prince Edward Island's unemployment rates have been consistently higher (in the low double digits) between 1999 and 2014 than those of their sister provinces New Brunswick and Nova Scotia, which usually have had unemployment rates just below 10 per cent. Employment rates in all four provinces (at 60 per cent or below) are low, especially when compared to western Canada where, for example, almost 70 per cent of the Alberta working-age population were employed in 2014.

The three larger Atlantic provinces had social assistance caseloads consistently in the range of 25,000–30,000 cases annually. These declined slightly over the 1999–2014 period. Newfoundland and Labrador had the highest dependency rate in 2012 at 8.9 per cent, New Brunswick's was 6.6 per cent, and Nova Scotia's was 5.6 per cent. Prince Edward Island's rate was lowest in Atlantic Canada at 4.2 per cent (Kneebone and White 2014). The economic downturn that started in 2008 seems to have had virtually no impact on social assistance caseloads in the four provinces. The number of people in receipt of federal Employment Insurance benefits in each province (except for Prince Edward Island) was greater than those in receipt of social assistance (10,000–15,000 more) and has held relatively steady over the period in question. In all provinces there was a slight increase in EI caseloads starting in 2008–9, with the most significant declines noticeable in 2013/14.

Effectiveness

LMDA funding allocations to provinces were set in 1996 on the basis of historical federal spending on active measures. Since then they have been adjusted slightly between jurisdictions – while retaining the same overall pot of money – to reflect changes in unemployment rates, EI claimant loads, etc. Until 2014 there had been no increase to the provincial allocations since 1996, other than in 2009/10 and 2010/11 as a result of the economic downturn. By 2011/12 the allocations and expenditures were back down to 1996 levels. Despite a significantly smaller population, Newfoundland's LMDA programming expenditures of over $115 million in 2014 were the largest in the Atlantic region, compared to $89 million in New Brunswick, $79 million in Nova Scotia, and $26 million in Prince Edward Island. In 2013/14 New Brunswick spent 76 per cent of its LMDA allocations on employment benefits (including measures like training), 13 per cent on short-term employment assistance services, and 11 per cent on labour market partnerships and research and innovation. Newfoundland's allocations to long-term employment benefits were highest of all provinces at 93 per cent. Nova Scotia had the smallest proportion of funding allocated to labour market partnerships and research and innovation at 2 per cent of the total.

Even as administrative responsibility transferred from federal to provincial government management during the 2009–10 period in Nova Scotia, Prince Edward Island, and Newfoundland and Labrador, the total number of clients served through LMDA funding remained relatively steady in the range of 15,000–20,000 clients annually in the two larger provinces and up to 5,000 in Prince Edward Island, although it did drop somewhat in Newfoundland and Labrador. In New Brunswick where the province was in charge throughout the entire period, the number of clients served using LMDA money has decreased over time to about 16,000 in 2013/14. LMA allocations were per capita and represented much less money, given the small populations of the Atlantic provinces. Using LMA funding, Nova Scotia served around 3,000 clients per year, Newfoundland and Labrador around 2,000, and Prince Edward fewer than 1,000. In 2013/14 New Brunswick served over 6,000 clients with the LMA funding.

The provincial LMA reports provided ample evidence that this funding was used so that provinces could reach out and serve underrepresented groups, including immigrants, Aboriginal persons, the disabled, older workers, and social assistance recipients. Most of the clients served through LMDA funding had an attachment to the EI program: that is they had a current EI claim or were a reach-back client. This did not substantially change over the period examined. In 1999 the portion of EI clients served ranged from 81 to 83 per cent; by 2014 this had declined somewhat such that this proportion was 71 per cent in New Brunswick; 74 per cent in Prince Edward Island and 73 per cent in Nova Scotia. However, in Newfoundland and Labrador the proportion of clients served with an EI attachment increased over the period from 81 to 84 per cent.

Like in the rest of Canada, how the LMDA money was used changed significantly over the 1999–2013 period. While the number of interventions in all Atlantic Canada provinces increased over time, the mix changed from long-term activities (like training or work experience) to short-term employment assistance services. In New Brunswick, in 1999 long-term interventions were 58 per cent of the total; by 2014 they were 23 per cent. In Prince Edward Island they were 59 per cent and in 2014 were at 29 per cent. In Nova Scotia they went from 46 to 14 per cent; in Newfoundland and Labrador from 63 to 40 per cent. There was no particular evidence in the data that there was any change in this trend as provinces took over control of the federal employment services; rather the trajectory already set was simply maintained. In three of the provinces, LMA interventions were focused primarily on long-term programming; unfortunately the Nova Scotia reports did not provide enough detail to assess the balance between long-term and short-term interventions.

In all provinces the targets set on returns to employment and unpaid benefits for EI clients through LMDA funding were largely met over the period and were sometimes exceeded. What was noteworthy was how modest the targets were, explaining why they were so easily attained. For example, in 2014 New Brunswick's target was to return 7,927 out of 40,460 EI regular clients to work; that is 20 per cent. Newfoundland's target was 15 per cent; PEI's was 23 per cent, and Nova Scotia's was 17 per cent. The targets selected in western Canada were much more aggressive at around 50 per cent, reflecting lower unemployment rates in those provinces.

In LMA programming the proportion of clients who completed their programming ranged in Newfoundland and Labrador between 37 and 66 per cent. New Brunswick had higher rates at over 70 per cent, and Prince Edward Island was higher still at between 82 and 86 per cent. Those employed in Newfoundland and Labrador were noted in that province at between 50 and 76 per cent; Prince Edward Island ranged from 68 to 88 per cent, Nova Scotia was at 68 per cent, and New Brunswick ranged from 50 to 78 per cent. Training helped 83 per cent of Nova Scotians, 88 per cent of Newfoundlanders, 92 per cent of Prince Edward Islanders, and around 83 per cent of New Brunswickers. Over 70 per cent of those served in Nova Scotia earned credentials as a result of the training; 39 per cent of New Brunswickers; between 46 and 63 per cent in Newfoundland and Labrador. In PEI it was an absolute number at 88 people in 2010/11 and 133 in 2012/13. In all provinces earnings reported were less than $15 per hour.

Moving beyond the LMDA and LMA performance data, provincial research and analysis on matters relevant to the provincial PES were also examined. Given their focus on poverty reduction through public engagement, Newfoundland and Labrador and New Brunswick had invested more time and effort in this area than Prince Edward Island and Nova Scotia. Memorial University researchers in St John's, Newfoundland, developed a system of "community accounts" that provided citizens and policymakers with a single comprehensive source of key social, economic, and health indicators. Not only did these allow Newfoundland communities to be compared to each other, the data also moved upwards to compare Newfoundland with other provinces in Canada, as well as with OECD countries. One respondent interviewed through this research characterized this undertaking as a "better, better-life index."[2]

New Brunswick invested in social policy research primarily through the New Brunswick Social Policy Research Network (NBSPRN), a partnership of the four publicly funded universities and the Government of New Brunswick housed at the University of New Brunswick.[3] Set up to advance an evidence-based approach to policy development, NBSPRN facilitates collaboration between governments, informed communities, and researchers in social and economic development matters within the province. A monthly newsletter keeps people informed; there are also regular conferences. Some of these broader initiatives affected labour market programming, especially on poverty and social assistance. No evidence of research initiatives such as these were uncovered in Prince Edward Island and Nova Scotia.

2 See http://nl.communityaccounts.ca/bli/ for more information.
3 See http://www.policyresearchnetwork.ca/ for more information.

Efficiency

In New Brunswick, with average annual LMDA expenditures of $92,758,000 over the period from 1999/2000 to 2013/14 and an average of 18,144 clients served each year, the cost per client served was calculated at $5,112. Using the same methodology, the cost per client was calculated at $4,774 in Nova Scotia, $5,923 in Prince Edward Island, and $8,006 in Newfoundland and Labrador.[4] These costs were remarkably higher than in western Canada, where, for example, Manitoba's cost per client served through LMDA funding was calculated at $1,740 and Saskatchewan's at $3,121. The return on EI investment was relatively modest in all Atlantic Canada provinces. In 2014, with spending of $26 million, PEI saved almost $8 million in EI benefits; in Nova Scotia it was $79 million vs $28 million in savings; in Newfoundland and Labrador $115 million in spending vs $26 million in savings; in New Brunswick $89 million in spending vs $29 million in savings. There are likely many reasons for these differences from one province to another; what is important is that the information is made available regularly so conversations can occur on best practices to foster improvements.

Client satisfaction indicators were available from LMA programming and were highly positive. Satisfied with the services in 2012/13 were 97 per cent in Nova Scotia, 95 per cent in Newfoundland and Labrador, 99 per cent in Prince Edward Island, and 96 per cent in New Brunswick. When asked about coherence *within* the provincial government, Nova Scotia officials were aware that improvements could be made to how the social services and employment departments coordinated programming. They also thought that work needed to be done to consolidate and streamline the wide array of employment services contracts. Prince Edward Island had already initiated some of these changes, but some respondents noted that further improvements were needed.

The OECD report on New Brunswick (Wood 2010) suggested that long-standing interdepartmental protocols had smoothed relations and referrals between the work, welfare, and workplace components of the provincial PES, as well as with the remaining federal Aboriginal and

4 Nova Scotia: average annual expenditures of $83,028,000 on 17,390 clients; Prince Edward Island: average annual expenditures of $27,100,000 on 4,575 clients; Newfoundland and Labrador: average annual expenditures of $130,777,000 on 16,335 clients.

youth programming. While in 2014 Newfoundland and Labrador had all component pieces of the PES under the responsibility of a single department, adjustments were still ongoing as the province further consolidated the provincial delivery system and redefined its external contractor relationships.

In 2014 each Atlantic Canada province had an association that provided professional support to career development practitioners. All of these self-organized community networks were within each province; there was no evidence of Atlantic Canada networks. Despite the fact that the provincial capitals of Halifax, Charlottetown, and Fredericton are less than five hours' driving distance of each other, there were few connections across provinces to share best practices through collective meetings. Respondents noted that this was because provincial funders generally would not fund out-of-province travel. Each Atlantic Canada career development practitioner's association had its own annual conference, with very limited cross fertilization. Although there were opportunities for national engagement through *Cannexus* – an annual career development conference held in Ottawa each year – it was very difficult for those working in the PES in Atlantic Canada to attend national conferences as the result of the cost of travel.

In both New Brunswick and Newfoundland and Labrador the province led in ensuring training for those working in the provincial PES. However, in Newfoundland this training was restricted to government workers and was not available to those working for not-for-profit agencies, whereas in New Brunswick training was available to all. Neither Prince Edward Island nor Nova Scotia provided training for the third-party contractors that delivered the bulk of their PES. This suggests that New Brunswick has the best trained PES in Atlantic Canada.

Democracy

The federal-provincial Labour Market Agreements prescribed that each province publicly release an annual plan and an annual report. The agreements also identified common indicators so that provincial performance could be compared. Every Atlantic Canada province publicly released an annual LMA plan spelling out its spending plans and consultation process; however, for the last year of the agreement (2013/14) only New Brunswick's and Newfoundland and Labrador's plans were available. All provincial LMA plans provided considerable information on how the province engaged with stakeholders – business, labour, service providers, other government departments, educators, sector councils, community organizations, and program consumers – in developing their annual LMA and LMDA initiatives.

Nova Scotia's description of its engagement strategy was the most comprehensive of the four provinces, outlining in detail not only whom it consulted with but the key messages heard. It was through engagement that Nova Scotia decided to develop "employability tables" to focus on the needs of specific disadvantaged groups. New Brunswick's engagement occurred at the regional as well as the provincial level, and was connected to its poverty-reduction strategy, its action plan to transform postsecondary education, the employment action plan for persons with disabilities, and the province's economic development plan.

Likewise, Newfoundland and Labrador's consultations noted the importance of the Labour Market Committee of the SPI as well as the provincial poverty-reduction strategy. Prince Edward Island's summaries highlighted key themes that emerged from the consultations, including a focus on postsecondary students, employer and industry engagement, and under-represented groups. There was clear evidence from the LMA plans that all four Atlantic Canada provinces had engaged with provincial stakeholders on their LMDA- and LMA-funded programming.

Despite a commitment in each province's Labour Market Agreement to report to its citizens on results – using common indicators – not every Atlantic province kept that commitment. Newfoundland and Labrador's LMA information was the most accessible, available on the provincial departmental website through a dedicated LMA performance report, updated and posted annually. The information was detailed, and all the indicators identified in the LMA agreement were reported on. Next most comprehensive was Nova Scotia's dedicated LMA performance report that, over time, came to report on most indicators. However, it was not accessible, as it could not be located on a provincial site, and the links on the federal site were broken. Some years were missing.

New Brunswick and Prince Edward Island reported on their LMA performance as part of their larger departmental annual report. In New Brunswick, this required a detailed read of a 30–90-page report, and even then the province reported on only two of the outcome indictors in the LMA agreement. It was also difficult to differentiate LMA results from its other programming. PEI's annual reports were even less accessible, as annual reports for 2011/12, 2012/13, and 2013/14 were still unavailable in the summer of 2015. To complete appendix K and M required follow-up contact with provincial civil servants. This analysis demonstrates that transparency and reporting was best in Newfoundland and Labrador and Nova Scotia.

Conclusion

Comparing PES governance choices and performance in the four Atlantic Canada provinces post-devolution was instructive, especially since one province – New Brunswick – took on the federal responsibilities in 1997, while it occurred twelve years later in Nova Scotia, Prince Edward Island, and Newfoundland and Labrador. Although by 2014 all provinces had come to the same place – responsible for the design and delivery of employment services to help its citizens back to work and assist employers secure the skilled workers they need – each developed a distinctive PES based on its own history, political culture, and provincial priorities.

While traditionalism and conservatism may be key features of Atlantic Canada's political culture, this chapter illustrates flashes of independence, especially when New Brunswick took on the federal programming earlier, and Newfoundland and Labrador completely revamped its provincial employment services system in order to ready itself for devolved LMDAs. It was only in Newfoundland and Labrador where a complete single-window delivery system had been implemented; in the other three provinces the PES was run in cooperation with the postsecondary education department, with social assistance and most employer supports delivered by sister departments.

Other than in New Brunswick, most decision making was relatively centralized. In two provinces – New Brunswick and Newfoundland and Labrador – the provincial PES was run mostly by government employees, while in the other two the services were contracted to third-party delivery agents. Partnerships and engagement beyond government were strongest in New Brunswick and Newfoundland and Labrador; this may be why these two provinces were more innovative in their governance choices than their sister provinces Nova Scotia and Prince Edward Island.

While all four Atlantic provinces were effectively serving clients through federal LMDA and LMA funding, Newfoundland and Labrador's programming was considered as the least efficient. On the other hand, it was the most transparent of the four provinces being compared in this chapter. All provinces were very active in engagement, ensuring that the PES programming selected met the needs of its citizens.

Chapter Eight

Aboriginal Employment Programs[1]

Since section 91 (24) of the Canadian constitution assigns jurisdictional responsibility for "Indians and the Land reserved for the Indians" to the Government of Canada, labour market services for Aboriginal people[2] were not part of the 1995 devolution offer to provinces. The Government of Canada first developed a Native employment policy and dedicated Aboriginal programming in the 1970s; in the 1990s most of these resources were placed under the direct control of Aboriginal labour market agencies through a devolved arrangement quite different from what was available to provinces and territories.

Over the past twenty-five years Pathways to Success, Regional Bilateral Agreements, the Aboriginal Human Resource Development Strategy, and the Aboriginal Skills and Employment Training Strategy (ASETS) have been used to ensure that labour market services for Aboriginal people were locally designed, flexible, and culturally sensitive. Managed and delivered in 2014/15 by eighty-five Aboriginal organizations through 600 points of delivery in urban, rural, and remote locations across the country, ASETS is Ottawa's flagship Aboriginal employment program. From time to time it has been supplemented by project-specific initiatives; there is also complementary programming

1 Some of the content in this chapter was published in Wood (2016).

2 The term *Aboriginal people* in this chapter refers to the Indigenous population of Canada and includes First Nations (status Indians), Inuit, and Metis people. Federal responsibility for Metis people was upheld by the Supreme Federal Court of Canada in the 2013 *Daniels vs Canada* decision.

through the Urban Aboriginal Strategy. All of this federally funded Aboriginal programming has defined time limits.

Canada's Aboriginal population is the fastest-growing cohort in Canada and could be a rich source of potential workers; however, all indictors demonstrate that Aboriginal people lag significantly behind their non-Aboriginal peers. Data from the 2011 National Household survey show that employment rates among the Aboriginal population were at 52.1 per cent, compared to the non-Aboriginal population at 61.2 per cent. The non-Aboriginal population had the lowest unemployment rate in 2011 at 7.5 per cent, compared to 15.0 per cent among the Aboriginal population and 22.0 per cent for those living on reserve (NAEDB 2015).

Given these problems, employers seldom consider Aboriginal people as a solution to fill their labour market gaps. Many look instead to temporary foreign workers. Aboriginal people continue to feel the effects of having been marginalized for most of Canada's history. Challenges include where they live, their low education levels, language and cultural barriers, and racism (Conference Board of Canada 2012). Many Aboriginal people remain trapped in a cycle of poverty, exacerbated by problems such as high rates of crime and substance abuse, as well as substandard housing and health. Aboriginal education levels are also low and are regularly singled out as a major channel through which improvements could occur.

So are Aboriginal employment and training programs for adults. These are the second-chance programs that pick up the pieces and provide access to new opportunities when the K–12 and postsecondary education systems fail. This chapter examines these federally funded Aboriginal employment and training programs. Running parallel to provincial and territorial labour market programming, they are a key component of Canada's public employment service, constituting about 12 per cent of all federal spending on workforce development. Because of Aboriginal people's disadvantage in the labour market, the share of funding allocated exceeds their proportion of the population, which in 2014 was 4.3 per cent.

The chapter starts by examining Canada's colonial legacy and its impact on Aboriginal people. Then a brief overview is provided on the political and economic context in which Aboriginal employment programs operate. Next, the programs themselves are looked at in some detail, including historical developments over time and the architecture under which they operated in 2014 and 2015. This includes an assessment of the federal-Aboriginal accountability regime. Relationships with the broader PES managed by provinces and territories are considered next, as well as industry partnerships. The chapter concludes by assessing outcomes achieved in Aboriginal employment programming over time, drawing on the available data.

The Colonial Legacy

Aboriginals were Canada's "first people," living on the land in organized societies when Europeans arrived in the 1500s. Recognizing that Indigenous people had certain rights to the lands they occupied, the British Royal Proclamation of 1763 regulated colonial expansion, requiring treaties to be signed between the Indigenous population and the government of the day. The eleven numbered treaties – all signed between the Government of Canada and various First Nations between 1871 and 1921 – covered all of Manitoba, Saskatchewan, and Alberta and parts of Ontario, British Columbia, and the Northwest Territories. Post-Confederation, these treaties were seen by Prime Minister John A. Macdonald as part of Canada's "national policy" of high tariffs and western settlement. Indians were to be controlled and subjugated and their land secured for immigrant settlement and railway building (Shewell 2004).

By the mid-1800s the spread of European diseases – especially smallpox and tuberculosis – had decimated the Aboriginal population such that by 1871 there were roughly 102,000 Aboriginal people living in the whole area of modern-day Canada, about 2.8 per cent of Canada's population of 3.69 million (Shewell 2004). Also affecting Aboriginal people was the collapse of the bison as their primary food source. As the treaties promised seeds, tools, food, medicine, and education, Aboriginal leaders saw them as a way to secure their well-being and as a bridge between reliance on the disappearing bison and conversion to agriculture (Daschuk 2013). In contrast, governments viewed the treaties – and the establishment of reserves – as a way to remove Aboriginal people from colonial society through first a policy of "insulation" followed by one of "assimilation" (Shewell 2004). The Indian Act of 1876 – under the constitutional control of the Government of Canada after Confederation in 1867– set the framework for these assimilation policies, where First Nations people were increasingly confined to reserves and subject to the severe and restrictive policies of the Department of Indian Affairs.

One key program of the Indian Affairs department was providing food rations or "relief." Shewell (2004, ix) maintains that relief was used to bribe Indians into taking treaty and entice them onto reserves. Despite being promised in the treaties, food was often withheld, such that in the 1880s there was widespread starvation and hunger among the First Nations population. In addition to restrictive relief policies, Indian Affairs banned religious and cultural rites and imposed new forms of political organization. Children were removed from their homes, placed into residential schools managed by religious organizations, and forbidden to speak their language. Crowding on reserves and in the Indian residential schools exacerbated disease and brought even more death (Daschuk 2013). As settlement of the west increased in the twentieth century, the "Indian problem" eventually seemed to disappear, quietly managed by the federal government in isolation from other policy issues of the day.

As part of building the Canadian welfare state, provinces modernized and expanded their social assistance policies in the 1960s with federal funding available through the Canada Assistance Plan. While the Department of Indian Affairs was keen to have provinces take over relief on reserve, only Ontario agreed to do so. Not only were provinces reluctant to take on an area of federal constitutional responsibility, First Nations were reluctant to lose their relationship with the Crown, as embodied in the Government of Canada.

Over time Indian Affairs policies were changed so that social assistance benefits and rates on reserve more closely mirrored those provided by its respective provincial government. However, there were few efforts on reserve to replicate the "activation turn" that most provinces started to focus on in the 1980s and the 1990s. Instead, attention was on administrative change, with band councils – not government administrators – taking over responsibility for the management and delivery of what over time became known as on-reserve "income support."

The special legislation, special land system, and separate administration for the Indian people – all under the control of the Department of Indian Affairs – continued with little notice by most Canadians until Ottawa released a White Paper on Indian policy in 1969. Increased assimilation was the plainly stated objective, outlining a plan for removing all rights specific to Indigenous people. The frankness of its intentions led to a surge in Aboriginal activism, which included the creation of the National Indian Brotherhood – the forerunner to the Assembly of First Nations – and the use of litigation to advocate and enforce Indigenous rights (Wilson 2015).

Political and Economic Context

The contemporary relationship between Indigenous people and Canada began in 1973, with the Supreme Court decision that recognized that, at the time of European settlement, Indigenous people had rights based on the fact that they were already living here in organized societies. The decision acknowledged that they had previously been self-governing, but had lost this capacity through coercion and colonization (Asch 2014).

In 1982 the written constitution of Canada was amended to explicitly recognize and affirm the existing Aboriginal and treaty rights of Indians, Inuit, and Metis, without defining those rights. From 1983 to 1992 intergovernmental negotiations to define the content of a constitutional right to Aboriginal self-government proved unsuccessful, leaving in its wake a host of unsettled questions affecting Aboriginal people.

Between 1991 and 1996 a Royal Commission on Aboriginal Peoples (RCAP) assessed past government policies towards Aboriginal people. Setting out a twenty-year agenda for change, the five-volume, 4,000-page report covered a vast range of issues; its 440 recommendations called for sweeping changes to the interaction between Aboriginal and non-Aboriginal people and their governments in a range of policy areas. Released in 1997, *Gathering Strength: Canada's Aboriginal Action Plan* committed the Government of Canada to renewal of the relationship, building on the principles of mutual respect, mutual recognition, mutual responsibility, and sharing as identified in RCAP (Canada 1997).

Federal policy since 1995 has recognized the inherent right to Aboriginal self-government, to be implemented through non-constitutional means. In exploring this concept Papillon (2014) identified three narratives over the past thirty years: self-government as self-administration, self-government as an inherent right, and self-government as coexisting sovereignties. His work demonstrates how federal and provincial governments appear to have backed away from their commitments to self-government in recent years, focusing instead on limited partnership arrangements.

As of the 2011 census, Aboriginal peoples in Canada totalled 1,400,685 people, or 4.3 per cent of the national population. In 2011, 49.8 per cent were Registered Indians (spread over six hundred recognized First Nations governments or bands), 15.5 per cent were non-status Indians, 29.9 per cent were Metis, and 4.2 per cent were Inuit. It is estimated that 54 per cent of Aboriginal people live in urban areas and that 70 per cent live off-reserve. Eight out of ten Aboriginal people reside in Ontario and the four western provinces.

Five National Aboriginal Organizations (NAOs) represent Aboriginal people at the intergovernmental table: the Assembly of First Nations (AFN), the Congress of Aboriginal people (CAP), the Metis National Council (MNC), the Inuit Tapiriit Kanatami (ITK), and the Native Women's Association of Canada (NWAC). During the constitutional discussions representatives of all five of these groups sat at the table with first ministers.

With the demise of the Charlottetown Accord in 1992, NAO representatives no longer come together regularly with first ministers. However, since 2002 they have met annually with premiers at their summer Council of the Federation meeting. The council does not include the prime minister, a key actor given federal constitutional responsibility for Aboriginal people. NAO representatives regularly come together with the federal government, the provinces, and territories at an Aboriginal ministers' table. In 2015 there were no Aboriginal representatives at the Forum of Labour Market Ministers' (FLMM) table, the institution used since 1983 to bring federal, provincial, and territorial governments together on labour market issues.

When the Harper Conservatives formed government between 2006 and 2015, relationships between the Government of Canada and Aboriginal peoples deteriorated. Most issues were determined – to the favour of Aboriginal people – through the courts. The Trudeau Liberals – elected with a majority in the fall of 2015 – have pledged to rebuild the relationship between the federal government and Indigenous peoples.

Historical Developments in Aboriginal Employment and Training Programming

As Aboriginal people began to reassert their rights over many aspects of their lives in the 1970s, they also sought control of the programming to help them prepare for, find, and keep a job. There have been five distinct phases in Aboriginal employment programming over time.

1970s and 1980s: The Employment Equity Period

In the 1970s and 1980s employment equity emerged as an issue, and an Employment Equity Act was passed in 1986. Targeted programs for Natives, women, and youth were created within the Employment and Immigration (EIC) department, including a 1977 Native Employment Policy, delivered by Aboriginal people recruited to serve as Native employment counsellors. Aboriginal outreach programs were also put in place. These employment programs did not reach Aboriginal people living on reserve, as passive income support – managed by First Nations bands and supervised by the federal Indian Affairs department – was the only focus.

By 1989–90 EIC was spending more than $139 million on employment programs and services for Aboriginal people. Despite this spending, many Aboriginal people felt that their unique needs were not being met. As detailed in chapter 2, in 1989 the Mulroney Progressive Conservatives implemented a new national Labour Force Development Strategy, creating non-government advisory boards (national, provincial, and local) to forge stronger partnerships between federal and provincial governments, business, and labour. Within this broader context an Aboriginal Employment and Training Working Group (AETWG) was created – bringing together senior Aboriginal representatives with federal officials – to improve the partnership (EIC 1990a).

1991–1996: Pathways to Success

Pathways to Success was born out of the work of the AETWG. Five partnership principles were collectively articulated and agreed to: local decision making, funding stability, Aboriginal infrastructure and delivery control, a proactive approach to employment equity, and reducing barriers to program access (EIC 1990a). These principles were important, as the Aboriginal community was not interested in being accountable for the administration of programs that were limited in scope and restrictive in criteria and intent. In 1991 national, regional, and local Aboriginal Management Boards were created in order to set training priorities for Aboriginal communities and develop partnership and co-management practices. Constitutional discussions – involving first ministers and national Aboriginal leaders – began when Pathways was still in its infancy, allowing Human Resources Development Canada, or HRDC (the successor department to EIC in 1993) to consider Pathways in the context of a broader vision (Eberts 1994).

Under Pathways all existing HRDC funding for Aboriginal labour market programming was gathered into one pot, and a notional budget of $200 million/year from the Consolidated Revenue Fund (CRF) (up from a baseline of $145 million) was established. A National

Aboriginal Management Board and Regional and Local Management Boards (consisting of an equal number of Aboriginal people and federal officials) were given a measure of control over most of this funding. Over one hundred local boards, twelve regional or territorial boards, and one national board were set up (Royal Commission 1996). The national board – a single table covering all Aboriginal groups (First Nations, Metis, and Inuit) – developed a formula to divide up the federal money by region and among the designated Aboriginal groups. During this period some of the regional and local boards evolved from an advisory role into incorporated service-delivery agents (Virtuosity Consulting 2003).

However, problems soon developed. Disputes arose over the allocation of funds across regions and to particular Aboriginal constituencies (Royal Commission 1996). The pan-Aboriginal approach did not recognize the separate Indian, Metis, and Inuit decision-making structures. Off-reserve Aboriginal people felt left out. And then there was the question of authority: were the Aboriginal labour market boards full self-government or were they merely advisory bodies? During 1994 and 1995 Ottawa initiated a review of Pathways. Out of this came new arrangements that represented a further step towards Aboriginal control (Royal Commission 1996).

1996–1999: Regional Bilateral Agreements (RBAs)

By 1996 the single Pathways table had fractured among the different Aboriginal constituencies, resulting in separate agreements between HRDC and the Assembly of First Nations, the Metis National Council, and the Inuit Tapirisat of Canada. These agreements outlined detailed financial accountability and results-based performance requirements for the employment programs and services on offer through their respective constituencies (Virtuosity Consulting 2003).

The national framework agreements between HRDC and the respective NAO set up the Aboriginal–government relationship, then service-delivery agreements were developed at the local level. As identified by the NAOs, fifty-four Regional Bilateral Agreements (RBAs) with local Aboriginal groups allowed them to design programs suited to their needs, providing they met HRDC program objectives. The RBAs effectively devolved responsibility for Aboriginal employment programming from the Government of Canada to the designated local Aboriginal organization. The Aboriginal programs were, by design, meant to run alongside mainstream employment programs delivered – at the time – by Canada Employment Centres (CECs) across the country. Even though they were not a NAO, Native Friendship Centres across Canada were included in the RBA funding envelope.

After the National Aboriginal Management Board was disbanded, responsibility for the allocation model went to an officials' working group. A new Employment Insurance Act was introduced in 1995. In addition to Consolidated Revenue funding, Employment Insurance, or EI part II funding was made available for Aboriginal employment programs, carving out a portion of services and clients to be charged to the EI account. This was also the time that Ottawa was negotiating the transfer of labour market programs to provinces and territories through Labour Market Development Agreements, or LMDAs, also charged to the EI account.

As identified earlier in this book, Alberta signed the first devolved agreement in 1996, followed shortly after by New Brunswick, Quebec, Manitoba, Saskatchewan, and the Northwest Territories. In the other provinces, CECs continued to manage the PES. Services for Aboriginal people – as well as youth and pan-Canadian programming – were not on offer to provinces. Unlike the devolved LMDAs, which had no defined time limits, the RBAs were three-year, time-limited agreements. There was also no transfer of federal delivery staff. However, some HRDC case managers were seconded to work with the various Aboriginal organizations.

As an outcome of *Gathering Strength*, in 1998 the Aboriginal Human Resource Council (AHRC) was founded as a non-profit national organization. Funded by the Government of Canada, AHRC was meant bring business, labour, academic, and Aboriginal experts together to encourage the private sector to share responsibility for improving Aboriginal access to the labour market (Royal Commission 1996). AHRC was set up specifically to develop partnerships and intermediate between employers, Aboriginal labour market organizations, educators, and others on a pan-Canadian and pan-Aboriginal basis. It was governed by a Council of Champions and a board of directors (HRSDC 2009).

1999–2010: Aboriginal Human Resource Development Strategy (AHRDS)

In 1999 Ottawa replaced the National Framework Agreements and RBAs with the five-year Aboriginal Human Resource Development Strategy

(AHRDS). This was an important part of the government response to RCAP. AHRDS was built upon six pillars: agreements with Aboriginal groups to transfer funds for labour market programming; partnerships between communities, the private sector and governments; the creation of the Aboriginal Human Resources Council (AHRC); internal HRDC program integration; Aboriginal capacity investments; and improved horizontal management between HRDC and other federal departments. It is noteworthy that there was no mention in the AHRDS principles of coordination with provincial governments, which were simultaneously taking on responsibility for mainstream employment services from the federal government. The two activities were undertaken in separate silos, managed by different teams of people at HRDC.

The framework agreements with the three NAOs were replaced by national protocols with now five national political organizations: the Assembly of First Nations, the Metis National Council, the Inuit Tapirisat of Canada, the Congress of Aboriginal Peoples, and the Native Women's Association of Canada. Left out from this funding envelope was the Friendship Centre movement, excluded by Ottawa as it was not a political organization. This caused great concern among the Friendship Centres who lost their employment services funding.

A number of programs were added to AHRDS, including youth, disability, capacity building, and an urban component. To support access to child care, the First Nations and Inuit Child Care Initiative was transferred from Health Canada and placed within the AHRDS envelope. With these changes, the federal HRDC annual allocation of $200 million a year under the RBAs increased to approximately $320 million. According to one Aboriginal informant interviewed through this research, this was viewed as a huge windfall for Aboriginal organizations. The priority of federal officials was to get the money out the door and off to the designated Aboriginal organizations.

In 2002 the Aboriginal Human Resource Council (AHRC) decided to work with a small number of AHRDS holders in western Canada, as opposed to expanding its activities across the country. It became known for organizing partnership workshops between private sector employers and Aboriginal organizations known as Workforce Connex (HRSDC 2009).

By 2003 ARHDS had set up seventy AHRDS agreements with 200 subagreements involving some 390 points of service (Virtuosity Consulting 2003). Over time this grew to seventy-nine AHRDS agreements, including status-blind urban agreements in Vancouver and Winnipeg. In 2003 the federal Indian Affairs department was authorized to begin offering employment supports on reserve; however, no additional funding was allocated to First Nations bands or AHRDS holders. As a result, income assistance on reserve remained resolutely passive. This contrasted with provincial approaches in which by now most had introduced specific measures to assist social assistance recipients to access the labour market.

Federal HRDC officials were always on hand to help Aboriginal organizations with AHRDS implementation, at both the regional and national level through pan-Canadian technical working groups. At that time, ensuring accountability for government expenditures was not a big priority. However, that changed in the late 1990s and early 2000s when HRDC was rocked by a grants and contributions crisis triggered by the release of a "soft audit" on the lack of management control in an unrelated pot of money. HRDC's tightened administrative procedures forced many AHRDS holders to realign resources from client services to administration.

However, the most important change occurred in 2003 when Ottawa decided to fund Aboriginal labour market programming outside the AHRDS umbrella through a new program called the Aboriginal Skills and Employment Partnership (ASEP), designed to increase access to job opportunities for Aboriginal peoples in major economic development initiatives. The federal government felt that ASEP was needed, as many potential projects crossed AHRDS boundaries and were beyond the capacity of individual AHRDS holders. Run directly by federal officials out of Ottawa, between 2003 and 2012 ASEP supported forty-five projects (HRSDC 2013b). To take on an ASEP project, bidders had to set up new legal entities. Private sector partners, provincial governments, and educational institutions also needed to contribute. In some cases AHRDS holders qualified to run or partner on ASEP projects, while in other places they became competitors.

The agreements were renewed in 2004 for another five years under AHRDS II. This involved a number of changes, including a new emphasis on supporting private-sector skills needs and a more stringent accountability framework. In 2005 the federal government decided to set up Service Canada, separating HRDC's service-delivery responsibilities across the country from strategic policymaking in Ottawa. Now AHRDS holders had three federal points of contact, two in Ottawa as well as local officials within the province.

In 2005 HRDC decided to move funding for the Aboriginal Human Resource Council from the AHRDS allocation to the more generic sector council program, effectively delinking the council from the AHRDS community. By 2009 most AHRDS holders were largely unaware of the mission and mandate of the AHRC, and many perceived the Workforce Connex forums to be of limited utility. An HRDC evaluation noted that the AHRC had had limited success in developing strategies that reflected the diversity of the AHRDSs in geography, size, economic opportunities available, and clientele (HRSDC 2009, 17).

It was during the AHRDS II period that Ontario finally came to an agreement with the federal government to take on a devolved Labour Market Development Agreement in 2005. In 2007 the Harper Conservatives offered all remaining provinces and territories the same deal, and by 2010 all had put public employment service-delivery systems in place suited to their needs. In 2008 Ottawa also offered provinces additional funding for employment services for non-EI clients through new Labour Market Agreements, or LMAs. This opened up new programming opportunities through the mainstream PES, and some provinces used the money to expand programs for their Aboriginal citizens, operating in partnership with their AHRDS holders.

2010–2016: Aboriginal Skills and Employment Training Strategy (ASETS)

The Harper Conservatives – elected in 2006 – inherited the AHRDS structure put in place by the federal Liberals. In response to the economic downturn, in 2008 they announced additional two-year funding – to be managed by AHRDS holders – through a new Aboriginal Skills and Training Strategic Investment Fund. This was followed in June 2009 with the release of a new federal framework for Aboriginal Economic Development. Further adjustments to Aboriginal employment programming came in 2010 when the Aboriginal Skills and Employment Training Strategy, or ASETS, was rolled out as the successor regime to AHRDS. A new Skills and Partnership Fund (SPF) was also announced to support smaller ASEP-like projects. In 2013 federal funding to the Aboriginal Human Resource Council (AHRC) ended when the larger sector council program was eliminated. The council continued into 2015 as a social enterprise that helped companies forge relationships with the Indigenous community.

Under ASETS the basic AHRDS infrastructure and the Aboriginal delivery agents remained the same. However, the principles behind the program were refocused on demand-driven skills development;

partnerships with the private sector and the provinces and territories; and accountability and results. Federal monitoring was also increased. All of this was very different from the Pathways, RBAs, and AHRDS I principles where Aboriginal organizations were expected to develop and implement their own employment and human resources programs. No new money was given to ASETS holders to operationalize these pillars.

The most employment-disadvantaged Aboriginal people are those receiving social assistance on reserve. Managed in 2014 by Aboriginal Affairs and Northern Development Canada (AANDC) and delivered by 541 First Nations bands, in 2012/13 there were approximately 82,000 cases and 162,000 people dependent on the program across Canada. Income Assistance on reserve is the fourth-largest welfare program in Canada, costing approximately $861 million per year, a significant increase over the past decade. While ASETS holders have always been available to provide employment supports on reserve, before 2013 there was no requirement for income-support recipients to participate. Given the colonial legacy outlined earlier in this chapter, in some communities the dependency rate is over 80 per cent (AANDC 2014b).

The 2013 federal budget formally brought AANDC and Employment and Social Development Canada, or ESDC (the successor to HRDC), together to enhance employment-related resources for people living on reserve. Only youth aged eighteen to twenty-four who required less than one year of training to become employable were eligible for the new programming. First Nations bands that met AANDC criteria received additional funding through a program called Enhanced Service Delivery. In 2014 ASETS holders were the designated delivery agent for employment and training supports, with dedicated funding provided through a new program called the First Nations Job Fund (FNJF).

Aboriginal Employment Programming Architecture in 2013/2014/2015

When Aboriginal leaders and the federal government developed the architecture in the 1990s for Aboriginal employment programs – first through the Aboriginal Employment and Training Working Group and then through the National Aboriginal Management Board – the ideas used in this book to compare provincial governance approaches – single window, decentralization, outsourcing, and partnerships – embedded the choices made.

Pathways/RBAs/AHRDS/ASETS clearly constituted a form of "single window," at least for employment and training services for Aboriginal people. In the early 1990s services being provided by federal Aboriginal staff were consolidated with Aboriginal outreach programs to form Aboriginal labour market agencies providing a single point of access for all Aboriginal people within a defined geographic area. However, this notion of single access fractured first in 1996 when the RBAs established local labour market agencies based on Aboriginal ancestry: First Nations, Metis, and Inuit. This made things particularly complicated for urban Aboriginal people. The notion of a single window was further overturned in 2003 when the federal government created the Aboriginal Skills and Employment Partnership (ASEP) as an additional program outside of the AHRDS umbrella, and required that new Aboriginal labour market organizations be set up to provide services to employers and potential trainees.

Decentralization and outsourcing were key elements of the Pathways to Success principles, demonstrated by the choices made to set up local, stand-alone, Aboriginal labour-market agencies, distributed across the country in relation to the size, location, and make-up of the Aboriginal population. Given the state of Aboriginal self-government at the time, the kind of decentralization chosen was a cross between political and managerial decentralization – as described in chapter 1 of this book – and constituted a form of devolution. The organizations that were established were all Aboriginal NGOs identified by their respective Aboriginal leadership, constructed quite specifically to deliver employment services to their constituents.

While the partnership principle was embedded in relation to the involvement of national Aboriginal organizations, the Government of Canada did not incorporate it with respect to business, union, and provincial involvement during the Pathways period. These groups became more involved with Aboriginal employment programming through the establishment of the Aboriginal Human Resource Council in 1998, in the 1999 AHRDS strategy, and the establishment of ASEP in 2003. The need to involve industry and provincial governments was reiterated even more strongly when the programming morphed into ASETS in 2010 and six principles were reduced to three. It continued with the Strategic Partnership Fund as well as the First Nations Job Fund. Table E outlines key elements of the Aboriginal employment programming architecture in 2013/14.

Table E. Federally Supported Aboriginal Employment and Training Programming, 2013/2014

Program name	Federal funding allocations	Responsibility	Comments
Aboriginal Skills and Employment Strategy (ASETS)	$342.8 million/year	ESDC	$93.1 million comes from EI account. Also covers $55 million for child care. Agreements ended in March 2015. Extended to March 2017.
Skills and Partnership Fund (SPF)	$92.5 million/year	ESDC	SPF allocations in 2013/14 were high as some of this money was re-profiled from previous years. SPF was renewed in the 2015 budget to 2020 at $50 million annually.
First Nations Job Fund and Enhanced Service Delivery	$27.2 million/year to ASETS holders and $33 million/year to First Nations bands	ESDC/ AANDC	Started in 2013. In place until 2017.
Aboriginal Human Resource Council	$675,000 for labour market information	ESDC	Delinked from ASETS under AHRDS II. Core federal funding ended in 2013.
Friendship Centres	None dedicated to employment and training	AANDC	The Urban Aboriginal Strategy has a strong employment and training focus.
Total federal funding allocated 2013/14	$496.1 million	ESDC/ AANDC	This number was higher than usual in 2013/14 as the result of SPF re-profiling.

Source: Funding allocations were taken from ESDC 2014d (*Report on Plans and Priorities*) and federal press releases.

Aboriginal Skills and Employment Training Strategy, or ASETS

The eighty-five ASETS agreements were distributed asymmetrically by jurisdiction and by Aboriginal identity group. Table F provides a summary in 2015, including the total value of the agreements.

The number of agreements by province was a direct result of the peculiarities of the governance structure in that location. In 2015, almost every ASETS holder had sub-agreement holders in their service area. For example, in Saskatchewan there was only one First Nations ASETS holder – the Saskatchewan Indian Training Association Group (SITAG) – while in British Columbia there were fifteen. With sixty-five sub-agreement holders, SITAG's allocation of about $24 million in annual funding rivalled that provided to the entire province of Saskatchewan, which received about $36 million from Canada through its LMDA. Given the large Aboriginal population of the three territories, ASETS allocations (almost $18.5 million) were almost double those provided by Ottawa to territorial governments under the LMDA (almost $9.5 million).

In 2015 there were fifty-seven First Nations, eight Inuit, seven Metis, and thirteen urban ASETS holders. Each Metis region represented in the Metis National Council – Ontario, Manitoba, Saskatchewan, Alberta, and British Columbia – had an ASETS agreement. The federal money was distributed about 65 per cent to First Nations, 18 per cent to Metis, 5 per cent to Inuit, and 12 per cent to urban ASETS holders. The distinctions-based approach is now embedded in ASETS. The generic National Aboriginal Management Board under Pathways was viewed as a failure and was replaced with framework agreements with each NAO. This change recognized that each Aboriginal people had a different history and culture and faced different labour market challenges.

Each ASETS holder is considered as an NGO with a community board and a non-political executive director who then hires the necessary staff. While ASETS executive directors are guided by their Aboriginal political leadership, they were all expected to provide the same Employment Benefits and Supports Measures (EBSMs) as provinces did under the LMDAs, with one key exception. Since 1996, First Nations and Inuit ASETS holders have been allocated about $55 million in dedicated child-care funding for day-care centres on reserve and in northern communities. Metis ASETS holders were excluded from this funding envelope.

Table F. Distribution of ASETS Agreements by Jurisdiction and Aboriginal Identity, 2015[3]

Jurisdiction and proportion of total Aboriginal population	First Nations	Metis	Inuit	Urban	Total no. of agreements	Value of agreements by jurisdiction ($000s)
British Columbia (15.5%)	13	1		1	15	39,613
Alberta (15.7%)	11	2			13	40,533
Saskatchewan (11.3%)	1	1			2	34,816
Manitoba (13.9%)	2	1		1	4	43,226
Ontario (21.5%)	13	1	1	3	18	57,718
Quebec (10.1%)	3		1	1	5	31,894
New Brunswick (1.6%)	3			1	4	4,074
Nova Scotia (2.4%)	1			1	2	4,827
Prince Edward Island (0.15%)	1				1	675
Newfoundland and Labrador (2.5%)	3		2	2	7	6,015
Northwest Territories (1.5%)	5	1	1		7	8,014
Yukon (0.5%)	1			1	2	3,120
Nunavut (1.9%)			3		3	7,334
National				2	2	4,000
Total number of agreements	57	7	8	13	85	
Value of agreements by Aboriginal identity (000s)	$188,668 (65%)	$51,456 (18%)	$14,294 (5%)	$31,442 (12%)		285,860[4]

3 Calculations based on financial information provided by ESDC in May 2015. Sums have been rounded. Some urban ASETS holders are also First Nations.

4 Does not include funding for the First Nations and Inuit Child Care Initiative and First Nations Job Fund.

The Skills and Partnership Fund (SPF)

Started in 2010 as a smaller version of ASEP, by 2014 SPF had had three calls for proposals. The first two were open and more general, while the third was targeted to projects in the natural resource sector, in particular mining and energy. In December 2013, eighty SPF projects were operating. These included projects in the Ring of Fire in Northern Ontario, shipbuilding in the Atlantic, and pipeline projects on the West Coast of BC.

Such projects are popular with politicians, as they result in "announceables" that provide opportunities to highlight government action and profile the responsible minister. Although all projects were due to expire in 2015, some were extended into 2016. The 2015 federal budget put SPF on a more permanent basis with annual funding of $50 million from 2016/17 to 2020.

While ASETS holders could bid on SPF projects, the separate organizations that were established often competed with each other. Many ASETS holders believed that SPF was an unnecessary add-on and the funding should have been given to them. A BC ASETS holder testified at the HUMA parliamentary hearing on 6 March 2014, "Among the things we see that are not working is the federal government contracting with other groups under the skills partnership fund that are in essence duplicating the work of the ASETS agreement holder … This creates a lot of confusion for the clients and employers … Employers are also asking who they should work with for the aboriginal communities."

First Nations Job Fund (FNJF)

As a partnership between two federal departments, Aboriginal Affairs and Northern Development Canada (AANDC) was responsible for ensuring that First Nations income assistance workers identified and monitored suitable clients, and implemented mandatory participation in employment programming through personalized case management. This was called Enhanced Service Delivery, or ESD. Employment and Social Development Canada (ESDC) was responsible for ensuring that ASETS holders provided the needed employment services through what was called the First Nations Job Fund, or FNJF. This task was challenging, as linkages between First Nations communities delivering income assistance on reserve and ASETS holders have traditionally been viewed as weak (AANDC 2007).

In 2015 the FNJF was supported by a federal interdepartmental governance and oversight structure comprising government officials only. There was no Aboriginal representation, from either First Nations Bands or ASETS holders. The FNJF was announced in 2013 without input or advice from the ASETS holders and took some time to roll out. The federal government put out a call for proposals to match suitable First Nations bands with willing ASETS holders; as a result, many projects did not become fully operational until 2014. Some ASETS holders objected to the threat of people losing their income assistance benefits and were reluctant to participate. While implementation was progressing in 2015, further review was underway to improve the program.

Aboriginal Human Resource Council (AHRC)

In its early years the AHRC failed to build connections with ASETS holders, with neither seeing a benefit to be gained and each doing its own thing. By 2014 the federal government was no longer providing core funding and did not consider AHRC as part of the Aboriginal employment infrastructure. However, in July 2014 $675,000 from ESDC was allocated to the council to provide labour market information on major projects located near Aboriginal communities.

Friendship Centres

Friendship Centres were mostly cut out of the AHRDS funding stream in 1999 but have remained in the employment services business as ASETS sub-agreement holders, recipients of SFP and other federal funding, and provincial government contractors. The Ontario Federation of Indian Friendship Centres has also maintained an ASETS agreement. In 2011/12 the National Association of Friendship Centres received ESDC funding to examine how the Friendship Centres might be more involved in Aboriginal human resource development programming.

Friendship Centres are supported primarily with annual funding provided by AANDC's Urban Aboriginal Strategy to the National Association of Friendship Centres (NAFC). They have retained a strong training-to-employment focus. In 2014 the 117 Friendship Centres across Canada provided a wide array of services to any Aboriginal person who walked in the door. Employment was one of three priority areas, with a 2012/13 report noting that over forty thousand urban and off-reserve Aboriginal people were helped into the labour market

(NAFC n.d.). In 2015 the Friendship Centres were keenly interested in regaining access to ASETS funding in order to build on their existing urban Aboriginal labour market service delivery.

Federal–Aboriginal Relationships and Accountability Requirements

Given the fragmentation and diffusion of Aboriginal employment programming service delivery across Canada, for it to be successful and sustainable, relationships between ASETS and SFP holders and the federal government – as well as relationships between the different Aboriginal groups offering employment programming – need to be well managed.

The Federal–Aboriginal Relationship

Over the years the national agreements and framework accords with the Assembly of First Nations (AFN), the Metis National Council (MNC), and the Inuit Tapiriit Kanatami (ITK) fell by the wayside. Instead, the AFN, MNC, and ITK received a regular funding allocation from ESDC to support technical working groups to assist with program management. For example, two to three times per year some of the fifty-seven First Nations ASETS holders – as well as Aboriginal politicians – met with federal officials. There were parallel and separate technical working groups for the other Aboriginal constituencies. While such meetings were useful for information sharing, Aboriginal informants interviewed through this research felt that limited action followed; for example, by 2015 few of the recommendations from a task force on reducing the reporting burden had been implemented.

In the early years of the Aboriginal labour market agreements Ottawa regularly hosted cross-Aboriginal conferences and sharing of best practices, especially under Liberal Ministers Bradshaw and Blondin-Andrews. There were national conferences in 1999, 2002, 2004, and 2007. However, engagement significantly diminished under the Harper Conservatives. A federal official characterized the relationship as one of "benign neglect" from Ottawa politicians. Diane Finlay – minister from 2006 to 2013 – showed little interest in the file. Collective engagement improved under Jason Kenney, minister from 2013 to 2015, and there were some regional consultations. However, Aboriginal informants interviewed through this research felt that the sessions on ASETS renewal were pro forma and failed to incorporate Aboriginal feedback.

Federal Accountability Provisions

The federal–ASETS relationship is defined through contribution agreements between each ASETS holder and the Government of Canada. In 2014 these were negotiated and managed by Service Canada officials working in each province. The smallest of the eighty-five agreements had a value of less than $500,000, while the largest was almost $25 million. Each agreement was largely the same, meant "to provide funding to Aboriginal organizations to support the costs of programs, services and other activities undertaken by those organizations which are designed to increase the participation in the Canadian labour market of the Aboriginal peoples served by those organizations" (ESDC n.d.).

In 2015 ASETS holders were subject to an extensive accountability regime involving direct oversight, monitoring, and correction of expenditures by federal staff and auditors. Service expectations, reporting, and accountability requirements were outlined in the individual agreements as well as in eight detailed annexes, in addition to four federally developed documents that formed part of the agreements: (1) an ASETS manual of instructions for the completion of annual operational plans, (2) ASETS guidelines on eligible expenditures, (3) ASETS recipient financial and activity monitoring guide, and (4) ASETS manual of instructions for the completion of annual reports. The agreements specified minimum levels of services to be provided, the amount of federal contributions to be provided, how funding could be reduced or terminated, and how money received from other sources was to be managed.

Substantial client information was collected by ASETS holders and uploaded to a database managed by ESDC. However, all that ASETS holders could access was their own data and national summaries, so results could not be compared. By 2015 changes promised by Ottawa to the client management system had not materialized, and many Aboriginal organizations had to develop their own alternative client reporting systems.

Service Canada staff made regular visits to ASETS holders for financial auditing and assurance that the organization's files were in good order. They also helped with complex accounting issues, especially those that arose when there were sub-agreement holders. While in the

1990s Aboriginal delivery of employment programming was conceptualized as a step towards self-government, in 2015 ASETS holders were viewed by the Government of Canada as hired contractors being paid for providing services through one of its many program lines. Ottawa's decision in 2003 to directly manage ASEP also effectively took control away from Aboriginal experts already charged with this responsibility.

In 2015 ASETS holders were almost completely dependent upon the federal government for their funding and significantly limited in their capacity to adopt policies outside the framework established by Ottawa. Given the power imbalance between the parties, ASETS did not even fit with Papillon's (2014) concept of self-administration as a form of delegated authority. With the closing of the constitutional window and the rise of neoliberal ideas in the 1990s, the focus in ASETS shifted from a rights-based view of self-government to autonomy based on "good governance" that emphasized accounting and reporting (125–6). The democratic input of the Aboriginal population into employment programming in 2015 was barely greater than the pre-devolution model of direct federal delivery. ASETS holders were significantly challenged to make room for culturally relevant employment and training programming choices.

Aboriginal–Aboriginal Relationships

Since the federal–Aboriginal relationship in 2015 was managed in silos – using the distinctions-based approach chosen in the late 1990s – finding a coordinated Aboriginal voice was challenging, as there were no institutional structures to support the work that would be required to overcome their differences. In the late 1990s this role was played by the National Aboriginal Management Board and the National Aboriginal Steering Committee (EIC 1990b). When these organizations were disbanded, they were replaced by bilateral relationships between each NAO and the federal government. While there were pan-Aboriginal and pan-Canadian organizations whose broad mandate encompassed labour market matters – for example, the National Aboriginal Economic Development Board, or NAEDB[5] – they did not focus particular attention on Aboriginal labour market programs.

5 Established in 1990, the NAEDB advises the federal government on matters relating to economic development. It reports to the minister of AANDC, not ESDC.

According to respondents interviewed through this research, over the past few years NAO officials from the Assembly of First Nations and the Metis National Council tried to collaborate and initiate pan-Canadian and pan-Aboriginal best practices sessions; however, this was difficult without federal funding. In 2015 the MNC took the initiative to host an ASETS conference in Vancouver, billed as the "first annual" spring ASETS conference. While over 150 people from across Canada (most of them ASETS holders) attended, it did not receive endorsement from the other NAOs. Some informants suggested that it was more of a business undertaking for the organizers.

At the operations level, Service Canada engagement with their respective provincial ASETS and SPF holders varied from one province to another. Federal officials in Ontario routinely brought all ASETS holders together on a quarterly basis. This was viewed as very helpful. This also used to occur in British Columbia, but stopped after Ottawa became more prescriptive about how Service Canada regions could use their funding. First Nations ASETS holders in BC still come together through the British Columbia Aboriginal Training Employment Alliance; however, non-First Nations ASETS holders are not part of the conversation.

Other Partnerships

Aboriginal employment programs are just one part of Canada's broader public employment service. For services to be effective, Aboriginal employment organizations need to connect with employers (who provide the jobs), as well as provincial governments who manage the mainstream PES and provide access to training through their post-secondary education and apprenticeship systems. These partnerships formally became one of three ASETS pillars in 2010.

Provincial-Aboriginal Partnerships

It is easy to see why partnerships between ASETS holders and the provinces are prescribed by Ottawa. Collectively provinces received about $2.7 billion annually from the federal government to run the provincial PES, reinforced by postsecondary education, social assistance, and child care programs funded primarily from the provincial tax base. Post-devolution provinces have developed expertise, competence, and capacity – in labour market information, training of career development practitioners, client management systems – that ASETS holders could benefit from. Federal officials no longer have this kind of expertise.

However, as outlined in chapters 4 to 7 of this book, in 2014 partnerships between ASETS and SPF agreement holders and provincial governments were weak. A federal official noted, "Building partnerships with the provinces [around Aboriginal employment programming] is our biggest challenge and weakness." ASETS holders seemed to agree. A 2014 regional engagement report on ASETS renewal noted that "with respect to partnerships with provincial and territorial governments, many agreement holders expressed that there were either no partnerships in place or they were not as beneficial as they could be" (ESDC 2014a, 4). A 2015 ESDC evaluation noted that while ASETS holders tended to collaborate with provinces, SPF agreement holders did not, citing a lack of inclusion in provincial strategies and friction from duplication of services. This has led to competition for clients (ESDC 2015a, 8).

Partnerships varied from one province to another. As already noted in this book, in 2014 New Brunswick had a long-standing Aboriginal Employment Strategy Initiative committee where all ASETS holders met quarterly with federal and provincial officials. In Quebec, ASETS holders formally engaged with the Commission des partenaires du marché du travail, or CPMT. However, federal officials were not involved. Relationships in other provinces were mostly ad hoc and locally based. While these could be productive, ASETS holders interviewed for this research would like to see a more formal relationship with their provincial governments, one that recognized them as a "partner" as opposed to being considered as just another "contractor."

Only the federal government can assist ASETS holders gain this kind of standing with provincial governments. Despite a commitment in each bilateral Canada Job Fund Agreement signed in 2014 – like the Labour Market Agreements that preceded it in 2008 – to "better coordinate the delivery of their respective programs for Aboriginal persons," up to 2015 Ottawa had not provided any guidance or support to operationalize the partnership in each province. There had been no attempts to develop a pan-Canadian employment framework to formalize the relationship, either through the Forum of Labour Market Ministers (FLMM) or with NAOs at the Aboriginal minister's table. Aboriginal coordination was not even on the agenda when federal/provincial/territorial governments met as the FLMM.

Private Sector–Aboriginal partnerships

A labour market demand component to ASETS has been supported by Ottawa since 1998 and was to have been nurtured through the establishment of the Aboriginal Human Resource Council, or AHRC. Ultimately this was not successful. While in 2015 there were no longer dedicated pan-Canadian resources assigned to this task, each Strategic Partnership Fund initiative required a formal partnership with business, including financial contributions. However, there were a number of challenges: a lack of labour market information; the fact that most Aboriginal clients are multi-barriered; political sensitivities between some First Nations and specific industries; and employer preferences to use temporary foreign workers rather than Aboriginal people (ESDC 2014a). Stop and start federal funding under ASEP and SPF was another barrier. The Metis National Council noted that CEOs of large firms seem to lack information about ASETS, and they had more success with small and medium-sized business. They wondered why tools such as the Canada Job Grant were not available to ASETS holders as a way to provide incentives for business engagement.

A 2012 Conference Board of Canada study on business engagement with Aboriginal workers identified that a significant portion of businesses surveyed (31.4 per cent) were not aware of, or had limited knowledge of, government funded programs for Aboriginal employment and training. It also noted that "the large number of Aboriginal organizations that exist in Canada acts as a labyrinth of information that is too complex for employers to navigate in their desire to reach out to potential Aboriginal workers" (Conference Board of Canada 2012, 17). A simplification of the points of contact between Aboriginal organizations and employers, as well as increased opportunities for sharing best practices among ASETS holders was recommended.

What Results Have Been Achieved?

The labour market downturn that began in the fall of 2008 lasted longer for Aboriginal people than for non-Aboriginal people. In their 2015 Economic Progress report, the National Aboriginal Economic Development Board (NAEDB) confirmed that little progress had been made between 2006 and 2011 in closing the socio-economic gap between Aboriginal people and their non-Aboriginal peers. For example, between 2006 and 2011 the Aboriginal gap in the employment rate actually increased from 9 to 9.1 percentage points. The unemployment rate gap showed a similar trend. Outcomes for First Nations on reserve had shown the least improvement, where the unemployment rate increased from 24.9 per cent to 25.2 per cent (National Aboriginal Economic Development Board 2015, 13).[6] The number of cases receiving income assistance on reserve peaked in 2009/10 at 84,970 and by 2013/14 had shown only a slight decline. These indicators demonstrate that Aboriginal people are not on track to achieving parity with non-Aboriginal Canadians.

Effectiveness

Finding results information on the Aboriginal employment programming detailed in this chapter was highly challenging as there was little consolidated information. A reference to RBAs/AHRDS/ASETS results has usually been included in the annual Employment Insurance Monitoring & Assessment Report. Annual ESDC planning and priority reports also sometimes included Aboriginal programming results. ESDC officials in Ottawa were very helpful in consolidating this information into a single document, summarized in appendix O.

Pre-devolution (in 1995/6) the federal government served just over 13,000 Aboriginal clients. By 1999/2000 – after the funding and programming had been consolidated under the AHRDS – this figure had jumped to 28,082 clients served. By 2005/6 it had increased substantially to 54,360 clients served. Over the past seven years about 52,000 clients have been served each year through AHRDS/ASETS funding, with an average 16,000 returned to work and 6,600 returned to school. These numbers have been fairly consistent from one year to the next. They peaked in 2008/9 and 2009/10 as a result of extra federal funding in response to the economic downturn.

ASEP/SPF has served an average of 6,400 clients since 2005/6, with an average of 2,200 employed. Very little information was available on Enhanced Service Delivery and the First Nations Job Fund. In 2014, twenty-seven Enhanced Service Delivery proposals, paired with twelve First Nations Job Fund proposals covering eighty-eight First Nation communities across Canada were implemented. Since 2013

6 These results vary by Aboriginal identify group. For example, outcomes for Metis, Inuit, and Aboriginal women have improved between 2006 and 2011. See National Aboriginal Economic Development Board (2015, 14).

1,300 clients have been served, of which 200 individuals have become employed and 40 have returned to school (Canada 2015).

AHRDS was evaluated in 2009, ASEP in 2013, and ASETS/SPF in 2015 (HRSDC 2009, 2013b; ESDC 2015a). These reports were positive and were available on ESDC's website. In contrast, the National Association of Friendship Centres surveyed its membership in 2009 and 2011 and concluded that ASETS was having limited success for urban Aboriginal people, and that there was a large urban service delivery gap that needed to be filled (NAFC 2012).

Efficiency

This research has noted inefficiencies in having separate ASETS and SPF programs, each with its own organizational structure and overhead. In many provinces ASETS programming was not well integrated with provincial programming. Concern was also expressed over a lack of attention to best practices learning, given that there had been no national Aboriginal conferences since 2007 and there was no pan-Canadian association to support ASETS holders in their work. Constrained by the distinctions-based approach and a lack of resources from the federal government, ASETS holders had not undertaken these activities on their own initiative.

It is not known the extent to which ASETS career development practitioners were qualified to perform their role. Unlike other communities that have self-organized, ASETS and SPF personnel did not appear to be highly engaged with the career development associations in their home province or with the umbrella employment-services organizations such as ASPECT in BC, ONESTEP and First Work in Ontario, or RQuODE and RCEE in Quebec. These organizations provide networking, conference, and policy advice to their membership and could include Aboriginal employment organizations within their province if they sought out membership. However, in 2015 ASETS holders generally saw themselves as separate from such provincial organizations, relying instead on the federal government for support.

ESDC – and HRDC before it – did produce a Labour Market Bulletin for ASETS and SFP constituents that examined, with an Aboriginal focus, general economic conditions, labour market and demographic trends, and current and potential employment opportunities at the national and regional levels. Available to the public, it often included feature articles on issues such as partnerships or entrepreneurship. In

2014 and 2015 there was one bulletin each year; in 2013 there were two. These facilitated some best practice learning (HRSDC 2013a). However, they were a far cry from the kind of connections available, such as in British Columbia through ASPECT and the BC Centre for Employment Excellence that respectively produced weekly and monthly bulletins for their employment services community.

Democracy

An Aboriginal informant interviewed through this research noted, "ASETS is Canada's greatest hidden asset, because almost no one knows about us." At least the Forum of Labour Market Ministers – representing federal, provincial, and territorial governments collectively – has its own web page. ASETS does not; other than a page on ESDC's departmental website listing the eighty-five ASETS holders that linked readers to each ASETS holder's individual website,[7] little consolidated information on ASETS was made available to the public by the Government of Canada. While ASETS/SPF holders had access to additional information through a password-protected Aboriginal portal, this was not available to the general public.

During 2013 and 2014 under the Conservatives and in 2016 under the Liberals the federal government consulted on the future of Aboriginal employment programming. However, participation was by invitation only. The report prepared by the federal government on the 2013 and 2014 roundtables was an internal document and not released to the public (ESDC 2014a). Both transparency and engagement were in short supply on Aboriginal employment programming in Canada. The federal stewardship role was very weak.

Conclusion

The twenty-five-year Pathways/RBA/AHRDS/ASETS legacy has provided Aboriginal labour market organizations with some degree of autonomy to ensure that labour market services for Aboriginal people are locally designed, flexible, and culturally sensitive. However, by

7 See https://www.canada.ca/en/employment-social-development/services/indigenous/agreement-holders.html. Each ASETS holder releases its own annual report.

2014 the federal commitment to expansion and growth – along with supporting Aboriginal control and empowerment evident in the late 1990s – had diminished significantly. There were important new actors in the game as provincial and territorial governments took on new labour market responsibilities. Federal funding arrangements tacked new programs onto the old, leading to greater fragmentation between the Aboriginal organizations delivering the programs. Up to 2015 no new resources had been allocated to deal with population growth and other costs of doing business. Over the past twenty years, federal support for capacity-building and coordination between the Aboriginal organizations on a pan-Canadian basis and within each province has become continuously weakened.

Despite these changes, there is an enduring commitment to retaining the current service delivery platform through the Aboriginal Skills and Employment Training Strategy (ASETS) – as heard at the HUMA parliamentary committee in 2014 and cross-Canada regional roundtables in 2013 and 2014 (ESDC 2014a). Whether this might change under the Trudeau Liberal commitment to nation-to-nation relationships with Indigenous people is not known.

Aboriginal employment programs are an essential component of Canada's PES. Aboriginal people are significantly disadvantaged in the labour market and are also the fastest growing cohort in the country. Without effective public employment services, employers will continue to bypass Aboriginal people, leading to their continued marginalization in Canadian society. Aboriginal leaders and governments across Canada have considerable work that needs to be undertaken to revitalize Aboriginal employment programming to make it fit for this task.

Chapter Nine

The Federal Role Post-Devolution

Chapters 4 to 8 of this book have described and assessed how between 1996 and 2015 provincial and territorial governments and Aboriginal labour market organizations took on the design and delivery of Canada's public employment service, or PES. Even with these arrangements, the Government of Canada continues to play the primary role, as it controls the money and sets the legislative, policy, and accountability framework under which the devolved programs operate. Ottawa is the only government with the legitimacy and capacity to convene national conversations on workforce development, including the PES. It has also retained responsibility for specific National Employment Services (NES) functions mandated under Part II of the EI Act, as well as "pan-Canadian programming."

These continuing federal responsibilities were described in the *2012 Canada Employment Insurance Monitoring and Assessment Report*:

> Canada plays a leadership role in active employment measures by ensuring accountability and evaluation of LMDA programming, and by developing labour market policy. In addition, the federal government plays a primary role in responding to challenges that extend beyond local and regional labour markets by delivering pan-Canadian activities and certain functions of the National Employment Service. Pan-Canadian activities fulfill three primary objectives: promoting an efficient and integrated national labour market and preserving and enhancing the Canadian economic union; helping address common labour market challenges and priorities of international or national scope that transcend provincial borders; and promoting equality of opportunity for all Canadians with a focus on helping underrepresented groups reach their full potential in the Canadian Labour Market. (CEIC 2012, 133)

This chapter examines the role that the Government of Canada has played in the public employment service in the twenty-year period post-devolution. It starts by assessing the accountability requirements in the federal/provincial and federal/Aboriginal labour market transfer agreements and how they have played out in practice. Next it looks at direct federal programming offered to youth through the Youth Employment Strategy and to persons with disabilities through the Opportunities Fund. Programming for these two client groups – as well as immigrants[1] – was specifically retained by Ottawa. Then developments and activities under the "pan-Canadian" funding umbrella are examined, with a particular focus over the past decade.

Intergovernmental coordination across Canada is assessed next, especially Ottawa's leadership in convening conversations between governments through the Forum of Labour Market Ministers and between other actors who deliver the PES, including community-based training organizations and career development practitioners. Unlike education and health care, employment services in Canada do not have a highly organized pan-Canadian policy community with powerful and mobilized stakeholders. The public employment service is also not a policy domain that affects all Canadians: most users of the service are unemployed and often poor and marginalized. The chapter concludes by considering how the views of program users and other stakeholders are secured at the national level. Especially important are the views of representatives of employers and workers whose contributions to the EI account fund most of the cost of the PES.

Federal/Provincial and Federal/Aboriginal Accountability

Federal-Provincial

As detailed in chapter 2 of this book, not only are the reporting and accountability regimes under the Labour Market Development Agreement (LMDA) and Labour Market Agreement (LMA) different, there are also different arrangements under the Labour Market Agreement for Persons with Disabilities (LMAPD) and the Targeted Initiative for

1 Employment programming for immigrants is a sub-component of immigrant settlement services and is directly managed by Immigration, Refugee and Citizenship Canada, not Employment and Social Development Canada.

Older Workers (TIOW). Federal and provincial civil servants interviewed through this research noted that the different accountability requirements in each agreement were very challenging to administer.

Post-devolution, Canada reported annually on results under the LMDAs through the *Employment Insurance Monitoring and Assessment Report*. Each province reported on its own on how it had used the LMA and LMAPD funding. For the TIOW the only public reporting was through federal evaluations, released by Ottawa from time to time. Provinces reported using three indicators under the LMDAs, while under the LMAs they reported on ten. The federal-provincial TIOW agreements are highly prescriptive. Results information is not publicly released. For the period that this book covers – 1995 to 2015 – provinces reported on common LMAPD indicators only as information was available. As part of the new generation of agreements negotiated in 2014, provinces agreed to report on ten new performance indicators and include additional federally prescribed information in their public reports.

The LMDAs decentralized (politically) the design and delivery of employment services for people with an EI attachment. While non-EI clients could be served, they were not eligible for longer-term and more expensive programming. Under the LMDAs, the federal government did not prescribe a specific program design, nor did it tell provincial governments which programs to utilize. Rather, the provinces designed their own programs, which were then subjected to a federal "test of similarity" to programs described in the federal EI Act. As noted, provinces were obliged to monitor and report their results according to three federally determined indicators, contextualized with local conditions and objectives. Targets were jointly determined by federal and provincial officials. There were no incentives – financial or otherwise – that would threaten provincial funding or cause them to adjust their behaviour on the basis of the chosen indicators.

From a comparative perspective, this is a relatively meagre performance review. European scholars who compared the federal-provincial accountability requirements in Canada to seven other federations characterized the Canadian accountability regime as "performance measurement" as opposed to "performance management" (Vandenbroucke and Luigjes 2016). For example, given the way that the LMDA funding has been distributed between provinces (a formula that has not changed since 1996), not only can poor activation performance by individual provinces be rewarded, the Government of Canada has no tools to ensure that provinces activate EI beneficiaries (and thereby reduce EI expenditure), as there are no incentives to target the programming to EI clients. In fact, provinces have an incentive to shift LMDA spending towards Employment Assistance Services, as this money can also be used to activate and reintegrate social assistance clients. This kind of interdependence between governments in multilevel systems is called "institutional moral hazard."[2] It is a factor in Canada. As shown in the latest EI Monitoring and Assessment Report, the non-insured beneficiary category continues to grow. In 1999/2000 21 per cent of clients served were non-insured; by 2013/14 this proportion had increased to 37 per cent.

In a recent report the OECD noted that "Canada holds a unique place in the OECD by virtue of its particular model of federation that features, in effect, two levels of sovereign government – federal and provincial – that must co-exist" (OECD 2010, 25). The exercise of federal oversight over the LMDA arrangements is deferential to the provinces as some, especially Quebec, question the authority of the federal government to impose conditions on provincial transfers. If in 1996 Ottawa had insisted on a more rigorous accountability regime, Labour Market Development Agreements would never have been signed in the first place.

Similar accountability issues applied to the LMAs; however, in this case there was no institutional moral hazard.[3] While it initially appeared that the federal government had imposed more accountability requirements through the Labour Market Agreements – including ten as opposed to three indicators that provinces were expected to report on – in 2012 Mosely described the Canadian arrangements under both the LMDA and LMA as "accountability light." Under the LMA Quebec did not even report using the same indicators as the rest

2 Institutional moral hazard arises in employment policy if there is a possibility for regions to influence unemployment insurance benefit costs borne by the central government. In a recent comparative study, the authors concluded that there has been limited federal concern in Canada, as a result of the relatively modest replacement rates of EI, the decreasing beneficiaries-to-unemployed ratio, and historical intergovernmental developments that precluded Ottawa from imposing conditions on provinces. See Vandenbroucke and Luigjes (2016, 24).

3 With the transformation of the Canada Assistance Plan into the Canada Health and Social Transfer in 1996, Ottawa's social assistance contributions are no longer determined by the size of provincial caseloads.

of Canada, nor was it expected to display its results so that Quebec could be compared to other provinces.

In examining the federal-provincial reporting scheme under the LMAPDs, Graefe and Levesque (2013) noted that the federal-provincial conflict inherent in reporting has led to a pro forma process of producing plans and reports that were little used by government or extra-governmental actors. In their view, this has stunted social policy innovation in Canada.

Federal-Aboriginal

In contrast, on the federal/Aboriginal side, the regime imposed by Ottawa on the ASETS holders was "accountability heavy." As described in chapter 8 of this book, ASETS holders were subject to an extensive accountability regime involving direct federal oversight, monitoring, and correction of expenditures by federal staff and auditors. Service Canada staff regularly visited ASETS holders for quality assurance and financial auditing. Given the strictness of the accountability regime, ASETS holders were extremely limited in their capacity to adopt policies outside the federally established framework that would have allowed them to make room for local and culturally relevant employment programming choices. Implementation of Aboriginal labour market programming in 2015 was far removed from the Pathways principles embracing Aboriginal self-government established in the mid-1990s.

Assessment of PES Accountability Regimes Post-Devolution

In two recent reports – one on employment services for disabled people and another on displaced workers – the OECD weighed in on accountability problems in Canada that they perceived had been exacerbated by devolution (OECD 2010, 2015b). Given that the federal government has no formal authority to monitor the performance of provinces, there was a minimal flow of information. Without a central coordinating mechanism there was no standardized yardstick to tell what is working or not. There was no easy way for the federal government to ensure that funding to provinces was spent in accordance with national policy priorities. There were no forums for disseminating information and engaging public debate, resulting in no tangible public expectations for improvement of outcomes. Having a multitude of programs meant that they were developed and administered in silos. With both governments involved, ultimate accountability to clients for policy performance and outcomes was divided and often blurred. In the OECD's view, one of the much-lauded virtues of federalism – that of promoting experimentation and innovative practices – was not happening in PES matters in Canada because data on outcomes were not comparable and information was not available in a transparent and timely fashion (OECD 2010).

There are other ways to ensure accountability, improve transparency, and facilitate policy learning in Canada's multi-tiered management of the PES besides layering more accountability requirements on the current structure of four separate federal-provincial labour market agreements. As will be identified in chapter 10 of this book, many of the federal-provincial dynamics that play out in Canada are also evident in the European Union. Sub-state autonomy – also a concern of provinces in Canada – is balanced alongside a pan-European policy dimension and EU-wide strategic direction by using the Open Method of Coordination as a governance technique. OMC approaches need to be studied more in Canada to see how some of these ideas might be translated into practice on this side of the Atlantic. Other suggestions to improve accountability in federal-provincial agreements are detailed in Graefe, Simmons, and White's edited 2013 book. Many of these ideas could also be transferred to the federal-Aboriginal context.

Direct Federal Programming That Supported Individual Clients

Despite acknowledging through devolution that provinces and territories were best placed to design and delivery labour market programming, in the mid-1990s the Government of Canada retained direct delivery responsibility for programs targeted to youth and persons with disabilities. These are funded through the Consolidated Revenue Fund, not the EI account.

Youth Employment Strategy

The Government of Canada has provided direct support for youth employment programs for over sixty years. As identified in chapter 2, it established a defined presence in the 1950s and expanded its initiatives for students, work-study, stay in school, youth at risk, and summer youth employment programs in the 1970s. By the late 1980s there were 100 federal youth centres on campuses across the country, funded primarily by the Government of Canada. Many argue that youth programs are the least logical for Ottawa to be providing directly, as the clientele is closest in age to the provincial school systems. If these systems have failed youth, then provinces should assume responsibility for their own failures (Lazar 2002).

When the federal Liberals cut Consolidated Revenue funding for equity groups as a result of program review in 1994/5, youth and Aboriginal employment programming were protected. In 1996 a ministerial task force, Take on the Future, recommended a revitalized federal Youth Employment Strategy (YES) and increased federal funding to youth-oriented initiatives. Implementing this recommendation meant that just as Ottawa was devolving programming to the provinces for one target group (EI clients), it was expanding its own direct involvement in employment services for a different target group (youth).

The objectives of YES are to enhance employability skills, encourage educational attainment, increase the number of skilled young Canadians aged fifteen to thirty, facilitate youth transition to the labour market, and provide labour market/employment information to youth. In 2014 federal officials identified YES as a $330-million initiative, led by Employment and Social Development Canada (ESDC) in collaboration with ten other federal departments (ESDC 2015c). There were three streams: Career Focus (for postsecondary graduates); Skills Link (for youth with barriers to employment); and Summer Work Experience (for high school and postsecondary students). The program is managed primarily by Service Canada offices across the country. YES was targeted to serve around fifty thousand clients each year (HRSDC 2014).

Provincial governments are also highly involved in youth employment programming. This varied from one province to another. An inventory of Canadian youth employment programs and services undertaken in 1997/8 identified $940 million in spending on activities by all jurisdictions, of which $417 million was from the federal government (as reported in McBride and Stoyko 2000, 229). As identified in earlier chapters of this book, Quebec, Newfoundland and Labrador, and Manitoba have retained specialized youth centres post-devolution. Youth employment programming run by the provinces is highly connected to their K–12 and postsecondary education systems. In its review of youth programming in Canada in 2008, the OECD noted federal and provincial overlap in youth employment programming and suggested that better coordination was needed (OECD 2008a). Efforts to do this in the late 1990s through the Forum of Labour Market Ministers failed. No further multilateral attempts have been made since.

Given that devolution resulted in provinces acquiring a large swathe of labour market programs, maintaining a separate system for youth on the federal side would seem to be needlessly redundant and result in the poor integration of services. In 2000 McBride and Stoyko suggested that folding federal youth programming into an arrangement similar to an LMDA would be logistically fairly simple. However, the authors also noted many reasons why the federal Liberals retained a direct federal role. First, they discerned considerable public support for enhancing education as an antidote to economic insecurity. Ottawa also spent heavily on postsecondary education through grants to enhance university research. Second, in contrast to conditional grants to provinces, direct federal spending provided high visibility and a way to receive political credit. Third, there was concern about the adverse effects of deficit reduction and public sector reforms on the younger generation. For federal Liberal politicians, youth programming was seen as a way of partially compensating those who did not have the opportunity to enjoy the same political supports that other generations did.

When the Conservative party under Stephen Harper came to power in 2006 it did not seem to support direct federal involvement in youth employment programming. Its new "labour market training architecture" – outlined in the 2007 budget – offered to "explore the feasibility of transferring to provinces and territories well over $500 million of annual funding associated with existing federal labour market programs for youth, older workers, and persons with disabilities" (Finance Canada 2007, 132). While provinces reacted positively to the idea of taking on this federal youth programming, ultimately there was no change in responsibility.

Instead, federal youth employment programming was expanded during the economic downturn between 2008 and 2010; however, by 2014/15 programming under the Conservatives had shrunk substantially. Hatt (2014) noted that summer hiring of students in the federal public service after 2009 had declined by more than a third. Federal Hire-a-Student offices were closed in 2011. In 2013/14 $30 million in Skills Link funding went unspent, leading to staff layoffs and closed offices in youth employment organizations (Wood 2015a). Despite the overlap with provincial programming noted in the 2008 OECD assessment, this research uncovered no evidence that the Government of Canada planned to stop running a national Youth Employment Program. A 2015 evaluation commissioned by the Government of Canada confirmed that the program remained relevant and that it continued to make a difference in the lives of Canadian youth (ESDC 2015c). The Trudeau Liberals – elected with a majority in 2015 – have committed to a significant expansion of federal youth employment programming.

Federal Disability Programming

An informant interviewed through this research noted that the disability community had been devastated by the federal cutbacks to provincial programming through the CHST in the mid-1990s, and what was perceived as the federal government walking away from its responsibilities to disabled people. As identified in chapter 2, as a result of these concerns, the federal-provincial Vocational Rehabilitation of Disabled Persons (VRDP) Agreement was left intact and not folded into the broader CHST transfer. In addition, the Government of Canada established a Federal Task Force on Disability Issues, chaired by Andy Scott, a prominent Liberal MP. Out of this came *In Unison: A Canadian Approach to Disability Issues,* accepted by all governments (except Quebec) as a framework for pan-Canadian action.

However, there was no new federal money available to implement this pan-Canadian vision. As an alternative, Ottawa made a modest reaffirmation of federal involvement in disability programming through the launch in 1997 of a new program – the Opportunities Fund (OF) – a directly managed federal initiative using money from the Consolidated Revenue Fund. Like YES, implementing a new federal disability program ran counter to the devolution of labour market programming to provinces through the LMDAs. OF was another example of the federal Liberals asserting leadership in a policy area it would otherwise have fully lost control of.

The Opportunities Fund aims to increase the labour force participation of Canadians with disabilities by supporting individuals who have no or little labour force attachment to prepare for, obtain, and keep employment or become self-employed. Eligible participants can access a range of interventions and services, including job search supports, coaching, counselling, résumé writing, interview preparation, job placements, tuition assistance, wage subsidies, and entrepreneurial training. These activities are similar to provincial interventions under LMAPD.

After the Harper Conservatives took control of government in 2006, the focus of Opportunity Fund programming shifted to wage subsidies. Funding for employer awareness activities was also available to eligible organizations. In 2015 the Opportunities Fund was delivered primarily at the regional level through Service Canada offices that distributed funds for projects through applications or calls for proposal. Some projects extended across provinces. It was a much smaller program than YES, with an annual allocation in 2013/14 of $38.7 million.

Intergovernmental momentum on disability issues died when the Harper Conservatives assumed power in 2006 and federal-provincial social services ministers stopped meeting. Instead the Conservatives made a number of changes to the federal tax system to offset disability-related costs. In 2012 they launched a Panel on Labour Market Opportunities for Persons with Disabilities that in 2013 produced a report to help companies accelerate success through the talents of people with disabilities. Out of this came the establishment of Canadian Business SenseAbility as a national, not-for-profit organization run by business for business. The federal government provided start-up funding.

For many years the Government of Canada provided direct grants to the disability advocacy community to offset their organizing costs so that they could engage in policy development. In the early 2000s about $5 million was available annually through the Social Development Partnerships Program. In 2012 the Conservatives started to phase out the program; by 2015 all federal funding had disappeared. The government noted that the federal role would change from funder to enabler. Organizations were encouraged to look instead to charities and the private sector (ESDC 2014c).

This significantly diminished capacity in the disability community. A respondent interviewed through this research noted that eliminating federal funding to the organizations was viewed by many in the disability community as a direct attack on the social contract that had been in place between government and social agencies since the Mulroney years. Levesque (2012) noted in particular the problems that have emerged over the past decade due to the lack of stable core funding for disability organizations. This limits their capacity for innovative programming.

A summative evaluation of the Opportunities Fund noted that between 2008 and 2013 the program had assisted 8,281 Canadians with disabilities to find employment. While the evaluation found that there was an ongoing need for labour market programming for persons with disabilities, it also suggested a "medium" level of overlap and lack of coordination with other programs, including those delivered by provinces under the LMA and LMAPD agreements. There was also overlap noted with the federal YES and ASETS programs. The evaluation concluded that the objectives of the Opportunity Fund remained relevant in the context of other ESDC labour market programming for persons with disabilities. However, attention should be given to better coordination and collaboration among programs (ESDC 2015d).

The OECD (2010) also explored this issue in an analysis of Canada's sickness and disability benefits systems, including employment services for persons with disabilities offered through the LMDAs, LMAs, LMAPDs, and the Opportunity Fund. It found policymaking in silos and poor coordination between federal and provincial governments. In 2010 it concluded that our system – as opposed to a client – focus in operational policymaking has produced a fragmented array of benefits and employment services that were difficult for clients to navigate and access, with too little systematic early detection and intervention to prevent the labour market detachment that often preceded long-term benefit dependency.

The OECD suggested that the remaining federal disability employment programs be handed over to the provinces, as then responsibility and spotlight would fall squarely on the latter to deliver. In its view, with both the federal and provincial governments involved, accountability to clients for policy performance and outcomes was divided and often blurred (OECD 2010). Levesque (2012) suggested another route: expanding the federal role by directly funding disability groups to meet social goals. There was no evidence detected through this research of changes in either direction, although federal funding for the Opportunities Fund increased marginally when the Conservatives were in charge between 2006 and 2015 (Wood 2015a).

Assessment of Federal Direct Involvement in Youth and Disability Programming

Despite devolution and OECD assessments of federal-provincial overlap and duplication, the Government of Canada has retained a direct delivery role in employment services through the Youth Employment Strategy (YES) and the Opportunities Fund (OF). While in 2015 YES was a large expenditure, OF was relatively small. Keeping these responsibilities has meant that Service Canada must maintain an infrastructure across Canada for developing and awarding grants, as the programs are delivered almost exclusively through third-party contracts to not-for profit organizations. Unlike ASETS programming, YES and OF are not delivered under a single brand through long-term contracts. With short-term competitive arrangements, few mechanisms have been put in place for agencies receiving the funding to provide input into federal policy or learn best practices from one place to another. Many of these same agencies also receive provincial funding, forcing them to confront two completely different contract management approaches. It was even more complicated in Ontario, where three levels of government were involved.

What is so special about these two groups that employment services were not devolved to the provinces along with the other federal programming? In my view it comes down to the political popularity of youth and the disabled versus the unpopularity of EI clients and other vulnerable groups (often perceived by the public as laggards and undeserving of government support); the attentiveness and organizational capacity of the respective stakeholder community; and the need for Ottawa to demonstrate to Canadians the continued relevance and salience of an ever-shrinking federal government role in labour market programming.

A federal presence in youth programming goes back over sixty years and has been seen by both Liberal and Conservative governments as a core federal responsibility. While provinces have challenged Ottawa to some degree on this, the issue has not captured public imagination as a problem that needs to be solved. Given sustained higher youth unemployment rates over time, any government action is seen as positive. Post-devolution, the federal youth programs have generally operated quietly under the radar, providing an opportunity for federal announcements and ribbon-cutting events by members of Parliament. While having two orders of government doing the same thing in the same policy domain has added complexity, many organizations that received the federal youth funding did not want Ottawa to withdraw, fearing the unknown of having the money administered by provincial governments. While funding under the Harper Conservatives was unreliable and some boards refused to allow their executive directors to apply, the additional dollars promised by the Trudeau Liberals offered new hope for increased opportunities in 2016.

Direct federal delivery of disability employment programming expanded only in the 1990s, so it does not have same historical roots and federal presence as youth programming with its stand-alone federal youth employment centres. Before the 1990s Ottawa was content to support disability programming through transfers to provinces, as well as grants to disability organizations to assist them in an advocacy role. A more direct federal role through the Opportunities Fund came about in 1997 as a way to demonstrate a federal commitment to disability issues in light of the large cutbacks made to provincial transfers. It was kept in place and expanded somewhat under the Conservatives through the lobbying efforts of national disability organizations. However, by 2014 most had lost their core federal funding.

There are also administrative and accounting issues that provide a rationale for a more direct federal role. Direct spending versus provincial transfers provides better accountability, as reporting by provinces on their spending on disability programming under VRDP/EAPD/LMAPD has always been problematic. Graefe and Levesque (2013) noted that provinces have assiduously protected their jurisdiction in disability programming, and that the reports they have provided to Ottawa over the years have been of little value. They wrote them only because they had to.

Pan-Canadian Programming

Every year since 2003 the *Employment Insurance Monitoring and Assessment Report* (*MAR*) has outlined federal spending on "pan-Canadian" activities, most supported with funding from the EI account. The most expensive pan-Canadian activity detailed in the *MAR* each year is programming provided by the ASETS holders. While other pan-Canadian activities have varied from one year to the next as specific initiatives waxed and waned, they were generally organized into three categories: (1) labour market partnerships; (2) federal elements of the National Employment Service; and (3) research and evaluation.

Labour Market Partnerships

Labour market partnerships were the most diverse component of pan-Canadian activities and the stream that has undergone the most change. One of the most important programs funded post-devolution was the Sector Council Program. At its peak in 2012, thirty-six national sector councils received core funding from the federal government, as well as an Alliance of Sector Councils that bound them together as a group. Directed by business and labour and supported by postsecondary institutions, sector councils developed national occupational standards as well as career products. Focused on the needs of their specific industry, the councils provided an opportunity for their members to come together to share ideas, concerns, and perspectives about industrial challenges for their sector and identify collective and sustainable solutions.

When it first took charge in 2006, the Harper Conservative government set up new councils in agriculture and forestry. However, it soon changed its mind about the value of the sector council initiative, and operational funding for all the councils ended on 31 March 2013. One informant suggested that the demise of the sector councils was a result of a number of factors: the small-government mindset of the Conservatives; a general reluctance to fund non-government organizations; a desire to reduce the voice of organized labour; a view that skills and labour market issues were a provincial, not a federal responsibility; and the fact that council members were too close to federal officials and inadequately engaged with politicians. Another informant suggested that funding was eliminated to serve the Conservatives' ideological agenda and business orientation.

Most sector councils were located in Ottawa or Toronto, and many failed to adjust to devolution by actively building linkages with provincial governments, now responsible for the design and delivery of most labour market programming. Given the loss of federal funding, by 2015 most sector councils had closed. Those that survived received their financial support from business, labour, and charitable foundations, as well as project funding from federal and provincial governments. Ottawa replaced the Sector Council Program with a much smaller Sectoral Initiatives Program, with funding available in a competitive process. By 2013/14 twenty-nine projects had been approved for dissemination and development of labour market information, national occupational certification, and/or accreditation in high-demand areas.

Also supported through labour market partnerships post-devolution were two skills tables: industry-driven organizations comprising key stakeholders focused upon specific initiatives. The Asia-Pacific Gateway Skills Table, located in British Columbia, was incorporated in the fall of 2008, with a mission to ensure that the labour force was equipped with the skills and training required to meet the needs of the Asia-Pacific Gateway (CEIC 2009). Between 2008 and 2013 the project received close to $6 million in funding from the federal government. Core funding was discontinued in March 2013 (CEIC 2013). The Yukon Skills Table Committee was added in 2011, responsible for cross-sectoral work to address key labour market priorities.

Pan-Canadian funding also supported a National Essential Skills Initiative. Focused on individuals with low literacy, the initiative provided practical tools and supports that employers, practitioners, and other stakeholders could use to improve literacy and essential skills. Funding supplemented resources already in place through the Office of Literacy and Essential Skills, as well as test social finance models that rewarded organizations that delivered pay-for-performance agreements that brought about the desired results (CEIC 2012/13).

Funding was also invested in the Interprovincial Standards Red Seal Program through the Canadian Council of Directors of Apprenticeship. Federal support to the Red Seal program was especially important to the Harper Conservative government given the priority it placed on apprenticeship. The Red Seal program was the main delivery platform for the federal Apprenticeship Incentive Grant and the Apprenticeship Tax Credit, introduced in 2007.

For many years an initiative called Youth Awareness was supported under pan-Canadian activities, meant to mobilize employers and communities to include youth in their response to labour market adjustment. Federal funding was regularly provided to Skills Canada, a national not-for-profit organization that organizes an annual skills competition intended to reposition trades and technical careers as a first-choice career option for youth. In 2014/15 the Youth Awareness program received its final year of funding through the pan-Canadian envelope. Starting in 2015/16 it was funded through the Youth Employment Strategy.

Labour mobility initiatives were also a key focus for pan-Canadian funding, to ensure that there were similar standards for occupations and professions – or at least a system of mutual recognition – across the country. Designing these standards is both costly and time consuming, involving regulatory agencies from all provinces, responsible for 400 professions and skilled trades. Pan-Canadian funding was used as a way to assist regulatory authorities to move to common standards and remove barriers to mobility, as set out in chapter 7 of the Agreement on Internal Trade. A number of forums were supported after 2011 using the Canadian Network of National Associations of Regulators. As part of that work, regulatory authorities from across Canada also considered the implications of the pan-Canadian Framework for the Assessment and Recognition of Foreign Credentials.

After the co-managed provinces entered into devolved agreements in 2008, money was allocated from pan-Canadian initiatives to ensure that they had proper systems support and connectivity to transfer data to the federal government and track provincial LMDA programming. This funding stream was later extended to support ASETS organizations. In 2012/13 a two-year project was initiated to modernize federal LMDA-related systems to ensure that EI claimants moved into the workforce quickly and improved their employability. This strengthened the links and coordination between federally delivered EI Part I (income support) and provincially delivered EI Part II EBSMs (CEIC 2012/13).

National Employment Service (NES)

Post-devolution, the federal government has maintained responsibility for two key functions of the NES: Job Bank and labour market information or LMI. Part II of the EI Act and regulations assigns the federal government responsibility for collecting and disseminating information on employment opportunities and labour market conditions, so that Canadians can access quality LMI about all areas of the country.

The National Job Bank opened in 1980. Maintained by federal officials in partnership with provincial and territorial officials, the electronic labour exchange provides access to job listings as well as specialized online career development tools such as Job Match, Résumé Builder, and Career Navigator. Merged with Working in Canada (WiC) in 2014, this free online service connects job seekers and employers from across the country and also helps individuals prepare for and carry out their return-to-work action plans. In 2013/14 Job Bank received more than 59 million visits and provided access to more than 1 million job postings. Over 116 million Job Alerts were sent to over 300,000 subscribers (CEIC 2013/14).

The LMI service provides local, regional, and national LMI information. Post-devolution, a regional network of analysts and economists employed by the Government of Canada continues to monitor and analyse socio-economic data and events to identify labour market trends. Utilizing pan-Canadian funding, national guidelines were employed to create LMI products. In 2012/13 a new National Work Plan for Regional LMI was implemented using pan-Canadian funding, including 11 LMI products in five key areas: labour market outlooks, labour market analysis, labour market news, occupational information, and support to Service Canada operations (CEIC 2012/13).

A key informant interviewed for this research noted that both pre- and post-devolution federal officials saw themselves as playing an active role in LMI as a catalyst, funder, and coordinator, responsible for bringing provinces and territories and key experts together on a number of initiatives. For example, Canada InfoNet was set up using funding provided by the Foreign Credentials Office as an online forum. It offered mentoring and access to resources and other services to help internationally educated business and trades people integrate into Canadian society and find jobs in their chosen profession. Another initiative focused on youth. While these were generally maintained, budgets became much tighter during the Harper Conservative years.

Research, Evaluation, and Innovation

Post-devolution, the Pan-Canadian Innovations Initiative (PCII) provided funding to organizations to carry out research and demonstration projects designed to test potential improvements to provincial EBSM programming. In 2008/09 twelve projects across Canada were approved, focused mainly on under-represented groups. Research and innovation funds were also used to support Learn$ave, a demonstration project that encouraged low-income Canadians to invest in their own human capital, thereby increasing their opportunities to find and maintain employment. After 2008 there was less demand for national PCII funding as provinces and territories focused on local priorities, using supplementary funding provided through the LMAs. PCII was wound down in 2011/12 (CEIC 2012).

A research project on the effectiveness of LMI was launched in 2008 and concluded in 2012, comprising a set of experimental projects to test the impact of various LMI interventions on diverse clients. Another measured the impact of career development services. A project examining the effect of motivational interviewing was implemented in 2011 (CEIC 2012). In 2011/12 the Foreign Credentials Recognition Loans pilot project was launched to create a base of evidence on financial barriers to internationally trained individuals. By the spring of 2013 nine project sites had been established in nine provinces, providing more than five hundred loans to internationally trained individuals (CEIC 2012/13).

The federal government and all provinces and territories also completed evaluations on the impact of Employment Benefits and Support Measures (EBSMs) under the LMDAs, focusing on the degree to which the interventions increased employment earnings and labour market attachment. Provincial formative and summative LMDA evaluations began to be posted on the federal website starting around 1998 and were subsequently noted in the *MAR* as they were released. In 2012 the *MAR* started to report on medium-term net and incremental impacts, that is impacts over a period of up to five years after a client's participation.

Assessment of Federal Involvement in Pan-Canadian Programming

Outside of ASETS, the 2013/14 *MAR* reported pan-Canadian spending of around $24 million, a significant decrease from previous years. For example, the 2010 *MAR* reported non-ASETS pan-Canadian expenditures of around $70 million. While many pan-Canadian activities have been described in this chapter, given this reduced level of investment, by 2015 Ottawa's pan-Canadian activities were a relatively minor element of PES spending in Canada.

Pan-Canadian programming declined substantially after the Harper Conservatives took control of government in 2006. Funding was withdrawn from the Sector Council Program, the Asia-Pacific Gateway Skills Table, youth awareness initiatives, and research and innovation. Some of this retreat was taken up through new, smaller pan-Canadian initiatives such as enhancing labour mobility, improving apprenticeship coordination, testing social finance models, and modernizing LMDA systems. There seemed to be a consistent federal investment in the Job Bank and LMI using pan-Canadian funding.

Federal Coordination and Leadership

Tracking federal spending on pan-Canadian activities funded through the EI account and reported in the *MAR* is one way to assess the federal PES role post-devolution. Another is to review federal leadership in pan-Canadian coordination and the development of national strategies for the PES. There are some things that provinces, acting together, cannot do. Given its constitutional competence and the financial resources available from the Employment Insurance account, only the Government of Canada has the legitimacy and capacity to lead pan-Canadian initiatives in labour market matters. While some money is necessary, more important is the mobilization of political will and interest among politicians, senior civil servants, and stakeholders.

There were considerable differences between the Liberals and the Conservatives in their views on the Government of Canada's leadership role in the federation. As outlined in chapter 2 of this book, between

1993 and 2006 the Chrétien/Martin Liberals were quite prepared to mobilize federal regulatory and spending powers to demonstrate leadership on a number of policy fronts. In contrast, the Conservative party, led by Stephen Harper between 2006 and 2015, believed in the "watertight" compartment approach to federalism. This meant that, in general, it did not engage collectively with the provinces to seek collaborative solutions to pressing policy issues. Over nine years in power, Prime Minister Harper convened only one first ministers' meeting with provincial premiers and territorial leaders. The Conservatives also did not value evidence-based research, as illustrated by their decision in 2011 to downgrade the Canadian census.

This attitude at the highest level sets the tone for activities at the policy level, whether in health care, environment, labour market, or any other policy field. Three strands were examined in order to assess federal coordination and leadership in PES matters over the 1995–2015 period: undertakings between federal/provincial/territorial governments through the Forum of Labour Market Ministers (FLMM); support for pan-Canadian coordination of not-for-profit (NGO) organizations involved with PES program delivery; and federal coordination of Canada's involvement in international activities.

Intergovernmental Coordination through the FLMM

As has been illustrated throughout this book, there is considerable interdependence between federal and provincial governments in Canada in labour market matters. This interdependence was evident before devolution. As a result, the Forum of Labour Market Ministers, or FLMM, was set up in 1983 as a federal/provincial/territorial forum to promote inter-jurisdictional cooperation and establish common goals on labour market issues; to promote a highly skilled, portable workforce; to facilitate adaptation to changes in skill requirements; and to provide a link to labour force development boards. As noted in chapters 2 to 8, these boards with business, labour, community, and Aboriginal organizations were all disbanded in the late 1990s. While the FLMM coordinated its work with other intergovernmental (IGR) forums (e.g., ministers of education and ministers of social services), given the demise of labour force boards it had no defined linkages with stakeholders outside of government.

The LMDA and LMA Agreements described and assessed in this book were negotiated bilaterally between the federal government and each province one at a time, not on a multilateral basis through a negotiated framework that was then customized for each province. The FLMM did, however, provide an institutional way pre- and post-devolution for jurisdictions to come together to discuss pan-Canadian issues, identify problems with the current arrangements, and propose solutions. For example, Quebec used an FLMM meeting in 1993 as a way to identify its concerns with federal delivery of labour market programming (Quebec 1993b). In 2002 provincial and territorial labour market ministers used the FLMM to develop a report calling for devolved LMDA agreements all around and for increased federal funding. In 2013 they came together to protest against the unilateral federal imposition of the Canada Job Grant (Provincial-Territorial Labour Market Ministers 2002, 2013).

Like all other IGR forums in Canada, the FLMM functions at the level of minister, deputy minister, and officials. In 2015 there were five working groups of officials: labour mobility, foreign credential recognition, effective employment services, workforce development, and labour market information. The FLMM is co-chaired by the federal government and a lead province; this lead province role rotates every two years. An equal split of federal and provincial/territorial resources provides funding for the lead province to hire two or three staff to perform a secretariat role.

Given these limited resources, the FLMM does not have the capacity to undertake independent research or other activities that might strengthen the PES on a pan-Canadian basis. Despite calls in 2009 for a stronger and more permanent FLMM secretariat to improve labour market information (Advisory Panel on Labour Market Information 2009), it took over six years for the FLMM to develop a Labour Market Information Council. In 2015 details on what the council would do, as well as its stakeholder advisory council and permanent secretariat, were still unclear. While the FLMM has developed and maintains two websites on labour market information and labour mobility – as well as a broader website for the forum as a whole – much of the information on the sites in 2014 was dated (Wood 2014).

According to the Canadian Intergovernmental Conference Secretariat, between 1996 and 2003 under the Liberals, the Forum of Labour Market Ministers generally met annually. For the ten-year period between 2003 and 2013 they met only once, leaving all work to the discretion and initiative of officials. Informants interviewed through this research suggested that the main reason that ministers did not meet between 2003 and 2013 was because of federal disengagement. When the Liberals were in power, the issue was federal refusal to negotiate a devolved LMDA with Ontario, as well as with the provinces and territories that had previously signed co-managed LMDAs. After the Conservatives took control in 2006 and offered devolved agreements all around, Diane Finlay – federal minister for a short period in 2006–7 and then re-appointed in October 2008 until July 2013 – preferred bilateral engagement. The FLMM has been more active in recent years, meeting once in 2013, twice in 2014, and once in 2015.

Writing in 2014, I assessed intergovernmental policy capacity through the FLMM as weak, compared to other forums like the Council of Ministers of Education Canada and the Employment, Social Policy, Health and Consumer Affairs Council (EPSCO) in the European Union (Wood 2015b). This was partly the result of federal disengagement with provinces and their preference for unilateral action. However, another reason is structural. With a secretariat that rotates every two years between provinces, FLMM work is significantly dependent on the competence, capacity, and interest of the provincial co-chair. Between 2003 and 2013 the forum was virtually invisible. While progress was made on labour mobility, by 2015 little had been achieved on labour market information. There was no evidence of any work by the FLMM to address key issues such as skills and labour shortages or Aboriginal unemployment. After 2013, provinces and territories forced the federal government to re-engage to resolve issues related to the transformation of the Labour Market Agreements into the Canada Job Grant (Provincial-Territorial Labour Market Ministers 2013). In this they were successful.

The Canadian Council of Directors of Apprenticeship (CCDA) also plays a role as an intergovernmental body in labour market matters, including management of the Red Seal program. The CCDA comprises provincial and territorial directors of apprenticeship. It has been meeting regularly for over thirty years, with secretariat services provided by federal ESDC officials. With funding from the Government of Canada, it sponsors an annual National Apprenticeship Stakeholders meeting. Supporting the CCDA is the Canadian Apprenticeship Forum (CAF). Established in the late 1990s as a subcommittee of the Canadian Labour Force Development Board and funded between 2000 and 2013 through the Sector Council Program, CAF is a national not-for-profit body that brings together all players in apprenticeship training from across the country. As a national voice for the apprenticeship community, CAF influences pan-Canadian apprenticeship strategies through research, discussion, and collaboration.

Core federal funding for CAF through the Sector Council Program ended in 2013. To survive without federal funding, CAF restructured and was able to secure ongoing financial support from business, unions, and provinces as well as short-term contracts. A respondent interviewed through this research noted that stakeholders refused to let the organization go under and rallied to save it. He suggested that being free of dependence on federal funding had made CAF stronger than ever. I am not so sure; the bottom line for this inquiry is that federal funding was withdrawn from one of the few long-standing collaborative initiatives that facilitated connections between governments and stakeholders on a pan-Canadian basis in workforce development.

Support to Pan-Canadian NGO Coordination

When the Government of Canada was still the main PES delivery agent across the country, it often provided funding and administrative support to facilitate connections between non-government organizations (NGOs) directly involved with PES program delivery in different provinces. Post-devolution – especially under the Harper Conservatives – almost all of this federal funding and support has disappeared.

One of these groups is the Canadian Coalition of Community-Based Employability Training (CCCBET),[4] a national, non-profit organization whose membership comprises representatives from provincial community-based employment and training associations. This includes organizations described in earlier chapters of this book such as ASPECT in British Columbia, First Work and ONESTEP in Ontario, and RQuODE in Quebec. Involvement in CCCBET is a way to maintain pan-Canadian connections, undertake advocacy on behalf of the community-based training sector, and facilitate best-practice learning across Canada. Many of the over one thousand community-based training organizations who delivered Canada's PES in 2015 (through contractual arrangements with federal and provincial governments) belonged to provincial umbrella organizations that come together under CCCBET.

Formally established in 1994, CCCBET has always been self-directed and self-organizing. It has never had a permanent secretariat or ongoing

---

4 See http://www.ccocde-cccbet.com/en/home/.

staff. However, it often qualified for federal grants for national projects and in this way built pan-Canadian connections. Post-devolution these national grants have faded away. As provincial agencies turned their attention towards their respective provincial governments who were now in charge of letting contracts under the federal LMDA and LMA funding, CCCBET as an organization faltered. Like the FLMM, it was re-energized in 2013 as the result of concerns about the impact of the Canada Job Grant on access to employment services for under-represented groups. However, with limited resources, the organization is highly vulnerable. Attempts between 2013 and 2015 to reach out to the Forum of Labour Market Ministers on behalf of the community-based training sector received limited response.

Even though the federal government has chosen to maintain direct oversight for youth, disability, and Aboriginal employment programming, post-devolution it has provided no leadership or funding support to assist these mostly not-for-profit delivery organizations to come together either collectively or within their separate streams to team-build and network, share best practices, and promote coordination. As detailed in chapter 8, annual conferences for ASETS holders stopped after 2007. Although youth organizations in Ontario come together under First Work to organize annual conferences, there is no federal funding support. Instead, some support for three years came from the Counselling Foundation of Canada. On the disability front, for over twenty years community organizations from across Canada managing supported employment programs for persons with developmental disabilities have come together each year in a conference organized under the auspices of the Canadian Association for Supported Employment, or CASE. In 2015 all efforts related to CASE came from the community organizations themselves; despite requests to the Government of Canada for funding support for its pan-Canadian conference and other initiatives, none was forthcoming.

One area where ongoing federal support had been provided on a pan-Canadian basis post-devolution was literacy. The National Literacy Secretariat was established in 1988 under the Progressive Conservatives, with $20 million allocated to literacy projects and organizations across the country. In 1997 funding was increased by 30 per cent as the Liberals moved to demonstrate federal leadership. With the Conservatives in charge, funding to local literacy organizations ended in 2006. By 2015, also gone was funding for national and provincial/territorial literacy coalitions. This has resulted in the closure of the Canadian

Literacy and Learning Network and Copian (a national clearinghouse) as well as several provincial literacy organizations. In 2015 the remaining literacy funding was routinely underspent as way to help balance the federal budget (Wood 2015a).

Another area of traditional federal strength in workforce development was its support for the career development practitioner (CDP) profession. In Canada, career and employment services are mostly publicly funded. While CDPs are employed by high schools, postsecondary institutions, or other organizations, most work for the public employment service.

Starting in the 1970s, the federal department responsible for the PES worked hard to develop a team of internal experts providing leadership, expertise, and funding to support CDP excellence. Government action was supplemented by four non-government organizations. Established in 1979, the Canadian Career Development Foundation (CCDF) develops and delivers training for career development practitioners; develops career education/development resources, programs, and tools; and conducts evidence-based research. It was instrumental in facilitating the development of Canadian standards and guidelines for CDPs. These outline the competencies that service providers need to deliver comprehensive career services to clients.

The CCDF also chairs the Canadian Council for Career Development (CCCD), an organization that brings together the nine provincial CDP associations as well as other players to work on pan-Canadian priorities such as certification, advocacy, and media penetration. While the CCDF received government grants in the past, it has always been self-supporting through project-based funding. CCDF is also the main conduit for Canada to relate to the International Centre for Career Development and Public Policy.

The Counselling Foundation of Canada (CFC) (a family foundation established by Frank G. Lawson and his estate in 1959) and the Canadian Education and Research Institute for Counselling (CERIC) are also key actors, providing funding to assist with the advancement of education and research in the field of career counselling and career development. Since 2007 CERIC has annually hosted Cannexus, Canada's largest bilingual career development conference. It also publishes the country's only peer-reviewed journal (the *Canadian Journal of Career Development*) and runs the free ContactPoint/OrientAction online communities, which provides learning and networking in the career field.

Before devolution, the federal government provided leadership to the CDP profession in a wide variety of ways, including training and support for federal staff working in the regions who delivered client services under the PES; developing labour market information systems such as CanWorkInfoNet (which later became CanWin); and hosting and funding NATCOM (the predecessor of Cannexus). It also provided financial support to various pan-Canadian bodies active in the field (Van Norman, Shepard, and Mani 2014). Post-devolution, informants interviewed through this research noted that federal direct action as well as partnerships had become much more limited and circumscribed. The Canada Career Consortium – a national leadership organization in career development – was the last federally funded organization to operate. In 2015 there was almost no federal project-based funding available to the four NGOs active in the career development field.

Federal support through the FLMM to help provinces develop the skills of their CDPs has also disappeared. As provinces took on the PES role, between 2007 and 2011 a federal/provincial/territorial FLMM Career Development Services (CDS) working group was established, with costs shared 50:50 between the provinces and the federal government. A key informant interviewed through this research who has worked in three provincial PES systems over the past fifteen years noted, "While on the working group I saw lots of duplication across the country, with people reinventing the wheel ... we have a hugely fragmented system that is becoming more so every day ... everything is segmented by province and Ottawa does not see itself playing a coordinating role. As a result, there is limited relationship-building happening to let partnerships develop between provinces ... Although Alberta tried, when Ontario withdrew from the CDS working group, federal funding ended and the working group was subsequently disbanded. While some of the work has transitioned to the FLMM workforce development working group, subject expertise has been lost and the focus on the needs of career development practitioners has diminished."

As identified in chapters 4 to 7 of this book, the support provided to career development practitioners by provincial governments varied considerably from one province to another, dependent upon the delivery model that had been chosen (in particular the degree to which the services were contracted out) and the strength and interest of its provincial career development association. Post-devolution the strongest support for the profession (and partnerships with organizations like the CCDF) came from Alberta, New Brunswick, Manitoba, and

Saskatchewan. In 2014 these all had a mixed PES delivery system comprising civil servants who provided front-door access to employment services supported by non-government organizations offering specialized services through contractual arrangements. Without federal leadership and funding through a structured process such as had been provided through the FLMM working group, best practice sharing between provinces on career development matters in Canada in 2015 was very much a hit-and-miss affair.

Coordinating International Connections

Unlike in education, labour, or health care, the international dimension of the public employment service in Canada is relatively minor and is rarely felt at the delivery level in services to the unemployed or employers. Post-devolution, Canada has regularly participated in research undertaken by the Organisation for Economic Cooperation and Development (OECD). As a founding member of the World Association of Public Employment Services (WAPES) in 1988, federal government officials also participated in WAPES events and activities. Ottawa is also obligated to report to the International Labour Organization (ILO) on conventions related to the PES and respond to concerns over implementation identified by employer organizations or organized labour.

OECD research on the PES is important as it enables Canada to benchmark its policies and programs against those of other countries at similar levels of development, thereby filling a knowledge gap in Canadian policy research. It also allows Canada to participate in forward-thinking international research. Ottawa funds projects deemed to have policy importance and are identified as a priority. Between 2003 and 2014, thirty-six OECD projects were funded by Employment and Social Development Canada (ESDC), usually between two to six projects per fiscal year.[5] This cost about $300,000 per annum. ESDC officials also worked extensively with five OECD committees/programs, providing Canadian input through these committees into OECD priorities and the selection of work projects and priorities (ESDC 2014b).

An evaluation in 2014 of Canada's involvement with OECD projects related to ESDC's mandate confirmed that the research provided "solid

5 This book cites eight of these studies.

recommendations that grasp the Canadian reality." It was considered as good value for money (ESDC 2014b, 6). The evaluation noted that few other organizations apart from the OECD had the capability to effectively analyse Canadian data and policies and compare them to other countries reliably. Value was noted "not only in relation to returns on investment and the quality of the products, but in terms of the uniqueness of the analysis and the strong perception of the neutrality of the OECD reports and findings" (10).

It was only in 2013/14 that ESDC put processes in place to distribute this OECD research – as well as updates on other international activities – to provincial and territorial officials and Service Canada offices through a newsletter that also went to the FLMM employment services working group. As there is no single network on Canada's PES that is regularly maintained and updated by the federal government or the Forum of Labour Market Ministers, Canadian academics or the PES policy community beyond government are seldom aware of OECD research comparing Canada to other places. This limits policy learning.

Also limiting policy learning was the fact that, starting in 2013/14, ESDC's OECD funding allocation was reduced to $100,000 per annum, a cut of about two-thirds. Those who contributed to the OECD evaluation expressed concern regarding the funding reduction. Not only did they fear the cut would compromise Canada's capacity to influence the OECD agenda, they also worried that it could constrain departmental thinking and policy work. In-house work was perceived as less efficient and comprehensive than OECD analytical work (ESDC 2014c).

The World Association of Public Employment Services (WAPES) is the only global network for the exchange of information on the public employment service, linking delivery research and practice in the fields of employment, migration, and training. In 2015, over ninety Public Employment Services from all over the world were members; the ILO and OECD as well as other international organizations were involved as observers. Canada is represented at WAPES conferences by ESDC officials who also serve on the executive. Quebec also participates directly through Emploi-Québec as an associate member. No other provincial government was directly represented, although Ontario and British Columbia had attended meetings and been involved in activities. There were a number of WAPES projects underway in 2015 relevant to Canada's PES, with input being sought from other federal departments as well as provinces and territories on how the benefits of WAPES membership could be maximized.[6]

As identified in chapter 1 of this book, Canada is signatory to two ILO conventions related to the public employment service: the Public Employment Service Convention 88 agreed to in 1950 and the Employment Policy Convention 122 agreed to in 1966. The ILO website noted concerns expressed by labour organizations in Canada about both conventions. Concerns with Convention 88 focused on Article 3 and insufficient local and regional employment offices. Concerns over Articles 4 and 5 focused on the absence of advisory committees to the PES involving business and labour.

In 2011 Canada responded by noting the presence of the Roundtable on Workplace Skills and the Sector Council program; however, these initiatives have since been defunded. In September 2015 the Canadian Labour Congress again expressed concern regarding Canada's lack of compliance with Convention 88. The government response submitted to the ILO detailed stakeholder engagement on apprenticeship matters, the LMDA retooling consultations held in 2014, small business engagement through the Canada Job Grant, and the development of a new LMI National Stakeholder Advisory panel (Canada 2015). However, these do not constitute "national advisory committees" as prescribed by ILO Convention 88.

Assessment of Federal Coordination and Leadership

This review of pan-Canadian coordination related to the PES demonstrates that the Government of Canada has provided weak leadership post-devolution. Under both the Liberals and Conservatives federal support to the Forum of Labour Market Ministers (FLMM) declined. With ministerial disengagement between 2003 and 2013 it was left to officials to keep up connections; without political interest and agreement authorizing travel to attend face-to-face meetings, building trust between fourteen jurisdictions by telephone was very challenging. Federal funding support for some key activities was withdrawn from an already meagre provincially managed secretariat.

---

6 For information on WAPES activities, see http://wapes.org/. Unfortunately, a 2015 report describing the Canadian PES contained factual errors and did not reflect the decentralized nature of the programming.

Post-devolution, the federal government provided neither funding nor encouragement to NGOs from across Canada involved with PES delivery – community-based training organizations, literacy organizations, youth, Aboriginal and disability employment agencies, and organizations for career development practitioners – to come together to share best practices, compare provincial approaches, and learn from their different devolution experiences. It has almost completely stepped back, leading to a highly provincialized view of programming by people working to deliver Canada's PES programs. All of these organizations have been left mostly on their own to initiate and fund pan-Canadian activities from their membership, private foundations, unions, and business. In the absence of funding to facilitate travel and support project activities, pan-Canadian NGO activities post-devolution have been very limited. While the FLMM would be a natural focus for this kind of pan-Canadian support, in 2015 it did not have enough money to support its own activities, let alone pan-Canadian NGO efforts.

While in the past decade the Government of Canada participated in OECD reviews, in 2013/14 the dollars available were cut by two-thirds. With the defunding of the sector councils and the Roundtable on Workplace Skills in 2013, Canada lost its last formal pan-Canadian institutional structures that demonstrated compliance with Articles 4 and 5 of ILO Convention 88 requiring social partner engagement through national advisory committees.

Pan-Canadian Stakeholder Involvement and Federal Investment in Research

Canada has a history of almost one hundred years of using institutional structures to ensure that the views of business and labour were heard on the operation and management of the PES. Many of these engagements also focused on labour market research. As outlined in chapter 2, this included formal advisory committees and research institutions involving a variety of stakeholders, as well as ongoing business and labour representation on the Canada Employment Insurance Commission (CEIC). Post-devolution, almost all of these pan-Canadian institutions have disappeared.

National Advisory Committees and Research

The early days of the public employment service saw the establishment of a number of formal advisory committees involving business, labour, and other organizations, including the National Employment Service Council (1918–40), the UI Advisory Committee (1940–76), the National Advisory Committee on Manpower (1951–5), and the Canada Employment and Immigration Advisory Committee (1976–92). In 1984 business and labour came together to establish the Canadian Labour Market Productivity Centre (later renamed the Canadian Labour and Business Centre) with federal funding support. In 1991 a series of consultations were held that led to the creation of the Canadian Labour Force Development Board (CLFDB), Aboriginal boards, sector councils, as well as labour market boards in all provinces except for Alberta, Prince Edward Island, and Manitoba.

By the time that the first group of provinces had taken on devolved LMDAs in the early 2000s, the national CLFDB board, as well as the Aboriginal and provincial boards, had faded away. Instead of creating formal advisory boards to government, the federal Liberals looked to task forces, discussion papers, and research brokering institutions. Canadian Policy Research Networks was created in 1994, and the Canadian Council on Learning or CCL was set up in 2002. University researchers came together with federal ESDC researchers in 2006 to create the Canadian Labour and Skills Researcher Network (CLSRN), with funding from the Social Sciences and Humanities Research Council (SSHRC).

These research institutions provided a new and different tool to reassert Ottawa's leadership in the federation (Boismenu and Graefe 2004). Expert interlocutors within these institutions, in tune with federal objectives, were able to position themselves to debate policy options with governments and other stakeholders, thereby setting agendas favourable to federal thinking. Many research papers and publications were prepared, with extensive recommendations made requiring government action, both federal and provincial.[7] Many provinces – especially Alberta and Quebec – were resistant to these federal initiatives and refused to participate.

After coming to power in 2006, it gradually became clear that the Harper Conservatives did not support Liberal directions on partnership-based research and engagement. Funding was withdrawn from one organization at a time, and by 2013 all research organizations had lost their federal funding. By 2015 most had closed. The Canadian

7 For example, over its six-year life (2004–10) the CCL created hundreds of products with its operating budget of about $20 million per year (Cooper 2014).

Labour and Business Centre closed down in 2007, the Canadian Policy Research Networks was disbanded in 2009, and the Canadian Council on Learning closed in 2012. As previously noted in this chapter, while the Sector Council Program ultimately grew to thirty-six sector councils, in 2013 core federal funding was withdrawn. The CLSRN academic network closed in the spring of 2015.

The Harper Conservatives chose instead to undertake consultations "as needed," with most conversations on labour market matters held privately between ministers, officials, and selected individuals and groups. When broader engagement or pan-Canadian conversations were deemed necessary, the House of Commons Standing Committee on Human Resources, Skills and Social Development and the Status of Persons with Disabilities (HUMA) was the preferred venue. Between 2011 and 2014 there were six dedicated HUMA studies related to workforce development: labour and skills shortages (2012), apprentices (2013), persons with disabilities (2013), older workers (2014), Aboriginal persons (2014), and LMDA renewal (2015). Witnesses and experts were called to present their views. Between 2013 and 2014 the federal government also organized fifteen engagement sessions across Canada on ASETS and eleven roundtables on LMDA renewal. In 2014 there was a National Skills Summit with over two hundred leaders from business, labour, and education.

All of these consultations were by invitation only, with limited notice given in advance of the sessions or broader advertising. Unlike the Liberals, no White or Green Papers were produced to stimulate the conversations. According to informants interviewed for this research, business had a privileged "insider" role. Labour and community-based organizations in particular would have liked more opportunities to present their views and have them heard.

After they came to power in 2015, the Trudeau Liberals took a different approach to consultation, organizing roundtables across Canada in the summer of 2016 with provinces and territories through the Forum of Labour Market Ministers. Using a discussion paper, the consultation focused on the four federal/provincial/territorial labour market agreements, seeking input to improve programming and inform future investments. Consultations on the ASETS agreements were also initiated.

The Canada Employment Insurance Commission (CEIC)

Established in 1940, the Canada Employment Insurance Commission (CEIC) has retained responsibility for managing the unemployment insurance program – now called Employment Insurance – including EI Part II, which details the national employment service and the active labour market programs funded from the account. In 2015 the CEIC had four members, two representing the interests of government and one each representing the views of workers and employers. Mandated to represent and reflect the views of their respective constituencies, the commissioners for workers and employers are appointed by the Governor-in-Council for terms of up to five years. The chairperson and vice-chairperson of the commission are respectively the deputy minister of ESDC and the senior associate deputy minister responsible for Service Canada. The vice-chairperson votes on decisions only if the chairperson is unavailable.

Although chosen by the minister of ESDC and appointed by Cabinet, the commissioners for employers and workers are nominated through a competitive process and their constituencies are canvassed to ensure that they have the support of employer and labour groups respectively. As Governor-in-Council appointees, the EI commissioners are independent of the federal public service, serving their terms on "good behaviour." They are subject to the Employment Insurance Act, which provides for ministerial direction in many areas. Their offices are situated within the ESDC department, providing proximity to both political and bureaucratic leaders in Ottawa.

As outlined on its website,[8] in 2015 the four EI commissioners had a wide array of responsibilities under the EI Act, including overseeing delivery of EI Part II pan-Canadian programming (including the National Employment Service); approving amendments to provincial and territorial EI Part II funding agreements; approving work-sharing agreements of $600,000 or more; employment services; and developing and using labour market resources. Collectively they were responsible for the review and approval of policies related to EI program administration, and monitoring and assessing the EI program through the annual EI *Monitoring and Assessment Report* (*MAR*). While implementation in all of these areas was carried out by public servants within ESDC, the commissioners for employers and workers were called upon to sign off on everything from EI regulations to cases destined for the federal court.

8 See https://www.canada.ca/en/employment-social-development/corporate/portfolio/ei-commission.html.

To fulfil these responsibilities, the EI commissioners for workers and employers have set up ways to establish and maintain working relationships with private and NGO organizations and individuals that are clients of, or affected by, ESDC programs. In 2014 the EI commissioner for employers issued a regular newsletter; in addition a thirty-member employer's forum met from time to time. Issues highlighted in the newsletters from that year included developments on LMDA renewal, the transformation of the LMAs into the Canada Job Fund Agreements, how to apply for apprenticeship tax credits, and changes to the temporary foreign worker program. The commissioner for employers also met regularly with employer groups.

The commissioner for workers holds an annual forum to bring the federal minister and senior federal officials together with labour stakeholders and other experts from across the country. The 2015 forum focused on EI funding. There was also a labour reference group, as well as opportunities for federal officials to provide briefing sessions on selected issues. The commissioner speaks at many union gatherings and connects regularly with organizations representing unemployed workers from across Canada. In 2014 each commissioners presented the views of their constituents at the HUMA committee examining LMDA renewal. They also attended all of the cross-Canada LMDA roundtables, as well as a Forum of Labour Market Ministers meeting.

As identified in chapter 2 of this book, business and labour influence over the Unemployment Insurance Commission was downgraded significantly in 1977. In 2015 the EI commissioner for employers saw the role as "an advocate for business that is embedded within the department." The commissioner for workers noted how the advocacy role goes beyond unionized workers to also include non-unionized labour. "The ombudsman role is the most rewarding part of my job ... speaking with advocacy groups keeps me grounded in the role." Both commissioners admitted to having to work very hard to influence EI policy, noting that the ESDC hierarchy from the bureaucracy to politicians did not typically include consideration of the views of the "independent commissioners" representing Canadian employers and employees.

Assessment of Pan-Canadian Stakeholder Involvement and Federal Investment in Research

Post-devolution, Canada has lost all of its federally supported institutions dedicated to pan-Canadian research and policy development on workforce development, skills, and learning, as well as formal institutions for governments to receive the views of labour, business, and other community-based organizations in a structured and ongoing way. This has taken place with both the Liberals and Conservatives in charge. The corporatist turn – primarily involving business and labour – built up under the Mulroney Progressive Conservatives between 1984 and 1993 was dismantled under the Chrétien/Martin Liberals between 1993 and 2006 and ultimately replaced with research-related institutional structures that went beyond the social partners to also include broader engagement with civil society organizations.

When the Harper Conservatives were in control of government between 2006 and 2015, it in turn dismantled these Liberal research institutions, replacing them with short-term, focused consultations as needed. By 2015 there were no active institutions beyond government providing input into PES deliberations from a pan-Canadian perspective. Other than the relatively hidden role played by the EI commissioners for workers and employers, Canada's PES and related workforce development programs were completely dominated by government executives, that is ministers and civil servants. Even elected members of Parliament were rarely heard, other than their limited involvement through the HUMA parliamentary committee.

As described in earlier chapters of this book, some provinces have created their own institutions to undertake research and connect their labour market partners with each other. This includes the Centre for Employment Excellence in British Columbia, l'Observatoire compétences-emplois in Quebec, and the Centre for Workforce Innovation in Ontario. Manitoba and Quebec have provincial labour market advisory boards. Ontario and Quebec have local boards, while Manitoba and Quebec have sector councils. The cost of these activities can be charged to labour market partnerships and research and innovation under the LMDA, and ranged from 1 per cent of expenditures in Alberta to 18 per cent in Quebec. In 2016 there were no mechanisms to formally link these activities on a pan-Canadian basis to facilitate coordination, share resources, and identify and fill gaps in research. Many provinces have chosen to not set up research and advisory structures for their PES, leaving knowledge gaps and an imbalance in their capacity to provide input on pan-Canadian matters.

The federal/provincial/territorial Labour Market Information (LMI) Council under the FLMM – announced in July 2015, complemented by a new National Stakeholder Council and a permanent secretariat – may fill in some of this role. In the fall of 2015, work was underway to develop a business implementation plan. By 2016 the LMI Council had still not been launched. However, as identified in chapter 1 of this book, LMI is but one PES function of many that would benefit from the knowledge, expertise, and advice of external stakeholders.

Conclusion

This chapter has analysed the role played by the Government of Canada in the public employment service post-devolution. A number of conclusions can be drawn. First, the federal-provincial and federal-Aboriginal accountability arrangements are inadequate. Different approaches need to be considered to ensure accountability, improve transparency, and facilitate policy learning. Second, despite the fact that devolution starting in 1996 resulted in provincial governments acquiring responsibility for a large swathe of labour market programs – such that by 2015 they controlled the design and delivery of over three-quarters of the federally funded programming – the Government of Canada was still highly involved through its direct management of programming for Aboriginal people, youth, immigrants, and persons with disabilities. This has created a highly complex and fragmented system.

Third, post-devolution Ottawa's role in pan-Canadian programming through national labour market partnerships, the National Employment Service, and research, evaluation, and innovation has diminished. Federal spending declined significantly when the Harper Conservatives were in charge between 2006 and 2015. On their watch pan-Canadian coordination and federal leadership also diminished, including intergovernmental activities through the Forum of Labour Market Ministers, support to NGOs for pan-Canadian activities, and international connections through the OECD.

Fourth, pan-Canadian stakeholder involvement as well as investment in labour market policy research has deteriorated significantly post-devolution. Since taking on constitutional responsibility for unemployment insurance in 1940, the Government of Canada has attempted different models of national stakeholder involvement, most notably advisory committees to the Unemployment Insurance Commission between 1940 and 1992 and dedicated labour market partnership boards and sector councils in the 1980s, the 1990s, and the 2000s. By the early 2000s the labour market partnership boards had disappeared;

the sector councils held on until 2013, when federal funding was withdrawn under the Harper Conservatives.

The Harper Conservatives did not support the research institutions put in place by the Chrétien/Martin Liberals in the 1990s to 2000s. By 2015 all organizations had lost their federal funding and no formal institutions were operating. Instead, defined consultations – usually through parliamentary committee hearings – took place. Many years before devolution occurred the influencing role of the EI commissioner for workers and the commissioner for employers had also diminished, transformed into one of acting behind the scenes as "insider" advocates for their respective communities. What the Trudeau Liberals will do in relation to the federal role in PES programming after 2016 is unclear. In research and institutions to secure stakeholder input they have almost a blank slate on which to work. On the youth programming front, they have announced that they plan to be very active.

Chapter Ten

Comparing with Australia, the United States, and the European Union

Much of the analysis done in social sciences as well as in everyday life is done by making comparisons. By using the comparative approach and more than one case, we can look at similarities and differences and think about the root causes of performance. Comparing political systems also provides an opportunity to think about what one country can learn from another. Although every nation is unique in its history, culture, and institutions, policy *concepts* (as distinct from their *application*) are ripe for borrowing: "All policy ideas have to be adapted to different cultural and institutional environments, improved and reshaped until sometimes their origins are unrecognizable … where most people recognize that things need to change, in these areas comparisons are essential, but they are more like explorations which provide insights" (Mulgan 2003, 2).

This book does not undertake a detailed comparison of Canada's public employment service or PES with other places. Rather, the purpose of this chapter is to give a flavour of how the PES in Australia, the United States, and the European Union (EU) operated in 2015 – including its relationship with other income support programs – with the thought that some of the governance ideas used might be transportable to Canada. These three places were chosen, as the PES in each is managed through two constitutionally defined orders of government considered as federal political systems that operate across a large geographic area. In 2011 Australia spent about the same amount as Canada on active labour market measures at 0.3 per cent of GDP, while the United States spent much less at 0.1 per cent.[1] Spending in European countries varied

1 American commentators often question these numbers, suggesting that they reflect only employment assistance services and leave out training and other supports.

considerably from a high of 2.3 per cent in Denmark to 0.2 per cent in Estonia (OECD 2013b).

Australia shares Canada's British colonial roots and Westminster-derived political rules and normative practices. The United States is our closest neighbour. While many people today routinely look to the United States as a mirror to reflect on Canadian practices, this was not the case when Canada's unemployment insurance (UI) and public employment service (PES) were being established in the interwar period. The thirty-sixth report of the UI Commission released in 1977 noted that "the European experience shaped Canada's original UI program. The American experience, only a few years older, offered no guidelines for further development. Thus, Canada had to rely mainly on its own perception of what an efficient UI system should be" (UIC 1976, 5). While Canada drew on the British model in its early years, as a unitary state the United Kingdom was very different from Canada back then and remains very different today in its constitutional structure. Much more applicable as a comparator is the broader European Union, a federal political system with many characteristics similar to Canada's.

Australia

Many scholars have compared the Canadian and Australian federations, noting how over time Canadian provinces have gained greater powers, while Australia has moved in the opposite direction, with a gradual transfer of power from the states to the federal government (Turgeon and Simeon 2015; Fenna 2012). This is clearly illustrated through an examination of Australia's protection and activation system for the unemployed. Where two elements of ours (social assistance and the public employment service) are designed and delivered by provincial governments (with some federal control and funding), and one (unemployment insurance) is managed and delivered by the federal government, in Australia all three elements are under the control and direct management of the Australian Commonwealth Government, equivalent to the Government of Canada. There is very limited involvement in any of these matters by the six Australian states.[2] Because all elements are federally financed and delivered, there are no horizontal

2 State governments are responsible for Indigenous policy as well as vocational training, housing, and disability supports.

transfers between governments, therefore there is no "political decentralization" as occurred in Canada. As described in chapter 1 of this book, all parts of Australia's system function within the context of "managerial decentralization."

In Australia, two large and powerful federal departments share responsibility for income support benefits for the unemployed and the public employment service: the Department of Employment and the Department of Human Services. Australia is different from most OECD countries in the sense that it does not have any substantial social assistance benefit scheme and its single most important unemployment-related benefit is flat-rate, means-tested, and near universal in terms of eligibility. It is financed out of government general revenues, not contributions from employers and workers. This contrasts with most other countries in the OECD world (including Canada) where there are separate benefit schemes for the unemployed involving contributory and non-contributory components.

The main unemployment benefit, called the Newstart Allowance, is for the long-term, mature unemployed. About half receiving benefits are subject to activation measures. There is a separate Youth Allowance for unemployed people under twenty-two. Benefits are administered by an arm's-length government agency called Centrelink, accountable to the Department of Human Services. Centrelink employs about 27,000 staff working out of 400 customer service offices and call centres across Australia. About one-third work on employment and employment-related services, and the rest deliver other social services functions. Centrelink is the first point of access for all people seeking to obtain publicly financed social services. Centrelink staff are responsible for initial and follow-up job-seeker interviews, unemployment benefit payments, and liaison with contracted employment service providers (OECD 2012).

After the Second World War, the Commonwealth Employment Service became responsible for matching supply and demand in the labour market and organizing a variety of labour market programs. This service was administered separately from the benefit administration function. By the early 1990s a body of opinion had developed inside and outside government that there were fundamental shortcomings in the government-delivered service, including institutional inertia and a lack of innovation. Spurred by ideologies of government administration such as New Public Management, in 1998 the commonwealth government under Prime Minister Howard introduced a "fully competitive employment services market" model (OECD 2012). The CES was closed and its function outsourced to predominately private and community providers. Initially these providers were to compete with the CES; however, over time all public providers disappeared. While there had been experimentation, some commentators have suggested that the decision to move to a wholly outsourced system was made without a robust evidence base to justify it (Farrow, Hurley, and Sturrock (2015).

Managed by a variety of governments with different political stripes, Australia's PES has been fully outsourced for almost twenty years. There have been a series of arrangements: from 1998 to 2009 it was called Job Network; between 2009 and 2015 it was called Job Services Australia, or JSA; in July 2015 it was rebranded as Jobactive. The rebranding that has occurred over time has been accompanied by changes to programming; for example, JSA was meant to focus resources on the most disadvantaged jobseekers. In all cases the commonwealth government funds the service for individual users, and there is a competitive market for these users to choose their service providers.

As detailed in chapter 3 of this book, among all OECD countries, Australia has the most extensive privatized "quasi-market" for labour market services, involving competitive tendering, pay-for-performance, a star rating system, and standardized government-defined work processes for service providers. A Job Seeker Classification Index is used to refer customers to services. Four streams of service – reduced to three in 2015 – are surrounded by a system of minimum requirements to ensure that the employment service providers do not cherry pick favourable clients and ignore hard-to-place clients. The accountability framework that has been put in place influences the selection and continuation of service providers. All of this is highly structured and codified and has become increasingly so over time. The tender call in 2015 for the renewal of arrangements under Jobactive ran to 228 pages.

The Department of Employment is responsible for setting employment policy, purchasing employment services, managing contracts, quality assurance and compliance, collecting and maintaining data, evaluating program performance, and administering complaints. In 2014 under Jobs Services Australia there were about 100 organizations delivering 650 contracts in 116 Employment Service areas across Australia (BCCfEE 2015). About half of the service providers were for-profit and half were not-for-profit. Commonwealth employment services contracts were worth about $1.3 billion Australian annually, and served approximately 1.6 million Australians annually. Compared to other countries, Australia has a small overall funding envelope for the PES. Over time there has been a steady reduction in costs to government per employment outcome (Farrow, Hurley, and Sturrock 2015, 28).

Assessments of the effectiveness of Australia's programming have been undertaken by (among others) the OECD (2012), the Australian Council of Social Services (2012), Jobs Australia (2013), the Advisory Panel on Employment Services Administration and Accountability (2012), the Centre for Policy Development (Farrow, Hurley, and Sturrock 2015), and academics (Considine et al. 2015).

In 2012 the OECD concluded, "Australia's unique approach to activating job seekers has yielded significant gains to the economy and society" (OECD 2012). Those closer to the system are more critical. The Australian Council of Social Services noted that the system was complex, over-engineered, and under-resourced, with too much focus on short-term employment outcomes and too little on long-term intensive work with job seekers and employers. The Centre for Policy Development noted that the outsourced model with its narrow focus on cost efficiency has fallen far short of delivering gains for the long-term unemployed. It also observed structural limitations in the outsourced arrangements, including the need for service providers to ration resources at the front end, resulting in "creaming" and "parking," and shrinkage of the employment services market.[3] It also recorded an erosion of public sector capability to provide strategic and operational direction and a lack of flexibility for service providers to create different policies if needed. In 2009 Australia was ranked among the OECD countries with the least flexibility available to agencies and departments operating below the national level (OECD 2009).

The peak industry bodies for Australia's public employment service are members of the National Employment Services Association (NESA), established in 1997 – which represents all employment and employment-related service providers – and Jobs Australia established in 1989, which represents the not-for-profit sector.[4] These bodies bring the needs and wishes of the employment services sector to the

---

3 Creaming and parking refers to helping jobseekers who are more "job ready" find work and ignoring everyone else. The British system, like that of Australia, is also extensively outsourced. The number of providers in Australia has shrunk from around 300 in 1998 to 66 in 2015. Large providers have significantly expanded their market share, and the diversity of smaller and locally connected providers has narrowed (Farrow, Hurley, and Sturrock 2015).

4 See http://www.nesa.com.au and https://ja.com.au.

Australian commonwealth government through advocacy, developing policy positions, providing a news service, offering industrial relations advice, and organizing professional training workshops and annual conferences. They also manage stakeholder engagement with the commonwealth government. The two associations collectively employ about thirty-five staff. Jobs Australia focuses more on the needs of the unemployed and advocacy in relation to system changes than NESA. Neither receives government funding.

There are a variety of other organizations important to the Australia PES. Local employment boards coordinate services for people with high support needs. Most significant as a forum for intergovernmental collaboration and decision making is the Council of Australian Governments (COAG) and its Industry and Skills Council. Similar to Canada's first ministers and the Forum of Labour Market Ministers (FLMM), these bodies involve politicians and civil servants from both the federal and state level.[5] The National Workplace Relations Consultative Council and the Regional Development Australia Committees focus on workplace relations and regional development. It is within these two tripartite and multipartite bodies that the views of business and unions are heard most strongly (OECD 2012).

Relevance to Canada

Australia's arrangements are closest to the way WorkBC operates in British Columbia, with its province-wide tendering system. There are also some similarities to the other provinces that outsource the front door of their PES (Ontario, Nova Scotia, and Prince Edward Island). However, when considered on a pan-Canadian basis, Australia's PES is completely different from Canada's. First, it is highly centralized, managed by the commonwealth government, not provinces and territories, as in Canada. With all authority under one government, there are no intergovernmental issues to deal with. Second, it is highly outsourced, as all services are contracted out, as opposed to the mixed model of provincial civil servants supported by specialized contracts, chosen by most provincial governments in Canada.

---

5 Unlike in Canada, where Prime Minister Harper avoided First Ministers' meetings, it would be unthinkable for an Australian prime minister to fail to attend an annual meeting of the COAG (Smith and Mann 2015).

Since it is up to each province to choose its PES service delivery model, the Australian governance model has little applicability on a pan-Canadian basis and so may be of limited interest to provinces that are not highly outsourced. However, British Columbia, Ontario, Nova Scotia, and Prince Edward Island would likely have much to learn by examining reports and studies on the challenges of contracting out under the Australia model. Likewise, given that employment services for Aboriginal people in Canada are contracted out by the federal government through ASETS terms and conditions that have also become increasingly prescriptive over time, lessons from the Australia experience may also be highly applicable to contracting arrangements under that model as well.

Where lessons from Australia might be more applicable to Canada is the organizations Australia has developed to support the for-profit and not-for profit employment service providers operating across the country, NESA and Jobs Australia. The latter bears a resemblance to what CCCBET could become if it had the necessary resources and support from governments across Canada. Also worth examining is the large body of work in Australia reflecting on how the system is working, with many studies completed over the past decade.

The United States

In 2015, public employment services in the United States operated under a common brand called American Jobs Centers (AJC), with over 2,500 local offices connected through fifty-three state-run networks that include Washington DC, Puerto Rico, and the Virgin Islands. The AJCs are mandated by federal legislation and overseen by state and local Workforce Development Boards (Wandner 2015).[6] The main pieces of the U.S. workforce development system are the unemployment insurance (UI) system, the U.S. Employment Service (ES), and job training under the Workforce Investment and Opportunity Act (WIOA).

All these pieces have both federal and state involvement. In the unemployment insurance system the federal partner holds the upper hand through federal requirements for compliance and conformity. State UI laws and actual state practices must conform with federal

6 The AJCs used to be referred to as "one-stop shops." The Workforce Development Boards used to be called Workforce Investment Boards.

laws. The Employment Service is federally funded through the Wagner-Peyser Act and delivers services through the local AJC. Along with job training, services are delivered at AJCs or through private contractors and managed by local workforce development boards with majority private sector membership. Last-resort social assistance – Temporary Assistance for Needy Families (TANF) – is separate from but collaborates with the workforce development system. While funded through formula-determined block federal grants, states determine their own rules within the federal TANF guidelines. Services are usually delivered through county social services offices (O'Leary and Eberts 2008). A growing player in ensuring basic needs in the United States is the Supplemental Nutrition Assistance Program (SNAP) program, previously known as Food Stamps.

Passed in the midst of the Great Depression, both the federal Wagner-Peyser Act of 1933 (which established the U.S. Employment Service) and the Social Security Act of 1935 (which established UI) put into law detailed arrangements whereby the federal government was responsible for setting the administrative framework for services and financing, and state governments were responsible for program administration and delivery. To fund the state services, a uniform tax collected under the Federal Unemployment Tax Act was imposed on employers (not workers), with 90 per cent of the revenue returned to states for UI benefit financing and 10 per cent retained to fund the employment service, state UI administration, and a federal UI loan account. Most states supplement the federal tax rebate with funding from state taxes. Federal funding is divided among the states, using a formula in the Wagner-Peyser Act and announced each year by the assistant secretary of labour for employment and training. The allocation to states is based on their share of the national labour force and unemployment (United States Department of Labour 2013).

The federal-state UI system is the first line of defence against unemployment. There are a multitude of different UI benefit replacement rates and durations. Federal conformity requirements include a rule that states must experience-rate employers in setting their UI tax rates, making them contingent on the relative incidence of unemployment among recent employees. For workers who qualify, the UI program has three elements: regular UI benefits, a permanent Extended Benefits program, and Emergency Unemployment Compensation in times of high unemployment. Regular UI must be financed by experience-rated taxes on employer payrolls. Extended Benefits is shared 50:50 by the states and federal government, and Emergency Unemployment Compensation is a federally financed discretionary program. Since states have the flexibility to determine eligibility, benefit levels and durations, and the rules for employer financing, there are considerable variations in coverage from one state to another. Compared to other countries, the generosity of the American UI scheme is relatively low, especially in duration of benefits and strictness of eligibility (Langenbucher 2015).

On the last resort/social assistance side, the main program is the state-administered Temporary Assistance for Needy Families (TANF), a federal block funded program created in 1996 to replace the open-ended Aid to Families with Dependent Children. Even with block funding, there are many federal rules that states must follow in administering the program. As TANF coverage has declined as the result of more restrictive eligibility rules, the federally run Supplemental Nutrition Assistance Program (SNAP) program has increased in importance. With an annual outlay of over $74 billion in 2013, the cost and importance of SNAP clearly outweighs TANF at $17 billion and unemployment insurance at about $35 billion.[7] The United States also has a federal earned income tax credit that supplements the wages of low-income earners who qualify. Nationwide, almost 26.7 million families received over $65 billion for the 2014 tax year (O'Leary 2015).

While all of these benefit programs have activation requirements, linkages with the U.S. Employment Service were historically not strong. Primarily a labour exchange service, in the 1960s the ES became involved through partnerships in two additional services: job training and labour market information. This relationship was short lived when the federal government established a separate nationwide network of local entities to design and administer training programs for economically disadvantaged and dislocated workers. In 1982 the training arrangements were transformed through the federal Job Partnership Training Act, intended to provide an array of targeted, more intensive training support to disadvantaged adults, displaced workers, and disadvantaged youth. Since the act gave state and local governments increased discretion over the operation of federally funded workforce programs, it required the majority participation of employers in local advisory committees (Barnow and Spaulding 2015).

7 These costs reflect a time of relatively low unemployment.

In 1998 the federal Workforce Investment Act (WIA) integrated the U.S. Employment Service and job training into a single system. Managed by the federal Department of Labor, the WIA prescribed the parameters of the new system, including a defined delivery model to be implemented across all of the United States. At the centre of the WIA was the concept of one-stop shops, where providers of various employment services – including the ES – were assembled under one roof so that job seekers did not have to visit multiple locations to get the services they needed. Every state was expected to set up a State Workforce Investment Board (SWIB) – led by the governor – to set out the strategic vision and policy for the state, designate local service delivery areas, and monitor performance. WIA gave state governors much more discretion over program design and coordination than they had had through the previous legislation, hence it effectively devolved many employment-related responsibilities. Services within each state were to be organized into local labour markets, known as Workforce Investment Areas (O'Leary and Eberts 2008).

With a minimum of four representatives on the board, state legislators were expected to approve a strategic workforce development plan and the distribution of federal funding within their state. Under the state boards are Local Workforce Investment Boards, mandated to develop strategies to connect with local employers as well as develop a local human capital plan. Local boards must be chaired by an employer, and business must make up more than 50 per cent of the board membership; others involved are educators, labour, community-based organizations, economic development agencies, and career centre agencies across the United States. In 2015 there were approximately 550 Workforce Boards with 12,000 business members. A National Association of Workforce Boards[8] with a small staff complement provides advocacy, communications, and capacity-building support.

Each Workforce Investment Area has a designated chief elected official (the highest ranking local elected official) responsible for the local board. Administration can be carried out by a local government or a designated local agency. In the most common set-up, policy development is done by the state board, program administration is done by the local board, and service delivery is carried out by vendors and/or state employees; however, this division is not mandatory. At every

8 See http://www.nawb.org/.

level of the system elected officials have the opportunity to weigh in and set policy direction for the federal funds that flow through the system. For many years direct linkages between the employment service and TANF, Food Stamps and UI were not mandatory. The federal government stepped up its concern for activation during the 2008–10 economic downturn, requiring states to deliver activation services for recipients of supplementary and emergency UI benefits. States were required to achieve certain work participation targets in their TANF caseloads. SNAP has its own activation program called SNAP Employment & Training and is an optional partner in the broader U.S. workforce development system.

After the Republicans swept both houses of Congress in 1994, the expected resources for the one-stop shops never materialized. WIA was always meant as a "work-first" program emphasizing employment over training. Any training available had to be short term and aimed at quick employment, not simply a degree or credentials. In the ensuing twenty years there has been a downward trend in federal funding for WIA programs. Training that does occur is mostly modest and short term. Where funding for Wagner-Peyser employment programs reached $839 million in 1995, by 2014 it had dropped to a low of $664 million. Funding under the WIA adult program has declined from $1.89 billion in 1984 to less than $800 million in recent years. Likewise the WIA Dislocated Worker program declined from $1.27 billion in 2000 to $1.0 billion in 2014. Most states are not in a position to replace the reduced federal funding. As a result, there has also been a shrinking in the program's basic infrastructure. Where in 2003 there were almost 3,600 one-stop shops, in 2014 there were just over 2,500. Likewise the number of LWIBs has been reduced. As local boards are expensive to operate, nine states have none, and all program administration has been transferred to the SWIB (Wandner 2015).

In 2014 the WIA Act was replaced by the Workforce Innovation and Opportunity Act (WIOA), bringing together into a unified system previously disconnected education and training pieces. This included the WIA programs administered by the Department of Labor (including the ES), as well as adult education and literacy programs, and services for persons with disabilities, disadvantaged youth, Native Americans, and immigrants previously administered by the federal Department of Education and the Department of Health and Human Services. Through WIOA the strategic role of the state and local workforce development boards has been streamlined and strengthened.

The Act also brought in new activities and requirements and codified federal guidance and regulations that already existed (Bird, Foster, and Ganzglass 2015). In addition, funding was increased, with about $3 billion in disadvantaged adult, disadvantaged youth, and dislocated worker programs authorized for fiscal year 2016 (Barnow and Spaulding 2015).

The advisory role of business is built into the U.S. system at all levels through the Workforce Boards; through this process there is also very significant political engagement in decision making. The National Association of State Workforce Agencies[9] (NASWA) also plays a significant advisory and coordination role. Founded in the early years of unemployment insurance and employment service programs, NASWA is an organization of state administrators who work in the publicly funded workforce development system managing unemployment insurance, employment services, training programs, employment statistics, and labour market information. For over eighty years it has provided a forum for states to exchange information and ideas about how to improve program operations; it also serves as a liaison between state workforce agencies and federal government agencies, Congress, business, labour, and intergovernmental groups. As the collective voice of state agencies on workforce policies and issues, the NASWA board is the closest that the United States has to a national workforce development board.

Initially supported by staff from the federal Department of Labor, in 1973 NASWA became an independent non-profit organization, financially supported by state membership fees allowed as a budget line in the federal funding envelope. With a staff of over forty, NASWA also carries out essential functions of the public workforce development system, including labour exchange activities. In 1994 the Center for Employment Security Education and Research was established as a consulting arm of NASWA to manage projects to help states streamline business processes, share best practices, undertake policy research and analysis, and provide state agencies with information technology support. NASWA represents the United States at meetings of the World Association of Public Employment Services (WAPES).

There are many other actors involved with implementing the WIOA across the United States beyond those already mentioned, including

9 See http://www.naswa.org/.

the National Governors Association, the American Public Human Services Association, the Council of State Administrators of Vocational Rehabilitation, the National Council of State Directors of Adult Education, the National Association of Counties, and the U.S. Conference of Mayors, to name just a few.

Relevance to Canada

The institutional structure of Canada's public employment service and surrounding income support programs (Employment Insurance and social assistance) is very different from the institutional structure in the United States. Federal control over all elements of the U.S. system – unemployment insurance, social assistance, the employment service, and job training – stands in stark contrast with Canada's arrangements in which Ottawa is directly responsible only for unemployment insurance or UI, has virtually no influence over provincial social assistance, and post-devolution wields only moderate control over provincial design and delivery of the PES and job training. In the United States the states are, in effect, the design and delivery agent for *all* of the federally determined programs. A national framework is set through federal legislation, debated and approved in a high-profile fashion through Congress in the national capital. As a result of this architecture, the federal grants provided to the states can be highly conditional and prescriptive.

This makes for an intergovernmental relationship in the United States ripe for tension, hence the need to establish NASWA as an intermediary organization to help manage the federal–state relationship. In some ways NASWA resembles the Council of Ministers of Education Canada (CMEC), established by provinces in the 1960s to manage the federal–provincial relationship in education matters. The main difference is that Ottawa does not fund K–12 education. With a staff of about sixty and a permanent secretariat, CMEC also undertakes research and manages some pan-Canadian activities such as the Canadian Information Centre for International Credentials. Given the direct involvement of provincial education ministers in CMEC, it is a more political organization than NASWA appears to be.

In the Canadian context, the only federal transfers that bear a resemblance to the U.S. system are those provided to provinces through the LMDA, LMA, LMAPD, and TIOW Agreements. The federal grant provided to support provincial social assistance costs is now rolled into the unconditional block Canada Social Transfer,[10] joining funds provided for postsecondary education and social services. With respect to the labour market transfer agreements, the parameters that set the relationship are outlined in each federal-provincial agreement and are not expressed as provinces implementing federal legislation. While the agreements do prescribe some elements of the services provinces are expected to deliver with the federal dollars – including who is eligible – provinces have great flexibility in deciding program design and service delivery arrangements.

The second big difference between Canada and the United States is the large degree of political and business engagement in the U.S. system, as prescribed first through the 1998 WIA Act and reinforced through its successor WIOA in 2014. The Canadian system is much more executive-dominated by politicians and civil servants. By requiring Workforce Boards at both the state and local level, politicians and business across the United States have been given defined ways to influence how federal workforce development dollars in their state are prioritized and spent. Compared to Canada, where labour is traditionally considered as one of three partners, business dominates in the United States.[11] Despite this access, recent evaluations have shown that employers do not typically play a major role in administering the boards and they effectively lack influence over workforce issues in their areas (Barnow and Spaulding 2015).

Canada has nothing that resembles the U.S. Workforce Development Boards; not even the Quebec and Manitoba labour market boards (in place in 2015) or the now defunct Canadian Labour Force Development Board (CLFDB) included politicians at the table. Instead the Canadian boards are seen as advisory to the political structure, with advice to be used or discarded according to the circumstances of the day. Every provincial government makes its own decisions on how business will be involved in workforce development and PES decision making. Unlike the United States, this cannot be federally imposed.

Looking to potential lessons for Canada from the U.S. experience, having an organization equivalent to NASWA might be a positive

10 The only requirement for the CST is that provinces must not impose a residency requirement on receipt of social assistance. This requirement is not policed.

11 For example, in 2015 the Michigan Workforce Development Board had twenty-two business members, compared to six representing organized labour out of forty-four voting members.

consideration, using the FLMM as the foundation. By examining the activities and projects that NASWA has undertaken over the years on workforce development and unemployment insurance, ideas might be generated on ways to improve FLMM activities on the PES and broader workforce development, including providing a mechanism for federal-provincial liaison on Employment Insurance Part I matters. With increased federal-provincial interdependence post-devolution, a more robust FLMM is needed now more than ever.

Although some have suggested that Canada emulate the U.S. Workforce Investment Boards, decisions of this nature would need to be taken within each province, not by the Government of Canada. Before a national board was set up, lessons from the demise of the CLFDB would need to be examined very carefully, as well as Quebec's and Manitoba's experiences with their provincial boards. The U.S. literature on the effectiveness of workforce development boards would be another key resource (Barnow and Spaulding 2015; O'Leary and Eberts 2008; Mulgan 2003; Wandner 2015).

The European Union

When Canadians think about other federations to which they can compare Canada, they typically think about Australia, the United States, or individual European countries like Switzerland, Germany, Belgium, or Austria. They seldom think about the broader entity – the European Union, or EU – to which three of these countries belong. There are key institutional and structural features in the EU that bear great similarity to how Canada's federation operates.

First is that in both systems competence of the constituent units – twenty-eight member states in the EU[12] and thirteen provinces and territories in Canada – is constitutionally defined, with their autonomy protected and affirmed by court decisions ranging over many years. This makes the constituent units in each political system very powerful, much more so than in the United States or Australia. Second is that responsibility for issues that matter most to citizens is held primarily by the constituent units, not the centre. In most areas the federal government in Canada and the European Commission (as authorized by

12 In June 2016 the United Kingdom voted through a referendum to leave the European Union.

the council) cannot impose pan-Canadian or pan-European approaches without broad agreement of all. Third is that moving forward on issues relies on a robust system of intergovernmental relations (IGR): processes where heads of state and ministers from across the political union come together to chart future directions and agree on their respective activities and roles. In Canada and the EU this means that many important decisions are made in these IGR forums, not in parliaments or legislative assemblies (Hueglin 2013).

The European Union as a defined entity did not even exist until 1950, when the European Coal and Steel Community started to unite European countries economically and politically. The EU was set up with the express aim of ending the frequent and bloody wars between neighbours, culminating in the Second World War. From six founding members in 1950 (Belgium, France, Germany, Italy, Luxembourg, and the Netherlands), by 2015 it had grown to twenty-eight member states. Given these historical developments, each European country has come to the EU table at a different time with various welfare states, both strong and weak. Most have long-standing contributory unemployment insurance (UI) schemes supplemented by last-resort social assistance programs. Like in Canada, the UI schemes are often funded by employer and worker contributions. In many countries social partners (business and labour) have defined advisory and administrative roles. Delivery responsibility for income support is often split between national governments and municipalities.

There is also a wide variation in each EU member state's PES. Like the unemployment insurance benefits scheme, the PES in many European countries is financed by social partner contributions. One of the first European-wide developments in the public employment service was the formal establishment in 1993 of the European Jobs Network (EURES) to provide information, advice, and job matching services to facilitate the free movement of workers. All EU member states participated, with coordination undertaken by the European Commission. However, it was completely up to each EU member state to determine how to manage its PES and associated employment and training programs; there was no pan-European coordination. The creation of the euro area, recession, and rising unemployment in the 1990s combined to stimulate the development of a White Paper on Competitiveness and Employment (European Commission 1993). Out of it the European Employment Strategy (EES) started to take shape. In 1997 the objective of a high level of employment became a specific EU priority. By building a pan-European dimension on top of existing member state activities, some elements of employment policy in the EU started to become "Europeanized."

Since the EU level was unable – as had occurred in Canada – to use the centre's spending power to convince the constituent units to move in a unified direction, a new governance instrument to achieve that goal was created, the Open Method of Coordination, or OMC. Designed to create convergence through benchmarking and policy learning, the OMC involves the development of EU-wide objectives, goals, guidelines, and indicators; their translation into member state national plans; peer review and mutual learning; and public reporting. While voluntary for the member states, the OMC process is compelling. It is managed through a defined IGR process that involves the European Commission, or EC – the EU's civil service – and the governments of each of the twenty-eight EU member states operating at various levels. EU social partners as well as civil society organizations also have a defined role, both at the European level and within each member state. The focus of the OMC is on policy convergence – not harmonization – of objectives, performance, and to some extent policy approaches – but not means (institutions, rules, and concrete measures) (Verdun and Wood 2013).

The European Employment Strategy is directed by ministers from the twenty-eight member states who comprise the Employment, Social Policy, Health and Consumer Protection Council (EPSCO).[13] With the assistance of staff from the European Commission, EPSCO ministers meet face-to-face four times a year (as well as twice a year in an informal setting), supported by the Employment Committee (EMCO), a treaty-based group made up of two senior civil servants per member state in addition to two representatives from the European Commission. These European IGR institutions bear substantial resemblance to the different layers of the Forum of Labour Market Ministers in Canada. Unlike Canada, in the EU there are also defined processes for EPSCO ministers and EMCO officials to meet with social partners and civil society organizations. The European Parliament also provides an opinion on the guidelines underpinning the EES; however, up to 2015 its impact on the process had been limited.

13 EPSCO is one of the formats under which the European Council meets. As a formal body and co-legislator within the EU institutions, EPSCO "must" meet regularly to play its legislative role.

Over time the improvement of PES performance has become an issue of highest priority for the European Employment Strategy and by 2015 was of particular relevance to Europe 2020, the EU's ten-year jobs and growth strategy. Launched in 2010 and agreed to by all European heads of state, five headline targets in various subjects have been agreed for the EU to achieve by the end of 2020. In employment, social inclusion, and poverty matters the Europe 2020 strategy (which encompasses the EES) aims to achieve an employment rate of 75 per cent (for ages twenty to sixty-four), a tertiary education completion rate of 40 per cent, a reduction in school dropouts to below 10 per cent, and lift a minimum of 20 million people from the risk of poverty and social exclusion. Progress on Europe 2020 and its targets is tracked within each member state and collectively at the EU level. Progress – or lack of – and comparisons between member states is routinized and subject to stakeholder and media attention and discussion.

In June 2014 the European Parliament and the European Council agreed on a *legal* measure (Decision No. 573/2014/EU) to strengthen cooperation between the Public Employment Services of the member states by establishing a European Network of Public Employment Services.[14] A formal network was required, as experience had shown that the informal network in place since 1997 under the EES did not sufficiently engage member states in mutual learning and benchmarking.

The cross-European public employment service network aims to: (1) compare PES performance through benchmarking, (2) identify evidence-based good practices and foster mutual learning, (3) promote the modernization and strengthening of PES service delivery, including the Youth Guarantee, and (4) prepare inputs to the European Employment Strategy and the corresponding national labour market policies. Defined PES qualitative and quantitative benchmarking indicators were included as an annex to Decision No. 573/2014/EU. The network is governed by a board, with two people from each member state and the commission and the EMCO chair as an observer. These are the heads of the PES or senior civil servants from each EU member state. The board meets twice a year to conduct strategic discussions and make decisions on the activities of the network. Contributions from the PES network are channelled through EMCO to EPSCO ministers. The

14 The PES network comprises all twenty-eight EU countries, in addition to Norway, Iceland, and the European Commission.

European PES network functions in a way similar to how a subcommittee of the FLMM functions in Canada.

In addition to the new PES network, "PES to PES dialogue" has for many years been the European Commission's mutual learning support program in the PES. Key activities include peer review meetings, dialogue conferences, and preparation of analytical papers and reports. Another process encourages EU-level dialogue to improve cooperation between public, private and non-profit employment services and help define fields where complementary services can be delivered.

In 2015 there was also a European Employment Policy Observatory (EEPO), which aims to improve European and national policymaking by providing information, analysis, and insight on the design, implementation, monitoring, and evaluation of policies. The main purpose of the EEPO is to produce high-quality research papers on the labour market and employment.[15] EEPO is managed by organizations selected through a competitive contract. The European Commission regularly releases a Social Europe newsletter to keep all stakeholders across Europe informed. Ministers' meetings documents and working papers are posted on the council website. Compared to Canada, there is much greater transparency and much more research and analysis on employment.

Funding for all of these EU activities is authorized through the PROGRESS/employment section of the EU Program for Employment and Social Innovation, through the European Social Fund, the Regional Development Fund, and Horizon 2020 (European Union 2014). EU-level funding also covers the cost of travel (but not accommodation) for government representatives from the twenty-eight EU member states as well as civil society organizations from across Europe. This contrasts with Canada, where each province must weigh the costs of intergovernmental travel to FLMM meetings in light of tight provincial budgets. As identified in chapter 9 of this book, there is no federal or provincial funding for NGO participation in pan-Canadian PES activities.

In addition to funding their participation in EES activities, civil society organizations in the European Union can also receive grants from the European Commission to cover their operating and activity costs. This ensures a process for long-term cooperation between the

---

15 All information detailed on the EU PES is available on the European Commission website at http://ec.europa.eu/social/main.jsp?catId=105&langId=en.

commission and the EU networks.[16] These contracts are normally let through a competitive bid process. For example, in 2013 there was a call for bids from organizations that were promoting the rights of persons with disabilities. These EU contracts would be similar to the Social Partnership grants that the Government of Canada used to provide to pan-Canadian disability organizations.

The EU system in employment matters is propelled by the Open Method of Coordination. The past twenty years has created an enormous wealth of academic and think tank literature about the effectiveness of the OMC. In their review of this literature, de la Porte and Pochet (2012) concluded that learning was the most effective part of the OMC, bringing together government and non-government actors to address common challenges, and facilitating deliberation and problem solving through socialization, reflexivity, and idea diffusion. Reflecting in 2014 on the OMC for a Canadian audience, Vanhercke (2015, 9) concluded, "No, the process is not perfect and has clearly failed to accomplish everything that participants had hoped for. As a tool of soft law, however – something undeniably necessary in the face of nations unwilling to surrender autonomy in the field of social policy – [the OMC] has indeed become a valuable policy instrument."

Relevance to Canada

I have written a number of articles on why I think the European Union is an appropriate comparator to Canada, and lessons that we might learn from the governance arrangements developed in its unique federal political system (Wood 2013a, 2013b). American authors considered the same possibility of how governance arrangements for TANF – its main welfare program – might be improved using EU approaches (Walker and Wiseman 2006). Learning could also go in the other direction. For example, what might the European Union learn from Canada, especially as the EU considers the potential for an EU-wide unemployment insurance benefits scheme to serve as a shock absorber for EU economies and a means to enhance social solidarity across the union?

---

16 Member states in the EU, like provinces in Canada, sometimes objected to European Commission funding of lobby groups and took the issue to court (van den Berg and Jenson 2015).

Both Canada and the EU are highly decentralized federal political systems. In 2016 provinces controlled and operated most social programs on their own, with limited pan-Canadian coordination or stakeholder involvement beyond their individual borders. While social programs in the EU are the responsibility of the member states, they are becoming increasingly coordinated on an EU-wide basis through the Open Method of Coordination. By developing common goals, benchmarking, comparison, and sharing best practices voluntarily, the OMC has shaped EU discourse, enhanced common understanding, and provided a way forward to tackle pan-European problems. All governments as well as stakeholders from across the union are involved.

These positive outcomes have been achieved while taking away no more autonomy from EU member states than they are willing to cede. This "collective action problem" is the perennial dilemma among Canada's often fractious fourteen governments where there is considerable autonomy at the same time as substantial interdependence. The traditional outcome in Canada in these circumstances – and certainly evident as it applies to employment policy matters, as detailed in this book – has been increased executive dominance of the policy field; unilateral federal action; limited ways for non-government actors to provide input into decision making; weak federal-provincial coordination; lack of transparency, reporting, and comparative research; and fragmentation and incoherence in the programming on offer.

There is much that Canada could learn from EU governance practices. The first step would be to examine in detail how the EU intergovernmental relations systems operates through EPSCO, as it bears a resemblance to the Forum of Labour Market Ministers (FLMM) in Canada. If we operated the FLMM like EPSCO, the most immediate result would be increased transparency, with FLMM initiatives and activities posted on public websites, and processes established for the FLMM to receive input from non-government entities such as the EI commissioners, ASETS organizations, and NGOS such as CCCBET. A second step would be to examine in some detail the recent work undertaken in the EU to implement a *legal* measure in place of the previous voluntary PES network, including new ways to compare PES performance through benchmarking (called "bench learning" in the EU PES jargon). Given its direct focus on the PES, the ready-made indicators already developed in the EU could be assessed for applicability in the Canadian context to stimulate conversations among the key players on actions needed to move policy-learning forward.

We could also learn a lot from the EU's willingness to invest in evidence-based research through institutional structures that bring the EU and member states together with each other, other levels of government, social partners, and civil society organizations. Also significant in this context is a willingness in the EU to fund part of the cost incurred by member state governments and NGO organizations to participate in these activities. In the EU this is seen as an essential cost of doing business in their highly complex union. In Canada, it's considered as a "frill," with pan-Canadian travel viewed by politicians and citizens as "junkets" of no value.

Conclusion

This chapter has analysed how Australia, the United States, and the European Union manage their respective PES, and assessed whether there were governance lessons that might translate to the Canadian context. It found such significant institutional differences between Canada, Australia, and the United States that lessons for improving Canadian PES governance were limited. Australia's PES is managed by the commonwealth government – not provinces and territories, as in Canada – so there are no intergovernmental issues to deal with. It is also highly outsourced, as opposed to the mixed model of provincial civil servants supported by specialized contracts, chosen by most provincial governments in Canada. Those provinces that have selected predominately outsourced models – British Columbia, Ontario, Nova Scotia, and Prince Edward Island – could learn from the challenges Australia has experienced in contracting out, as could the federal government in relation to the ASETS arrangements; for the rest, the lessons are slim. A more useful lesson from Australia could be gleaned from the organizations developed to support the for-profit and not-for-profit organizations that deliver the PES. These resemble what the Canadian Coalition for Community Based Employment Training (CCCBET) could become if it had the necessary resources and support from governments across Canada.

Likewise, U.S. lessons for Canada are slim. Federal control over all elements of the U.S. system – unemployment insurance, the employment service, job training, and social assistance – stands in stark contrast to Canada, where Ottawa is directly responsible only for unemployment insurance and has no responsibility for social assistance. The various labour market transfers do bear some resemblance to the conditional grants and legislative controls imposed by the U.S. federal government on state-run employment and job training services. However, the Canadian agreements do not prescribe detailed program delivery arrangements to be implemented by provinces, including uniform branding through the American Jobs Centres overseen by employer-dominated Workforce Development Boards. Given provincial autonomy, this kind of detailed federal oversight would be untenable in the Canadian constitutional context.

Likewise, prescribing employer involvement alongside politicians, as in the United States, would not fit well with the executive dominance that has come to characterize Canadian public administration. Where lessons might be learned from the United States – like in Australia – are in relation to pan-Canadian coordination. The long-standing U.S. arrangements that bring state administrators together through NASWA is an institutional structure that the FLMM might want to consider examining in some detail.

Ideas from the European Union were more persuasive, especially given its recent emphasis on the PES and the establishment of a new legal mechanism to facilitate improved collaboration among the EU member states. The constitutional structure of Canada and the EU have much in common, especially the autonomy held by the constituent units – twenty-eight member states in the EU and thirteen provinces and territories in Canada – over employment policy matters and related income support programming. The federal spending power as a way to persuade provinces to do the bidding of the centre is much less compelling in 2016 than it was in the post-war years. In the wake of the 1995 Quebec referendum, Canada has become a much more decentralized nation.

Pan-Canadian collective action will occur only if provinces consider it to be in their best interest. Techniques like the Open Method of Coordination could provide a way to overcome the "collective action program" that so often prevents us from moving forward on issues of common concern. There is also learning from the EU's intergovernmental structures, approach to research, and willingness to offset the administrative and travel costs incurred in managing their complex political union.

Chapter Eleven

Conclusion

By 2015 Canada's public employment service or PES was back to where it started almost a hundred years ago: a provincially run service supported by federal transfers. It has been a remarkable journey: from a national network of provincially managed but federally funded services between 1918 and 1940; to an arm's-length organization between 1940 and 1977 under federal control; to direct federal management under a government department between 1977 and 1996; and back to provincial design and delivery using federal funding, starting in 1996.

As outlined in this book, the reality is much subtler than this broad statement, including the emergence in the 1990s of another key actor: Aboriginal labour market agencies delivering services under federal management. Unlike the United States and Australia with their countrywide American Jobs Centres and Jobactive Australia, in Canada each province and territory has its own PES brand. The only national brand is PES services for Aboriginal people, delivered in 2015 under the Aboriginal Skills and Employment Training Strategy (ASETS) banner.

Despite this change in governance, what has not changed is the fundamental place of the PES as a key component of the Canadian welfare state. PES basic functions include job brokering and labour exchange; assembling and interpreting labour market information; and facilitating labour mobility. These services are used by all citizens – both employed and unemployed – as well as by Canadian businesses and non-government organizations. However, the most important function of a PES is to broker access to "second chance" adjustment programs for people without a strong labour market connection: youth, older workers, persons with disabilities, immigrants, Aboriginal people, and those receiving government income support benefits. Without timely and adequate access to job search, counselling, training, work experience, and other labour market interventions, millions of Canadians would miss out on opportunities for productive work and continue to live at high risk for long-term unemployment, erratic income, and poverty.

In just twenty short years Canada has implemented highly decentralized arrangements to deliver these PES functions, with three-quarters of the programming in 2015 designed and delivered by the provinces and territories and 12 per cent under Aboriginal delivery. The architecture used to support the arrangements was rolled out by the Government of Canada between 1995 and 2013, one initiative at a time, with no "grand plan" debated and considered multilaterally between governments, let alone with parliamentarians, social partners, or citizens. Offered under the federal Liberals between 1995 and 2006 and consolidated by the Conservatives between 2006 and 2015, decentralization of the Canadian PES is now deeply entrenched. While in the early 2000s Lazar (2002, 65) noted that "the roots of the decentralization … are not yet very deep in the federal capital," this is not the case in 2015.

The OECD has been the biggest champion of decentralized PES decision making, noting how operational efficiency is improved when there is administrative flexibility to cope with the differentiated patterns of labour markets at the local level. However, it also identified trade-offs: cross-regional inequity, an increased funding burden at the local level, disparity in PES management skills, loss of consistency, and duplication of services (OECD 1998). In his assessment of devolution in Canada in 2002, Lazar (66) drew a similar conclusion: "While the design and delivery of active labour market measures may well make sense as a provincial responsibility, duplicating the design of much of the infrastructure (occupational standards, training programs, techniques of prior assessment and recognition of foreign credentials, information systems etc.) on a province by province basis makes much less sense."

This book has looked at Canada's PES from a number of perspectives. Chapter 1 identified why a *public* employment service is important, the low level of Canadian investment compared to other countries, and key actors involved in the sector. Chapter 2 walked through the history of Canada's PES, how devolution played out between 1995 and 2015, and the parameters of the four federal-provincial agreements through which most of the PES was delivered post-devolution. Chapter 3 examined the literature on federalism and activation and its relevance to the devolution of the PES.

Chapters 4 through 8 are at the heart of the book, and looked at how British Columbia and Alberta (the Far West), Saskatchewan and

Manitoba (the Midwest), Ontario and Quebec (the Middle), New Brunswick, Nova Scotia, Prince Edward Island, and Newfoundland and Labrador (the East), and Aboriginal labour market organizations took on the federal programs and adapted them to meet their respective needs. It also looked at the results achieved. Chapter 9 reflected on the role of the Government of Canada post-devolution. Chapter 10 assessed how the United States, Australia, and the European Union manage their PES compared to Canada. It also looked for transferable governance ideas.

This final chapter takes the various strands of the PES story and knits them into a coherent pan-Canadian assessment of devolution by reflecting back on the questions posed in chapter 1:

1. What governance choices did provinces make in taking on the federal programming? What outcomes have been achieved? How do they compare?
2. How do the devolved PES services – now under provincial, territorial, and Aboriginal control – collectively compare to when they were under federal delivery?
3. How is the federal government managing the pieces of the PES it retained, including oversight of Aboriginal Labour market programming?
4. How does Canada's public employment service fit together as a whole? What challenges remain as it moves into the twenty-first century?

The book concludes by reflecting on how an examination of devolution of the PES illustrates the workings of Canadian federalism over the past two decades. Canada's political culture is one of evolutionary change: gradual, incremental, and iterative (Wiseman 2007, 11). The new Liberal federal government – elected with a majority in 2015 – will need to take the past *and* the present into account as it works with provinces, territories, Aboriginal organizations, and other stakeholders to retrofit Canada's PES for the next hundred years.

Different Governance Choices in Different Places: Comparing Provinces

In taking on the federal PES programming, every province had to make a number of governance choices to ensure that the programs they assumed were as successful as possible. This included deciding which provincial government department would hold prime responsibility for managing and organizing the services; the extent to which work and welfare programs would be managed as one-stop shops; the degree of flexibility regional and local offices would be given in implementing program objectives; whether the services would be contracted out or delivered by provincial civil servants; and how external partnerships and networks would influence provincial policymaking. These public administration decisions built upon the legacy of existing provincial programming for related areas such as postsecondary education, social assistance, and economic development. They also reflected the province's political culture.

Single Gateways or One-Stop Shops

As detailed in chapter 3, this theme examines the scope of the PES and the extent to which job brokering and exchange, benefit administration, and active employment measures are integrated. The OECD considers "one-stop" or "single gateway" access to these three functions as a way to increase convenience for clients and employers, reduce duplication, facilitate information sharing, and improve overall program effectiveness.

Devolution deliberately severed federal Employment Insurance benefit delivery from provincially managed employment services. For a while co-located federal-provincial sites were maintained so that EI benefits and employment services could be accessed from the same site; however, over time Service Canada left the shared sites to consolidate federal-only services in the same location. Connecting federal EI recipients with employment services offered by the provinces now needed to be done through different approaches.

Upon assuming the federal responsibilities, every province had to decide where to position the new programming with related provincial activities. By 2014 three provinces had implemented "one-stop" PES shops as described by the OECD: Quebec, Alberta, and Newfoundland and Labrador. Here, access to PES services was provided through a government office staffed by provincial civil servants where social assistance benefits and employer services were also available. Quebec had 158 Local Employment Centres, Alberta had fifty-three Alberta Works Centres,[1] and Newfoundland and Labrador had twenty-seven

1 In 2014 Alberta transferred responsibility for LMA programming from Human Services to a newly established Jobs, Skills, Training, and Labour Department. Other programming followed in 2016.

Employment Skills Centres. All PES services were managed by a single provincial government department that also held responsibility for social matters. All federal LMDA and LMA funding was also under the control of this same provincial government department.

While in Manitoba and New Brunswick social assistance and PES responsibilities were in different organizational structures, strong and defined linkages had been established to ensure that social assistance recipients took advantage of the PES programming on offer. By 2014 Manitoba had transferred social assistance responsibility to the economic development department that was also responsible for the PES under the sixteen Manitoba Jobs and Skills Development Centres. New Brunswick developed defined protocols between the postsecondary education department (responsible for the PES through nineteen Career Information Centres) and the social services department (responsible for social assistance). The Manitoba PES centres also provided supports for employers, whereas in New Brunswick they were the responsibility of economic development agencies. However, clear and defined linkages with the PES had been established, including staff positions funded through the PES.

Although the interdepartmental structure that supported Prince Edward Island's six Career Development Centres, Nova Scotia's sixty-eight Careers Nova Scotia Centres, and Saskatchewan's nineteen Canada-Saskatchewan Career and Employment Services Centres was somewhat similar to Manitoba's and New Brunswick's arrangements, key informants interviewed through this research noted that the linkages between the PES, activation supports for social assistance recipients, and services for employers were not as strong as it could be.

In 2014 Ontario and British Columbia were furthest away from having "one-stop" shops that integrated the three PES functions as promoted by the OECD. While British Columbia placed delivery responsibility for LMDA programming under 101 WorkBC Employment Services Centres operating under the responsibility of the social services department, access to social assistance benefits was through another door. LMA-funded PES programming for non-EI recipients was managed and delivered by the BC skills ministry, not the social services ministry that managed the LMDA-funded programming. By 2014 BC had put protocols in place to coordinate PES programming across the two provincial government departments responsible. Employer supports in BC were the responsibility of various provincial ministries.

Figure 3. One-Stop Shops

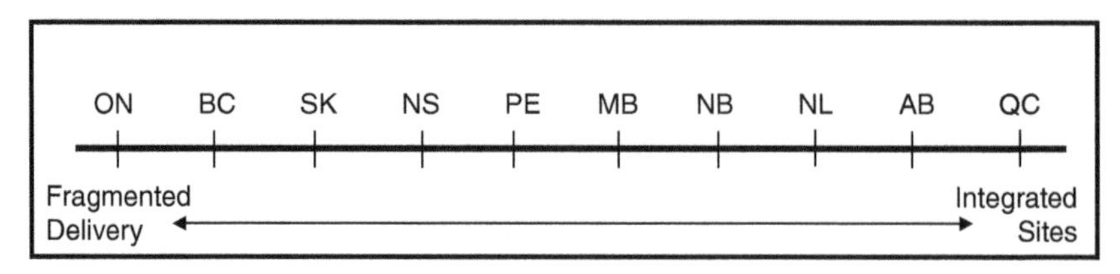

There was even greater fragmentation in Ontario, where in 2014 three doors offered access to provincial PES services. The mainstream PES (under the postsecondary education department) was offered through 170 Employment Ontario service providers across the province. This business line was managed separately from employment services for social assistance claimants, which were offered through forty-seven municipalities, or by contractors working directly for the provincial social services department. Each of these organizations connected individually with employers as needed. Unlike BC, there was no formal interdepartmental process to coordinate the different parts of Ontario's PES. In 2015 a review was underway examining realignment of the system and how the Employment Ontario network could be strengthened.

Figure 3 places provinces in a continuum, where Quebec was closest to having "one-stop" shops as described by the OECD and Ontario was the farthest away.

Decentralization

One key objective of devolution was to ensure that PES services were flexible and met local and regional needs. This not only included policy flexibility, but also the capacity for local partners to integrate supports based on individual client and local organizational needs.

In 2014 Quebec, Alberta, New Brunswick, Manitoba, and Saskatchewan all had decentralized delivery arrangements, where regional and local offices of the provincial department responsible for the PES had significant authority to make contracting decisions and facilitate PES programming suited to local needs. All had put management processes in place that ensured that regional and local office personnel played a formal role in provincial policy development.

The presence of seventeen regional labour market councils (CRPMTs) in Quebec – matched to support each of Emploi-Québec's regional

Figure 4. Decentralization

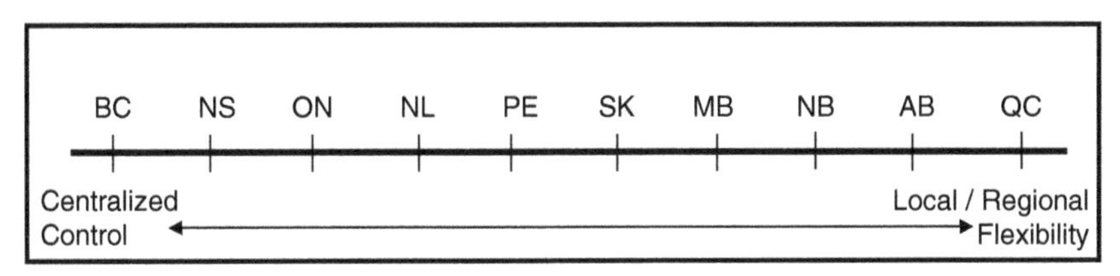

offices – further strengthened the decentralized nature of the Quebec arrangements. Their presence ensured that business, labour, educational institutions, and the community sector – working alongside government – played a role in shaping regional action plans that directed Emploi-Québec spending decisions.

British Columbia had the most centralized PES arrangements of all of the provinces, with contracting managed and controlled out of the provincial capital under a defined province-wide business model. The Employment Program of BC – established in 2012 to replace the legacy provincial and federal programs – was implemented through a province-wide request for proposal in order to ensure that similar services were available across the province. Nova Scotia, Ontario, and Prince Edward Island were not as centralized as BC; however, informants interviewed for this research noted that most PES decisions were made in the provincial capital, with limited flexibility at the regional and local level.

Figure 4 places provinces along a continuum, where Quebec was considered as having the most decentralized PES arrangements and British Columbia the most centralized.

Outsourcing or Contracting Out

Outsourcing or contracting out divides up the roles of service purchaser (e.g., the PES) and service provider (e.g., a private company or non-government organization). In PES matters, outsourcing arrangements are "quasi-markets," as purchasing power does not come from consumers of the services (unemployed people), but from the government.

In 2014 British Columbia's PES, followed by that of Ontario, Nova Scotia, and Prince Edward Island was almost completely outsourced, with the entire service contracted out to third-party organizations that were the public "face" of the provincial PES. All other provinces had a

Figure 5. Outsourcing

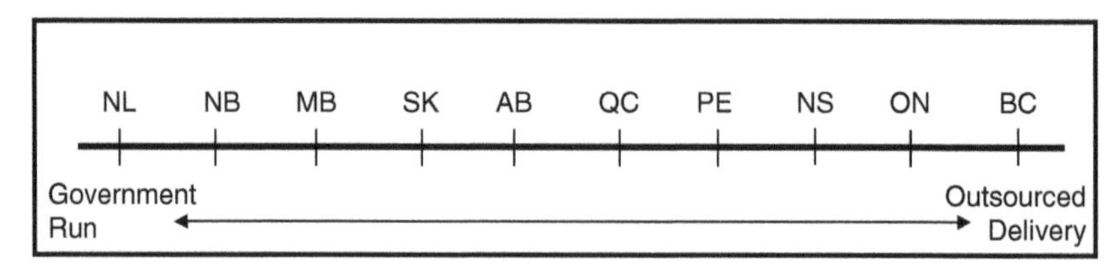

"mixed" delivery model consisting of provincial civil servants providing "front door" access to the service, supported by contacted delivery agents providing specialized services. In Newfoundland and Labrador and New Brunswick most of the services were provided by provincial civil servants. Post-devolution Newfoundland and Labrador cancelled many of the contracts inherited from the federal government to take PES services in-house. Alberta, Quebec, Saskatchewan, and Manitoba fit somewhere in the middle along the continuum, as illustrated in figure 5.

British Columbia, Ontario, Nova Scotia, and Prince Edward Island had more outsourcing as, by the time that devolved agreements were signed between 2005 and 2008, Service Canada had already begun to aggressively contract out PES service delivery. Pre-devolution, British Columbia and Ontario also had contracted delivery models for services targeted to social assistance recipients and youth. After their provincial governments agreed to take on the federal contracts, the first task confronting officials was how to rationalize the basket of federal and provincial contracts providing employment supports to the different client groups.

British Columbia was the boldest of all jurisdictions. To deal with the 400 "legacy" programs, the province undertook consultations and then developed a new delivery model consisting of "prime" and "sub" contractors and pay for performance. It then put the entire system out for open bidding. This required forced partnering among the various BC employment agencies. While Ontario, Nova Scotia, and Prince Edward Island faced the same dilemma, they took a much more incremental approach to change. Ontario used a "capacity assessment" process that resulted in about eighty agencies leaving the system. By 2015 specialized disability contracts had still not been integrated into the mainstream PES. Prince Edward Island undertook a bidding process for the main employment services contract; however, the same contractor was successful. By 2015 Nova Scotia had still not made changes to the contractors inherited from the federal government, although changes were made to the contract conditions.

Partnerships and Networks

The final governance theme examined in this book looks at how public and private actors – beyond politicians and civil servants – are involved in designing, directing, influencing, and managing the provincial PES. Partnerships can be formal or informal, with the specific arrangements often detailed in defined institutions set out in legislation.

In 2014 Quebec had the most developed partnership structure of all provinces. This included a national board (Commission des partenaires du marché du travail, or CPMT), seventeen regional labour market councils (CRPMTs), and twenty-nine sectoral workforce committees (CSMOs), all with defined representation from labour, business, the community, and academia. This partnership structure was detailed in legislation with defined linkages to the provincial government department responsible, the Ministère du Travail, de l'Emploi et de la Solidarité sociale (MTESS) and its delivery arm Emploi-Québec. Manitoba also had a well-developed and long-standing partnership structure with business and unions – also in legislation – consisting of a Minister's Advisory Council on Workforce Development as well as seventeen sector councils.

Since 2008 New Brunswick's Economic and Social Inclusion Corporation has provided non-government partners with structured access to government decision making that may include PES matters. Until its demise in 2012 Newfoundland and Labrador's Strategic Social Partnership provided business and labour with similar access. While Ontario lost its provincial labour market board and sector councils in 1996, it has retained twenty-six local workforce boards. However, the local boards played a limited role in the design and delivery of employment and training initiatives in the province (OECD 2014b). In 2015 their role was being recast.

Partnership arrangements in the rest of the provinces were more informal. Nova Scotia and Prince Edward Island retained remnants of the sector councils established by the federal government. Saskatchewan, British Columbia, and Alberta set up industry advisory groups; however, in 2014 their roots were shallow, and activities ebbed and flowed, dependent upon the political environment. There was limited

Figure 6. Partnerships

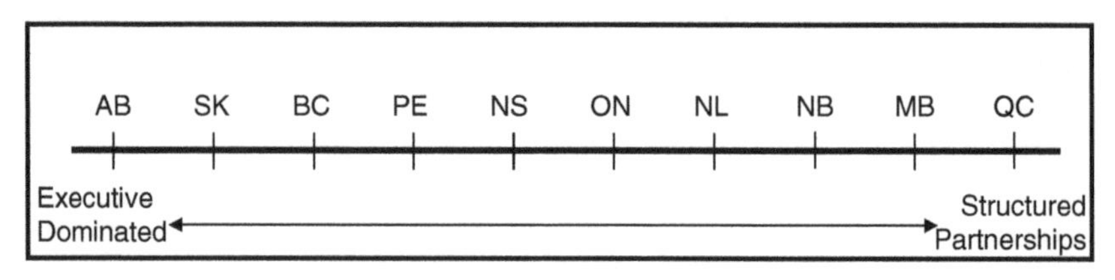

funding support provided. This contrasts with Quebec and Manitoba that provide provincial funding to support their PES partnership arrangements.

Provinces have established various mechanisms to connect with the third-party contractors who deliver most of the PES. Quebec had formal protocols to link external contractors and the associations that represented them with Emploi-Québec. British Columbia, Ontario, and Nova Scotia set up defined ways to solicit input and seek feedback. Quebec, British Columbia, and Ontario also had umbrella provincial associations that linked their community-based training organizations with each other and with their provincial government. More informal mechanisms were used in other places. Figure 6 ranks provincial partnerships with business, labour, community organizations, and academia on PES matters along a continuum.

Why Were Different Governance Choices Made?

Unlike in the United States where the federal government required states to establish "one-stop shops" supervised by employer-dominated Workforce Investment Boards, provinces in Canada were free to select their own governance arrangements. Some aligned the programming with their social services responsibilities (Quebec, Alberta, and Newfoundland and Labrador); others associated it with their postsecondary education departments (New Brunswick, Nova Scotia, Prince Edward Island, and Ontario); and others aligned PES programs with their economic development department (Manitoba and Saskatchewan). British Columbia split the federally funded programming between its social services and skills departments.

These choices have changed over the years. While this kind of flexibility is fully consistent with provincial constitutional autonomy, the result has been considerable churning in PES programming as it is shifted within a province from one department to another as premiers under different political parties build and rebuild Cabinets. It also prevents the development of a strong identify and brand for PES programming, either on a provincial or pan-Canadian basis. Until the Canada Job Grant dispute in 2013, most Canadians did not even realize that the federal government no longer delivered the PES. Their confusion is understandable, given that Ottawa has maintained direct responsibility for Aboriginal, youth, immigrant, and disability programming.

The governance choices made by provinces post-devolution built upon the arrangements they inherited when the federal programs transferred over. British Columbia, Ontario, Nova Scotia, and Prince Edward Island have a primarily outsourced PES, as they had no choice. It took considerable political courage in Newfoundland and Labrador to cancel existing third-party contracts and take the services in-house. Likewise, decentralized versus centralized arrangements are a function of the size of the provincial government department responsible, whether the services were outsourced or not, and whether the outsourcing was done at the provincial or local level. Partnerships and networks reflected the larger political culture of the province.

The Government of Canada was wise not to insist on standardization of these service delivery arrangements, which would have been an impossible task, given that the LMDAs were voluntary arrangements implemented one jurisdiction at a time, in a federal political system comprising semi-sovereign governments. In the political climate following the Quebec referendum in the late 1990s, it would have been unfeasible to develop a pan-Canadian multilateral framework acceptable to all.

Different Outcomes in Different Places: Comparing Provinces

Chapters 4 to 7 placed provinces into groups – the Far West, the Midwest, the Centre, and the East – and compared PES programming outcomes using publicly released data under the LMDA and LMA agreements. In some places supplementary information – especially OECD reports – was also used. The analysis in each chapter was detailed and subjective. It represented a first attempt to compare PES programming outcomes from one province to another and assess the results achieved (or not). Now that the data have been assembled for this book, readers are encouraged to challenge my interpretations and develop their own.

On the basis of the information assembled, I made judgments on the effectiveness of the province's PES programming (i.e., how

Table G. Comparing Provincial PES Performance

Jurisdiction	Performance to 2014
Alberta vs British Columbia	Alberta's PES programs were more effective and efficient than British Columbia's. BC's were more democratic.
Manitoba vs Saskatchewan	Both Manitoba and Saskatchewan had effective programs. Manitoba's were more efficient and democratic.
Ontario vs Quebec	Quebec's programming was more effective, efficient, and democratic than Ontario's.
New Brunswick, Nova Scotia, and Prince Edward Island vs Newfoundland and Labrador	Effectiveness was similar in all provinces. Newfoundland and Labrador had the least efficient PES programming and New Brunswick had the most efficient. Newfoundland and Labrador's programming was the most democratic.

useful it was to those being served); whether it was efficient (i.e., that things were done in the most optimal way); and whether it was democratic (i.e., that stakeholders and others were involved). I then compared provinces in groups. Table G provides a high-level summary. Readers are encouraged to review the detailed analysis in chapters 4 to 7.

Devolved Delivery Compared to When the Government of Canada Was in Charge

Between 1996 and 2010 over 2,600 federal government staff and almost 1,000 contracts transferred from the Government of Canada to the provinces and territories as they took on devolved LMDAs. From over 500 federally managed Canada Employment Centres in the late 1990s, by 2014 there were 637 provincially managed main sites where Canadians could access employment services, supplemented by 85 Aboriginal labour market organizations operating under the Aboriginal Skills and Employment Training Strategy (ASETS) banner offering over 600 points of service. In 2014 over 1,100 contracted service delivery providers were engaged in providing PES services. Appendix P provides more information on these pan-Canadian statistics.

To cover the cost of designing, delivering, and managing these employment services, in 2013/14 the Government of Canada transferred over $2.7 billion annually to provinces and territories through four labour market transfer agreements. An additional $496 million was provided to Aboriginal labour market organizations. Seventy-five

Figure 7. Comparing Clients Served Pre- and Post-Devolution

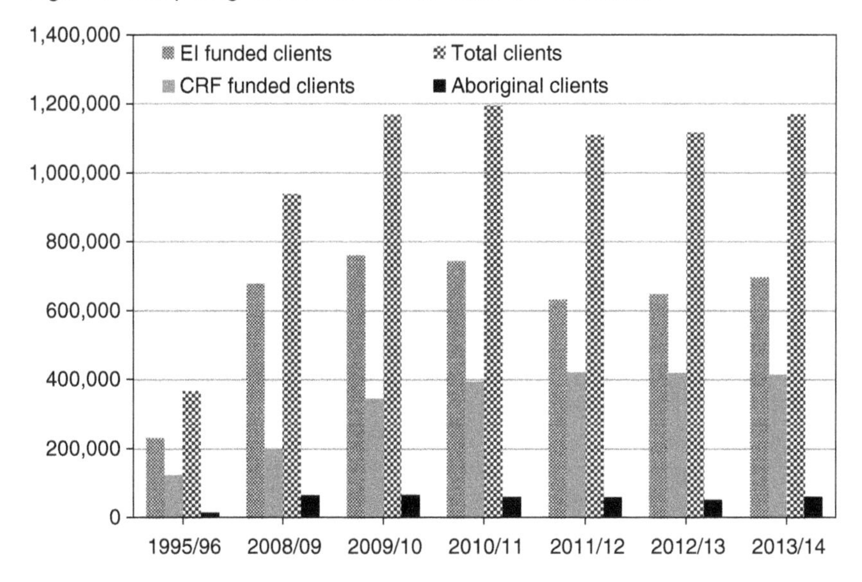

per cent of this money came from employer and employee contributions to the Employment Insurance (EI) account.

Comparing Clients Served and the Type of Intervention

PES usage has increased dramatically post-devolution. As shown in figure 7 and summarized in appendix S, more than triple the number of clients were served by the PES in 2013/14 under provincial/territorial/Aboriginal management compared to 1995/6 when the Government of Canada was directly responsible.[2]

When in 1995/6 Canada Employment Centres offered employment services paid for through the Unemployment Insurance Development Uses (UIDU) program, 231,000 clients were served. As detailed in appendix Q, in 2013/14, 695,745 Canadians used Employment Insurance (EI) Part II Employment Benefits and Support Measures (EBSMs)

2 These numbers are based on eighteen years of data from the EI Monitoring and Assessment reports, six years of data from provincial LMA reports, in addition to information on Aboriginal programming provided by federal officials.

offered by provinces and territories, taking part in 1,112,031 interventions. The number of clients served reached a peak of 758,761 in 2009/10 when additional federal funding was allocated for two years to deal with the economic downturn.

By 2010 all provinces and territories had signed onto devolved Labour Market Development Agreements and taken on the federal responsibilities. In 1999/2000 79 per cent of clients served were active EI recipients or reach-back clients, and 21 per cent were non-insured. The proportion of EI-attached clients has dropped every year since then, such that by 2013/14, 63 per cent of clients served were EI clients and 27 per cent were non-insured.

This change in the number of clients served needs to be read in conjunction with a change to the nature of the programming provided. In 1995 – when the PES was still solely federally managed – 68 per cent of interventions were long-term "employment benefits" that included skills development, wage subsidies, and self-employment supports. By 2013/14, long-term interventions had dropped to just 14 per cent. The most common service was "light-touch" Employment Assistance Services (EAS), reflecting a "work-first" philosophy emphasizing a speedy return to work.

This change in programming emphasis is a result of the three indicators put in place through the 1995 federal EI reform. Explicitly designed to reduce EI expenditures, the indicators chosen were based on an expectation that most unemployed people would search for a job in a relatively autonomous fashion with government help restricted primarily to EAS-like activities such as résumé writing and job clubs. More intensive training and work-related supports were to be offered sparingly. This trajectory occurred in all jurisdictions under both federal and provincial management. The results also reflected the fact that – other than in relation to the economic downturn for two years starting in 2009/10 – there has been no increase to the LMDA funding allocations since they were set twenty years ago. The only way that more clients requesting services could be assisted with the same amount of money was by changing the interventions provided to those that cost less, regardless of effectiveness and client need.

The change in the nature of the intervention provided has resulted in a decline in the cost per participant in LMDA funded programming from $7,359 in 1995/6 to $2,794 in 2013/14. Results versus targets on returns to employment and EI unpaid benefits demonstrated considerable steadiness in outcomes over the entire period examined in this book. Almost every year post-devolution – under both federal and provincial management – these jointly determined federal-provincial targets have been achieved and often exceeded.

In addition to money from the EI account, before 1995 considerable funding from the Consolidated Revenue Fund (CRF) was allocated by the federal government to provide employment services for "designated groups" (women, persons with disabilities, Aboriginal people, and visible minorities) who had not developed an EI attachment, as well as youth, social assistance recipients, and older workers. A report prepared by the Canadian Labour Force Development Board in 1998 (but never released) indicated that in 1993/4 306,920 people had been served through federal CRF funded programming. By 1995/6 the numbers had dropped dramatically to 136,472 clients served (with 13,096 of them being Aboriginal people) as a result of reduced funding due to federal fiscal restraint.

Pan-Canadian statistics on the number of clients served under the Labour Market Agreements (LMAs) using Consolidated Revenue Funding (CRF) are summarized in appendix R, drawing on the public reports released by provinces between 2008 and 2014 and Emploi-Québec annual reports. Funding provided to provinces through the Labour Market Agreements was, in effect, a partial replacement for the CRF funding that had been cut in the mid-1990s, as the client group served was similar. It took provinces a while to ramp up the services on offer through the LMAs with only 198,229 clients served in 2008/9. By 2013/14 when the funding ended (to be replaced by the Canada Job Fund Agreements), this figure had more than doubled to 413,639 clients served.

Aboriginal employment programming was funded through both the Consolidated Revenue Fund and the EI account. Before the Regional Bilateral Agreements were implemented in 1996, the federal government offered Aboriginal employment programming as one of its designated groups, with 13,096 clients served in 1995/6. As identified in appendix O, in 2013/14 59,243 people were served through ASETS programming, the Skills and Partnership Fund, and the First Nations Job Fund.

Adding all of these numbers together, in 2013/14, 1,168,227 Canadians used PES services managed by provinces, territories, and Aboriginal organizations. This contrasts with the 367,472 Canadians who used the services when they were managed directly by the Government of Canada in 1995/6. Devolving the PES to provinces, territories, and Aboriginal organizations has substantially broadened access and increased the number of Canadians served far beyond what was available when the services were federally managed. This is a positive outcome.

Qualitative Assessments of Federal versus Devolved Service Delivery

Chapter 2 of this book detailing the history of the public employment service has identified many comments on the effectiveness of Canada's PES. Reflecting on provincial delivery, Struthers (1983, 40) noted, "After 1924 the Employment Service of Canada was little more than a patronage-ridden clearing house for casual help." Under Unemployment Insurance Commission management after 1940 the National Employment Service limped along "severely hampered by lack of adequate staff and facilities" (Dupré et al. 1973, 47). To overcome these problems, as recommended by the Gill Commission, in 1962 the PES was made the direct responsibility of an operating department of the federal government.

The Dodge Report in 1981 noted that the PES still did only a "fair" or "poor" job in helping the unemployed find work, and employers preferred informal hiring channels. The Neilson Report in 1985 was also critical, noting a "high level of dissatisfaction with the quality of the screening and referral service of the Canada Employment Centres" (Canada 1985, 78). The Forget Commission weighed in 1986, noting that the CEC placement service should either be revitalized or cancelled. A 1986/7 evaluation identified that the PES could not efficiently provide its services to every component of the labour market. "It is mainly the equity role of the NES which should be emphasized ... there is a rationale for maintaining a publicly funded network of CECs which provide services not otherwise available to client groups experiencing job search or recruitment difficulties" (Employment and Immigration Canada 1989, 8–9). Problems with the federally managed PES continued into the 1990s, with the 1994 Social Security review identifying that there was "an urgent need to re-think employment services so that they focus squarely on one objective: helping people to find good jobs" (HRDC 1994, 30).

In *none* of these reports was devolution to the provinces suggested as a solution to PES problems. However, given political circumstances, that was what ultimately transpired. The question people are most interested in knowing the answer to is whether devolution has improved

PES outcomes. The answer from regular reports as well as evaluation studies over the past fifteen years is a clear "yes." Appendix T provides a summary of federally sponsored evaluation reports on provincial and Aboriginal PES programming completed between 1998 and 2015. The outcomes achieved were highly positive.

A Fragmented and Complex Delivery System

However, the results were largely hidden, as the focus on individual programs does not provide a holistic "big picture" of what has happened with Canada's PES over the past twenty years. While a summary of the provincial summative evaluations was prepared, no pan-Canadian evaluation on the Labour Market Development Agreements (LMDAs) has ever been commissioned. The Labour Market Agreement evaluation was considered by the media only in the context of the larger federal-provincial disagreement on the Canada Job Grant. No academic or think tank studies have been undertaken on the PES, as has occurred in Australia, the United States, and the European Union.[3]

Post-devolution, Canada's public employment service has become highly complex, involving in 2015 fifty-two bilateral LMDA/LMA/CJFA/LMAPD/TIOW agreements as well as eighty-five federal-Aboriginal agreements under the Aboriginal Skills and Employment Training Strategy. Even though Aboriginal employment programming looks like one-stop shops offered through ASETS holders across the country, in 2015 it was even more fragmented than what occurred in the provinces. Part of the fragmentation was due to the federal decision to have the Skills and Partnership Fund managed by separate and distinct Aboriginal labour market organizations, as opposed to ASETS holders. In addition, the desire of Aboriginal organizations to segment programming on a "distinctions" basis resulted in fifty-seven First Nations, seven Metis, eight Inuit, and thirteen urban ASETS holders across Canada. Employers find it very hard to know whom to contact, especially with regards to Aboriginal workers.

In her testimony at the HUMA hearings in 2014, the EI commissioner for employers noted, "At least one business associate has worked hard to garner information about LMDA-funded programming by visiting ESDC and provincial territorial websites, writing to Ministers involved,

3 See chapter 10 of this book for more information and references.

and consulting the monitoring and assessment report. Despite this, they have found it virtually impossible to get a concrete picture of what programs are offered using LMDA money that may apply in their industry, let alone how well that money is being spent" (HUMA 2014).

The EI commissioner noted that a key objective was to improve comparative provincial reporting under the *MAR* to better inform employers and unemployed workers. This will be challenging. As noted in the preface to this book, provincial governments do not want the federal government to compare them. They view the Canada Employment Insurance Commission as being the same as the Government of Canada. By established protocol, the annual *MAR*s require provincial approval before they are publicly released. This means that provinces can block comparative assessment on their PES programming from being shared with Canadians through the *MAR*.

Federal Management of the PES Pieces It Retained

LMDA results are just one piece of Canada's PES. Post-devolution, the Government of Canada remains directly involved in very important ways. It provides direct oversight and direction to employment programming for Aboriginal people, youth, immigrants, and persons with disabilities. It retained responsibility for pan-Canadian labour market partnerships; elements of the National Employment Service; and research, evaluation, and innovation. As the national government and the main funder of the PES, Ottawa also plays a coordinating role: between governments through the Forum of Labour Market Ministers (FLMM), between governments and national program delivery organizations, and between Canada and international organizations. To be in conformance with ILO Convention 88, Ottawa is expected to ensure that business and labour views are heard on national PES issues through advisory committees.

As detailed in chapters 8 and 9 of this book, the Government of Canada's performance post-devolution has been weak. Federal oversight of Aboriginal employment programming became more controlling, with ASETS holders subjected to an extensive accountability regime involving direct oversight, monitoring, and correction of expenditures. There was little evidence of "co-production" of policy, as had been aspired to in the early days of the federal-Aboriginal agreements. The democratic input of Aboriginal people into employment programming in 2015 was barely greater than the pre-devolution model of direct federal delivery through Native employment counsellors. Over the past twenty years federal support for capacity building and coordination between Aboriginal organizations on a pan-Canadian basis and within each province became progressively weaker.

Employment and Social Development Canada has also held onto direct delivery responsibility for youth programming through the Youth Employment Strategy, and disabled people through the Opportunities Fund. While its role in youth programming predates devolution, it developed a defined federal funding envelope for employment services for disabled people only *after* provinces were offered responsibility for EI clients. This occurred despite the presence of a long-standing federal-provincial agreement that provided federal funding to provinces for disability employment programming. As noted by the OECD (2015b), the result in all of this is a fragmented "system-oriented" institutional framework – as opposed to a client-oriented one – that is difficult for unemployed workers to navigate and challenging for governments to monitor and evaluate.

The federal presence in national aspects of the labour market – an area where most Canadians would agree that federal leadership is appropriate – has diminished significantly post-devolution. Under both Liberal and Conservative governments, federal ministers were often disengaged from their provincial colleagues through the Forum of Labour Market Ministers. Ottawa provided limited support and funding to help pan-Canadian umbrella NGOs directly involved with delivering the PES – community-based training organizations, youth, disability, and Aboriginal employment agencies, and organizations for career development practitioners – come together to share best practices, compare provincial approaches, and learn from their different experiences across Canada.

While the Liberals were prepared to reinforce and strengthen the federal role in labour market research and knowledge-brokering institutions, the Conservatives did not share this perspective. The Canadian Labour and Business Centre closed down in 2007. Canadian Policy Research Networks was disbanded in 2009, and the Canadian Council on Learning closed in 2012. Federal spending on pan-Canadian activities through the EI account dropped from $70 million in 2010 to $24 million in 2013/14. By 2013/14 federal funding for Canadian participation in OECD reviews had been cut by two-thirds.

Although some provinces have created their own research institutions – the Centre for Employment Excellence in British

Columbia, l'Observatoire compétences-emplois in Quebec, and the Centre for Workforce Innovation in Ontario – in 2015 there were no mechanisms for them to link on a pan-Canadian basis to ensure coordination, resource sharing, and assurance that gaps in the big picture were identified and filled. Since other provinces have chosen not to invest, an imbalance in provincial capacity to contribute to the workings of the federation is being created.

The corporatist turn under the Mulroney Progressive Conservatives during the 1980s and 1990s represented the pinnacle of formal stakeholder involvement in Canada's PES, involving dedicated labour market boards at the national, provincial, and local level. There were also sector councils and Aboriginal labour market boards. By 2000 the national board, the Aboriginal boards, and all of the provincial boards had disappeared. By 2013 most sector councils were gone. The only institutionalized way that stakeholder input was secured on a national basis in 2015 was through the presence of the EI commissioners for workers and employers on the Canada Employment Insurance Commission. This provides very limited access.

How Canada's PES Fits Together as a Whole

Figure 8 presents a picture of how Canada's PES fit together as whole in 2015, based on the research and analysis undertaken for this book.

At the core of the wheel are the two institutions responsible for funding, strategy, policy development, and program design of the PES: the Canada Employment Insurance Commission, or CEIC, and the Forum of Labour Market Ministers, or FLMM. The CEIC has four commissioners responsible under the Employment Insurance Act for the management of Canada's EI program, including EI Part II Employment Benefits and Support Measures (EBSMs). The CEIC reports to the minister of employment and social development Canada. The FLMM is the intergovernmental body responsible for pan-Canadian coordination. It operates at the level of federal/provincial/territorial ministers, as well as at the level of deputy ministers and officials. The only linkage between the two bodies is through the presence of the federal ESDC deputy minister who sits on both. Only recently have the EI commissioner for workers and the EI commissioner for employers attended an FLMM meeting. Missing from the core is representation from Aboriginal labour market organizations, a key new player post-devolution.

Figure 8. Mapping Key Institutions (2014–15) in Canada's Public Employment Service*

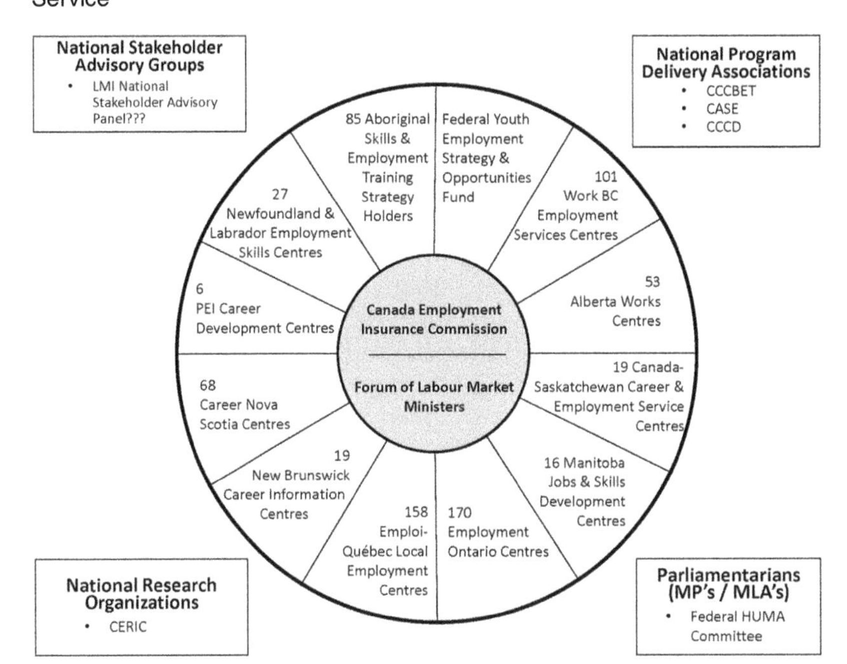

*PES arrangements in the Northwest Territories, Yukon, and Nunavut were not examined in detail in this book.

In the outer spoke of the wheel are the provincial and Aboriginal service delivery organizations that present as the "face" or "front door" of the PES across Canada. These are the entities that, in most provinces, are responsible for the delivery of federally funded LMDA/LMA/CJFA/LMAPD/TIOW programming. As identified earlier in this chapter, every province has made different choices on how to organize its service delivery arrangements. The Aboriginal labour market arrangements under ASETS are also distinct. Also included as a spoke are the federally delivered Youth Employment Strategy (YES) and Opportunities Fund (OF) programs. Unlike ASETS and the provincial arrangements, these are not delivered under a single brand across Canada and so are a more hidden part of Canada's PES arrangements.

As identified in the top left, in 2015 there were no national institutions to ensure that the views of employers, workers, and other stakeholders were heard on labour market matters. While the Stakeholder Advisory Panel to the Labour Market Information Council may be an improvement over the status quo, labour market information is just one piece of Canada's PES. The lack of institutionalized involvement by non-government actors into Canada's PES contrasts with the approach of the United States, where employer influence is federally mandated through a majority employer presence on Workforce Investment Boards. There are also distinct processes in the European Union to ensure that the voice of a wide variety of EU stakeholders is heard.

Moving to the top right, three pan-Canadian organizations representing PES delivery were identified through this research. The Canadian Coalition of Community-Based Employability Training (CCCBET) comprises representatives from provincial community-based employment and training associations. The Canadian Association for Supported Employment (CASE) represents provincial organizations managing supported employment programs for persons with developmental disabilities. The Canadian Council for Career Development (CCCD) brings together the nine provincial Career Development Practitioner associations. None of these organizations had defined linkages with the government-run PES structure. This contrasts with how Jobs Australia and the National Employment Services Association connected PES service delivery organizations with each other and with government in Australia.

Moving to the bottom right, there are few ways for federal and provincial politicians – beyond those designated as federal and provincial ministers or parliamentary secretaries responsible for the labour market policy file – to participate in PES decision making. The only federal politicians directly involved were those serving on the Standing Committee on Human Resources, Skills and Social Development and the Status of Persons with Disabilities (HUMA). Other than those designated as Cabinet ministers, provincial politicians usually engaged in the PES only as issues arose. This contrasts with both the U.S. and EU systems that provide a wide variety of ways for legislators to influence PES programming choices.

On the bottom left are national research organizations. The only pan-Canadian institution in place in 2015 focusing specifically on employment matters was the Canadian Education and Research Institute for Counselling (CERIC), focused on career counselling and career development. It is funded by a private foundation, not government. All other research institutions have been defunded. Those left operate at the provincial level only. Our international partners do a much better job in this area. Since implementing the European Employment Strategy in 1997, the European Union has placed great emphasis on comparative research through its PES to PES dialogue and institutes such as the European Employment Policy Observatory. In the United States the endowment-funded W.J. Upjohn Institute has for eighty-five years been undertaking research on the causes and consequences of unemployment.

Final Reflections

In 1995 – through the Quebec independence referendum – Canada came close to falling apart. Provincial control over employment and training was a key Quebec demand. Efforts to change jurisdictional responsibility by constitutional means through the Charlottetown Accord in 1992 had failed. What happened between 1995 and 2015 through devolution of the PES illustrates the practical tools that governments in Canada used to keep the country together and mitigate some of the irritants that were causing problems.

Instead of constitutional change, on the labour market front action was taken one step at a time through bilateral intergovernmental agreements that did not require all provinces to do the same thing. What was on offer to Quebec was on offer to all, precluding the development of highly asymmetrical arrangements that applied only to Quebec. Announced by the Chrétien Liberal government as part of larger changes to transform unemployment insurance into Employment Insurance, the bilateral Labour Market Development Agreements were implemented quietly by executive edict, with negotiations confined to federal and provincial ministers and senior civil servants. It was up to each provincial government to decide whether to take on the federal programs or just work to improve federal-provincial coordination within its province.

The views of parliamentarians and other external stakeholders were ignored, including the Canadian Labour Force Development Board concerned at the time that the potential for extreme decentralization and fragmentation of Canadian labour market programming under the LMDAs would reduce access to employment services for disadvantaged groups and lead to what Herman Bakvis (2002) called "checkerboard federalism." Thomas Klassen (2000a) was more optimistic, characterizing the arrangements that had been put in place by the late

1990s as a "brave new model of collaboration." Writing a decade later and reflecting on almost fifteen years of Quebec responsibility for PES programming, Alain Noel (2012) concluded that bilateralism and asymmetry in employment programs had yielded positive outcomes from both a policy and governance standpoint and had allowed for experimentation, change, learning, and diffusion.

Canada is now into phase three of devolution of its PES and related workforce development programming. Phase one under the Chrétien/Martin Liberals starting in 1995 involved the initial offer to the provinces of employment services for EI clients under the new Employment Insurance legislation and the transfer of federal staff, assets, contracts, and programming responsibilities to Alberta, New Brunswick, Quebec, Saskatchewan, Manitoba, Northwest Territories, Nunavut, and Ontario under devolved Labour Market Development Agreements. It also involved setting up and supporting Aboriginal labour market organizations under Pathways to Success and AHRDS, the establishment of pan-Canadian research organizations to assure federal leadership, and the affirmation of federal direct delivery of youth and disability programming. Federal-provincial transfer agreements for persons with disabilities were updated and modernized through the development of a pan-Canadian framework.

Phase two under the Harper Conservatives after 2006 focused on consolidation and improvement of the delivery architecture, including implementing similar devolved LMDA arrangements in British Columbia, Nova Scotia, Prince Edward Island, Newfoundland and Labrador, and the Yukon Territory. This moved the asymmetrical arrangements under the Liberals to a relatively similar approach in all jurisdictions across Canada, removing the checkerboard nature of the previous arrangements. The Conservatives also allocated additional money to all jurisdictions through Labour Market Agreements so that Canadians without an EI attachment could be better served through the provincial PES. They also reaffirmed existing federal-provincial transfer agreements for older workers. These arrangements put more money into the provincial system to enhance employment services for many disadvantaged groups.

However, the Conservatives left much unfinished business in that they ultimately did not transfer responsibility for youth and disability programming to the provinces as promised, thereby retaining a fragmented system. When it came to implementation they found that disability organizations did not support transferring the Opportunities

Fund to the provinces, concerned that a weakened position for the federal government relative to the provinces was not in the best interests of persons with disabilities (McColl and Roberts 2015). Federal relationships with Aboriginal labour market organizations became more controlling and fraught. The Conservatives also undermined the federal leadership role by reducing funding for pan-Canadian initiatives and the youth employment program, closing research institutions, defunding disability advocacy groups, and disengaging with the Forum of Labour Market Ministers.

Their unilateral action in 2013 to replace provincial funding under the successful Labour Market Agreements (LMAs) with the untested Canada Job Fund Agreements (CJFA) heightened the intergovernmental tension that had been significantly reduced after 1996 through implementation of the LMDAs. Dealing with these federal changes forced provinces and territories to come together to work towards improvements to the federal offer to better satisfy their needs. Allowing Quebec – but not other provinces – to roll over its LMA illustrated a willingness to treat Quebec differently, justified on the grounds that it already had extensive employer participation in its PES through various partnership networks. While this is true, it also applies to Manitoba.

Future developments regarding the LMDAs, LMAs, CJFAs, LMAPDs, TIOWs, and ASETS will now be decided by the Trudeau Liberals, elected to a four-year term with a majority government in the fall of 2015. In cooperation with provinces and territories, in the summer of 2016 they undertook consultations on programs funded through the labour market transfer agreements. It is expected that the Liberals will govern very differently from the Conservatives. Commentators expect a return to an active federal government and the development of stronger public institutions (Graves 2016). On labour market matters the Liberal campaign platform committed to increase LMDA, LMA, and ASETS funding – the first base-funding increase in more than twenty years. It also promised a significant expansion of the Youth Employment Program and new employment services for veterans.[4]

---

4 The 2015 Liberal platform committed to an increase of $500 million annually for the LMDAs, $200 million for LMAs, $50 million for ASETS, and $300 million more for youth programming for three years. It also promised $25 million for training facilities delivered in partnership with unions, $40 million for student co-op placements, and $80 million to create a new Veterans Education Benefit.

There is no shortage of issues in implementing these promises. An important first question is whether the existing four federal/provincial/territorial labour market transfer agreements could be consolidated and streamlined, thereby reducing fragmentation in PES programming. Devolving federal programs for youth and persons with disabilities to provinces and territories would also support this goal. Recognizing the PES and how its various pieces fit together would be much easier to understand if governments committed to an overarching framework agreement and vision for employment, as occurs in the agriculture and immigration sectors, two other policy areas where jurisdiction is shared between federal and provincial governments. On top of the basic architecture, the next question is how any federal money is distributed between provinces and territories. As detailed in this book, the LMDA allocation formula has not been updated since 1996 and is considered as unfair by some provinces. The fragmented accountability arrangements for the different agreements affect transparency and public understanding of Canada's PES. They also impede best practice learning.

Also important is finding the right balance between Aboriginal autonomy and federal accountability, as well as considering whether the current architecture of eighty-five ASETS organizations across Canada – with programming supplemented through project-based initiatives awarded to different Aboriginal organizations – is the right choice, given the commitment of the Trudeau government to a nation-to-nation relationship with Indigenous people. In addition, new ways need to be found to build capacity among Aboriginal labour market organizations so that they can engage with provincial governments – now responsible for most of the PES programming on offer – with each other, and with their key funder, the Government of Canada.

Just as important is reaching consensus on the federal role in labour market programming. The Liberals are starting with almost a blank slate on national research organizations that support labour market intelligence and decision making, since most of these were defunded by the Harper Conservatives. There are no longer any national advisory bodies. Without some sort of national stakeholder advisory committee, not only are we in violation of ILO Convention 88, PES programming will continue to be suboptimal without business and labour input. While no commitments were made in their election platform, the Liberals will soon have to decide what else is needed to improve pan-Canadian PES institutions beyond the LMI Council and its stakeholder advisory panel announced in the summer of 2015. Since PES responsibility is an area of shared federal-provincial jurisdiction, these decisions cannot be made by the federal government acting alone.

I consider a vibrant *public* employment service as a critical component of Canada's welfare state, essential to keeping unemployment rates low and labour market participation rates high. Canada's PES is now designed, managed, and delivered at the level where decisions are best made: provincial, regional, local, and Aboriginal. This is its core strength. At the same time, its pan-Canadian dimension as well as overall coordination needs to be improved. Moving forward over the next hundred years on these issues is a job not only for governments but also for business, unions, civil society organizations, researchers, and ordinary Canadians. Hopefully the information assembled in this book will help them to do this job as they collectively embark on Devolution Part Three.

Appendices

Appendix A. Interviews Held across Canada, 2012–2015, Dedicated to Research for Devolution Book

Place	PG	FG	R	AB	BU	UN	NGO	AC	PO	Total meetings[1]	Total people
British Columbia	10	2	5	4	2		9	4		34	49
Alberta	5	1		1	1		1			9	10
Saskatchewan	1		2	1	1		3			8	9
Manitoba	4			2			2	2		10	12
Ontario	6[2]			1	1		5	3		16	18
Quebec	8			1	1	1	3	4		18	21
New Brunswick	2			1			1	1		5	9
Nova Scotia	3			1			3			7	9
Prince Edward Island	2			1						3	5
Newfoundland and Labrador	3			1		1	1	1		7	8
National Capital Region		4		3	1	2	3	1	1	15	20
Total	44	7	6	17	7	4	29	16	1	132	170

PG = Provincial government officials
FG = Federal government officials
R = Retired
AB = Aboriginal officials
BU = Business representatives
UN = Union representatives
NGO = Representatives of non-government organizations
AC = Academics and representatives of policy think tanks
PO = Representatives of political parties

1 Most meetings were with one individual. However, in some cases, two to four individuals participated. I met with some individuals more than once. These are not included in the totals above.

2 This includes one meeting with two people from the City of Toronto.

Appendix B. Government Reports Used for Data Analysis

Federal Government Reports

1996/97 Employment Insurance Commission Monitoring and Assessment Report
1997/98 Employment Insurance Commission Monitoring and Assessment Report
1998/99 Employment Insurance Commission Monitoring and Assessment Report
1999/2000 Employment Insurance Commission Monitoring and Assessment Report
2000/1 *Employment Insurance Commission Monitoring and Assessment Report*
2001/2 Employment Insurance Commission Monitoring and Assessment Report
2002/3 Employment Insurance Commission Monitoring and Assessment Report
2003/4 Employment Insurance Commission Monitoring and Assessment Report
2004/5 Employment Insurance Commission Monitoring and Assessment Report
2005/6 Employment Insurance Commission Monitoring and Assessment Report
2006/7 Employment Insurance Commission Monitoring and Assessment Report
2007/8 Employment Insurance Commission Monitoring and Assessment Report
2008/9 Employment Insurance Commission Monitoring and Assessment Report
2009/10 Employment Insurance Commission Monitoring and Assessment Report
2010/11 Employment Insurance Commission Monitoring and Assessment Report
2011/12 Employment Insurance Commission Monitoring and Assessment Report
2012/13 Employment Insurance Commission Monitoring and Assessment Report
2013/14 Employment Insurance Commission Monitoring and Assessment Report
Canada's Labour Market Agreements: A National Report for 2008/9 and 2009/10

Provincial Government Reports

Canada–British Columbia Labour Market Agreement Performance Report, 2008/9, 2009/10, 2010/11, 2011/12, 2012/13, and 2013/14
Canada-Alberta Labour Market Agreement Performance Measures Final Report, 2008/9, 2009/10, 2010/11, 2011/12, 2012/13, and 2013/14
Canada-Saskatchewan Labour Market Agreement Performance Measures, Annual Report 2008/9, 2009/10, 2010/11, 2011/12
Canada-Manitoba Labour Market Agreement (LMA) Public Annual Report, 2008/9, 2009/10, 2010/11, 2011/12, 2012/13, and 2013/14
Canada-Ontario Labour Market Agreement (LMA) Outcomes Report on LMA, Incremental Investments 2008/9, 2009/10, 2010/11, 2011/12, 2012/13, and 2013/14
Québec Ministère du Travail, de l'Emploi et de la Solidarité Sociale, *Rapport statistique sur les individus, entreprises et organismes participant aux*

interventions des Services publics d'emploi, 2008/9, 2009/10, 2010/11, 2011/12, 2012/13, and 2013/14

New Brunswick Postsecondary Education, Training and Labour Annual Report, 2008/9, 2009/10, 2010/11, 2011/12, 2012/13, and 2013/14

Canada–Nova Scotia Labour Market Agreement Report, 2008/9, 2009/10 2010/11, 2011/12, 2012/13, and 2013/14

Prince Edward Island Advanced Education and Learning Annual Report, 2008/9 2009/10, and 2010/11

Canada–Newfoundland and Labrador Labour Market Agreement Performance Indicators Report, 2008/9, 2009/10, 2010/11, 2011/12, 2012/13, and 2013/14

Appendix C. Summary of Federal/Provincial/Territorial Labour Market Transfer Agreements[1]

Province	LMDA date[2]	2013/14 LMDA allocations	2013/14 LMA allocations	2013/14 LMAPD allocations	2011/12 TIOW allocations	Total[3]
Newfoundland and Labrador	2 Nov. 2009	$129,219,000	$7,349,000	$4,578,367	$2,380,282	$143,526,000
Prince Edward Island	5 Oct. 2009	$26,084,000	$2,094,000	$1,375,659	$535,959	$30,088,000
Nova Scotia	1 July 2009	$79,014,000	$13,599,000	$8,290,346	$1,940,237	$102,843,000
New Brunswick	1 Apr. 1997	$89,763,000	$10,836,000	$5,958,848	$1,944,252	$108,501,000
Quebec	1 Apr. 1998	$581,242,000	$115,462,000	$45,892,915	$13,346,355	$755,942,000
Ontario	1 Jan. 2007	$565,471,000	$193,603,000	$76,411,477	$16,429,066	$851,914,000
Manitoba	27 Nov. 1997	$43,507,000	$18,162,000	$8,964,971	$1,067,822	$71,700,000
Saskatchewan	1 Jan. 1999	$36,426,000	$15,481,000	$10,852,608	$922,343	$63,681,000
Alberta	1 Nov. 1997	$109,143,000	$55,529,000	$25,190,332	$2,828,636	$192,690,000
British Columbia	2 Feb. 2009	$280,647,000	$66,263,000	$30,744,084	$5,890,448	$383,544,000
Northwest Territories	1 Oct. 1, 1998	$3,143,000	$621,000	–	$488,200	$4,252,000
Yukon	1 Feb. 2010	$3,482,000	$518,000	–	$488,200	$4,488,000
Nunavut	1 Apr. 2000	$2,859,000	$483,000	–	$488,200	$3,830,000
Total		$1,950,000,000	$500,000,000	$218,254,000	$48,820,000	$2,717,000,000

1 LMDA/LMA/LMAPD allocations are from Zon (2014, 16 and 17). TIOW allocations are from ESDC 2014e. 2013/14 TIOW numbers were not available.

2 LMDA implementation date from *2013/14 EI Monitoring and Assessment Report*, 278.

3 Total amounts are rounded.

Appendix D. Employment Benefits and Supports Measures Descriptions[1]

Employment benefits	**Targeted Wage Subsidies** assist insured participants to obtain on-the-job work experience by providing employers with financial assistance towards the wages of participants. This benefit encourages employers to hire unemployed individuals whom they would not normally hire in the absence of a subsidy. **Targeted Earnings Supplements** encourage unemployed persons to accept employment by offering them financial incentives. Quebec offers a similar measure – Return to Work Supplement – to help with expenses related to returning to work (e.g., new tools, office materials, or clothing). **Job Creation Partnerships** projects provide insured participants with opportunities to gain work experience that will lead to ongoing employment. Activities of the project help develop the community and the local economy. **Skills Development** helps insured participants to obtain employment skills by giving them direct financial assistance that enables them to select, arrange for, and pay for their own training. **Self-Employment** provides financial assistance and business planning advice to EI-eligible participants to help them start their own business. This financial assistance is intended to cover personal living expenses and other expenses during the initial stages of the business.
Support measures	**Employment Assistance Services** provide funding to organizations to enable them to provide employment assistance to unemployed persons. The services provided may include individual counselling, action planning, job search skills, job-finding clubs, job placement services, the provision of labour market information, case management, and follow-up. **Labour Market Partnerships** provide funding to help employers, employee and employer associations, and communities to improve their capacity to deal with human resource requirements and to implement labour force adjustments. These partnerships involve developing plans and strategies, and implementing adjustment measures. **Research and Innovation** supports activities that identify better ways of helping people to prepare for or keep employment and to be productive participants in the labour force. Funds are provided to eligible recipients to enable them to carry out demonstration projects and research for this purpose.

1 From *2013 EI Monitoring and Assessment Report*, 210.

Appendix E. British Columbia PES Performance Data
(Implemented Devolved LMDA 2 February 2009, population 2014 was 4,631,000)

Category	1999/2000	2005/6	2008/9	2009/10	2010/11	2011/12	2012/13	2013/14
Unemployment rate[1]	8.3%	4.8%	7.7%	7.6%	7.5%	6.7%	6.6%	6.1%
Employment rate[2]	60.1%	62.2%	60.5%	60.5%	60.2%	60.6%	59.9%	59.5%
Social assistance cases[3]	156,992	98,867	110,353	126,878	133,803	136,005	134,410	134,591
EI regular beneficiaries[4]	71,330	53,010	102,290	98,420	83,030	71,330	60,800	58,000
LMDA information[5]								
Expenditures ($000s)								
Employment benefits	$143,284	$175,960	$161,729	$202,797	$186,749	$141,568	$136,834	$158,503
Employment assistance services	$84,897	$107,267	$113,250	$127,341	$130,008	$114,849	$71,230	$95,976
Other support measures	$11,185	$2,789	$2,688	$2,857	$4,555	$10,863	$14,830	$21,293
Total	$239,366	$286,016	$277,667	$332,995[6]	$321,312	$267,280	$222,894	$276,402
Clients served								
EI	47,255	54,841	54,288	78,917	68,261	49,873	45,256	45,948
Non-insured	20,932	31,051	41,736	35,795	38,415	29,068	31,522	35,680
Total	68,187	85,892	96,024	114,712	106,676	78,941	76,778	81,628
New interventions and mix								
Long term	30,237	22,439	26,184	28,313	22,286	17,250	16,975	18,993
Short term	60,875	115,320	122,331	152,170	146,827	102,708	197,676	205,855
Total	93,193	137,759	148,515	180,483	169,113	119,958	214,651	224,848
Returns to employment								
Target	28,536	29,820	29,660	20,000	20,000	30,000	30,000	24,000
Total clients	43,309	30,747	31,607	38,931	42,082	33,580	16,777	20,040
Results vs targets	152%	103%	107%	195%	210%	112%	56%	84%
EI unpaid benefits ($000s)								
Target	$131,190	$113,000	$120,000	$50,000	$241,700	$124,000	$124,000	$104,000
Total	$118,210	$123,710	$161,800	$241,600	$228,400	$146,400	$112,500	$121,800
Result vs target	89%	109%	135%	483%	95%	118%	91%	117%

LMA information[7]						
Allocations ($000s)	$65,600	$65,600	$65,600	$65,600	$65,600	$65,600
Clients served						
Employment services	10	2,910	1,130	873	1,403	2,019
Skills development for unemployed	889	3,765	2,389	4,295	4,139	3,286
Work experience	0	0	0	0	0	0
Combination	159	4,964	4,736	6,691	1,100	15,081
Skills development for employed	0	459	454	716	10,951	225
Total	1,058	12,098	8,709	12,575	17,593	20,611
Clients satisfied	n/a	92%	94%	95%	96%	98%
Clients completed	n/a	80%	86%	85%	87%	78%
Clients employed	n/a	43%	n/a	n/a	n/a	70%
Training helped	n/a	n/a	n/a	n/a	n/a	94%
Earned credentials		54%	2757	5553	6,110	72%
Average hourly earnings		n/a	n/a	n/a	n/a	$17.53

1 Statistics Canada, table 282-0086.
2 Statistics Canada, table 282-0002.
3 From Makhoul (2015, 36). Case counts exclude children and spouses.
4 From Statistics Canada, table 276-0020, March data. Regular beneficiary count excludes maternity, etc.
5 From the *Employment Insurance Monitoring & Assessment Report*. These records go back to 1998/9.
6 LMDA allocations were increased for two years, starting in 2009/10, to deal with the economic downturn.
7 From *Canada-BC Labour Market Agreement Performance Reports*. LMA funding began in 2008/9.

Appendix F. Alberta PES Performance Data (Implemented Devolved LMDA 1 November 1997, population 2014 was 4,121,700)

Category	1999/2000	2005/6	2008/9	2009/10	2010/11	2011/12	2012/13	2013/14
Unemployment rate[1]	5.7%	3.4%	6.6%	6.5%	5.5%	4.6%	4.6%	4.7%
Employment rate[2]	68.6%	70.9%	69.4%	68.1%	69.7%	70.0%	69.7%	69.3%
Social assistance cases[3]	56,900	59,900	69,680	80,585	81,775	79,753	80,873	–
EI regular beneficiaries[4]	38,740	26,180	58,160	65,710	49,350	35,110	31,720	33,170
LMDA information[5]								
Expenditures ($000s)								
Employment benefits	$75,873	$71,749	$57,293	$98,365	$114,402	$76,468	$78,795	$80,055
Employment assistance services	$30,782	$36,767	$47,021	$39,144	$36,163	$29,623	$28,102	$27,089
Other support measures	$13,748	$1,175	$1,484	$1,340	$966	$833	$1,781	$2,000
Total	$120,403	$109,691	$105,798	$138,849[6]	$151,531	$106,924	$108,678	$109,143
Clients served								
EI	44,269	51,599	62,630	79,671	71,600	62,360	58,057	59,291
Non-insured	37,519	51,075	69,072	76,097	72,284	65,098	62,404	63,516
Total	81,788	102,674	131,702	155,768	143,884	127,458	120,461	122,807
New interventions and mix								
Long term	19,598	19,310	30,748	27,536	24,023	21,264	21,383	22,816
Short term	114,509	156,842	238,816	341,766	310,070	264,427	235,175	233,876
Total	135,592	176,152	269,564	369,302	334,093	285,691	256,558	256,692
Returns to employment								
Targets	20,540	24,000	24,874	32,275	32,000	21,000	–	22,000
Total clients	25,268	23,292	27,869	31,341	29,890	25,776	23,686	25,092
Results vs targets	123%	97%	112%	97%	93%	123%	–	114%
EI unpaid benefits ($000s)								
Targets	$91,060	$150,000	$199,000	$258,700	$348,000	$230,000	–	$200,000
Total	$110,520	$162,630	$254,400	$357,900	$329,600	$223,600	$219,600	$249,300
Result vs target	121%	108%	128%	134%	95%	97%	–	125%

LMA information[7]						
Expenditures ($000s)	$30,397	$90,615	$68,280	$55,601	$58,793	$66,954
Clients served						
Employment and training services	5,223	20,104	25,697	20,763	23,122	30,990
Workforce partnerships	222	372	360	816	14,384	15,001
Immigrant programs	1,059	2,749	2,920	2,489	2,197	2,976
Total	6,504	23,225	28,977	24,068	39,703	48,967
Clients satisfied[8]	89%	88%	90%	81%	92%	93%
Clients completed	84%	82%	89%	81%	74%	76%
Clients employed	57%	48%	75%	59%	68%	39%
Training helped	78%	79%	85%	81%	73%	81%
Earned credentials	n/a	n/a	285	249	324	468
Average hourly earnings	n/a	n/a	$15.00/hr	$18.13/hr	$15.00/hr	$16.00hr

1 Statistics Canada, table 282-0086.
2 Statistics Canada, table 282-0002.
3 From Makhoul (2015, 31). Case counts exclude children and spouses.
4 From Statistics Canada, table 276-0020, March data. Regular beneficiary count excludes maternity etc.
5 From *Employment Insurance Monitoring & Assessment Reports*. These records go back to 1998/9.
6 LMDA allocations were increased for two years, starting in 2009/10, to deal with the economic downturn.
7 From *Canada-Alberta Labour Market Agreement Performance Reports*. LMA funding began in 2008/9.
8 Percentages that follow have been averaged to simplify presentation.

Appendix G. Saskatchewan PES Performance Data (Implemented Devolved LMDA 1 November 1997, population 2014 1,125,400)

	1999/2000	2005/6	2008/9	2009/10	2010/11	2011/12	2012/13	2013/14
Unemployment rate[1]	5.1%	4.7%	4.8%	5.2%	5.0%	4.7%	4.0%	3.8%
Employment rate[2]	63.3%	65.6%	66.7%	66.3%	65.7%	66.2%	67.2%	67.0%
Social assistance cases[3]	33,363	27,079	25,901	26,857	26,494	26,687	27,821	–
Employment Insurance regular claimants[4]	17,420	13,840	17,010	18,150	15,340	13,980	12,410	12,780
LMDA information[5]								
Expenditures ($000s)								
Employment benefits	$27,461	$30,509	$30,506	$39,098	$36,062	$29,753	$28,322	$27,836
Employment assistance services	$1,578	$5,003	$4,103	$4,796	$6,897	$5,491	$6,817	$5,566
Other support measures	$16,906	$3,497	$4,123	$3,867	$3,792	$2,522	$1,953	$3,024
Total	$45,945	$39,009	$38,732	$47,761[6]	$46,750	$37,766	$37,082	$36,426
Clients served								
EI	5,292	12,027	14,497	14,069	12,885	13,892	12,949	12,995
Non-insured	1,727	648	351	640	577	870	748	798
Total	7,019	13,575	14,848	14,709	13,462	14,762	13,697	13,793
New interventions and mix								
Long term	5,652	6,826	8,224	9,239	8,896	8,396	8,034	8,200
Short term	2,152	13,132	9,293	12,516	8,678	12,294	10,495	10,403
Total	8,763	19,958	17,517	21,755	17,574	20,690	18,529	18,603
Returns to employment								
Targets	5,175	4,500	4,700	5,750	5,640	4,925	4,850	5,000
Total clients	3,542	6,453	4,956	6,432	6,692	6,083	5,784	6,038
Results vs targets	68%	143%	105%	112%	119%	124%	119%	121%
Employment Insurance unpaid benefits ($000s)								
Targets	$16,450	$21,000	$27,000	$30,900	$64,700	$35,000	$35,000	$44,000
Total	$14,400	$27,320	$42,800	$64,700	$63,600	$54,100	$55,600	$60,800
Result vs target	87%	130%	159%	209%	98%	155%	159%	138%

LMA information[7]						
Expenditures ($000s)	$14,005	$15,240	$15,328	$15,339	n/a	n/a
Clients served						
Foundational skills	1,245	862	1,440	1,378	759	748
Skills training	815	778	794	630	804	657
Labour market needs	4,381	3,844	5,613	5,964	7,510	8,042
Total	6,441	5,484[8]	7,847	7,972	8,673	9,447
Clients satisfied	84%	95%	95%	94%	97%	85%
Clients completed	71%	74%	76%	83%	87%	81%
Clients employed	n/a	42%	62%	53%	59%	n/a
Training helped	n/a	90%	89%	88%	81%	n/a
Earned credentials	n/a	n/a	54%	48%	61%	n/a
Average hourly earnings	n/a	$13.52	$14.90	$15.19	n/a	n/a

1 Statistics Canada, table 282-0086.
2 Statistics Canada, table 282-0002.
3 From Makhoul (2015, 27). Case counts exclude children and spouses.
4 From Statistics Canada, table 276-0020, March data. Regular beneficiary count excludes maternity, etc.
5 From *Employment Insurance Monitoring & Assessment Reports*. These records go back to 1998/9.
6 LMDA allocations were increased for two years, starting in 2009/10, to deal with the economic downturn.
7 From public *Canada-Saskatchewan Labour Market Agreement Performance Reports*. 2012/13 and 2013/14 data provided internally to author. LMA funding began in 2008/9.
8 Includes people served through the Strategic Training & Transition Fund (STTF).

Appendix H. Manitoba PES Performance Data (Implemented Devolved LMDA 1 November 1997, population 2014 1,282,000)

	1999/2000	2005/6	2008/9	2009/10	2010/11	2011/12	2012/13	2013/14
Unemployment rate[1]	5.0%	4.3%	5.2%	5.4%	5.4%	5.3%	5/4%	5.4%
Employment rate[2]	64.5%	65.5%	65.5%	65.9%	65.5%	65.4%	65.0%	64.2%
Social assistance cases[3]	35,277	32,406	31,096	32,829	34,147	35,427	35,523	35,611
Employment Insurance regular claimants[4]	19,780	15,370	20,420	21,750	18,100	17,400	15,870	15,530
LMDA information[5]								
Expenditures ($000s)								
Employment benefits	$32,575	$33,465	$32,768	$42,928	$42,062	$29,000	$25,981	$29,595
Employment assistance services	$8,917	$8,341	$8,804	$8,783	$9,398	$10,316	$10,300	$7,488
Other support measures	$13,742	$5,543	$4,628	$5,719	$5,391	$5,502	$7,806	$6,424
Total	$55,254	$47,399	$46,200	$57,430[6]	$56,851	$44,818	$44,086	$43,507
Clients served								
Employment Insurance	13,379	17,173	17,300	19,700	18,985	15,609	15,588	14,567
Non-insured	7,287	9,195	11,180	12,546	14,153	13,704	13,369	13,540
Total	20,666	26,368	28,480	32,246	33,138	29,313	28,957	28,107
New interventions and mix								
Long term	8,190	5,565	7,284	8,673	8,830	6,635	6,755	6,480
Short term	20,375	30,930	33,114	37,268	42,050	45,013	45,916	47,243
Total	28,965	36,495	40,398	45,941	50,880	51,648	52,671	53,723
Returns to employment								
Targets	9,486	9,700	9,000	10,000	9,000	9,000	9,000	8,500
Total clients	14,153	9,293	9,256	10,043	9,950	8,714	8,056	7,526
Results vs targets	149%	96%	103%	100%	111%	97%	90%	89%
Employment Insurance unpaid benefits ($000s)								
Targets	$26,180	$35,000	$32,000	$35,500	$68,000	$50,000	$45,000	$40,000
Total	$28,740	$33,610	$46,000	$68,000	$63,400	$41,000	$43,500	$44,300
Result vs target	110%	96%	144%	192%	93%	82%	97%	111%

LMA information[7]						
Expenditures ($000s)	$9,805	$14,834	$18,110	$16,807	$23,862	$23,879
Clients served						
Skills development	n/a	n/a	1,715	1,255	1,904	3,845
Employer HR capacity	n/a	n/a	4,908	4,677	5,655	7,038
Community capacity	n/a	n/a	287	241	594	260
Labour supply	n/a	n/a	1,728	1,210	4,545	3,126
Skills utilization	n/a	n/a	154	54	52	21
Total	3,230	7,074[8]	8,495[9]	7,298	9,093	11,214
Clients satisfied	n/a	n/a	95%	96%	95%	93%
Clients completed	n/a	n/a	n/a	n/a	n/a	n/a
Clients employed	n/a	n/a	68%	70%	69%	66%
Training helped	n/a	n/a	72%	65%	69%	72%
Earned credentials	n/a	n/a	61%	n/a	n/a	n/a
Average hourly earnings	n/a	n/a	$15.88	$17.88	$18.19	$19.85

1 Statistics Canada, table 282-0086.
2 Statistics Canada, table 282-0002.
3 From Makhoul (2015, 24). Case counts exclude children and spouses.
4 From Statistics Canada, table 276-0020, March data. Regular beneficiary count excludes maternity, etc.
5 From *Employment Insurance Monitoring & Assessment Reports*. These records go back to 1998/9.
6 LMDA allocations were increased for two years to deal with the economic downturn.
7 From *Canada-Manitoba Labour Market Agreement Performance Reports*. LMA funding began in 2008/09.
8 Includes participation using the Strategic Training & Transition Fund.
9 Totals for all years in this row may not add up, as people may participate in more than one intervention.

Appendix I. Ontario Performance Data (Implemented Devolved LMDA 1 January 2007, population 2014 was 13,678,700)

Category	1999/2000	2005/6	2008/9	2009/10	2010/11	2011/12	2012/13	2013/14
Unemployment rate[1]	5.7	6.3	9.0	8.7	7.8	7.8	7.5	7.3
Employment rate[2]	63.2	63.2	61.1	61.3	61.6	61.3	61.4	61.0
Social assistance cases[3]	451,975	410,435	449,657	499,143	527,471	550,442	562,552	566,800
EI regular claimants[4]	149,320	182,130	319,440	286,830	242,840	213,440	205,050	199,540
LMDA information[5]								
Expenditures ($000s)								
Employment benefits	$275,330	$251,788	$300,307	$493,298	$341,059	$325,797	$286,775	$278,933
Employment assistance services	$138,517	$184,717	$221,187	$243,179	$392,866	$216,434	$258,435	$271,860
Other support measures	$72,361	$10,099	$11,283	$12,421	$22,833	$10,458	$14,754	$14,677
Total	$486,208	$446,604	$532,777	$748,898[6]	$756,758	$552,689	$559,964	$565,471
Clients served								
EI	134,044	103,448	121,684	140,475	99,604	85,854	87,455	84,834
Non-insured	19,350	34,145	37,923	27,682	92,788	46,170	66,703	74,533
Total clients	153,394	137,593	159,607	168,157	192,392	132,024	154,158	159,367
New interventions and mix								
Long term	50,314	36,870	40,557	51,031	52,218	37,245	31,490	30,040
Short term	130,552	210,930	232,028	229,729	213,749	108,570	142,224	149,001
Total interventions	182,356	247,800	272,585	280,760	265,967	145,815	173,714	179,041
Returns to employment								
Targets	69,335	65,160	54,000	56,500	60,000	56,700	62,230	33,700
Total clients	114,053	53,510	56,562	58,333	73,855	33,347	36,112	36,018
Results vs targets	165%	82%	105%	103%	123%	59%	58%	107%
EI unpaid benefits (000s)								
Targets	$294,480	$297,000	$213,000	$264,000	$408,500	$296,700	$325,000	$216,000
Total	$465,250	$214,050	$264,400	$408,500	$315,800	$221,700	$227,700	$237,600
Result vs target	158%	72%	124%	155%	77%	75%	70%	110%

LMA information[7]						
Expenditures ($000s)	$141,000	$359,000	$283,800	$203,500	$193,500	$192,400
Additional clients served						
Immigrant integration	1,300	26,600	17,750	15,000	2,299	1,000
Foundation skills	56,000	87,000	138,800	205,300	188,755	162,600
Technical skills training	29,400	63,400	30,000	30,700	33,033	32,500
Total clients served	86,000	177,000	219,908	251,040	224,087	196,242
Infrastructure projects	80	80	86	67	60	268
Apprenticeship bonus	n/a	1,450	4,895	5,366	6,104	3,674
Clients satisfied	n/a	94%	90%	91%	91%	91%
Clients completed	n/a	75%	73%	67%	66%	65%
Clients employed	n/a	59%	65%	61%	65%	55%
Training helped	n/a	94%	83%	83%	95%	95%
Earned credentials	n/a	n/a	9,413	4,399	5,980	4,761
Average hourly earnings	n/a	n/a	$18.89	$22.44	$19.26	$18.76

1 Statistics Canada, table 282-0086.
2 Statistics Canada, Table 282-0002.
3 From Makhoul (2015, 20). Case counts exclude children and spouses.
4 Statistics Canada, table 276-0020, March data. Regular beneficiary count excludes maternity, etc.
5 From *Employment Insurance Monitoring & Assessment Reports*. Only selected years are displayed.
6 LMDA allocations were increased for two years starting in 2009/10 to deal with the economic downturn.
7 This is a composite of Ontario's public LMA reports, as well as internal reports shared with the author. Results for 2009/10 and 2010/11 include the Strategic Training & Transition Fund. Sometimes client numbers do not add up. Infrastructure projects supported capital investment. Apprenticeship bonuses ($1,000) were paid to employers.

Appendix J. Quebec PES Performance Data (Implemented Devolved LMDA 1 April 1998, population 2014 was 8,214,700)

Category	1999/2000	05/06	08/09	09/10	10/11	11/12	12/13	13/14
Unemployment rate[1]	8.5	8.1	8.5	8.0	7.8	7.8	7.6	7.7
Employment rate[2]	57.8	60.1	59.8	60.2	60.1	60.0	60.3	59.7
Social assistance cases[3]	396,141	341,314	330,401	335,105	334,791	330,707	323,127	319,601
EI regular claimants[4]	228,380	227,930	270,510	254,150	233,440	218,760	205,010	203,040
LMDA information[5]								
Expenditures ($000s)								
Employment benefits	$408,277	$384,206	$374,269	$472,994	$452,006	$353,495	$335,769	$347,619
Employment assistance services	$78,226	$111,963	$115,549	$128,551	$135,219	$129,318	$139,711	$139,752
Other support measures	$131,234	$99,880	$108,781	$127,448	$122,740	$106,342	$108,567	$93,870
Total	$617,737	$596,049	$598,599	$728,992[6]	$709,965	$589,155	$584,048	$581,242
Clients served								
EI	86,785	153,855	150,920	163,244	154,070	146,188	144,852	174,175
Non-insured	4,255	34,485	37,408	42,167	37,859	47,049	54,519	63,162
Total clients	91,040	188,340	188,328	205,411	191,929	193,237	199,371	237,337
New interventions and mix								
Long term	53,681	47,857	48,953	62,015	48,882	43,268	41,321	40,285
Short term	63,597	169,775	167,449	173,297	166,845	182,141	196,423	243,873
Total interventions	117,915	217,632	216,402	235,312	215,727	225,409	237,744	284,158
Returns to employment								
Targets	53,222	60,469	50,855	55,537	59,547	50,900	50,900	50,900
Total clients	56,244	51,175	51,383	53,081	54,239	52,872	49,757	55,043
Results vs targets	106%	85%	101%	96%	91%	104%	98%	108%
EI unpaid benefits (000s)								
Targets	$117,340	$156,200	$156,200	$198,500	$285,800	$156,200	$156,200	$200,000
Total dollars	$128,050	$172,140	$188,300	$285,800	$307,800	$219,400	$230,500	$252,400
Results vs target	109%	110%	121%	144%	108%	140%	148%	126%

Under-represented groups[7]						
LMA Allocations (000s)	$116,300	$116,300	$115,900	$115,700	$115,500	$115,980
Clients served						
Social assistance recipients	78,464	84,716	81,603	81,456	88,292	93,853
Youth less than 25	27,186	31,266	30,511	30,445	30,476	30,719
Persons over 55	5,359	6,656	6,656	7,847	7,973	8,382
Immigrants	24,816	30,532	30,215	30,849	31,002	30,853
Disabled people	7,607	9,871	10,734	11,694	11,715	12,158
Total clients served	93,880	108,722	106,731	109,976	111,455	114,913
Clients employed	57%	57%	n/a	n/a	n/a	n/a
Clients satisfied	88%	88%	n/a	n/a	n/a	n/a

1 Statistics Canada, table 282-0086.

2 Statistics Canada, table 282-0002.

3 From Makhoul (2015, 16). Case counts exclude children and spouses.

4 Statistics Canada, table 276-0020, March data. Regular beneficiary count excludes maternity, etc.

5 From *Employment Insurance Monitoring and Assessment Reports*. Only selected years are displayed.

6 LMDA allocations were increased for two years, starting in 2009/10, to deal with the economic downturn.

7 Canada and Quebec agreed that the regular Emploi-Québec (EQ) management report would be used to report LMA results. These do not separate LMA results from other PES results. Numbers noted for under-represented groups – the LMA target group – are obtained by subtracting EI clients from total clients served. Client participation costs could be funded through LMA, Quebec funds, or other labour market agreement (excluding LMDA). Sources are: Ministère du Travail, de l'Emploi et de la Solidarité Sociale, *Rapport statistique sur les individus, entreprises et organismes participant aux interventions des Services publics d'emploi*, 2008–9, 2009–10, 2010–11, 2011–12, 2012–13, 2013–14. Quebec did not participate in the pan-Canadian LMA evaluation released by ESDC in March 2013. Clients employed and satisfied in 2008/9–2009/10 are from an evaluation report released in October 2010 (Jolicoeur & Associés 2010).

Appendix K. New Brunswick PES Performance Data (Implemented Devolved LMDA 1 April 1997, population 2014 was 753,900)

Category	1999/2000	2005/6	2008/9	2009/10	2010/11	2011/12	2012/13	2013/14
Unemployment rate[1]	10.0%	8.7%	8.8%	9.3%	9.5%	10.2%	10.4%	9.9%
Employment rate[2]	55.4%	57.7%	58.6%	57.7%	56.8%	56.6%	56.6%	56.9%
Social assistance cases[3]	30,519	25,371	23,137	23,576	24,581	25,121	24,765	24,421
EI regular beneficiaries[4]	49,470	46,630	48,390	48,610	47,160	46,570	43,110	40,460
LMDA information[5]								
Expenditures ($000s)								
Employment benefits	$61,133	$75,985	$76,923	$94,326	$92,318	$74,240	$55,764	$68,214
Employment assistance services	$7,860	$10,925	$10,455	$9,199	$8,580	$10,704	$10,193	$11,282
Other support measures	$25,319	$5,332	$5,318	$3,318	$2,561	$4,494	$7,929	$9,725
Total	$94,292	$92,242	$92,686	$106,843[6]	$103,458	$89,438	$73,886	$89,220
Clients served								
EI	15,528	11,629	13,618	16,959	14,817	12,824	11,699	11,662
Non-insured	3,070	3,390	3,512	5,679	5,001	4,217	3,844	4,876
Total	18,598	17,852	17,130	22,638	19,818	17,041	15,543	16,538
New interventions and mix								
Long term	13,469	10,202	10,084	13,560	11,285	9,472	7,901	7,712
Short term	9,588	27,760	26,018	31,700	25,558	24,318	23,857	25,824
Total	23,197	37,962	36,102	45,260	36,843	33,790	31,758	33,536
Returns to employment								
Targets	6,889	8,611	8,786	8,850	9,245	8,950	8,700	8,410
Total clients	11,684	9,892	9,422	9,367	10,193	9,017	8,015	7,927
Results vs targets	169%	115%	107%	106%	110%	101%	92%	94%
EI unpaid benefits dollars ($000s)								
Targets	$15,880	$23,050	$29,400	$25,800	$43,700	$35,200	$34,200	$31,200
Total dollars	$20,610	$28,030	$34,000	$43,700	$41,300	$30,900	$27,600	$28,700
Result vs target	130%	122%	115%	169%	95%	88%	81%	92%

LMA information						
Expenditures ($000s)[7]	$2,700	$20,614	$18,742	$10,261	$11,988	$15,692
Clients served[8]						
Skills development (SD) and upgrading	86	2,510	2,507	1,660	272	2,631
Work experience	86	1,700	611	200	280	29
SD and work experience	49	183	539	83	724	3,442
Employment services		2,567	3,015	135	609	136
Total	221	6,960	6,672	2,078	1,885	6,238
Clients satisfied[9]	[10]	84%	84%	very	very	96%
Clients completed		n/a	n/a	n/a	77%	70%
Clients employed		71%	62%	78%	57%	50%
Training helped		78%	80%	86%	88%	88%
Earned credentials		24%	27%	43%	34%	69%
Average hourly earnings		$536/wk	$13.27	$13.56	$12.50	$12.56

1 Statistics Canada, table 282-0086.
2 Statistics Canada, table 282-0002.
3 From Makhoul (2015, 12). Case counts exclude children and spouses.
4 From Statistics Canada, table 276-0020, March data. Regular beneficiary count excludes maternity, etc.
5 From *Employment Insurance Monitoring and Assessment Reports*. These records go back to 1998/9.
6 LMDA allocations were increased for two years, starting in 2009/10, to deal with the economic downturn.
7 From *Post-secondary Education, Training and Labour Annual Reports* (2008/9–2013/14).
8 From PETL's *LMA Performance Indicator Report* (internal) (2008/9–2013/14).
9 All indicators that follow are from PETL's *LMA Evaluation Reports* (twelve-month follow-up results, with the exception of 2013/14, with three-month follow-up results).
10 Combined with 2009/10 results.

Appendix L. Nova Scotia PES Performance Data (Implemented Devolved LMDA 1 July 2009, population 2014 was 942,700)

Category	1999/2000	2005/6	2008/9	2009/10	2010/11	2011/12	2012/13	2013/14
Unemployment rate[1]	9.1%	7.9%	9.2%	9.3%	8.8%	9.0%	9.0%	9.0%
Employment rate[2]	55.7%	57.7%	58.4%	58.2%	58.1%	58.4%	58.1%	57.2%
Social assistance cases[3]	42,000	29,800	26,800	28,000	28,200	28,700	28,700	28,500
EI regular beneficiaries[4]	40,750	40,260	43,770	43,990	42,560	41,660	36,680	33,630
LMDA information[5]								
Expenditures ($000s)								
Employment benefits	$50,655	$60,384	$56,617	$75,562	$72,997	$58,069	$51,681	$54,542
Employment assistance services	$8,655	$18,766	$21,640	$20,935	$22,138	$21,154	$25,980	$23,491
Other support measures	$11,621	$1,442	$1,424	$1,449	$1,054	$1,047	$1,945	$1,980
Total	$70,931	$80,592	$79,681	$97,946[6]	$96,189	$80,270	$79,606	$79,014
Clients served								
EI	15,311	10,515	12,874	15,531	14,844	13,339	13,479	12,092
Non-insured	2,207	3,042	4,101	4,155	4,429	4,247	4,410	4,545
Total	17,518	13,557	16,975	19,686	19,273	17,586	17,889	16,637
New interventions and mix								
Long term	11,004	6,526	5,605	6,579	5,805	5,118	6,088	4,740
Short term	12,090	13,816	27,720	32,625	32,662	30,167	29,598	28,423
Total	23,765	20,342	33,325	39,204	38,467	35,285	35,686	33,163
Returns to employment								
Targets	11,145	5,000	6,160	6,127	6,000	6,800	6,500	6,000
Total clients	11,995	5,323	6,100	5,908	6,942	6,734	5,259	5,680
Results vs targets	108%	106%	99%	96%	116%	99%	81%	95%
EI unpaid benefits ($000s)								
Targets	$33,060	$12,670	$21,000	$25,000	$30,100	$33,000	$25,000	$22,000
Total dollars	$28,440	$16,660	$24,700	$30,100	$33,300	$25,400	$25,700	$28,100
Result vs target	86%	131%	118%	120%	111%	77%	103%	128%

LMA information[7]						
Expenditures ($000s)	$4,500	$8,100	$15,400	$20,000	$16,500	$19,000
Clients served						
Client access and service provision	n/a	n/a	n/a	n/a	n/a	n/a
Labour market skills development	n/a	n/a	n/a	n/a	n/a	n/a
Workforce attachment and retention	n/a	n/a	n/a	n/a	n/a	n/a
Workforce development	n/a	n/a	n/a	n/a	n/a	n/a
Total	805	2,200	2,500	3,000	3,200	3,800
Clients satisfied	n/a	majority	90%	90%	97%	81%
Clients completed	n/a	n/a	n/a	n/a	n/a	n/a
Clients employed	n/a	n/a	n/a	n/a	68.2%	68%
Training helped	n/a	80%	80%	90%	83.8%	92%
Earned credentials	n/a	n/a	n/a	70%	70%	77%
Average hourly earnings	n/a	n/a	n/a	$15.76/hr	$12–16/hr	$12–16/hr

1 Statistics Canada, table 282-0086.
2 Statistics Canada, table 282-0002.
3 From Makhoul (2015, 6). Case counts exclude children and spouses.
4 From Statistics Canada, table 276-0020, March data. Regular beneficiary count excludes maternity, etc.
5 From *Employment Insurance Monitoring & Assessment Reports*. These records go back to 1998/9.
6 LMDA allocations were increased for two years, starting in 2009/10, to deal with the economic downturn.
7 From *Canada–Nova Scotia Labour Market Agreement Annual Reports*. LMA funding began in 2008/9.

Appendix M. Prince Edward Island PES Performance Data (Implemented Devolved LMDA 1 October 2009, population 2014 was 146,300)

Category	1999/2000	2005/6	2008/9	2009/10	2010/11	2011/12	2012/13	2013/14
Unemployment rate[1]	12.0%	11.1%	12.1%	11.2%	11.3%	11.3%	11.5%	10.6%
Employment rate[2]	58.7%	60.9%	59.3%	60.3%	60.4%	60.4%	61.3%	61.4%
Social assistance cases[3]	4,668	5,142	4,570	4,749	4,881	5,148	5,069	4,964
EI regular beneficiaries[4]	13,480	12,490	12,480	13,290	12,480	12,200	10,680	9,740
LMDA information[5]								
Expenditures ($000s)								
Employment benefits	$17,732	$20,460	$20,095	24,348	$23,640	$20,403	$19,203	$19,837
Employment assistance services	$1,524	$4,007	$4,796	4,921	$4,790	$4,941	$4,935	$4,517
Other support measures	$3,526	$1,811	$2,042	1,622	$1,802	$1,794	$2,329	$1,730
Total	$22,782	$26,278	$26,933	30,891[6]	$30,232	$27,138	$26,467	$26,084
Clients served								
EI	3,819	3,220	3,547	3,227	3,454	3,495	3,740	3,666
Non-insured	516	948	1,072	885	1,071	1,340	1,316	1,285
Total	4,335	4,168	4,619	4,112	4,525	4,835	5,056	4,951
New interventions and mix								
Long term	3,614	2,377	2,291	2,459	2,494	2,224	2,120	2,136
Short term	2,457	3,328	4,047	3,604	3,376	4,980	5,526	5,276
Total	6,080	5,705	6,338	6,063	5,870	7,204	7,646	7,412
Returns to employment								
Targets	2,224	2,027	2,035	–	2,123	1,949	1,901	1,624
Total clients	3,022	1,833	2,186	1,841	2,183	2,034	1,939	2,194
Results vs targets	135%	90%	107%	–	103%	104%	102%	135%
EI unpaid benefits ($000s)								
Targets	$4,430	$4,820	$6,000	–	$8,900	–	$8,500	$8,400
Total dollars	$5,000	$5,400	$7,700	$8,900	$9,100	$8,200	$7,500	$7,700
Result vs target	112%	112%	128%	–	102%	–	89%	93%

LMA information[7]					
Expenditures ($000s)	$351	n/a	$5,718	$3,424	$2,860
Clients served					
Skills development	n/a	n/a	n/a	212	107
Work experience	n/a	n/a	n/a	61	91
Combination	n/a	n/a	n/a	36	35
Skills development for employed	n/a	n/a	n/a	184	418
Total	n/a	1,000	1,200	493	651
Clients satisfied	n/a	n/a	83%	98%	99%
Clients completed	n/a	n/a	n/a	82%	86%
Clients employed	n/a	n/a	88%	68%	74%
Training helped	n/a	n/a	94%	92%	91%
Earned credentials	n/a	n/a	n/a	88	133
Average hourly earnings	n/a	n/a	n/a	$14.04	$14.01

1 Statistics Canada, table 282-0086.
2 Statistics Canada, table 282-0002.
3 From Makhoul (2015, 9). Case counts exclude children and spouses.
4 From Statistics Canada, table 276-0020, March data. Regular beneficiary count excludes maternity, etc.
5 From *Employment Insurance Monitoring & Assessment Reports*. These records go back to 1998/9.
6 LMDA allocations were increased for two years, starting in 2009/10, to deal with the economic downturn.
7 2008/9, 2009/10, and 2010/11 LMA data are from *PEI Innovation & Advanced Learning Annual Report*. 2011/12 and 2012/13 data are from internal information provided by PEI Innovation & Advanced Learning. Includes Strategic Training & Transition (STTF) funding for 2009/10 and 2010/11.

Appendix N. Newfoundland and Labrador PES Performance Data (Implemented Devolved LMDA 1 October 2009, population 2014 was 527,000)

Category	1999/2000	2005/6	2008/9	2009/10	2010/11	2011/12	2012/13	2013/14
Unemployment rate[1]	16.6%	14.7%	15.5%	14.4%	12.7%	12.5%	11.4%	11.9%
Employment rate[2]	46.3%	50.4%	49.8%	51.2%	52.6%	53.9%	54.2%	53.8%
Social assistance cases[3]	30,830	27,412	24,333	24,530	25,092	24,802	24,320	23,528
EI regular beneficiaries[4]	47,120	51,310	52,240	50,290	47,060	43,730	39,270	40,340
LMDA information[5]								
Expenditures ($000s)								
Employment benefits	$93,759	$111,359	$111,142	$126,965	$125,670	$106,318	$104,293	$108,162
Employment assistance services	$8,477	$13,008	$17,149	$17,454	$16,129	$20,864	$18,849	$4,557
Other support measures	$12,776	$6,363	$3,394	$3,326	$4,109	$4,682	$6,374	$3,038
Total	$115,012	$130,730	$131,685	$147,745[6]	$145,908	$131,864	$127,516	$115,757
Clients served								
EI	14,546	17,832	14,529	16,580	13,943	12,432	11,116	10,759
Non-insured	3,493	2,346	2,561	2,302	2,171	2,031	2,046	1,980
Total	18,039	20,178	17,090	18,882	16,134	14,463	13,162	12,739
New interventions and mix								
Long term	15,904	13,218	9,414	11,307	8,913	7,652	6,683	7,441
Short term	7,284	25,765	15,497	16,959	14,020	12,605	12,369	11,000
Total	25,179	38,983	24,911	28,266	22,933	20,257	19,052	18,441
Returns to employment								
Targets	8,133	7,675	7,350	7,936	6,438	7,600	5,800	5,800
Total clients	9,372	6,677	7,995	6,526	6,857	6,335	6,114	5,918
Results vs targets	115%	87%	109%	82%	107%	83%	105%	102%
EI unpaid benefits ($000s)								
Targets	$14,820	$19,900	$21,500	$30,100	$32,900	$25,000	$24,500	$24,500
Total	$17,210	$19,740	$26,800	$32,900	$31,200	$26,700	$30,400	$25,700
Result vs target	116%	99%	125%	109%	95%	107%	124%	105%

LMA information[7]						
Expenditures ($000s)	n/a	$7,400	$18,600	$8,900	$17,300	$16,400
Clients served						
Employment supports	n/a	84	863	1,114	852	604
Jobs/workplace skills	n/a	107	311	531	742	702
Training/skills development	n/a	248	339	361	378	616
Work placement/supported employment	n/a	33	48	20	247	285
Total	n/a	472	1,561	2,026	2,219	2,207
Clients satisfied	n/a	96.2%	97.6%	96.0%	94.5%	96.4%
Clients completed	n/a	65%	66%	59%	43%	36.7%
Clients employed	n/a	60.9%	50.6%	52%	76%	53%
Training helped	n/a	92.3%	93.6%	88.0%	88%	86.5%
Earned credentials	n/a	n/a	63.3%	46.2%	n/a	n/a
Average hourly earnings	n/a	$12.35/hr	$15.53/hr	$14.67/hr	$16.82	$14.60/hr

1 Statistics Canada, table 282-0086.
2 Statistics Canada, table 282–0002.
3 From Makhoul (2015, 3). Case counts exclude children and spouses.
4 From Statistics Canada, table 276-0020, March data. Regular beneficiary count excludes maternity, etc.
5 From *Employment Insurance Monitoring & Assessment Reports*. These records go back to 1998/9.
6 LMDA allocations were increased for two years, starting in 2009/10, to deal with the economic downturn.
7 From *Canada–Newfoundland and Labrador Labour Market Agreement Performance Reports*. Although LMA funding began in 2008/9, programming did not commence until the fall of 2009.

Appendix O. Performance Data for Aboriginal Employment Programs[1]

Category	1995/6	1997/8	1999/2000	2005/6	2008/9	2009/10	2010/11	2011/12	2012/13	2013/14
Unemployment rate[2]	n/a	n/a	n/a	14.8%	n/a	n/a	15.0%	n/a	n/a	n/a
Employment rate	n/a	n/a	n/a	53.7%	n/a	n/a	52.1%	n/a	n/a	n/a
On-reserve social assistance cases[3]	n/a	70,927	73,974	80,905	75,277	84,970	84,504	83,580	82,624	82,634
RBA/AHRDS/ASETS[4]										
Spending (000s)	n/a	$224,500	$320,000	$340,000	$351,600	n/a	n/a	$344,400	$347,600	$347,600
Clients served	13,096	14,200	28,082	54,360	59,986	60,737	49,005	48,014	45,380	47,420
Returns to work	n/a	n/a	10,028	15,977	17,865	16,162	14,315	16,323	13,589	18,017
Returns to school	n/a	n/a	n/a	5,624	7,639	8,122	7,174	5,272	4,286	8,060
Unpaid EI benefits (000s)		n/a	$7,700	$15,400	$18,900	$24,600	$19,000	$11,700	$14,400	$15,800
ASEP[5]										
Spending (000s)	–	–	–	$24,800	$23,100	$31,400	$74,300	$59,400		
Clients served	–	–	–	1,693	3,316	4,010	9,434	10,372		
Employed	–	–	–	217	2,459	1,265	2,737	4,755		
Returns to school	–	–	–	–	–	–	–	–		
SPF[6]										
Spending (000s)									$2,200	$32,600
Clients served									5,300	10,523
Employed									861	3,195
Returns to school									301	320

ESD/FNJF[7]										
Spending (000s)										n/a
Clients served										1,300
Employed										200
Returned to school										40
# of First Nations bands participating										88
Total clients served	13,096	14,200	28,082	56,053	63,302	64,747	58,439	58,386	50,680	59,243

1 Aboriginal employment programs are funded from both the Employment Insurance account and the Consolidated Revenue Fund.

2 Employment and unemployment rates are from National Aboriginal Economic Development Board (2015, 15 and 17), using Statistics Canada 2011 National Household Survey and 2006 Census.

3 Numbers for 1997–2006 are from Indian and Northern Affairs 2007. Numbers for 2007–14 are imputed using beneficiary numbers from Aboriginal Affairs and Northern Development Canada (2014a).

4 1995/6 data from CLFDB unreleased report (14). All other data provided directly to author by Employment & Social Development Canada. Includes Regional Bilateral Agreements (RBAs), Aboriginal Human Resource Development Agreements (AHRDSs), and Aboriginal Skills and Employment Strategy (ASETS). Data for all years between 1997/8 and 2013/14 are available; only selected years are presented. Spending allocations exclude federal stimulus funding through ASTIF.

5 Data provided by ESDC. The Aboriginal Skills and Employment Partnership (ASEP) program started in 2003.

6 Data provided by ESDC. The Skills and Partnership Fund (SPF) started in 2010.

7 Enhanced Service Delivery (ESD) and the First Nations Job Fund (FNJF) started in 2013. The number of bands participating was provided by AANDC. Participant numbers are from Canada report to ILO on Convention 88, 2015.

Appendix P. Public Employment Service: Comparative Provincial Data 2014

Province	Federal FTEEs transferred[1]	Federal contracts transferred[2]	LMDA funding[3]	LMA funding[4]	ASETS funding[5]	Total federal funding	Number of ASETS holders	Points of provincial service delivery[6]	Contracted service providers[7]
British Columbia	250	350	$280,647,000	$66,263,000	$39,613,000	$386,523,000	15	101	140
Alberta	156	n/a	$109,143,000	$55,529,000	$40,533,000	$205,205,000	13	53	53
Saskatchewan	97	n/a	$36,426,000	$15,481,000	$34,816,000	$86,723,000	2	19	n/a
Manitoba	118	n/a	$43,507,000	$18,162,000	$43,226,000	$104,895,000	4	16	154
Ontario	600	400	$565,471,000	$193,603,000	$57,718,000	$816,792,000	18	170	283
Quebec	1,022	n/a	$581,242,000	$115,462,000	$31,894,000	$728,598,000	5	158	350
New Brunswick	124	n/a	$89,763,000	$10,836,000	$4,074,000	$104,673,000	4	19	n/a
Nova Scotia	125	65	$79,014,000	$13,599,000	$4,827,000	$97,440,000	2	68	70
Prince Edward Island	40	13	$26,084,000	$2,094,000	$675,000	$28,853,000	1	6	17
Newfoundland and Labrador	75	70	$129,219,000	$7,349,000	$6,015,000	$142,583,000	7	27	42
Northwest Territories	24	n/a	$3,143,000	$621,000	$8,014,000	$11,778,000	7	n/a	n/a
Yukon	n/a	n/a	$3,482,000	$518,000	$3,120,000	$7,120,000	2	n/a	n/a
Nunavut	n/a	n/a	$2,859,000	$483,000	$7,334,000	$10,676,000	3	n/a	n/a
National	n/a	n/a	n/a	n/a	$4,000,000	$4,000,000	2	n/a	n/a
Total	2,607	898	$1,950,000,000	$500,000,000	$285,860,000	$2,735,860,000	85	637	1,109

1 Staff numbers from provinces that signed devolved agreements before 1998 are from Klassen (2000b, 178). Other provincial numbers were gathered through interviews and documents reviewed through this research.

2 From interviews and documents reviewed through this research. The total is incomplete.

3 From *CEIC Monitoring and Assessment Report* (2013/14, 278).

4 From Zon (2014, 16).

5 Calculations done by the author on the basis of information provided by ESDC in May 2015. Excludes funding for the First Nations and Inuit Child Care Initiative and First Nations Job Fund.

6 As identified on provincial websites in 2014–15.

7 This is an approximate number. It includes not-for-profit and for-profit third-party organizations providing PES services, including those contracted by the province, ASETS holders, the federal government, and (in Ontario) municipalities. It does not include postsecondary institutions.

Appendix Q. Pan Canadian PES Performance Data Summary Employment Services Funded through Employment Insurance (EI) Part II[1]

Category	1995/6[2]	1996/7	1999/2000	2005/6	2008/9	2009/10	2010/11	2011/12	2012/13	2013/14
Expenditures (billions)	$1,700	$1,200	$1,878	$2,016	$2,110	$2,605[3]	$2,605	$2,081	$2,075	$1,987
Clients served										
EI[4]	n/a	n/a	380,661	456,989	484,182	568,130	486,696	431,708	420,426	446,326
Non-insured	n/a	n/a	100,621	170,714	209,871	209,020	269,350	214,587	241,834	264,716
Regular EBSMs total	231,000	305,000	481,282	611,420	676,842	758,761	742,907	631,522	647,127	695,745
Aboriginal pan-Canadian	n/a	n/a	n/a	16,283	17,211	18,389	13,139	14,773	15,133	15,297
Canada total	231,000	305,000	481,282	627,703	694,053	777,150	756,046	646,295	662,260	711,042
Proportion of EI-attached clients	n/a	n/a	79%	73%	70%	73%	64%	67%	63%	63%
New interventions[5]										
Long term	158,000	148,000	212,090	171,936	190,078	221,847	194,471	159,279	149,521	149,576
Short term	31,000	113,000	423,798	968,253	878,254	1,033,557	965,082	988,779	901,063	962,455
Other	42,000	44,000	n/a	n/a	n/a	n/a	n/a	n/a	n/a	n/a
Regular EBSMs total	231,000	305,000	635,888	940,189	1,068,332	1,255,404	1,173,923	948,058	1,050,584	1,112,031
Aboriginal pan-Canadian	n/a	n/a	9,951	18,657	19,522	21,235	15,966	14,615	25,687	26,378
Canada total	231,000	305,000	645,839	958,846	1,087,854	1,276,639	1,175,519	962,673	1,076,271	1,138,409
Proportion of long-term interventions	68%	68%	49%	33%	18%	17%	17%	17%	17%	14%
Returns to employment										
Results vs targets (%)	n/a	n/a	136%	91%	105%	109%	116%	93%	90%	103%
EI unpaid benefits										
Result vs target	n/a	n/a	124%	96%	127%	167%	93%	101%	126%	118%
Cost per participant[6]	$7,359	$3,934	$3,902	$3,211	$3,040	$3,351	$3,445	$3,219	$3,133	$2,794

1 All information in this table is taken from the *Canada Employment Insurance Monitoring and Assessments Reports*, issued annually. It covers programming delivered by provinces and territories under the LMDAs, as well as pan-Canadian (which includes activities delivered by Aboriginal labour market organizations operating under AHRDS and ASETS agreements). *MARs* are available for the entire 1995/6–2013/14 period. To save space, yet show trends over time, only selected years are reported.

2 Expenditures in 1995/6 and 1996/7 were called Unemployment Insurance Developmental Uses. All other years include expenditures under the LMDAs, as well as pan-Canadian.

3 LMDA and ASETS allocations were increased for two years, starting in 2009/10, to deal with the economic downturn.

4 Includes current EI claimants, as well as reach-back clients.

5 Clients may take more than one intervention.

6 Calculated as total expenditures divided by clients served.

Appendix R. Pan-Canadian PES Performance Data Summary Employment Services Funded through the Consolidated Revenue Fund for Non-Employment Insurance Clients[1]

	1995/6	2008/9	2009/10	2010/11	2011/12	2012/13	2013/14
Allocation (millions)	n/a	$500	$750[2]	$750	$500	$500	$500
Clients served[3]							
British Columbia	n/a	1,058	12,098	8,709	12,575	17,593	20,611
Alberta	n/a	6,504	23,225	28,977	24,068	39,703	48,967
Saskatchewan	n/a	6,441	5,484	7,847	7,972	8,673	9,447
Manitoba	n/a	3,320	7,074	8,495	7,278	9,093	11,214
Ontario	n/a	86,000	177,000	219,908	251,040	224,087	196,242
Quebec[4]	n/a	93,880	108,722	106,731	109,976	111,455	114,913
New Brunswick	n/a	221	6,960	6,672	2,078	1,885	6,238
Nova Scotia	n/a	805	2,200	2,500	3,000	3,200	3,800
Prince Edward Island	n/a	n/a	1,000	1,200	493	651	n/a
Newfoundland and Labrador	n/a	n/a	472	1,561	2,026	2,219	2,207
Total clients served	136,472	198,229	344,235	392,600	420,506	418,559	413,639

1 Data for 1995/6 have been extracted from a chart developed by staff of the Canadian Labour Force Development Board (CLFDB) for its first annual report in December 1998. This report was never released. The CLFDB report focused specifically on federal spending under the Consolidated Revenue Fund. All of these services were managed by the Government of Canada. Of the 136,472 clients served, 13,096 were Aboriginal and are noted in appendix O. Information for 2008/9–2013/14 summarizes results calculated by the author from provincial LMA performance reports, as well as Emploi-Québec's annual report. Numbers do not include programs for youth and disabled people that were directly managed by the federal government. It is noteworthy that the single federal LMA report released in August 2011 calculated that 198,271 clients were served in 2008/9, and 350,234 in 2009/10. These numbers are very close to the calculations noted above.

2 LMA allocations were increased for two years, starting in 2009/10, to deal with the economic downturn.

3 Clients served by the Government of Canada in 1995/6 included women, visible minorities, social assistance recipients, and older workers. Aboriginal client numbers served by Canada in 1995/6 have been extracted and are reported separately in appendix O. Provincial LMA clients served between 2008/9 and 2013/14 were from similar but not identical groups.

4 Quebec does not report LMA results separately from the rest of their PES reporting. LMA numbers for Quebec are for under-represented groups – the LMA target group. They have been obtained by subtracting EI clients from total clients served. See appendix J for more details.

Appendix S. Comparison of Total Clients Served Pre- and Post-Devolution

	1995/6	2008/9	2009/10	2010/11	2011/12	2012/13	2013/14
Clients served using EI funding[1]	231,000	676,842	758,761	742,907	631,522	647,127	695,745
Clients served using CRF funding[2]	123,376	198,229	344,235	392,600	420,506	418,559	413,639
Aboriginal clients served[3]	13,096	63,302	64,747	58,439	58,386	50,680	59,243
Total clients served	367,472	938,373	1,167,743	1,193,946	1,110,414	1,116,366	1,168,627

1 EI-funded client numbers are from annual CEIC *MAR*. They exclude pan-Canadian (Aboriginal) clients, which are reported separately. In 1995/6 all services were under federal control. By 2010/11 all services were being delivered by provinces and territories. See appendix Q for more details.

2 CRF-funded clients in 1995/6 are from chart developed by CLFDB. It separated Aboriginal from non-Aboriginal clients. All clients served in subsequent years are from provincial LMA reports. See appendix R for details.

3 Aboriginal client numbers in 1995/6 are from CLFDB report. All other years are from information provided by ESDC. See appendix O for more details. Aboriginal funding comes from both the EI and CRF accounts.

Appendix T. Summary of Evaluation Reports[1]

Labour Market Development Agreements

The following are excerpts from Employment Insurance Monitoring and Assessment Reports that highlighted Employment Benefits and Support Measures (EBSM) results under the provincial Labour Market Development Agreements (LMDAs).

1998 The evidence shows that EBSMs are effective, with more clients being served at a lower cost per client.

1999 The flexibility to tailor programs and services to local needs appears to be one of the major successes of the LMDAs. Early evaluations suggest that growing partnerships between governments have resulted in successful harmonization of federal and provincial programs.

2000 Overall, results indicate that EBSMs are effective in the short term. Satisfaction levels with EBSMs are relatively high. Over three-quarters of participants rated service as good or excellent, while only one in 10 expressed dissatisfaction.

2003 Preliminary findings indicate some positive impacts with regard to former clients on employment, earnings and social assistance, but there is insufficient evidence to conclude positive impacts on employment and earnings for active EI clients.

2004 EBSMs appear to yield some modestly positive net impacts on the participants, dependent on the program, client type and jurisdiction.

---

1 Under the LMDAs every province agreed to co-operate with the federal government to evaluate its programming. In the early devolution days, formative evaluations were used to inform the transition from federal to provincial delivery, detailing lessons learned. These were followed by more comprehensive summative evaluations in all thirteen jurisdictions between 1999 and 2009. Even jurisdictions with co-managed LMDA agreements – where Ottawa retained direct oversight of the programming – were evaluated. In 2008 provinces and territories – except for Quebec, which undertook its own evaluation – also worked with the federal government to evaluate LMA programming. Unlike the LMDAs, an evaluation of LMA programming was a pan-Canadian effort from the start. On Aboriginal employment programming, AHRDS was evaluated in 2009, ASEP in 2013, and ASETS/SPF in 2015 (HRSDC 2009; HRSDC 2013b; ESDC 2015a).

2005 EBSM evaluations confirm the importance of a combination of work experience and training ... they also underscore the important effect of local labour market conditions and client characteristics on the range of programming offered and on program outcomes. Tailoring programs to local needs is important.

2006 Summative evaluations reported generally high levels of client satisfaction and increased skills levels as a result of EBSM participation. Targeted wage subsidies worked best, followed by skills development and self-employment.

2009 EBSMs appeared to yield some modest positive impacts for participants, although such findings were not consistent across all jurisdictions. Skills development was the most effective for increasing earnings for active claimants. Targeted wage subsidy was most effective in increasing employment and earnings for former claimants.

2013/14 With the exception of self-employment and job creation partnerships for former claimants, EBSMs were effective in improving the labour market experience of participants (i.e., higher earnings and incidence of employment, as well as lower EI use). There was an incremental impact of $3,000 in average annual earnings.

By 2010, summative LMDA evaluations had been completed in all jurisdictions and a second evaluation round, called "net impact analysis," was implemented. This involved linking administrative data from EI Part I and EI Part II with data from the Canadian Revenue Agency. By using a comparison group, the difference that participation made, compared to non-participation, could be assessed. These results also demonstrated that Targeted Wage Subsidies worked best, followed by Skills Development and Self-employment.

Labour Market Agreements

After 2008, provinces and territories – except for Quebec, which undertook its own evaluation – also worked with the federal government to evaluate the LMA programming. Unlike the LMDAs, an evaluation of LMA programming was a pan-Canadian effort from the start, carried out by a single contractor under the supervision of an advisory committee with representation from ESDC, nine provinces, and the three territories. The contractor carried out a literature and document review, interviewed thirty key informants, undertook secondary data analysis, and conducted a survey with participants who had completed one or more LMA programs or services between April 2008 and September 2010. The survey obtained 7,000 completions.

The executive summary of the LMA evaluation report released in March 2013 noted,

> *A strong and continuing need exists for LMA programs and services ... At the time of the survey 86% of LMA participants were employed, 9% were unemployed and 5% were not in the labour force (retired, in school). Employment levels improved from 44% at the start of participation to 86% at the time of the survey ... On average participants increased their earnings by $323 per week after participation compared to the one year prior to participation ... Dependence on social assistance is reduced ... A majority of participants experienced positive life changes since they began participation ... Overall 87% of participants were satisfied with their participation.* (ESDC 2013, v–vii)

Aboriginal Labour Market Programming

On Aboriginal employment programming, AHRDS was evaluated in 2009, ASEP in 2013, and ASETS/SPF in 2015 (HRSDC 2009, 2013b; ESDC 2015a). Like the provincial evaluation reports, most comments were positive. The ASETS/SPF evaluation had the following overarching comment: "The evaluation findings demonstrate that ASETS and SPF are relevant. They are meeting the priorities of the Government of Canada, and there continues to be a demonstrable need for labour market programming for Aboriginal Canadians. The evidence indicates that both programs are working towards achieving their intended outcomes" (ESDC 2015a, v).

References

Aboriginal Affairs and Northern Development Canada (AANDC). 2007. "Evaluation of the Income Assistance Program." http://www.aadnc-aandc.gc.ca/eng/1100100011999/1100100012006.

– 2014a. "Income Assistance: Key Facts." https://www.aadnc-aandc.gc.ca/eng/1369766807521/1369766848614.

– 2014b. "On Reserve Income Assistance." Internal document.

Advisory Panel on Employment Services Administration and Accountability (APESAA). 2012. *Final Report of the Advisory Panel on Employment Services Administration and Accountability*. http://servicedelivery.dss.gov.au/2012/09/24/final-report-of-the-advisory-panel-on-employment-services-administration-and-accountability-released/.

Advisory Panel on Labour Market Information. 2009. *Working Together to Build a Better Labour Market Information System for Canada*. http://publications.gc.ca/collections/collection_2011/rhdcc-hrsdc/HS18-24-2009-eng.pdf.

Alberta. 2006. "Building & Educating Tomorrow's Workforce." Alberta's Ten-Year Strategy. http://work.alberta.ca/department/betw.html.

Alberta Strategic Planning and Research Branch. n.d. "A Case Study of the Canada-Alberta Agreement on Labour Market Development." Internal document. Edmonton: Information and Policy Services Division, Alberta Advanced Education and Career Development.

Asch, Michael. 2014. *On Being Here to Stay: Treaties and Aboriginal Rights in Canada*. Toronto: University of Toronto Press.

Askim, Jostein, Anne Lise Fimreite, Alice Moseley, and Lene Holm Pedersen. 2011. "One-Stop Shops for Social Welfare: The Adaption of an Organizational Form in Three Countries." *Public Administration* 89 (4): 1451–68. https://doi.org/10.1111/j.1467-9299.2011.01933.x.

Atkinson, Michael, Daniel Beland, Gregory Marchildon, Kathleen McNutt, Peter Phillips, and Ken Rasmussen. 2013. *Governance and Public Policy in Canada: A View from the Provinces*. Toronto: University of Toronto Press.

August, Rick. 2015. "Social Assistance in Saskatchewan: Developments, Reform and Retrenchment." In *Welfare Reform in Canada: Provincial Social Assistance in Comparative Perspective*, edited by Daniel Béland and Pierre-Marc Daigneault, 177–92. Toronto: University of Toronto Press.

Australian Council of Social Services. 2012. *Towards More Efficient and Responsive Employment Services: Submission to APESAA*. http://www.acoss.org.au/images/uploads/ACOSS_submission_to_APESAA_Jan_2012.pdf.

Bakvis, Herman. 1996. "Shrinking the House of HRIF: Program Review and the Department of Human Resources Development." In *How Ottawa Spends 1996–97: Life under the Knife*, edited by Gene Swimmer, 133–70. Ottawa: Carleton University Press.

– 2002. "Checkerboard Federalism? Labour Market Development Policy in Canada." In *Canadian Federalism: Performance, Effectiveness and Legitimacy*, edited by Herman Bakvis and Grace Skogstad, 197–219. Don Mills, ON: Oxford University Press.

– 2014. "Canada: A Crisis in Regional Representation?" *Tocqueville Review* 35 (2): 51–77. https://doi.org/10.1353/toc.2014.0013.

Bakvis, Herman, and Peter Aucoin. 2000. *Negotiating Labour Market Development Agreements*. Research no. 22. Ottawa: Canadian Centre for Management Development.

Bakvis, Herman, Gerald Baier, and Douglas Brown. 2009. *Contested Federalism: Certainty and Ambiguity in the Canadian Federation*. Don Mills, ON: Oxford University Press.

Banting, Keith. 2012. "Introduction: Debating Employment Insurance." In *Making EI Work: Research from the Mowat Centre Employment Insurance Task Force*, Queen's Policy Studies Series, edited by Keith Banting and Jon Medow, 1–36. Montreal and Kingston: McGill-Queen's University Press.

Banting, Keith, and Jon Medow. 2012. *Making EI Work: Research from the Mowat Centre Employment Insurance Task Force*, Queen's Policy Studies Series, edited by Keith Banting and Jon Medow. Montreal and Kingston: McGill-Queen's University Press.

Banting, Keith, and John Myles. 2013. "Introduction." In *Inequality and the Fading of Redistributive Politics*, edited by Banting and Myles, 1–42. Vancouver: UBC Press.

Barbier, Jean-Claude, and Wolfgang Ludwig-Mayerhofer. 2004. "Introduction: The Many Worlds of Activation." *European Societies* 6 (4): 423–36. https://doi.org/10.1080/1461669042000275845.

Barnow, Burt S., and Shayne Spaulding. 2015. "Employer Involvement in Workforce Programs: What Do We Know?" In *Transforming U.S. Workforce Development Policies for the 21st Century*, edited by Carl Van Horne, Tammy Edwards, and Todd Greene, 231–64. Kalamazoo, MI: W.E. Upjohn Institute for Employment Research.
Belanger, Paul, and Magali Robitaille. 2008. *A Portrait of Work-Related Learning in Québec*. Ottawa: Canadian Council on Learning's Work and Learning Knowledge Centre.
Berdahl, Loleen, and Roger Gibbons. 2014. *Looking West: Regional Transformation and the Future of Canada*. Toronto: University of Toronto Press.
Bernard, Jean-Thomas. 2012. *The Canadian Equalization Program: Main Elements, Achievements and Challenges*. https://ideefederale.ca/documents/Equalization.pdf.
Bird, Kisha, Marcie Foster, and Evelyn Ganzglass. 2015. *New Opportunities to Improve Economic and Career Success for Low-Income Youth and Adults: Key Provisions of the Workforce Innovation and Opportunity Act (WIOA)*. http://www.clasp.org/resources-and-publications/publication-1/KeyProvisionsofWIOA-Final.pdf.
Black, Edwin R., and Alan C. Cairns. 1966. "A Different Perspective on Canadian Federalism." *Canadian Public Administration* 9 (1): 27–44. https://doi.org/10.1111/j.1754-7121.1966.tb00919.x.
Boismenu, Gérard, and Peter Graefe. 2004. "The New Federal Tool Belt: Attempts to Rebuild Social Policy Leadership." *Canadian Public Policy* 30 (1): 71–89. https://doi.org/10.2307/3552581.
Bramwell, Allison. 2008. "Under the Radar: Workforce Development Networks and Urban Governance in Ontario." Paper presented to Canadian Political Science Conference, 5 June. http://citeseerx.ist.psu.edu/viewdoc/download?doi=10.1.1.529.9100&rep=rep1&type=pdf.
– 2010. "Networks Are Not Enough: Urban Governance and Workforce Development in three Ontario Cities." PhD diss., University of Toronto.
– 2012. "Adult Training for the 21st Century: EI Reform, Decentralization and Workforce Development." In *Making EI Work: Research from the Mowat Centre Employment Insurance Task Force*, Queen's Policy Studies series, edited by Keith Banting and Jon Medow, 393–420. Montreal and Kingston: McGill-Queen's University Press.
British Columbia Centre for Employment Excellence (BCCfEE). 2014. *Accessible Services for Specialized Populations in One-Stop Employment Models: Learning from Other Jurisdictions*. http://cfeebc.org/files/Accessible-Services-for-Specialized-Populations-in-One-stop-Employment-Centres-Reference-Report.pdf.
British Columbia Construction Association. 2007. BC and Yukon Territory Building and Construction Trades Council. Human Resources Development Committee. Overview of the Alberta Apprenticeship System.

Brodkin, Evelyn Z., and Gregory Marston. 2013. *Work and the Welfare State: Street-Level Organizations and Workfare Politics*. Washington, DC: Georgetown University Press.

Campeau, Georges. 2005. *From UI to EI: Waging War on the Welfare State*. Translated by Richard Howard. Vancouver: UBC Press.

Canada. 1962. *Report of the Committee of Inquiry into the Unemployment Insurance Act* (Gill Report). Ottawa: Queen's Printer.

– 1985. *Job Creation, Training and Employment Services*. A Study Team Report to the Task Force on Program Review. Ottawa: Supply and Services Canada.

– 1986. *Summary Report of the Commission of Inquiry on Unemployment Insurance* (Forget Commission). Ottawa: Supply and Services Canada.

– 1997. *Gathering Strength: Canada's Aboriginal Action Plan*. http://www.ahf.ca/downloads/gathering-strength.pdf.

– 2015. *Report for the Period June 1, 2014 to May 31, 2015 by the Government of Canada to the ILO on Employment Service Convention No. 88*. Internal document.

Canada Employment Insurance Commission (CEIC). Various years. *Employment Insurance Monitoring and Assessment Report*. https://www.canada.ca/en/employment-social-development/corporate/portfolio/ei-commission.html.

Canadian Labour Force Development Board (CLFDB). 1998. "The First Annual Report of the Canadian Labour Force Development Board on the State of Labour Market Programs and Services in Canada." Draft.

Carcillo, Stephane, and David Grubb. 2006. "From Inactivity to Work: The Role of Active Labour Market Policies." OCED Social Employment and Migration Working Paper no. 36. http://www.oecd-ilibrary.org/social-issues-migration-health/from-inactivity-to-work_687686456188.

Conference Board of Canada. 2012. *Understanding the Value, Challenges and Opportunities of Engaging Métis, Inuit and First Nations Workers*. Report, July, by Alison Howard, Jessica Edge and Douglas Watt. http://www.conferenceboard.ca/e-library/abstract.aspx?did=4886.

Considine, Mark, Jenny M. Lewis, Siobhan O'Sullivan, and Els Sol. 2015. *Getting Welfare to Work: Street-Level Governance in Australia, the UK, and the Netherlands*. London: Oxford University Press. https://doi.org/10.1093/acprof:oso/9780198743705.001.0001.

Considine, Mark, and Siobhan O'Sullivan. 2014. "Introduction: Markets and the New Welfare: Buying and Selling the Poor." *Social Policy and Administration* 48 (2): 119–26. https://doi.org/10.1111/spol.12052.

Conway, Aidan D., and J.F. Conway. 2015. "Saskatchewan: From Cradle of Social Democracy to Neoliberalism's Sandbox." In *Transforming Provincial*

Politics: The Political Economy of Canada's Provinces and Territories in the Neoliberal Era, edited by Bryan M. Evans and Charles W. Smith, 226–54. Toronto: University of Toronto Press.

Cooper, Amanda. 2014. "Knowledge Mobilisation in Education in Canada: A Cross-Case Analysis of 44 Research Brokering Institutions." In *Evidence and Policy* 10 (1): 29–59.

Council of Atlantic Premiers Employment Insurance Advisory Council. 2014. *Pan-Atlantic Study of the Impact of Recent Changes to Employment Insurance Advisory Panel Final Report*. http://www.cap-cpma.ca/images/AdvisoryPanelFinalReport.pdf.

Coward, John. 2013. *Environmental Scan of Employment Programs in BC*. Prepared for the BC Centre for Employment Excellence. http://cfeebc.org/reports/Environmental-Scan-BC-Employment-Programs.pdf.

Daschuk, James. 2013. *Clearing the Plains: Disease, Politics of Starvation, and the Loss of Aboriginal Life*. Regina: University of Regina Press.

de la Porte, Caroline, and Phillippe Pochet. 2012. "Why and How (Still) Study the OMC." *Journal of European Social Policy* 22 (3): 336–49. https://doi.org/10.1177/0958928711433629.

Dennison, Donald G. 2005. "Intergovernmental Mechanisms: What Have We Learned?" Paper presented at the Conference for the Institute of Intergovernmental Relations, Queen's University, Kingston.

Dingledine, Gary, 1981. *A Chronology of Response: The Evolution of Unemployment Insurance from 1940 to 1980*. Ottawa: Minister of Supply and Services Canada.

Dion, Stephane. 1992. "Explaining Québec Nationalism." In *The Collapse of Canada?* edited by R. Kent Weaver, K. Banting, S. Dion, and A. Stark, 77–8. Washington, DC: Brookings Institute.

Doern, Bruce. 1969. "Vocational Training and Manpower Policy." *Canadian Public Administration* 12 (1): 63–71. https://doi.org/10.1111/j.1754-7121.1969.tb00240.x.

Dunn, Christopher. 2016. "Introduction." In *Provinces: Canadian Provincial Politics*, 3rd ed., edited by Christopher Dunn, xv–xxvi. Toronto: University of Toronto Press.

Dupré, Stefan, David Cameron, Graeme McKechnie, and Theodore Rotenberg. 1973. *Federalism and Policy Development: The Case of Adult Occupational Training in Ontario*. Toronto: University of Toronto Press.

Eberts, Tina. 1994. "Pathways to Success: Aboriginal Decision Making in Employment and Training." In *Aboriginal Self-Government in Canada: Current Trends and Issues*, edited by John H. Hylton, 130–44. Toronto: Purish Publishing.

Eichhorst, Werner, and Regina Konle-Seidl. 2008. "Contingent Convergence: A Comparative Analysis of Activation Policies." Discussion Paper Series. Bonn: Institute for the Study of Labor.

Elkins, David, and Richard Simeon. 1980. *Small Worlds: Provinces and Parties in Canadian Political Life*. Toronto: Methuen.

Employment and Immigration Canada (EIC). 1981. *Labour Market Development in the 1980s* (Dodge Report). A Report of the Task Force on Labour Market Development, prepared for the minister of employment and immigration.

– 1989. *Evaluation of the National Employment Service: An Overview Report*. Program Evaluation Branch.

– 1990a. "Pathways to Success: Aboriginal Employment and Training Strategy: A Background Paper."

– 1990b. "Pathways to Success: Aboriginal Employment and Training Strategy: A Policy and Implementation Paper."

Employment and Social Development Canada (ESDC). 2014a. *Aboriginal Skills and Employment Training Strategy (ASETS) Regional Engagement Thematic Report*. Prepared by Aboriginal Affairs Directorate/Aboriginal Programs Operations Directorate.

– 2014b. *Evaluation of the Organization for Economic Co-operation and Development Named Grants Final Report*. Evaluation Directorate, Strategic Policy and Research. http://publications.gc.ca/collections/collection_2014/edsc-esdc/Em20-1-2014-eng.pdf.

– 2014c. *Evaluation of the Social Development Partnerships Program, Final Report*. Evaluation Directorate, Strategic Policy and Research. http://publications.gc.ca/collections/collection_2015/edsc-esdc/Em4-2-2014-eng.pdf.

– 2014d. *Report on Plans and Priorities*. Ottawa: ESDC.

– 2014e. *Summative Evaluation of the Targeted Initiative for Older Workers*. http://publications.gc.ca/site/eng/469501/publication.html.

– 2015a. *Evaluation of the Aboriginal Skills and Employment Training Strategy and the Skills and Partnership Fund, Final Report*. Evaluation Directorate, Strategic Policy and Research Branch. https://www.canada.ca/en/employment-social-development/corporate/reports/evaluations/2015-aboriginal-skills.html.

– 2015b. *Retooling Labour Market Development Agreements: Stakeholder Consultations Report – Roundtables*. https://www.canada.ca/en/employment-social-development/programs/social-finance/consultations-various-retooling-lmda.html.

– 2015c. *Summative Evaluation of the Horizontal Youth Employment Strategy, Final Report*. Evaluation Directorate, Strategic Policy and Research. https://www.canada.ca/en/employment-social-development/corporate/reports/evaluations/2015-youth-employment.html.

– 2015d. *Summative Evaluation of the Opportunities Fund for Persons with Disabilities, Final Report.* Evaluation Directorate, Strategic Policy and Research. http://publications.gc.ca/site/eng/9.629830/publication.html.
– n.d. "Aboriginal Skills and Employment Training Strategy Funding Agreement between Her Majesty the Queen in Right of Canada and [Legal Name of Recipient Organization]."
European Commission. 1993. "Growth, Competitiveness, Employment: The Challenges and Ways Forward into the 21st Century." White Paper COM (93)700, 5 December. Brussels: Commission of the European Communities.
– 2013. "Successful Partnerships in Delivering Public Employment Services: Analytical Paper, PES to PES Dialogue." European Commission, Mutual Learning Programme for Public Employment Services.
European Union. 2014. "Decision No 573/2014/EU of the European Parliament and of the Council of the European Union on Enhanced Coordination between Public Employment Services (PES)." http://eur-lex.europa.eu/legal-content/EN/TXT/PDF/?uri=CELEX:32014D0573&from=EN.
Evans, Bryan M., and Charles W. Smith. 2015. "'The Transformation of Ontario Politics: The Long Ascent of Neoliberalism." In *Transforming Provincial Politics*, edited by Evans and Smith, 162–94. Toronto: University of Toronto Press.
Farrow, Kelly, Sam Hurley, and Robert Sturrock. 2015. *Grand Alibis: How Declining Public Sector Capability Affects Services for the Disadvantaged.* Centre for Policy Development. https://cpd.org.au/wp-content/uploads/2015/12/Grand-Alibis-Final.pdf.
Fenna, Alan. 2012. "Centralising Dynamics in Australian Federalism." *Australian Journal of Politics and History* 58 (4): 580–90. https://doi.org/10.1111/j.1467-8497.2012.01654.x.
Finance Canada (FC). 2007. *Budget 2007.* http://www.budget.gc.ca/2007/pdf/bp2007e.pdf.
Finn, Dan. 2011. *Sub-contracting in Public Employment Services: Review of Research Findings and Literature on Recent Trends and Business Models.* PES to PES Dialogue, European Commission Mutual Learning Programme for Public Employment Services, DG Employment, Social Affairs and Inclusion.
Flanagan, Kathleen. 2015. "The State of Social Assistance in Prince Edward Island." In *Welfare Reform in Canada: Provincial Social Assistance in Comparative Perspective*, edited by Daniel Béland and Pierre-Marc Daigneault, 255–72. Toronto: University of Toronto Press.
Fortin, Pierre. 2010. "Québec Is Fairer: There Is Less Poverty and Less Inequality in Québec." *Inroads* 26:58–65.

Froy, Francesca, Sylvain Giguère, Lucy Pyne, and Donna E. Wood. 2011. *Building Flexibility and Accountability into Local Employment Services: Synthesis of OECD Studies in Belgium, Canada, Denmark and the Netherlands.* http://www.oecd-ilibrary.org/docserver/download/5kg3mkv3tr21-en.pdf?expires=1504573470&id=id&accname=guest&checksum=FCD737E293A9DF2A656CF920BE293FCF.

Galarneau, Diane, and Thao Sohn. 2013. *Long-term Trends in Unionization.* Statistics Canada. http://www.statcan.gc.ca/pub/75-006-x/2013001/article/11878-eng.pdf.

Garcea, Joseph, and Ken Pontikes. 2004. "Federal-Municipal-Provincial Relations in Saskatchewan: Provincial Roles, Approaches and Mechanisms." In *The State of the Federation, 2004: Municipal Federal-Provincial Relations in Canada*, 333–70. Kingston: Institute of Intergovernmental Relations, Queen's University.

Gibbons, Roger. 1998. "Alberta's Intergovernmental Relations Experience." In *Canada: The State of the Federation 1997*, edited by Harvey Lazar, 247–70. Kingston: Institute of Intergovernmental Relations.

– 2001. "Staying the Course? Historical Determinants of Debt Management Strategies in Western Canada." In *Deficit Reduction in the Far West the Great Experiment*, edited by Paul Booth and Bradford Reid, 111–34. Edmonton: University of Alberta Press.

Gold, Jennifer, and Matthew Mendelsohn. 2014. *Better Outcomes for Public Services: Achieving Social Impact through Outcomes-Based Funding*. Toronto: Mowat Centre. https://mowatcentre.ca/better-outcomes-for-public-services/.

Graefe, Peter. 2014. "Economic Development Policies in Ontario and Québec: Thinking about Structures of Representation." In *Comparing Canada: Methods and Perspectives on Canadian Politics*, edited by Luc Turgeon, Martin Papillon, Jennifer Wallner and Stephen White, 271–91. Vancouver: UBC Press.

– 2015a. "Québec Nationalism and Québec Politics, from Left to Right." In *Transforming Provincial Politics*, edited by Bryan Evans and Charles Smith, 137–61. Toronto: University of Toronto Press.

– 2015b. "Social Assistance in Ontario." In *Welfare Reform: Provincial Social Assistance in Comparative Perspective*, edited by Daniel Beland and Pierre-Marc Daigneault, 111–26. Toronto: University of Toronto Press.

Graefe, Peter, and Mario Levesque. 2013. "Accountability in Labour Market Policies for Persons with Disabilities." In *Overpromising and Underperforming? Understanding and Evaluating New Intergovernmental Accountability Regimes*, edited by Peter Graefe, Julie M. Simmons, and Linda A. White, 127–43. Toronto: University of Toronto Press.

Graves, Frank. 2016. "The Reinstatement of Progressive Canada." Montreal: Ekos Politics, in cooperation with the Institute for Research on Public Policy. http://www.ekospolitics.com/index.php/2016/01/the-reinstatement-of-progressive-canada/.

Gunderson, Morley, and Rafael Gomez. 2016. "Labour Market Policies in the Provinces." In *Provinces: Canadian Provincial Politics*, 3rd ed., edited by Christopher Dunn, 522–47. Toronto: University of Toronto Press.

Gunderson, Morley, and Andrew Sharpe. 1998. "Introduction." In *Forging Business-Labour Partnerships: the Emergence of Sector Councils in Canada*, edited by Gunderson and Sharpe, 3–30. Toronto: University of Toronto Press.

Haddow, Rodney. 1997a. "The Saskatchewan Labour Force Development Board: Reforming Labour Market Governance in a Cold Climate." In *Social Partnerships for Training: Canada's Experiment with Labour Force Development Boards*, edited by Andrew Sharpe and Rodney Haddow, 189–216. Kingston: School of Policy Studies, Queen's University.

– 1997b. "Worth the Candle? Labour Force Development Boards in Nova Scotia and New Brunswick." In *Social Partnerships for Training: Canada's Experiment with Labour Force Development Boards*, edited by Andrew Sharpe and Rodney Haddow, 85–124. Kingston: School of Policy Studies, Queen's University.

– 2000a. "How Malleable Are Political-Economic Institutions? The Case of Labour Market Decision-making in British Columbia." *Canadian Public Administration* 43 (4): 387–411. https://doi.org/10.1111/j.1754-7121.2000.tb01151.x.

– 2000b. "Labour Market Training: Is a High Skills Future Feasible for Nova Scotia?" In *The Savage Years*, edited by P. Clancy, James Bickerton, Rodney Haddow, and Ian Stewar, 170–98. Halifax: Formac.

– 2004. "Canadian Labour Market Policy: Federalism and Policy Re-alignment at the Millennium." In *Federalism and Labour Market Policy: Comparing Different Governance and Employment Strategies*, edited by Alain Noel, 235–70. Montreal and Kingston: Institute of Intergovernmental Relations, McGill-Queen's University Press.

– 2015. *Comparing Québec and Ontario: Political Economy and Public Policy at the Turn of the Millennium*. Toronto: University of Toronto Press.

Haddow, Rodney, and Thomas Klassen. 2006. *Partisanship, Globalization, and Canadian Labour Market Policy: Four Provinces in Comparative Perspective*. Toronto: University of Toronto Press. https://doi.org/10.3138/9781442678279.

Haddow, Rodney, Steffen Schneider, and Thomas Klassen. 2006. "Can Decentralization Alleviate Labour Market Dysfunctions in Marginal

Jurisdictions? Active Labour Market Policies in Nova Scotia and Saxony-Anhalt." *Canadian Public Policy* 32 (2): 318–34.
Haddow, Rodney, and Andrew Sharpe. 1997. "Canada's Experiment with Labour Force Development Boards: An Introduction." In *Social Partnerships for Training: Canada's Experiment with Labour Force Development Boards*, edited by Andrew Sharpe and Rodney Haddow, 3–23. Kingston: School of Policy Studies, Queen's University.
Hatt, Kayle. 2014. *Help Not Wanted: Federal Public Service Cuts Have Hit Students Hard*. Ottawa: Canadian Centre for Policy Alternatives. https://www.policyalternatives.ca/publications/reports/help-not-wanted.
Holden, Bill, Nicola Chopin, Carmen Dyck, and Nick Fraser. 2009. *Poverty-Reduction Policies and Programs*. Ottawa: Canadian Council on Social Development.
Hood, Christopher. 1991. "A Public Management for All Seasons?" *Public Administration Review* 69 (1): 3–19. https://doi.org/10.1111/j.1467-9299.1991.tb00779.x.
Hudson, Carol-Anne, and Peter Graefe. 2011. "The Toronto Origins of Ontario's 2008 Poverty-Reduction Strategy: Mobilizing Multiple Channels of Influence for Progressive Social Policy Change." *Canadian Review of Social Policy* 65/66:1–15.
Hueglin, Thomas. 2013. "Treaty Federalism as a Model of Policy Making: Comparing Canada and the European Union." *Canadian Public Administration* 56 (2): 185–202. https://doi.org/10.1111/capa.12013.
Human Resources Development Canada (HRDC). 1994. "Improving Social Security in Canada: A Discussion Paper." Ottawa: Ministry of Supply and Services Canada.
– 1995. *A 21st-Century Employment System for Canada: Guide to the Employment Insurance Legislation*. Ottawa: Support and Services Canada.
Human Resources and Skills Development Canada (HRSDC). 2009. *Formative Evaluation of the Aboriginal Human Resources Development Agreements, Final Report*. Ottawa: Evaluation Directorate.
– 2012. *Formative Evaluation of Provincial Benefits and Measures under the Canada-Ontario Labour Market Development Agreement, Final Report*. Ottawa: Evaluation Directorate, Strategic Policy and Research Branch.
– 2013a. *Aboriginal Labour Market Bulletin* 2 (2). https://www.canada.ca/content/dam/canada/employment-social-development/migration/documents/assets/portfolio/docs/en/aboriginal/bulletins/almb.pdf.
– 2013b. *Summative Evaluation of the Aboriginal Skills and Employment Partnership Program*. http://publications.gc.ca/collections/collection_2014/edsc-esdc/HS28-193-2013-eng.pdf.

– 2014. *Supplementary Information Tables in the 2013–14 Report on Plans and Priorities.*
Human Resources, Skills and Social Development and the Status of Persons with Disabilities (HUMA) Standing Committee. 2014. *Opportunities for Aboriginal Persons in the Workforce.* http://www.ourcommons.ca/DocumentViewer/en/41-2/HUMA/report-4.
Hunter, John. 1993. *The Employment Challenge: Federal Employment Policies and Programs 1900–1990.* Ottawa: Government of Canada.
Huo, J. 2009. *Third Way Reforms: Social Democracy after the Golden Age.* New York: Cambridge University Press. https://doi.org/10.1017/CBO9780511581045.
Ibbitson, John. 2015. "The Incredible Shrinking Region." *Globe and Mail,* 21 March.
Indian and Northern Affairs Canada. 2007. Evaluation of the Income Assistance Program. Audit and Evaluation Section, Project 07/06.
Informetrica Ltd. 1993. "Labour Market Development and Training." Paper no. 5, prepared for the Ontario Ministry of Intergovernmental Affairs, by M.C. McCracken and R.A. Jenness.
Institute on Governance. 2011. "Defining Governance." http://iog.ca/defining-governance/.
International Labour Organization (ILO). 1950. "Employment Services Convention, 1948 (No. 88)." http://www.ilo.org/dyn/normlex/en/f?p=NORMLEXPUB:12100:0::NO::P12100_INSTRUMENT_ID:312233.
– 1964. "Employment Policy Convention, 1964 (No. 122)." http://www.ilo.org/dyn/normlex/en/f?p=NORMLEXPUB:12100:0::NO:12100:P12100_INSTRUMENT_ID:312267:NO.
Jackson, Andrew, and Sylvian Schetagne. 2010. *Is EI Working for Canada's Unemployed? Analyzing the Great Recession.* Ottawa: Canadian Centre for Policy Alternatives. https://www.policyalternatives.ca/sites/default/files/uploads/publications/reports/docs/Is_EI_Working_For_Canadas_Unemployed.pdf.
Jobs Australia. 2013. *Reforming Employment Assistance: Blueprint for the Future.* Victoria: Jobs Australia.
Johnson, Andrew F. 1997. "Towards a Renewed Concertation in Québec: La Société Québécoise de développement de la main-d'oeuvre." In *Social Partnerships for Training,* edited by Andrew Sharpe and Rodney Haddow, 125–46. Kingston: School of Policy Studies, Queen's University.
Jolicoeur & Associés. 2010. Enquête sur la Situation Postintervention de Participants et Participantes aux Interventions de Services Publics d'Emploi, *Rapport de Researche Donnee Globales.*

Kenworthy, Lane. 2010. "Labour Market Activation." In *The Oxford Handbook of the Welfare State*, edited by Francis G. Castles, Stephan Leibfried, Jane Lewis, Herbert Obinger, and Christopher Pierson, 435–47. Oxford: Oxford University Press.

Klassen, Thomas R. 2000a. "The Federal-Provincial Labour Market Agreements: Brave New Model of Collaboration?" In *Federalism, Democracy and Labour Market Policy in Canada*, edited by Tom McIntosh, 159–201. Kingston: School of Policy Studies, Queen's University.

– 2000b. *Precarious Values: Organizations, Politics and Labour Market Policy in Ontario*. Montreal and Kingston: School of Policy Studies, McGill-Queen's University Press.

Kneebone, Ron, and Katherine White. 2014. *The Rise and Fall of Social Assistance Use in Canada 1969–2012*. School of Public Policy, SPP Research Papers. Calgary: University of Calgary.

Langenbucher, K. 2015. *How Demanding Are Eligibility Criteria for Unemployment Benefits, Quantitative Indicators for OECD and EU Countries*. Paris: OECD. http://www.oecd-ilibrary.org/social-issues-migration-health/how-demanding-are-eligibility-criteria-for-unemployment-benefits-quantitative-indicators-for-oecd-and-eu-countries_5jrxtk1zw8f2-en.

Lazar, Harvey. 2002. *Shifting Roles: Active Labour Market Policy in Canada under the Labour Market Development Agreements – A Conference Report*. Ottawa: Canadian Policy Research Networks.

Levesque, Mario. 2012. "Assessing the Ability of Disability Organizations: An Interprovincial Comparative Perspective." *Canadian Journal of Nonprofit and Social Economy Research* 3 (2): 82–103. https://doi.org/10.22230/cjnser.2012v3n2a119.

Lord, Stella. 2015. "Welfare Reform in Canada: Nova Scotia." In *Welfare Reform in Canada: Provincial Social Assistance in Comparative Perspective*, edited by Daniel Béland and Pierre-Marc Daigneault, 223–38. Toronto: University of Toronto Press.

Lysenko, Ekaterina. 2012. "Labour Market Development in Newfoundland & Labrador: Regional Challenges and Active Solutions." MA thesis, Memorial University.

Maddock, S. 2012. "The DWP Work Programme: The Impact of the DWP Procurement Model on Personal Service Innovation." MIOIR Case Study on Public Procurement and Innovation. https://www.centreforwelfarereform.org/uploads/attachment/344/dwp-work-programme.pdf.

Makhoul, Anne. 2015. *Social Assistance Combined Summaries, 2014*. Caledon Institute of Social Policy. http://www.caledoninst.org/Publications/PDF/1062ENG.pdf.

Manitoba. 2008. "The Advisory Council on Workforce Development Act." http://web2.gov.mb.ca/laws/statutes/ccsm/a006-5e.php.
– 2013. *Entrepreneurship Training and Trade: Annual Report 2012–2013*. https://www.gov.mb.ca/jec/reports/2007_2016_fiscal/2007-16_pdfs/12_13_ett_ar.pdf.
Manitoba Department of Education and Training. 1997. *Transfer of Employment and Training Programs*.
Marsh, Leonard. 1943. *Report on Social Security for Canada, Prepared by L.C. Marsh for the Advisory Committee on Reconstruction*. Ottawa: E. Cloutier.
Martin, John. 2014. "Activation and Active Labour Market Policies in OECD Countries: Stylized Facts and Evidence on Their Effectiveness." Policy Paper no. 84. IZA Policy Paper Series.
Martin, John, and Mark Pearson. 2005. "Time to Change: Towards an Active Social Policy Agenda." *OECD Observer* 248.
McBride, Stephen. 1992. *Not Working: State, Unemployment and Neo-conservatism in Canada*. Toronto: University of Toronto Press.
McBride, Stephen, Rianne Mahon, and Gerard W. Boychuk. 2015. "Introduction." In *AFTER 08 Social Policy and the Global Financial Crisis*, edited by McBride, Mahon, and Boyckuk, 3–20. Vancouver: UBC Press.
McBride, Stephen, and Peter Stoyko. 2000. "Youth and the Social Union: Intergovernmental Relations, Youth Unemployment and School-to-Work Transitions." In *Federalism, Democracy and Labour Market Policy in Canada*, edited by Tom McIntosh, 205–68. Kingston: School of Policy Studies, Queen's University.
McColl, Mary Ann, and Lynn Roberts. 2015. *Policy Governing Employment Supports for People with Disabilities Canada*. Kingston: Canadian Disability Policy Alliance.
McDonald, G.P.A. 1966. "Labour, Manpower and Government Reorganization." *Canadian Public Administration* 10 (4): 471–98.
McDonald, Jessica. 2014. *The Industry Authority and Trades Training in BC: Recalibrating for High Performance*. http://www.itabc.ca/sites/default/files/docs/about-ita/ITA_Review_Final_Report.pdf.
Mendelsohn, Matthew, and J. Scott Matthews. 2010. "The New Ontario: The Shifting Attitudes of Ontarians toward the Federation." Mowat Centre for Policy Innovation: Mowat Note. https://mowatcentre.ca/wp-content/uploads/publications/1_the_new_ontario.pdf.
Mosely, Hugh. 2012. "Accountability in Decentralised Employment Services Regimes." OECD Local Economic and Employment Development (LEED) Working Papers, OECD Publishing. http://www.oecd.org/leed-forum/publications/WP%20-%20Accountability%20in%20Decentralised%20Employment%20Service%20Regimes.pdf.

Mulgan, G. 2003. "Global Comparisons in Policy-making: The View from the Centre. openDemocracy. https://www.opendemocracy.net/democracy-think_tank/article_1280.jsp.

National Aboriginal Economic Development Board (NAEDB). 2015. *The Aboriginal Economic Progress Report*. http://www.naedb-cndea.com/reports/NAEDB-progress-report-june-2015.pdf.

National Association of Friendship Centres. 2012. *NAFC AHRDS/ASETS Survey Report 2011/12 Update*. Ottawa: NAFC.

– n.d. *Labour Market Opportunities for Urban Aboriginal People*. Ottawa: NAFC.

National Association of State Workforce Agencies (NASWA). 2012. "A History of the National Association of State Workforce Agencies." https://www.naswa.org/assets/utilities/serve.cfm?gid=bcdb456f-54c8-4570-b844-d02ce2c1cf58.

Nikiforuk, Andrew. 1987. "The New Quarterback." In *Running on Empty: Alberta after the Boom*, edited by Andrew Nikiforuk. Edmonton: NeWest.

Noel, Alain. 2012. "Asymmetry at Work: Québec's Distinct Implementation of Programs for the Unemployed." In *Making EI Work: Research from the Mowat Centre Employment Insurance Task Force*, edited by Keith Banting and Jon Medow, 421–48. Queen's Policy Studies Series. Montreal and Kingston: McGill-Queen's University Press.

– 2015. "Québec: The Ambivalent Politics of Social Solidarity. In *Welfare Reform: Provincial Social Assistance in Comparative Perspective*, edited by Daniel Beland and Pierre-Marc Daigneault, 127–42. Toronto: University of Toronto Press.

Obinger, Herbert, Stephan Leibfried, and Francis Castles. 2005. "Introduction: Federalism and the Welfare State." In *Federalism and the Welfare State: New World and European Experiences*, edited by Obinger, Leibfried, and Castles, 1–48. Cambridge: Cambridge University Press. https://doi.org/10.1017/CBO9780511491856.003.

O'Leary, C. 2015. "Presentation to Centre for European Policy Studies Workshop on the Potential for a European Unemployment Benefits Scheme." Brussels.

O'Leary, C., and R. Eberts. 2008. *The Wagner-Peyser Act and U.S. Employment Service: Seventy-Five Years of Matching Job Seekers and Employers*. Report prepared for the Center for Employment Security Education and Research and National Association of State Workforce Agencies. Kalamazoo, MI: W.E. Upjohn Institute for Employment Research Publisher.

Ontario. 2003. Standing Committee on Public Accounts. Testimony from K. Constante, W. Forward, and P. Redmond, 12 February 2003.

Ontario, Ministry of Community and Social Services (MESS). 2012. "Discussion Paper 2: Approaches for Reform." Commission for the Review of Social Assistance in Ontario.

– 2013. *Final Report: Ontario Works Employment Assistance Services Report.* Policy Research and Analysis Branch.

Ontario, Ministry of Finance. 2012. "Commission on the Reform of Ontario's Public Services." http://www.fin.gov.on.ca/en/reformcommission/.

Ontario, Ministry of Training, Colleges and Universities (MTCU). 2006. "New Skills Strategy Simplifies Access to Training and Supports Economic Growth and Prosperity." News release, 17 January. https://news.ontario.ca/archive/en/2006/01/17/New-Skills-Strategy-Simplifies-Access-To-Training-And-Supports-Economic-Growth-A.html.

– 2014. *Employment Services: Service Provider Guidelines.* Ministry of Training, Colleges and Universities. http://www.tcu.gov.on.ca/eng/eopg/publications/es_2014_2015_sp_guidelines.pdf.

Organisation for Economic Cooperation and Development (OECD). 1994. *The Jobs Study.* Paris: OECD.

– 1998. *Local Management for More Effective Employment Policies.* http://www.oecd-ilibrary.org/urban-rural-and-regional-development/local-management-for-more-effective-employment-policies_9789264162723-en.

– 2001. "Labour Market Policies and Services in Canada: A New Collaborative Approach." In *Labour Market Policies and the Public Employment Service: Proceedings of the Prague Conference.* Paris: OECD. http://www.oecd.org/employment/emp/labourmarketpoliciesandthepublicemploymentserviceproceedingsofthepragueconferencejuly2000.htm.

– 2008a. *Jobs for Youth: Canada 2008.* Paris: OECD. http://www.keepeek.com/Digital-Asset-Management/oecd/employment/jobs-for-youth-des-emplois-pour-les-jeunes-canada-2008_9789264046498-en#page4.

– 2008b. *More Than Just Jobs: Workforce Development in a Skills-Based Economy.* Paris: OECD. http://www.oecd.org/cfe/leed/morethanjustjobsworkforcedevelopmentinaskills-basedeconomy.htm.

– 2009. *Flexible Policy for More and Better Jobs.* Paris: OECD. http://www.oecd.org/publications/flexible-policy-for-more-and-better-jobs-9789264059528-en.htm.

– 2010. *Sickness, Disability and Work: Breaking the Barriers: Canada: Opportunities for Collaboration.* Paris: OECD. http://www.oecd.org/canada/sickness-disability-and-work-breaking-the-barriers-9789264090422-en.htm.

– 2012. *Activating Jobseekers: How Australia Does It.* Paris: OECD. http://www.oecd-ilibrary.org/employment/activating-jobseekers_9789264185920-en.

– 2013a. "Activating Jobseekers: Lessons from Seven OECD Countries." In *Employment Outlook 2013.* Paris OECD Conference, Directorate for Employment, Labour and Social Affairs, 4–5 April, chap. 3.

– 2013b. "Public Expenditure on Active Labour Market Policies (% of GDP)." OECD database, Employment and Labour Markets: Key Tables from OECD.
– 2014a. *Education at a Glance: Canada.* http://www.oecd.org/edu/Canada-EAG2014-Country-Note.pdf.
– 2014b. *Employment and Skills Strategies in Canada.* Paris: OECD Publishing. http://www.keepeek.com/Digital-Asset-Management/oecd/employment/employment-and-skills-strategies-in-canada_9789264209374-en#page1.
– 2015a. *Employment Outlook 2015: How Does Canada Compare?* http://www.oecd.org/canada/Employment-Outlook-Canada-EN.pdf.
– 2015b. *Back to Work: Canada: Improving the Re-employment Prospects of Displaced Workers.* Paris: OECD Publishing.
– 2015c. "Strengthening Public Employment Services." Paper prepared for the G20 Employment Working Group, Istanbul, 24 April 2015. http://g20.org.tr/wp-content/uploads/2015/11/Strengthening-Public-Employment-Services.pdf.
– 2016. "Employment and Skills Strategies in Saskatchewan and the Yukon, Canada." Paris: OECD Publishing. http://www.oecd.org/canada/employment-and-skills-strategies-in-saskatchewan-and-the-yukon-canada-9789264259225-en.htm.
Ostry, Jonathan D., Prakash Loungani, and Davide Furceri. 2016. "Neoliberalism Oversold?" *Finance and Development* 53 (2). http://www.imf.org/external/pubs/ft/fandd/2016/06/ostry.htm.
Pal, Leslie. 1983. "The Fall and Rise of Developmental Uses of UI Funds." *Canadian Public Policy* 9:81–93.
– 1988a. "Sense and Sensibility: Comments on Forget." *Canadian Public Policy* 14 (1): 7–14. https://doi.org/10.2307/3550448.
– 1988b. *State, Class and Bureaucracy: Canadian Unemployment Insurance and Public Policy.* Montreal and Kingston: McGill-Queen's University Press.
Palameta, Boris, Karen Myers, and Natalie Conte. 2013. *Applying Performance Funding to Essential Skills: State of Knowledge Review.* Social Research and Demonstration Corporation. http://www.srdc.org/publications/Applying-performance-funding-to-Essential-Skills-State-of-knowledge-review-details.aspx.
Papillon, Martin. 2014. "The Rise (and Fall?) of Aboriginal Self Government." In *Canadian Politics,* 6th ed., edited by James Bickerton and Alain G. Gagnon. Toronto: University of Toronto Press.
Paquet, Mireille. 2014. "The Federalization of Immigration and Integration in Canada." *Canadian Journal of Political Science* 47 (3): 519–48. https://doi.org/10.1017/S0008423914000766.

Parliamentary Budget Office (PBO). 2011. *Fiscal Sustainability Report 2011.* http://publications.gc.ca/collections/collection_2011/dpb-pbo/YN2-1-2011-eng.pdf.

– 2012. *Renewing the Canada Health Transfer: Implications for Federal and Provincial-Territorial Fiscal Sustainability.* http://www.pbo-dpb.gc.ca/web/default/files/files/files/Publications/Renewing_CHT.pdf.

– 2015. *Labour Market Assessment 2015.* http://www.pbo-dpb.gc.ca/en/blog/news/Labour_Market_Assessment_2015.

Patten, Steve. 2015. "'The Politics of Alberta's One-Party State." In *Transforming Provincial Politics: The Political Economy of Canada's Provinces and Territories in the Neoliberal Era,* edited by Bryan M. Evans and Charles W. Smith, 255–83. Toronto: University of Toronto Press.

Pivan, Frances Fox. 2015. "Neoliberalism and the Welfare State." *Journal of International and Comparative Social Policy* 31 (1): 2–9. https://doi.org/10.1080/21699763.2014.1001665.

Porter, Ann. 2003. *Gendered States: Women, Unemployment Insurance and the Political Economy of the Welfare State in Canada, 1945–1997.* Toronto: University of Toronto Press. https://doi.org/10.3138/9781442675216.

Prince, Michael. 2016. *Inclusive Employment for Canadians with Disabilities: Towards a New Policy Framework and Agenda.* IRPP Study no. 60. http://irpp.org/research-studies/study-no60/.

Provincial-Territorial Labour Market Ministers (FLMM). 2002. *Skill Investments for All Canadians: The Future of the Labour Market Development Agreements.* FLMM.

– 2013. *Building Skills Together: A Report from Provincial and Territorial Labour Market Ministers.* http://novascotia.ca/lae/pubs/docs/FLMM.pdf.

Quebec. 1993a. "Communiqué." Federal-Provincial-Territorial Conference of Ministers Responsible for Labour Market Matters, Toronto, 19–20 January.

– 1993b. "Québec's Position on Labour Force Development Issues." Federal-Provincial-Territorial Conference of Ministers Responsible for Labour Market Matters, Toronto, 19–20 January.

– 2006. "Memorandum of Recognition and Partnership between Emploi-Québec and the Community Organizations Working in the Employability Field." Emploi-Québec internal document.

Raiq, Hicham, Paul Bernard, and Axel van den Berg. 2012. "Québec's Distinct Welfare State." *Inroads Journal: The Canadian Magazine of Opinion* 31:59–68.

Rees, James, Adam Whitworth, and Eleanor Carter. 2013. *Support for All in the UK Work Programme? Differential Payments, Same Old Problem ...* Third Sector Research Program, Working Paper 115. http://www.birmingham.ac.uk/generic/tsrc/documents/tsrc/working-papers/working-paper-115.pdf.

Reichwin, Baldwin. 2002. *Benchmarks in Alberta's Public Welfare Services: History Rooted in Benevolence, Harshness, Punitiveness and Stinginess*. http://www.canadiansocialresearch.net/Alberta_welfare_history.pdf.

Rice, James J., and Michael Prince. 2013. *Changing Politics of Canadian Social Policy*. 2nd ed. Toronto: University of Toronto Press.

Robinson, Andrew. 2013. "Negative Reaction to Employment Program Changes." *Telegram*, 5 March.

Royal Commission. 1996. *Report of the Royal Commission on Aboriginal Peoples (RCAP)*. http://www.collectionscanada.gc.ca/webarchives/20071115053257/http://www.ainc-inac.gc.ca/ch/rcap/sg/sgmm_e.html.

Royal Commission on the Economic Union and Development Prospects for Canada. 1985. *Report*. Vol. 2. Ottawa: Minister of Supply and Services Canada.

Saint-Martin, Denis. 2009. *Quebec's Social Model: A Case of Europeanization Outside Europe?* Canada-Europe Transatlantic Dialogue Policy Brief. https://labs.carleton.ca/canadaeurope/2009/policy-brief-quebecs-social-model-a-case-of-europeanization-outside-europe-by-denis-saint-martin/.

Sheldrick, Bryon M. 2015. "The Manitoba NDP and the Politics of Inoculation: Sustaining Electoral Success through the Third Way." In *Transforming Provincial Politics: The Political Economy of Canada's Provinces and Territories in the Neoliberal Era*, edited by Bryan M. Evans and Charles W. Smith, 195–225. Toronto: University of Toronto Press.

Shewell, Hugh. 2004. *Enough to Keep Them Alive: Indian Welfare in Canada, 1873–1965*. Toronto: University of Toronto Press.

Simpson, Wayne. 2015. "Social Assistance in Manitoba." In *Welfare Reform in Canada: Provincial Social Assistance in Comparative Perspective*, edited by Daniel Béland and Pierre-Marc Daigneault, 193–208. Toronto: University of Toronto Press.

Smith, Andrew, and Jatinder Mann. 2015. "Federalism and Sub-National Protectionism: A Comparison of the Internal Trade Regimes of Canada and Australia." Institute of Intergovernmental Relations Working paper. http://www.queensu.ca/iigr/sites/webpublish.queensu.ca.iigrwww/files/files/WorkingPapers/NewWorkingPapersSeries/SmithAndrewWorkingPaper2015.pdf.

Social Research Demonstration Corporation (SRDC). 2013. *Employment and Training Services Review: Phase Two Final Report*. Ottawa: SRDC.

Stanford, Jim. 2013. "Canada's Sluggish Labour Market and the Myth of the Skills Shortage." In *Academic Matters* (November). http://academicmatters.ca/2013/11/canadas-sluggish-labour-market-and-the-myth-of-the-skills-shortage/.

Starr, Richard. 2014. *Equal as Citizens: The Tumultuous and Troubled History of a Great Canadian Idea*. Halifax, NS: Formac Publishing.

Statistics Canada. 2014. *Population by Year, by Province and Territory*, CANSIM table 051-0001.

– 2015. *Employment Services 2013*. CANSIM tables 361-0042 to 361-0044.

– 2017a. "Median Total Income, by Family Type, by Province and Territory." http://www.statcan.gc.ca/tables-tableaux/sum-som/l01/cst01/famil108a-eng.htm.

– 2017b. "Table 282-0020: Labour Force Survey Estimates (LFS), by Sex and Detailed Age Group." http://www5.statcan.gc.ca/cansim/a26?lang=eng&id=2820002.

Struthers, James. 1983. *No Fault of Their Own: Unemployment and the Canadian Welfare State, 1914–1941*. Toronto: University of Toronto Press.

Terpstra, J. 2002. "Cooperation between Social Security and Employment Services: Evaluation of a Reform Strategy in the Netherlands." *International Social Security Review* 55 (3): 39–55. https://doi.org/10.1111/1468-246X.00131.

Thériault, Luc, and Hélène Le Breton. 2015. "Social Assistance in New Brunswick: Origins, Developments, and Current Situation." In *Welfare Reform in Canada: Provincial Social Assistance in Comparative Perspective*, edited by Daniel Béland and Pierre-Marc Daigneault, 209–22. Toronto: University of Toronto Press.

Thomas, Paul. September 2008. "Leading from the Middle: Manitoba's Role in the Intergovernmental Arena." *Canadian Political Science Review* 2 (3): 29–50.

Thuy, Phan, Ellen Hansen, and David Price. 2001. *The Public Employment Service in a Changing Labour Market*. Geneva: International Labour Organization.

Toneguzz, Mario. 2015. "Alberta Entrepreneurs Canada's Most Active in Starting Up New Businesses." *Calgary Herald*, 18 June 2015. http://calgaryherald.com/business/local-business/alberta-entrepreneurs-canadas-most-active-in-starting-up-new-businesses.

Torjman, Sherry. 1995. "Milestone or Millstone? The Legacy of the Social Security Review." Caledon Institute of Social Policy, keynote address, 7th Social Welfare Policy Conference, Vancouver.

Toronto. 2012. *Working as One: A Workforce Development Strategy for Toronto*. City of Toronto.

Turgeon, L., and R. Simeon. 2015. "Ideology, Political Economy and Federalism: The Welfare State and the Evolution of the Australian and Canadian Federations." In *Understanding Federalism and Federations*, edited by Alain Gagnon, Soeren, Keil, and Sean Mueller. New York: Routledge.

Unemployment Insurance Commission (UIC). 1976. *Unemployment Insurance Commission 36th Annual Report*. Ottawa: Government of Canada.

United States Department of Labour (DOL). 2013. *Unemployment Compensation: Federal-State Partnership*. Washington: United States Department of Labour, Office of Unemployment Insurance Division of Legislation.

Vaillancourt, Francois, and Mathieu Laberge. 2010. "Québec: Equitable Yes, Sustainable No." *Inroads* 26:74–83.

van Berkel, Rik, and Vando Borghi. 2008. "Introduction: The Governance of Activation." *Social Policy and Society* 7 (3): 331–40.

van Berkel, Rik, Willibrord de Graaf, and Tomás Sirovátka, eds. 2011. *The Governance of Active Welfare States in Europe*. New York: Palgrave Macmillan. https://doi.org/10.1057/9780230306714.

– 2012. "Governance of the Activation Policies in Europe." *International Journal of Sociology and Social Policy* 32 (5/6): 260–72. https://doi.org/10.1108/01443331211236943.

Van den Berg, Axel, and Jason Jenson. 2015. "A Tale of Two Federalisms: Social Policy in Canada and the European Union." In *Social Europe: A Dead End: What the Eurozone Crisis Is Doing to Europe's Social Dimension*, edited by Arnaud Lechevalier and Jan Wielgohs, 103–32. Copenhagen: Djof Publishing.

Vandenbroucke, Frank, and Chris Luigjes. 2016. *Institutional Moral Hazard in the Multi-Tiered Regulation of Unemployment and Social Assistance Benefits and Activation: A Summary of Eight Country Case Studies*. Brussels: Centre for European Policy Studies.

Vanhercke, Bart. 2015. "Social Policy Coordination in Canada: Learning from the EU." Policy Paper for the Canada-Europe Transatlantic Dialogue. https://labs.carleton.ca/canadaeurope/2015/policy-paper-social-policy-coordination-in-canada-learning-from-the-eu-by-bart-vanhercke/.

Van Norman, Marilyn, B. Shepard, and P. Mani. 2014. "Historical Snapshots in the Emergence of Career Development in Canada." In *Career Development Practice in Canada: Perspectives, Principles, and Professionalism*, edited by Blythe Shepard and Priya Mani, 11–34. Toronto: Canadian Education and Research Institute for Counselling.

Venn, D. 2012. "Eligibility Criteria for Unemployment Benefits: Quantitative Indicators for OECD and EU Countries." OECD Working Papers, 131. http://dx.doi.org/10.1787/5k9h43kgkvr4-en.

Verdun, Amy, and Donna E. Wood. 2013. "Governing the Social Dimension in Canadian Federalism and European Integration." *Canadian Public Administration* 56 (2): 173–84. https://doi.org/10.1111/capa.12012.

Virtuosity Consulting. 2003. "History of Federal Employment Policies and Programs 1985–2002." Draft final report, under contract to Strategy and Coordination Human Resources Development Canada.

Walker, Robert, and Michael Wiseman. 2006. "Opening Up American Federalism: Improving Welfare the European Way." http://mlwiseman.com/?p=141.
Wandner, Stephen A. 2015. "The Future of the Public Workforce Investment in a Time of Dwindling Resources." In *Transforming U.S. Workforce Development Policies for the 21st Century*, edited by Carl Van Horn, Tammy Edwards, and Todd Greene, 129–68. Kalamazoo, MI: W.E. Upjohn Institute for Employment Research.
Watts, Ronald L. 1999. *Comparing Federal Systems*. 2nd ed. Kingston: Institute of Intergovernmental Relations, School of Policy Studies, Queen's University.
Whitcomb, Ed. 1982. *A Short History of Manitoba*. Ottawa: From Sea to Sea Enterprises.
– 2005a. *A Short History of Alberta*. Ottawa: From Sea to Sea Enterprises.
– 2005b. *A Short History of Saskatchewan*. Ottawa: From Sea to Sea Enterprises.
– 2006. *A Short History of British Columbia*. Ottawa: From Sea to Sea Enterprises.
– 2007. *A Short History of Ontario*. Ottawa: From Sea to Sea Enterprises.
– 2009. *A Short History of Nova Scotia*. Ottawa: From Sea to Sea Enterprises.
– 2010a. *A Short History of New Brunswick*. Ottawa: From Sea to Sea Enterprises.
– 2010b. *A Short History of Newfoundland & Labrador*. Ottawa: From Sea to Sea Enterprises.
– 2010c. *A Short History of Prince Edward Island*. Ottawa: From Sea to Sea Enterprises.
– 2012. *A Short History of Québec*. Ottawa: From Sea to Sea Enterprises.
Wilder, Matt, and Michael Howlett. 2016. "Province Building and Canadian Political Science." In *Provinces: Canadian Provincial Politics*. 3rd ed. Edited by Christopher Dunn. Toronto: University of Toronto Press.
Wilson, Daniel. 2015. "Irreconcilable Differences: First Nations and Harper Government's Energy Superpower Agenda." In *The Harper Record 2008–2015*, Canadian Centre for Policy Alternatives. https://www.policyalternatives.ca/Harper_Record_2008-2015/02-HarperRecord-Wilson.pdf.
Wiseman, Nelson. 2007. *In Search of Canadian Political Culture*. Vancouver: UBC Press.
– 2016. "Provincial Political Cultures." In *Provinces: Canadian Provincial Politics*. 3rd ed., edited by Christopher Dunn, 3–45. Toronto: University of Toronto Press.
Wolfe, David. 1997. "Institutional Limits to Labour Market Reform in Ontario: The Short Life and Rapid Demise of the Ontario Training and Adjustment

Board." In *Social Partnerships for Training*, edited by Andrew Sharpe and Rodney Haddow, 155–88. Kingston: School of Policy Studies, Queen's University.

Wood, D.E. 2010. "Building Flexibility and Accountability into Local Employment Services: Country Report for Canada." OECD Local Economic and Employment Development (LEED) Working Paper.

Wood, Donna. 2008. "The Workability of Intergovernmental Administrative Arrangements: A Comparison of Labour Market Policy in Post-Devolution Canada and the United Kingdom." PhD diss., University of Edinburgh.

Wood, Donna E. 2013a. "Comparing Employment Policy Governance Regimes in Canada and the European Union." In "Governing the Social Dimension in Canadian Federalism and European Integration," special themed issue, *Canadian Public Administration* 56 (2): 286–303.

– 2013b. "Could European Governance Ideas Improve Federal-Provincial Relations in Canada?" Research paper prepared for EURAC Institute for Studies of Federalism and Regionalism. https://core.ac.uk/download/pdf/16756231.pdf.

– 2014. "Comparing Intergovernmental Institutions in Human Capital Development." In *State of the Federation 2012: Regions, Resources and Resiliency*, edited by Loleen Berdahl, André Juneau, and Carolyn Tuohy, 119–44. Kingston: Institute for Intergovernmental Relations, Queen's University.

– 2015a. "Recasting Federal Workforce Development Programs under the Harper Conservatives." In *The Harper Record, 2008–2015*, 183–200. Canadian Centre for Policy Alternatives. https://www.policyalternatives.ca/Harper_Record_2008-2015/11-HarperRecord-Wood.pdf.

– 2015b. "The State of Social Assistance in Alberta." In *Welfare Reform in Canada: Provincial Social Assistance in Comparative Perspective*, edited by Daniel Beland and Pierre-Marc Daigneault, 161–78. Johnson-Shoyama Series on Public Policy. Toronto: University of Toronto Press.

– 2016. "From Pathways to 'ASETS' in Aboriginal Employment Programming." In *How Ottawa Spends, 2015–2016: The Liberal Rise and the Tory Demise*, ed. Christopher Stoney and G. Bruce Doern, 398–443. Ottawa: School of Public Policy and Administration, Carleton University. https://carleton.ca/sppa/wp-content/uploads/HOW-OTTAWA-SPENDS-2015-2016.pdf..

Wood, Donna E., and Thomas Klassen. 2012. "The Governance Problem in Employment and Training Policy in Canada." In *Making EI Work: Research from the Mowat Centre Employment Insurance Task Force*, edited by Keith Banting and Jon Medow, 449–76. Toronto, Montreal: Mowat Centre for

Policy Innovation, Queen's School of Policy Studies, McGill-Queen's University Press.
Zizys, Tom. 2014. *Better Work: The Path to Good Jobs Is through Employers.* Toronto: Metcalf Foundation.
Zon, Noah. 2014. *Slicing the Pie: Principles for Allocating Transfer Payments in the Canadian Federation.* Mowat Centre, Research #90. https://mowatcentre.ca/wp-content/uploads/publications/90_slicing_the_pie.pdf.

Index

Page references in *italics* indicate a figure; page references in **bold** indicate a table.

The Institute of Public Administration of Canada Series in Public Management and Governance

Networks of Knowledge: Collaborative Innovation in International Learning, Janice Stein, Richard Stren, Joy Fitzgibbon, and Melissa Maclean
The National Research Council in the Innovative Policy Era: Changing Hierarchies, Networks, and Markets, G. Bruce Doern and Richard Levesque
Beyond Service: State Workers, Public Policy, and the Prospects for Democratic Administration, Greg McElligott
A Law unto Itself: How the Ontario Municipal Board Has Developed and Applied Land Use Planning Policy, John G. Chipman
Health Care, Entitlement, and Citizenship, Candace Redden
Between Colliding Worlds: The Ambiguous Existence of Government Agencies for Aboriginal and Women's Policy, Jonathan Malloy
The Politics of Public Management: The HRDC Audit of Grants and Contributions, David A. Good
Dream No Little Dreams: A Biography of the Douglas Government of Saskatchewan, 1944–1961, Albert W. Johnson
Governing Education, Ben Levin
Executive Styles in Canada: Cabinet Structures and Leadership Practices in Canadian Government, edited by Luc Bernier, Keith Brownsey, and Michael Howlett
The Roles of Public Opinion Research in Canadian Government, Christopher Page
The Politics of CANDU Exports, Duane Bratt
Policy Analysis in Canada: The State of the Art, edited by Laurent Dobuzinskis, Michael Howlett, and David Laycock
Digital State at the Leading Edge: Lessons from Canada, Sanford Borins, Kenneth Kernaghan, David Brown, Nick Bontis, Perri 6, and Fred Thompson
The Politics of Public Money: Spenders, Guardians, Priority Setters, and Financial Watchdogs inside the Canadian Government, David A. Good
Court Government and the Collapse of Accountability in Canada and the UK, Donald Savoie
Professionalism and Public Service: Essays in Honour of Kenneth Kernaghan, edited by David Siegel and Ken Rasmussen
Searching for Leadership: Secretaries to Cabinet in Canada, edited by Patrice Dutil
Foundations of Governance: Municipal Government in Canada's Provinces, edited by Andrew Sancton and Robert Young
Provincial and Territorial Ombudsman Offices in Canada, edited by Stewart Hyson
Local Government in a Global World: Australia and Canada in Comparative Perspective, edited by Emmanuel Brunet-Jailly and John F. Martin

Behind the Scenes: The Life and Work of William Clifford Clark, Robert A. Wardhaugh
The Guardian: Perspectives on the Ministry of Finance of Ontario, edited by Patrice Dutil
Making Medicare: New Perspectives on the History of Medicare in Canada, edited by Gregory P. Marchildon
Overpromising and Underperforming? Understanding and Evaluating New Intergovernmental Accountability Regimes, edited by Peter Graefe, Julie M. Simmons, and Linda A. White
Governance in Northern Ontario: Economic Development and Policy Making, edited by Charles Conteh and Bob Segsworth
Off and Running: The Prospects and Pitfalls of Government Transitions in Canada, David Zussman
Deputy Ministers in Canada: Comparative and Jurisdictional Perspectives, edited by Jacques Bourgault and Christopher Dunn
The Politics of Public Money, Second Edition, David A. Good
Commissions of Inquiry and Policy Change: A Comparative Analysis, edited by Gregory J. Inwood and Carolyn M. Johns
Leaders in the Shadows: The Leadership Qualities of Municipal Chief Administrative Officers, David Siegel
Funding Policies and the Nonprofit Sector in Western Canada: Evolving Relationships in a Changing Environment, edited by Peter R. Elson
Backrooms and Beyond: Partisan Advisers and the Politics of Policy Work in Canada, Jonathan Craft
Fields of Authority: Special Purpose Governance in Ontario, 1815–2015, Jack Lucas
A Quiet Evolution: The Emergence of Indigenous–Local Intergovernmental Partnerships in Canada, Christopher Alcantara and Jen Nelles
Canada's Department of External Affairs, Volume III, Innovation and Adaptation, 1968–1984, John Hilliker, Mary Halloran, and Greg Donaghy
Federalism in Action: The Devolution of Canada's Public Employment Service, 1995–2015, Donna E. Wood

Lightning Source UK Ltd.
Milton Keynes UK
UKHW011058080819
347609UK00001B/352/P